"As more and more colleges, seminari teaching the foundations of church hi......, ..., ... need for scholarly but accessible one-volume introductions to the discipline that are also contemporary and global in scope has risen. Dr. Early has provided a balanced and valuable resource in this important area."

—*William Loyd Allen, professor of Church History and Spiritual Formation,*
James and Carolyn McAfee School of Theology, Mercer University

"The most prolific young church historian in evangelicalism has given us a generous book—one that offers the reader much in information and passion but by its readability and energetic pace requires little from him in effort. This book is faithful Christian history in both senses. It is faithfully Christian. It is faithfully historical."

—*Bart Barber, pastor, First Baptist Church, Farmersville, Texas*

"Joe Early's new survey of church history moves easily and smoothly across the expanse of the Christian centuries. Very readable for the entry-level student, *A History of Christianity* also contains details to inform the more experienced scholar. As he covers the breadth of church history, Dr. Early pauses occasionally to profile significant individuals in such a way that the reader can see not only their contributions to the church but also their human flaws and foibles. Readers, whether in the classroom or the church, who are eager to learn about God's work in the past two thousand years, will find much to applaud in this new resource."

—*Rex D. Butler, professor of Church History and Patristics,*
New Orleans Baptist Theological Seminary

"When teaching church history I have regularly asked myself the following questions: How can I make everything I know about this topic manageable and meaningful for my students? What information should I include to teach the subject well? What aspects should I leave out to keep the narrative flowing? What details should I include to keep it interesting? Most importantly, what will they think about Christ and his church along the way? Joe Early's *A History of Christianity* addresses this ongoing dilemma by providing a resource that is filled with information for the professor without becoming like lead for the student; it is written with the seriousness of a researcher but with clarity for the learner; it answers questions for the novice while inviting discussion for the curious; and it is designed to help every reader appreciate the faithfulness of God in promoting, protecting, and preserving the church."

—*Anthony Chute, associate dean and professor of Church History,
School of Christian Ministries, California Baptist University*

"I am delighted to see the arrival of Joseph Early's *A History of Christianity* after many years in the making. Too often academic presentations of the history of Christianity are a mere pile of bones containing the necessary facts and figures but without any life. Early's contribution has commendably assembled these bones and put life and flesh around them in a way that will inspire and instruct. Right in the center of it all is Early's very own heart for the relevance of the study of the past for the people of God in the present. As a result, *A History of Christianity* will challenge and change all who read it."

—*Jason G. Duesing, provost, Midwestern Baptist
Theological Seminary and College*

"Most Christians are woefully ignorant of the history of Christianity. Church historians have the important (and enjoyable) task of showing believers that the God of the Bible continued to work in and through his people—warts and all—after the time of the Bible and on through to our present era. Joe Early has written a fine introductory textbook to church history that serves this purpose well. Professors will appreciate how Early covers the most important figures, themes, doctrines, and controversies from a perspective that is convictionally Protestant, but appreciative of all the branches of the Christian family tree. Students will appreciate that the text is easy to read and avoids unnecessarily technical discussions for a survey textbook."

—*Nathan A. Finn, associate professor of Historical Theology and
Baptist Studies, Southeastern Baptist Theological Seminary*

"In this powerful antidote to historical amnesia, Joseph Early gives a vivid and compelling memory of God's purposeful work in the past. It is rare to find a history of Christianity that avoids being overly academic and cumbersome on the one hand, or overly simplistic and sweeping on the other. But this balanced blend of breadth and depth fills the gap masterfully and should be a go-to book for pastors, professors, students, and laity."

—*Christian T. George, assistant professor of Historical
Theology, Midwestern Baptist Theological Seminary*

"Joe Early's work provides evangelicals an up-to-date survey of the history of Christianity. While reformers like Martin Luther are given extensive treatment, each era of Christian history and a wide variety of movements and groups are afforded good attention. Emphases to note include several sections on Christian worship, missions, and the global nature of contemporary faith. The study combines history and historical theology (not many Christian histories highlight as many theologians as Early does) and will function as an accessible, easy-to-read handbook for students or for Christian education of the laity in local churches—both good goals of the author."

—*Doug Weaver, professor of Religion and director of Undergraduate Studies, Department of Religion, Baylor University*

A HISTORY OF
CHRISTIANITY

AN INTRODUCTORY SURVEY

A HISTORY OF CHRISTIANITY

AN INTRODUCTORY SURVEY

JOSEPH EARLY JR.

ACADEMIC

NASHVILLE, TENNESSEE

A History of Christianity: An Introductory Survey
Copyright © 2015 Joseph Early Jr.

B&H Publishing Group
Nashville, Tennessee
All rights reserved

ISBN: 978–1–4336–7221–7

Dewey Decimal Classification: 270
Subject Heading: CHURCH HISTORY\CHRISTIANITY

Printed in the United States of America

For Dr. Robert E. Johnson,
my first professor of church history

CONTENTS

FOREWORD

If the church is always one generation away from extinction, historical amnesia threatens its demise as much as spiritual complacency. A call to renewed commitment must necessarily be a summons to remember. In every age the church must recall its mission and identity as it imparts the tradition and disciples a new generation of believers. The study of church history is essential for this continuity. Many ardent believers know little about the history of their own Christian faith. It is a peculiar temptation for Baptist Christians and others in the free-church tradition to leapfrog mentally over hundreds of years of history and to place in limbo within historical parentheses everything that happened between the age of the apostles and the faith of their grandparents.

The study of church history is a way of remembering and a constructive effort to repair the condition of a broken memory, which has been a reality of the modern world since the Enlightenment. What memory is to the individual, history is to the church, and a careful and engaging examination of the church's history is an invaluable resource for transmitting the faith to the next generation. It challenges the kind of pride that discounts the faith of our mothers and fathers and so easily falls prey to the cult of novelty, which is a shortcoming of modern evangelicals. Knowing our history provides perspective and a broader context for understanding Christian identity and the ministry of the church.

By returning to the past, the study of church history prepares us for what lies ahead by confronting us with the inevitability of change. It frees us from what C. S. Lewis called "chronological snobbery" by providing coordinates and reference points. Perhaps more than any other academic discipline within Christian education, church history is holistic and integrationist in nature. It encompasses the study of theology, ethics, philosophy, pastoral ministry, preaching, missions, and evangelism, as well as others. Church history helps us better understand Scripture because it is a further unfolding—through many cultures, times, and places, of biblical history—of the story of God's working in the world among His people.

Joe Early's book is an overview of the history of the church, a hedge against the extinction that menaces every generation of Christians, and a welcomed and needed resource in the battle to remember. This is a book that instructs, informs, inspires, challenges, and raises critical questions for engagement. Covering two millennia of history is a daunting task, but Dr. Early has done this comprehensively while maintaining a concentrated focus on the broad sweep of movements, ideas, events, and key figures in the story. Reflecting his abilities as both a seasoned scholar and an effective teacher, it is a well-researched and balanced presentation of Christian history with a judicious use of both primary and secondary sources and is conveyed in an accessible and engaging style that is enjoyable to read. An additional asset is that this work serves as a ready resource for future reference, the kind of volume one can return to again and again for information and research. This is a versatile book that is ideal as an introductory text for college and seminary classes in religion and church history but can meet a critical educational need for small groups and discipleship classes in local congregations.

More than ever the church needs skilled historians who remind us that God has always been at work among His people and provide the necessary means of scholarship for affirming Christian identity, passing on the faith to the next generation and enabling the church to navigate the shoals of societal and cultural change. Joe Early's work is a resource in remembering and extending the witness of the church and will serve a new generation of students, church leaders, and inquiring Christians seeking to learn more about the history of their faith. Read this book and join the fight against historical amnesia and ecclesial extinction.

J. Bradley Creed

Provost and Executive Vice President and Professor of Religion

Samford University

Birmingham, Alabama

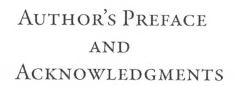

Author's Preface
and
Acknowledgments

W riting a history of Christianity proved to be more difficult than I had expected. While the research, writing, and proofing were certainly challenging from a believer's perspective, other issues beyond academics were equally difficult. Throughout Christian history there have been incidents and even entire eras where church leaders appeared to place personal objectives over what God has depicted in Scripture. To achieve his goals, man often construed Christianity to fit his own purpose. These are the eras when man has attempted to make God in his own image. During these times Christian leaders attempted to make the church organization more powerful than the gospel. As a historian I am often asked where God was during these times. After twenty years of rumination, I believe the answer is that God was present all the time calling man and the church back to the Bible.

The other part of my challenge is to make sure God's activities in the lives of men are visible. This is difficult because if one studies the pure history of the church it is possible to become cynical. After all, it's hard to see the hand of God in the Inquisition. The problem for most observers is the way we look at any history. We look at facts and dates and fail to take the long view.

As we view the history of the church over 2,000 years, we can see bad things happen when man ignores or minimizes the Scriptures and instead relies on power, tradition, and the government. Many church leaders acted purely in their own selfish interests, but others believed they were doing what was necessary and best for the church. For them the ends justified the means. If the means are not biblically based, however, the ends can never be justified. Invariably, the brightest times in the history of the church are those when man allowed himself to be led by the Scriptures and the Holy Spirit.

When one takes the long view of history, it is easier to see that, regardless of what was going on in the organized church, there have always been those who seek to find God's will for the church. As a Christian and a historian, I hope the readers of this book will be able to see the bright light of the gospel shining throughout the lives of heroic Christians no matter how dark the times may be. After all, in the end we are promised that the light of the gospel will obliterate the darkness. One of man's problems with interpreting history is his understanding of time. We want God to work on our timetable. It is clear, however, that in the history of the church God has his own concept of time that is not dependent on man.

Often man's view of church history may appear to be just a progression of evolutionary activities. When one looks closely, the light of God's ultimate will for man has always been espoused by men of faith and conviction in every era. Sometimes they are hard to find, but they are always present, seeking and serving God. So when you are reading this text and things appear to be grim, remember, in a few pages or chapters God will bring someone along who will bring the church back in line.

I first became enamored with church history while working on my master of divinity degree at Midwestern Baptist Theological Seminary in the mid 1990s. Dr. Robert Johnson was my professor, and he made the history come alive. I could not learn enough about popes, monks, martyrs, Reformers, the birth of denominations, and the development of doctrine. Early in my studies, I began to realize that what we believe as Christians was based in one way or another on the Bible, but also our theology and beliefs developed over a much larger period of time. Church fathers, creeds, councils, theologians, governments, Reformers, and pastors played a major role in the continual development of Christianity in its various shades over the previous two millennia. I had never really realized this before. I suppose I assumed Christians, Baptists in particular, had always held to the basic beliefs we accept today. As a professor, I can now see that my students are in the same situation I was once in all those years ago. For the most part Christians have no idea of their history, why they believe what they believe, and why they are members of particular denominations other than that their parents were members. I hope this book will encourage Christians to seek answers to these matters.

Another reason I wrote this book was the need. Most general church history textbooks currently in print were either written by Catholic scholars and come from their perspective or are so overly academic that the faith element of Christianity has been significantly reduced. Protestant works such as Kenneth Scott Latourette's *A History of Christianity* and Robert A. Baker's *A Summary of Christian History* are excellent but dated. As a Protestant (Baptist) believer, I hope I have filled this current need. With that said, please do not think I am merely promoting Protestant dogma and treating all things Protestant in a hagiographic manner. This is a history, not a book of highlights. Protestants have their warts, and I have not glossed over them.

When writing this text, I considered several elements. First, the ever-present problem of word count and my desire that this work be published in one book rather than a multivolume series. For this reason I was forced to make choices in what was included and what was omitted. Some people will be disappointed with my choices. Second, rather than bog down the text with endless footnotes, I chose to note only the primary source documents. All the books employed or examined in this text are listed in the bibliography. Third, when dealing with many individuals from antiquity, finding a consensus for birth and death dates can be difficult. The dates in this text were heavily weighed, and I believe they are as close to the actual dates as possible. In addition, the dates for monarchs and popes coincide with their reigns. When discussing everyone else, birth and death dates are provided.

I need to thank many people for helping me in this endeavor. First, I'm grateful that my wife, Tiffany, allowed me to spend the last six months of our engagement and the first six months of our marriage writing. Not only did she allow me to write, but she also proofed chapters and encouraged me to keep working rather than taking extended breaks. My father, Dr. Joe Early Sr., always deserves mentioning. As he has on all my previous books, he proofed the entire work and provided great insight. I also asked nine of my friends and professors to look over my work before it went to press: Dr. John Hurtgen (Campbellsville University), Dr. Shane Garrison (Campbellsville University), Dr. Twyla Hernandez (Campbellsville University), Dr. Dwayne Howell (Campbellsville University), Dr. Rex Butler (New Orleans Baptist Theological Seminary), Dr. Robert Johnson (Central Baptist Theological Seminary), Dr. Paul Gritz (Southwestern Baptist Theological Seminary), Dr. James Leo Garrett (Southwestern Baptist Theological Seminary), and Dr. John Storey (Lamar University). These professors are excellent scholars, provided a valuable critique, and kept me true to task. My secretary, Emma Calvert, prepared my bibliography and did an excellent job. I'm also grateful to my dean, Dr. John Hurtgen, and colleagues in the School of Theology for their encouragement.

Joseph Early Jr., Ph.D.

Associate Professor of Religion, Campbellsville University

What is past is prologue. —William Shakespeare, *The Tempest*

CHAPTER ONE

JESUS AND THE WORLD INTO WHICH HE WAS BORN

Jesus Christ and Christianity were born into the volatile world of Palestine. Then as now, the region was a religious and political powder keg, constantly on the verge of explosion. Although Judaism had dominated the area for more than a thousand years, the Jewish people often found themselves under the rule of foreign powers vying for Palestine's important position as a land bridge that connected Asia, Europe, and Africa. In turn, the Babylonians, Persians, Greeks, and, at the time of Christ, the Romans ruled the region. The cultures of these occupiers deeply affected Jews and the region's other inhabitants.

FIRST-CENTURY JUDAISM

Because Jesus and his first followers were Jewish, Judaism had a strong impact on the foundation of Christianity. Early Christianity stressed the laws of Moses, the Passover, and the importance of the Abrahamic covenant. Jesus, however, chose to interpret Old Testament teachings in a more spiritual and less legalistic manner than did some Jewish sects. Though first-century Judaism was fragmented by the dispersion of Jews throughout the world and internal arguments among the religious elite, many of its core concepts laid the groundwork for Christianity.

The Hebrew Scriptures were the basis of Judaism. The *Tanakh* (*Torah*, *Nevi'im*, and *Ketuvim*), or Old Testament, provided Jews with the story of their national birth, the explanation of their special standing as Yahweh's chosen people, their religious requirements, and their hope for the future. Jesus and his disciples had deep respect for and frequently quoted from the *Tanakh*. These thirty-nine books, often in their Greek form (the Septuagint), provided Christianity with its first literature.

The Tanakh helped establish Christian monotheism. As stressed in Deuteronomy 6:4–9, Christianity believed in only one God, Yahweh; and as Yahweh was invisible, no graven images were permitted. For both Jews and Christians, pagan gods were nothing more than figurines with no true power.

The concept of covenant was also important to Judaism and Christianity. A covenant was a vow or agreement made between a deity and a group of people. God made key covenants in the Old Testament with Noah, Abraham, Moses, and David. The covenants with Abraham and David were of special importance. The Abrahamic Covenant (Gen 12:1–3) promised the descendants of Abraham that they would have a homeland, be a great and numerous people, and be blessed by God. The Gospels stressed the importance of this covenant in, for example, Matthew 3:9 and 8:11 and Luke 1:73–74. The Davidic covenant (2 Samuel 7) stated that the Messiah would come from the line of David. As noted throughout the New Testament (e.g., Acts 2:29–31), Jesus was the Messiah prophesied in the Davidic covenant. He fulfilled the Old Testament covenants and inaugurated the new covenant predicted in Jeremiah 31.

Around the time of the Babylonian captivity, anticipation of the Messiah became a prominent feature of Judaism. It reached a fever pitch in the first century. The term *Messiah* as used in the Hebrew Bible means "anointed one," and in the Septuagint it is translated as "Christ." In the Jewish context the Messiah or Christ was to be God's tool for the purification of Judaism, a liberator, and a Davidic warrior. Old Testament figures like the judges, Saul, David, and the prophets prefigured the ultimate Messiah. Like these Old Testament heroes, Jews expected that the one to come would be human.

The most important site for Judaism was Solomon's temple in Jerusalem. It was the central site for Yahweh worship, the only location where sacrifices could be offered by faithful Jews. In 722 BC, Assyria defeated the ten northern tribes of Israel and took many Jews back to their homeland as slaves. In 586 BC, Babylon destroyed Jerusalem and the temple of Solomon and transported thousands of enslaved Jews back to Babylon. This displacement of Jews became known as the Diaspora. Even after a few Jews were permitted to return from exile and rebuild the temple, many remained in foreign lands. Synagogues were built for these displaced people who could not visit the temple. In synagogues the Scriptures were read, oral traditions were passed on, and Jews received religious education. In the Roman Empire synagogues served as outposts of Jewish culture amid a pagan society. They were pivotal in the spread of Christianity. During the apostle Paul's missionary journeys, he often shared the gospel in synagogues. In Palestine, however, Herod's temple remained the center of Judaism until its destruction in AD 70.

Not only were the Jewish people separated by great distances, but they were also split into factions that often despised one another. The most prominent factions were Pharisees, Sadducees, Zealots, and Essenes.

During the life of Jesus Christ, the Pharisees (the separated ones) were a nonpriestly group that numbered about 6,000. They were legalistic, hoping to hasten the Messiah's coming by purifying Judaism. They accepted not only the Torah but also Jewish oral traditions as authoritative, they believed in the physical resurrection of the body, and they observed Sabbath laws meticulously. They were deeply admired by the average Jew but opposed by the Sadducees. Because of their legalism, the Pharisees frequently clashed with Jesus. Tradition maintains that Ezra—who reinstituted the law, led many exiled Jews home, and organized the rebuilding of the temple—was the father of the Pharisees. In the development of Christianity, the apostle Paul was the most important Pharisee.

The Sadducees controlled the priesthood and observed the sacrificial system strictly. They only accepted the Torah and not ancient traditions as authoritative, did not believe in the physical resurrection of the body, did not affirm the existence of angels or demons, and said there was no judgment after death. Because of their connection with the priesthood and the temple, the Sadducees tended to mediate between the Jewish populace and the Roman authorities. Like the Pharisees, the Sadducees were at odds with Jesus and thus were not depicted in a flattering light by the New Testament writers.

The Zealots were a radical fringe of the Pharisees that sought to remove the Romans from Palestine by force. They believed God would reestablish Israel as a political power only when defiling Gentiles were removed from the land. Their violent resistance to Roman rule played a major role in inciting the Romans to destroy Jerusalem in AD 70.

The Essenes likely originated from the Pharisees but were even more radical. They came to believe the Pharisees were corrupt and broke from them. A group known as the Qumran community, who lived in the Judean desert near the Dead Sea, appears to have been a group of Essenes. In 1947 more than 900 of their texts were found, revealing that they were highly apocalyptic, held messianic expectations, wore white clothing, and conducted baptismal ceremonies similar to those of John the Baptist. The Qumran community was massacred by the Romans in AD 67.

Hellenism

Greek (i.e., Hellenic) culture saturated the ancient Near East in the first century. First, Philip of Macedon (359–336 BC) consolidated all the squabbling Greek city-states into a cohesive nation with a unified identity. Then his son Alexander the Great (336–323 BC) conquered most of the known world and infused it with Greek culture, establishing colonies characterized by Greek philosophy, medicine, architecture, and, most importantly, the Greek language. By the time of Jesus, most people in the Mediterranean region spoke basic, or *koine*, Greek. As a result, in cosmopolitan cities like Alexandria, Egypt, people from different areas of the world lived together. Diaspora Jews, or Hellenistic Jews, were among these groups. Greek may not have been their first language, but it was the universal language. The apostle Paul found this helpful on his missionary journeys.

The prominence of Greek culture also had negative effects. If a young man wanted an education or to become important in politics or society, he had to be fluent in Greek language and conversant with Greek culture. This led many Hellenistic Jews to compromise their Jewish identity and even their moral standards, as when young Jewish athletes competed with Greeks in the nude.

Many Hellenistic Jews became so Greek that they forgot the Hebrew language. This was a major problem since Yahweh inspired Jewish prophets to write the Scriptures in Hebrew. To date no one had translated the Hebrew Bible into another language, and Jewish leaders were faced with the dilemma of either allowing Judaism to die or permitting the Scriptures to be translated into Greek.

After much deliberation Jewish scholars determined that a Greek translation of the Hebrew Bible was permissible. This translation, known today as the Septuagint, became the Bible used by writers of the New Testament. The name *Septuaginta* is Latin for "seventy" and refers to the Jewish tradition that seventy (or seventy-two) Jewish elders produced the translation. Thus, the

Septuagint is often referred to as the "LXX"—the Roman numeral for seventy. Dating the Septuagint is difficult, but scholars believe the entire Old Testament was translated between the third and second century BC.

Greek philosophy was prominent in the Mediterranean world and had displaced the classical Greek religions as the source of answers to life's ultimate questions. The Greek religions' demise was hastened by their inability to answer difficult questions like, What happens after death? The pantheon was replaced by Platonism, Epicureanism, Stoicism, and Cynicism. These philosophies influenced and clashed with traditional Judaism.

Plato (427–347 BC) provided much of the framework for Greek philosophy. His most important idea was "Forms" or "Ideas." Forms, for Plato, are the archetypes of which material objects are just approximations. Only the perfect Forms are real, and they are not perceptible by the senses. What we perceive through our senses is an illusion. Plato also taught a radical dualism that stressed the eternity and superiority of the soul and the temporality and inferiority of the body. The soul is imprisoned inside the body and longs to escape. Though Plato is vague when it comes to details, he taught that good souls return to the realm of true Forms and evil souls are placed into inferior, material creatures.

Founded by Epicurus of Athens (342–270 BC), Epicureanism taught that the gods exist but do not care about humanity. Everything is physical or material, and nothing exists after death. Not only does the human body die, but so does the soul. Therefore, there are no eternal rewards or punishments. The greatest goal of the Epicurean was to avoid pain and to enjoy mental pleasures, which outlast physical ones. In Acts 17, the apostle Paul debated with Epicureans at Mars Hill in Athens.

Zeno of Citium (ca. 311 BC) was the father of Stoicism. The Stoics practiced self-control, freedom from passions, and doing right in order to be right. Their ultimate goal was to train the body to be in harmony with nature and the mind to face the difficulties of the world. The *Logos* was an important aspect of Stoicism. It was a cosmic intelligence or active reason that united the world and made it intelligible to humans. Human souls are endowed with a portion of the divine *Logos*. This principle plays a significant but altered role in the New Testament and in the writings of the early church fathers.

For the lack of a better description, the Cynics ("dogs") were the hippies of the first-century world. They advocated a simple lifestyle, moral virtue, self-sufficiency, and harmony with nature. They also believed that all authority should be questioned. Their distinctive appearance made them easy to identify—one cloak, a walking stick, a beggar's bag, and a long beard.

ROMAN POLITICAL AND RELIGIOUS INFLUENCE

In the first century, the Roman Empire extended as far west as Britain and Spain and as far east as the border of the Persian Empire in modern-day Iran. The Romans referred to the Mediterranean Sea as *Mare Nostrum* (our sea), and they built roads that connected their vast empire. These roads proved to be safe and were essential in the transmission of the gospel. Rome controlled Palestine from 63 BC, when General Pompey (106–48 BC) conquered Jerusalem. Local authority was granted to a puppet king, Herod the Great, who ruled from 37 to 4 BC and is mentioned in Matthew 2. Herod was known for his cruelty but also for his building projects such as the temple, which Jesus frequented. The Romans provided Palestine with aqueducts, safety, and a stabilizing presence. The Jews, however, viewed Rome as an occupying force and hoped for a Messiah to deliver them.

The old Roman religions of Jupiter, Saturn, and Apollo remained popular. Many temples and statues of these gods were erected throughout the empire. These gods, however, were capricious, capable of being bribed to gain favor, and often immoral. They did not offer the worshipper a personal relationship with deity.

Mystery religions were also popular in the first century and became even more popular in the following two centuries. Unlike the traditional Roman religions, the mystery religions promised union with a god. Generally, they were not for women and were secretive. Within these religions tales of virgin births and resurrections were common. They offered forgiveness and a new life to their adherents and immortality to those who truly believed and dedicated themselves to a god. These mystery religions thus bore some superficial similarities to Christianity.

The deity Mithras, for example, was of Persian origin and was popular with the Roman legions. He supposedly killed a mystical bull, which, as he was dying, expelled the seed of life upon the earth. Followers of Mithras held ceremonies in caverns that involved bathing in a bull's blood and eating its raw flesh. To the followers of Mithras, the sacrificial killing of the bull symbolized regeneration.

Dionysus was the god of wine. Ceremonies among his followers were marked by drunken orgies and drinking the blood of a bull. Supposedly, Dionysus was murdered by the Titans and raised from the dead. He offered eternal life to those who followed him. His followers believed that drinking bull's blood allowed them to participate in Dionysus's divinity.

Rome used religion to unify the empire and promote loyalty to the emperor, so emperor worship fit well into its cultic system. An excellent administrator and stabilizer of the empire, Augustus Caesar (63 BC–AD 14) was the first emperor to be posthumously worshipped as a god. He was followed by Tiberius (AD 14–37), the insane Caligula (37–41), Claudius (41–54), and Nero (54–68), some of whom insisted on being worshipped as gods.

The Jews viewed emperor worship as idolatry and would not participate. Because of their staunch belief in one God and their willingness to revolt for this principle, they were exempt from emperor worship and other Roman religious rites. For the Romans, imposing their religion on the Jews was not worth the trouble. In many ways the Romans left Judaism alone. If the Jews did not mount an insurrection, they were permitted to practice their religion and worship at the temple. Yet because of the Jews' radical monotheism and loyalty to an unseen God, the Romans viewed them, and later the Christians, with suspicion.

JESUS CHRIST

Jesus' birth and genealogy are recorded in the Gospels of Matthew and Luke. His earthly parents were Mary and Joseph. They are depicted as common people, righteous, and the best Judaism had to offer. God was Jesus' heavenly father. The Gospels demonstrate that he was God incarnate and born to Mary when she was a virgin. This pregnancy caused much consternation for Joseph, her husband. After the divine conception was explained by the angel Gabriel though, Joseph believed. Jesus was born in Bethlehem in a sequence of events signaling the arrival of someone important. Indeed, he fulfilled Hebrew prophecies about the coming Messiah. Following Jesus' birth, the holy family fled to Egypt to escape the murderous King Herod, who tried to kill him as a rival to the throne. Other than one story of Jesus in the temple when he was twelve years old, there is no scriptural record of the first thirty years of his life. Scholars assume he learned carpentry under his father as he "increased in wisdom and stature, and in favor with God and with people" (Luke 2:52).

When Jesus was approximately thirty years old, he was baptized in the Jordan River by his cousin John the Baptist. As prophesied in Malachi 3:1, Matthew presents John the Baptist as the Elijah figure who was to come before the Messiah. Following his baptism, which was witnessed and approved by the Holy Spirit in the form of a dove, Jesus went into the wilderness where he was tempted by Satan for forty days.

After resisting Satan's temptations and returning from the wilderness, Jesus began his earthly ministry, which lasted approximately three years. He called twelve disciples and began an itinerant preaching tour, mostly around the Sea of Galilee. Often in the form of parables, Jesus' teachings centered on the kingdom of God, repentance from sin, and warnings of God's impending judgment. All of Jesus' teachings were tempered with love and a desire to reconcile humanity with God. As the sinless Son of God, Jesus' ultimate act of love occurred when he took the sins of humankind upon himself and died on the cross in humanity's stead. Those who follow Jesus are justified and attain salvation by trusting him as Savior and Lord (John 3:16).

Jesus holds the offices of prophet, priest, and king. As prophet, he communicated the will of the Father to his followers (Deut 18:18). In Luke 18:31–33, he prophesied his own imminent death. As priest, he offered himself as the perfect and final sacrifice for humanity's sins (Heb 7:24–27). As stated in 1 Timothy 2:5, his sacrifice and priestly role allow him to serve as an advocate for people before God. Jesus also reigns over his people as king (Matt 21:4–5; 27:11; John 18:36–37). The genealogy that opens the book of Matthew demonstrates his royal lineage as a descendent of King David (Matt 1:1–17). Jesus, however, is more than an earthly king. He also has power to forgive sin (Mark 2:1–12), heal the sick (Luke 4:40), and raise the dead (John 11:1–45). He reigns over the kingdom of God and will return to judge the living and the dead (2 Tim 4:1). Jesus' divinity was demonstrated by the miracles he performed and by his resurrection, which was witnessed by many of his followers. Before ascending to heaven, Jesus instructed his disciples to continue his mission (Matt 28:16–20).

The Apostle Paul

The apostle Paul was the most important early convert to Christianity. He was the author of at least thirteen New Testament books, the first missionary to the Gentiles, and Christianity's greatest theologian. Previously known as Saul, Paul had been a Pharisee who persecuted Christians and was present at the stoning of Stephen, the first Christian martyr. While Paul was traveling to Damascus, he met the risen Christ and underwent a dramatic conversion. In that moment Paul went from a great enemy of Christianity to its staunchest advocate.

On his three missionary journeys, Paul taught that Jesus was the sinless, all-sufficient Creator and Redeemer, the manifestation of God, and predicted his imminent return. Paul said salvation was open to Gentiles and not dependent on keeping Old Testament laws. He taught that salvation came through faith in Jesus alone. One did not have to become a Jew before becoming a Christian. Thus, Paul opposed mandatory circumcision for Gentile converts. In addition to being Christianity's first great theologian, Paul was a significant apologist in both Greek and Jewish circles.

CHAPTER TWO

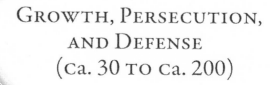

GROWTH, PERSECUTION, AND DEFENSE (ca. 30 TO ca. 200)

During the life of Christ and for three centuries thereafter, Rome had no major rival, ruling most of the known world. In *The Twelve Caesars* (Julius Caesar, 49–44 BC, through Hadrian, AD 117–138) Roman historian Suetonius (AD 70–130) labeled five Caesars of this period as capable rulers and the other seven as weak. The greatest of the Caesars was Octavian, or Augustus (27 BC–AD 14), who united the empire after its great civil war. Caligula (AD 37–41) and Nero (AD 54–68) were among the weak Caesars, whose major emphases were self-gratification, narcissism, and a desire to protect their thrones from rivals.

During the era of the twelve Caesars (49 BC–ca. AD 138), Roman literature, architecture, and science flourished. Roman highways connected the far-flung empire, and aqueducts provided water to its cities. In matters of religion, the mystery religions, particularly Mithras, grew in popularity. Because Christianity was also growing, it caught the eye of the Roman authorities, who looked at it with disdain and suspicion.

WHY DID CHRISTIANITY GROW?

Christianity spoke to humanity's most basic needs. It offered a new hope for the oppressed because Christ too had been oppressed. To those with guilt, Christianity offered forgiveness of sin. For those in poverty with no hope in this world, it promised another world free from want and suffering. It taught that one could commune with God and that he listened to and cared about his followers. Finally, Christianity offered a warm community atmosphere that included anyone who followed Jesus, regardless of gender, social rank, or political status.

Even the illiterate could understand Christianity's simple symbols. Baptism visibly expressed the washing away of sins, the inner cleansing of the soul, and entrance into the Christian community. The Eucharist portrayed communion with God.

Though Christianity was a new religion, it bore similarities to older religions. Because of its monotheism and the invisibility of its God, Christianity appealed to people who were attracted to Judaism but were not Jews. Known as Godfearers, these individuals had not undergone the Jewish rite of circumcision. While they could attend a synagogue, they were barred from worshipping with the Jews. Christians, however, taught that anyone who believed in Christ had access to God, even if he was not circumcised. In fact, the issue of circumcision was a major discussion in the early church. Did a believer in Christ who was not Jewish have to be circumcised? Were the rites of Judaism still to be imposed on Christians? The apostle Paul answered these questions by preaching against the necessity of circumcision and experienced great success with the Godfearers. As attested in Acts 15 and by Christian practice since, Paul's teaching won the day.

Christianity's similarity to Greek philosophy also helped it gain followers. Paul's writings had many Platonic ideas, and those of John stressed the *Logos*, a principle with connections to Stoicism. To Greek-minded people these philosophical elements were attractive.

Women found a home in Christianity that many other religions denied them. Most mystery religions were exclusive to males, and Judaism placed women in a subservient position. For these reasons Christianity attracted many women, who in turn often brought their husbands and children to the faith.

Christian love also contributed to the growth of Christianity. In an age when plague was rife, the stricken were often deserted as the healthy fled to safer regions. In many circumstances the sick were abandoned by their own families. Christians though did not abandon their families and often provided care for non-Christians with plague. To observers of this and many other acts of love, Christianity became increasingly attractive.

The early Christians demonstrated their strong belief in Christ by following him even if it meant martyrdom. Rather than deny Christ and swear an oath to the emperor, many Christians chose death at the hands of the Romans. Such faith impressed many and attracted Tertullian of Carthage (160–225). According to the second-century church father Tertullian, "The more we are hewn down by you, the more numerous do we become. The blood of martyrs is the seed of Christians."[1]

WHERE CHRISTIANITY GREW

In Christianity's earliest days, Christians and Jews intermingled and often worshipped together. Christians attended the synagogues and went to the temple. In some instances Christians led the services. James, the brother of Jesus, was permitted to preach in the temple in Jerusalem. Hellenized Jews were particularly attentive to the message of Christ, especially at feasts and festivals. This was the case at Pentecost (Acts 2), when thousands of Hellenized Jews from all over the Roman Empire traveled to Jerusalem.

Christians in Jerusalem continued to worship with Jews at the temple until the martyrdom of Stephen (ca. 35). Since Stephen was a Hellenized Christian, the Hellenized Christians in Jerusalem feared a similar fate and fled to Antioch and surrounding regions, where they created their own communities to propagate the gospel message.

Christians further distinguished themselves from Judaism following the failed Jewish revolt of AD 66 that led to the destruction of the temple in 70. Many Jewish Christians fled to Pella in Perea on the east side of the Jordan River. Wherever these Christians fled, they brought the Christian message with them.

The Romans believed Christianity was a Jewish sect. So to avoid both religious confusion and the wrath of Rome, Christians fled Palestine to cities throughout the empire. Many of these Diaspora Christians took refuge in Rome, Antioch, and Alexandria.

The apostle Paul's three missionary journeys are another reason for the growth of Christianity. He preached throughout Palestine, Asia Minor, Greece, Rome, and perhaps as far west as Spain. In each of these regions, he began at the synagogue where frequently he found an eager audience in the Godfearers.

According to extrabiblical sources, other apostles spread Christianity across the empire too. According to the *Acts of Peter*, Peter organized and led the first Christians in Rome. This legend was later used as evidence that Peter was the first pope. Another legend claimed that the apostle John and Mary the mother of Jesus founded the church in Ephesus. This tradition became so strong that pilgrims still visit a house venerated as the home of Mary and a grave believed to be John's. The *Acts of Thomas* says Thomas founded churches in Syria and possibly India.

Early Christian Worship (Liturgy)

The first Christians in Jerusalem continued many traditional Jewish practices. They prayed three times a day, fasted two days a week, and professed monotheism. Under James the brother of

Jesus, the Christian community indeed appeared to resemble a Jewish sect. These early Christians worshipped at the temple and synagogues and continued to observe Jewish law. This continued until the martyrdom of James in 62, when Christianity's break from Judaism was accelerated. The rupture was all but complete by 100.

After their separation from the temple and synagogues, Christians usually met and worshipped in homes. In order not to attract the attention of Romans and hostile Jews, these house churches were almost always small and had limited contact with one another. The lack of contact resulted in some liturgical diversity. Certain common elements, however, remained.

All Christians accepted the Old Testament Scriptures but interpreted them in light of the new revelation of Christ. The structure of a Christian worship service was similar to that of the synagogue, including reading and exposition of Scriptures. Christians confessed Christ, fasted, shared meals, and were generous to the poor. Jewish songs and psalms were adapted for a Christian context. Baptismal ceremonies stressed the birth, death, and resurrection of Christ, entrance into the Christian community, and an eschatological hope.

THE APOSTOLIC FATHERS

The apostolic fathers were church leaders believed to have had direct contact with the apostles. For this reason their teachings and writings were accepted as orthodox, though they did not gain canonical status. When theological controversies arose, their authority often was invoked to settle differences. They linked the original twelve apostles to second-century Christianity.

The writings of the apostolic fathers were mostly epistles, pastoral in nature, and informal. They were meant to solve specific problems or meet certain needs within the Christian community. With the exception of Ignatius of Antioch (ca. 35–107), the apostolic fathers relied on the Old Testament as their primary source of authority.

Clement of Rome (fl. ca. 96)

Clement of Rome appeared in early succession lists as either the second or third bishop of Rome. The historian Eusebius of Caesarea (260–340) claimed that he served as the bishop of Rome from 92 to 101. Clement's letters demonstrate that he was well educated, knew the Septuagint, and was a capable administrator. His most important contribution to the early church was his *First Epistle to the Corinthians* or *First Clement* (ca. 96). The letter was a response to an earlier letter sent from the Corinthian church to Clement describing several problems. Younger members were removing older members as presbyters without justification, thus threatening the church's survival. Clement ordered the church to reinstate the presbyters, punish the agitators, and obey the legitimate presbyters who had been appointed by the successors of the apostles. Clement argued:

> Let us realize how near he is, and that nothing escapes him, either of our thoughts or of the plans that we make. It is right, therefore, that we should not be deserters from his will. Let us offend foolish and senseless people, who exalt themselves and boast in the arrogance of their words, rather than God. Let us fear the Lord Jesus Christ, whose blood was given for us. Let us respect our leaders; let us honor the older men; let us instruct the young with instruction that leads to the fear of God. Let us guide our women toward that which is good.[2]

Though Clement did not press the matter, the epistle demonstrated that as early as the first century, churches were appealing to Rome as an authority. For a time Clement was believed to have written *Second Clement*, but the scholarly consensus has changed.

Second Clement might be a sermon delivered in Corinth and then attached to *First Clement* in later collections of early Christian writings. Traditions about Clement's later life and death abound. According to one tradition he was banished to Crimea to work in the mines. Another tradition claimed that he was tied to an anchor and drowned in the Black Sea.

HERMAS OF ROME (SECOND CENTURY)

Hermas was most likely a Christian slave in the home of a wealthy Roman woman.[3] He was granted his freedom, married, and became a successful merchant. His business dealings, however, led his church to denounce him. Because of his faith, Hermas was persecuted by the Romans and lost all his possessions. He then repented and returned to the church. *The Shepherd* (ca. 110) was his most influential writing. Popular in the East, the work told of an angel of repentance appearing to him in the guise of a shepherd. *The Shepherd* is an allegory meant to demonstrate the importance of repentance and that forgiveness after baptism is possible if repentance was sincere.

IGNATIUS OF ANTIOCH (35–107)

Ignatius was a pupil of the apostle John and was believed to have been one of the little children Christ held in his arms and blessed. Because he would not renounce his Christianity, he was arrested and transported from Antioch, where he served as bishop, to Rome for execution. His seven epistles recounted his journey. He was allowed to preach in the cities he passed through, and even his guards were converted. Ignatius was asked to swear allegiance to Rome in exchange for a pardon, but he refused and was executed.

Ignatius's epistles were important in the development of early Christian ecclesiology and were among the first to assert the authority of the bishop. Ignatius maintained that the bishop was the singular leader over all the house churches, presbyters, and deacons in a city and its surrounding region. He said that all human desires and ambitions should be put aside in order to follow the ways and teachings of God, which were expressed by the bishop. He wrote,

> Be eager to do everything in godly harmony, the bishop presiding in the place of God and the presbyters in the place of the council of the apostles and the deacons, who are especially dear to me, since they have been entrusted with the ministry of Jesus Christ, who before the ages was with the Father and appeared at the end of time.[4]

For this reason the Catholic Church often cites Ignatius as a witness to the legitimacy of its episcopal structure.

Ignatius also emphasized the importance of martyrdom. In his *Letter to the Romans*, he told the Roman Christians that he sought martyrdom so he could be with God:

> I am writing to all the churches and I am insisting to everyone that I die for God of my own free will—unless you hinder me. I implore you: do not be unseasonably kind to me. Let me be food for the wild beasts, through whom I can reach God. I am God's wheat, and I am to be ground by the teeth of the wild beasts, so that I may prove to be pure bread.[5]

With Ignatius as its authority, a theology of martyrdom began to develop. Christians began to seek martyrdom rather than flee persecution. Ignatius was also the first church father to use to term *catholic* (universal) for the developing Christian church.

POLYCARP OF SMYRNA (69–155)

Bishop of Smyrna in Asia Minor, Polycarp was reported by Irenaeus of Lyons (140–202) to have been a student of the apostle John. Only one of his letters to the Philippians has survived. Polycarp went to Rome to help settle the debate over the date of Easter, known as the Quartodeciman controversy. The party known as Quartodecimans celebrated Easter on the day of the Jewish Passover no matter what day of the week it fell. The Roman practice was to celebrate Easter on the first Sunday following the Jewish Passover. In the end it was decided that each church should maintain its own date for Easter. Polycarp viewed this as a victory for the churches in Asia Minor. Unlike Ignatius, Polycarp did not promote an episcopal structure for the emerging church. When arrested, put on trial in Smyrna, and asked to renounce his faith, he said: "For eighty-six years I have been [Christ's] servant, and he has done me no wrong. How can I blaspheme my King who saved me?"[6] He was then tied to a stake to be burned, but legend has it that the fire did not burn him. So he was stabbed and died a martyr.

Epistle of Barnabas (ca. 132–135)

The pseudonymous *Epistle of Barnabas* is named for the apostle Paul's traveling companion. It took an extreme stance against Mosaic law and warned Christians not to return to Judaism. It went so far as to accuse Moses of idolatry for creating the bronze serpent. Furthermore, Jewish observance of the Mosaic law and temple rites had been taken beyond God's intentions, it said. Sacrifices were no longer necessary as Jesus' sacrifice was all sufficient. Since the Jews rejected God's covenant, the epistle claimed that Christians had become God's chosen people. Christians were to interpret the law in a spiritual rather than a legalistic manner as the Jews had erroneously done. For example, circumcision was of the heart, not of the flesh. Thus, the Old Testament itself supports Christianity and repudiates Jewish interpretations, according to the epistle. The *Epistle of Barnabas* made heavy use of allegorical interpretation of Scripture.

THE DIDACHE OR THE TEACHING OF THE TWELVE (CA. 110)

Popular in the postapostolic period and believed to be Syrian in origin, the author of the *Didache* is unknown. This work provided instructions on how Christians should live their lives, encompassing morality, fasting, the Eucharist, community, and church affairs. Baptism was to be performed by immersion in cool running water if possible, it said. If running water was not available, pouring water on the head three times in the name of the Father, Son, and Holy Spirit was permitted. It also contained a section on how to treat traveling bishops, deacons, and prophets. The majority of the *Didache* was composed as early as AD 70, but it appears that some material was added later.

PERSECUTION OF CHRISTIANITY

JEWISH PERSECUTION OF CHRISTIANS

Jews were the first group to persecute the early Christian community. Perceived as heretics, Christians were often harassed and oppressed by Jews. These persecutions were most severe between AD 30 and 70. The initial phase of Jewish persecution took place when Peter and John were imprisoned for preaching that Jesus had been resurrected from the dead (Acts 5). At the urging of the high priest (Acts 5), Peter and other apostles were arrested and imprisoned. They were later freed, rearrested, and flogged. Peter was arrested (Acts 12) and was imprisoned but released by an angel. In order to satisfy the Jewish leaders in Jerusalem, James the son of Zebedee and brother of John, was executed by Herod Agrippa (Acts 12:2). The apostle Paul, then known as Saul, held the coats of the Jews who stoned Stephen to death (Acts 7).

After his conversion to Christianity, Paul faced persecution at the hands of his former brethren. On his missionary journeys he was followed by Jews who attempted to sabotage his work. While in Jerusalem, Paul was beaten and only escaped death when the Romans intervened (Acts 21). There was also a Jewish plot to kill him (Acts 23). Paul was arrested for agitating the Jews and remained in prison two years (Acts 24–26).

The leader of the first Christian community in Jerusalem, James the brother of Jesus, was martyred in AD 62. His death at the temple accelerated Christianity's break from Judaism.

ROMAN PERSECUTION OF CHRISTIANS

Because Christianity was different from any other religion practiced in the empire, Rome did not understand it and reacted with suspicion. Most persecutions were localized until the third century, when they became empire-wide. The Romans persecuted Christians for several reasons.

First, Christians worshipped a man whom they claimed had been raised from the dead. The Romans put no stock in the stories of Jesus' resurrection. In their eyes Christians were ignorant and superstitious. Moreover, Jesus had been executed for treason against Rome. The authorities feared that if Jesus was a traitor, so were his followers.

Second, the Romans viewed Christianity as another Jewish sect. The Palestinian Jews rebelled against Rome in AD 66 and again in 135, making Christians guilty by association. In each case the Romans committed thousands of soldiers to squelch the rebellion. Wars cost money, took time, slowed commerce, and stopped the flow of tribute. Naturally, Rome opposed any group believed to cause such trouble.

Third, Christians steadfastly held to monotheism and thus refused to participate in Roman religious festivals. As these events were often state supported and participation in them was seen as an expression of loyalty to the gods and the empire, Christians were perceived as disloyal citizens.

Fourth, Christianity was a universal religion. It placed no emphasis on class, gender, or race. In fact, many of the earliest Christian converts were women, slaves, and the less fortunate. Rome, in contrast, was a class-oriented society, and the idea of equality was anathema. The Romans associated Christianity with weaklings, women, and slaves.

Fifth, many Christians did not believe in killing. This led them to avoid arenas and public executions. It also kept many from enlisting in the army. The Romans viewed this as the ultimate civic disloyalty and used it as a reason for the great persecution, which began under Diocletian in 303.

Sixth, Christians were often accused of awful practices. The Eucharist symbolism of eating Christ's flesh and drinking his blood led many Romans to believe Christians were cannibals. In Roman society everyone followed some religious system. Atheism was perceived negatively. Since Christians worshipped an invisible God, many Romans perceived them as atheistic. Christians were also accused of incest because Christian spouses often called each other "brother" and "sister."

Nero (54–68). Romans had high hopes for Nero, and many believed he would be a good emperor. His reign began well, but he soon became fearful that someone might try to take his throne and executed anyone who posed a threat, including his mother. In the early 60s, Nero began to lose his mind. He declared himself a god, built himself a golden palace, and claimed he had conversations with Apollo. In 64, sections of Rome were destroyed by fire. Many scholars believe Nero caused the fire so he could build a new Rome. In any case he blamed the fire on Christians. The Roman historian Tacitus (AD 56–117) said no one believed this, but Christians were hated because of their abominations.[7] Nero then began to persecute Christians in increasingly cruel ways. He often had them dressed in animal skins and thrown into the arena to be eaten by wild animals. He crucified them, set them on fire, and then used them for torches at public events. Church tradition maintains that Peter and Paul were martyred in Rome under Nero. He was killed by his own bodyguards in 68.

Domitian (81–96). Domitian was a cruel, arrogant, and superstitious emperor who demanded to be worshipped as a god. He supported the state-sanctioned religions as a way to ensure civic loyalty. All foreign gods and religions were viewed as potential avenues to treason and revolt. Church tradition dates the apostle John's exile to Patmos and the persecutions of Revelation 2–3 to the time of Domitian.

Trajan (98–117). Trajan had no overt hatred of Christianity, but he feared secret religions. An interesting exchange of letters between Trajan and Pliny the Younger (61–ca. 112), the governor of Pontus/Bithynia, discussed what to do with the growing population of Christians. Pliny told Trajan:

> They have been accustomed to meet before daybreak, and to recite a hymn antiphonally to Christ, as to a god, and to bind themselves by an oath, not for the commission of any crime but to abstain from theft, robbery, adultery, and breach of faith, and not to deny a deposit when it was claimed. After the conclusion of this ceremony it was their custom to depart and meet again to take food; but it was ordinary and harmless food, and they had ceased this practice after my edict in which, in accordance with your orders, I had forbidden secret societies. I thought it the more necessary, therefore, to find out what truth there was in this by applying torture to two maidservants, who were called deaconesses. But I found nothing but a depraved and extravagant superstition, and I therefore postponed my examination and had recourse to you for consultation.[8]

Trajan told Pliny that there should be no deliberate searching out of Christians. If arrested, those who recanted could go free.

Anonymous accusations of Christians were forbidden. Simeon (62–107), bishop of Jerusalem, and Ignatius, bishop of Antioch, were martyred under Trajan.

Marcus Aurelius (161–180). During the reign of Marcus Aurelius, Christianity continued to grow, particularly among the upper classes, and it became more aggressive in its apologetics and its evangelism. Faced with several military defeats, Marcus Aurelius blamed Christianity, saying it precipitated the decline of traditional Roman religions that had always protected the empire. The most severe persecutions of Christians during this period occurred in Asia Minor and the region of Lyons in modern-day France. Justin Martyr (103–165) was put to death under Marcus Aurelius.

Septimius Severus (193–211). After returning from campaigns in Egypt and Palestine, Septimius Severus became concerned over the lack of reverence for state religions, so he prohibited conversions to Christianity and Judaism. Though the Severian persecutions were not as devastating as others, Christians in North Africa were martyred, including the female martyrs Perpetua (181–203) and Felicitas (d. 203).

Trajan Decius (249–251). Trajan Decius wanted to return Rome to its former glory. In order for this to occur, he believed the old Roman religions would need to be revived and Christianity would need to be annihilated. Knowing that Christians were unbending in their monotheism, Trajan Decius made everyone in the empire offer a small sacrifice to the state gods. Some Christians offered sacrifices, others burned incense, and still others refused and were martyred. Trajan Decius died in battle with the Goths in 251, and the persecutions ceased.

Valerian (253–260). Valerian initially tolerated Christianity. However, after several military defeats he began to use it as a scapegoat. He attempted to exile the Christians in 257, but this was unsuccessful so he began to persecute them. Valerian's plan was to kill Christian leaders in hope that this would destabilize the entire

Christian movement. Cyprian of Carthage (d. 258) was martyred, but the plan ultimately failed.

Diocletian (285–305). Diocletian began to persecute Christians in 295 for their refusal to join the army. All Christian officers were removed from the army in 303. Then he began the Great Persecution (ca. 303–311). Diocletian executed not only church leaders but all classes of Christians. He ordered the burning of all Christian churches and Scriptures. The persecutions ceased when co-emperor Galerius (305–311) became ill and asked the remaining Christians to pray for him.

INTELLECTUAL PERSECUTION

Skilled in rhetoric, pagan writers and philosophers mocked Christianity. Christ's miraculous birth, resurrection, and miracles were all targets of ridicule. Christianity was depicted as an irrational religion for the ignorant. The best-known critics were Lucian of Samosata (fl. 165), Celsus (late second century), and Porphyry (232–305). Celsus argued that Christianity was a radical Jewish sect that was attempting to unravel the fabric of Roman society. Jesus was a fraud who learned magic in Egypt, he said. Rather than support persecution, Celsus tried to persuade Christians to be good citizens and return to the traditional Roman deities.

THE APOLOGISTS

The apologists defended Christianity from misrepresentation and attack. Just as the New Testament fulfilled the Old Testament, the apologists believed Christianity was the logical culmination of Greek philosophy. But to persuade Roman opponents of this was a daunting task. The apologists also sought to demonstrate the fallacy of pagan religions and the truth of Christianity. Their knowledge of both pagan religions and Christianity made them adept defenders of the faith. They explained that Christians posed no threat to Rome and asked for Christianity to exist in peace.

The apologists were well versed in Greek philosophy. Their ability to explain the *Logos* principle demonstrated how Jesus could be understood philosophically. Apologetic writings also explained that Christianity was not new because Jesus was the prophesied Messiah of the Old Testament. The Romans respected institutions that stood the test of time and had virtue.

Justin Martyr (100–165). Justin Martyr was the most influential apologist. Born in Flavia Neapolis (in modern-day Israel), he studied philosophy. One day while walking along the beach in Ephesus, he met an old man who explained to him how Jesus was the Messiah who had been prophesied in the Old Testament. Justin was converted and began to consider himself a philosopher for Christ. He spent most of his remaining years in Rome. His most famous encounter with pagan philosophy was his debate with a Cynic philosopher named Crescens (fl. second century). A friend of emperor Marcus Aurelius, Crescens had Justin and six followers arrested. Since they would not renounce Christ, they were beheaded.

Justin's writings are painstakingly logical, reconciling faith and reason. He maintained that the ethics and *Logos* principle of Stoic philosophy had much in common with Christianity. All rational beings are endowed with the divine *Logos*, according to Justin, and men like Plato, Socrates, and Abraham were "Christians" before Christ.

In his *First Apology*, Justin made a strong case for Christianity's right to exist and refuted pagan accusations of immorality. His *Second Apology* explained why God allowed his followers to suffer at the hands of nonbelievers. In *Dialogue with Trypho, A Jew*, Justin argued that Jesus fulfilled Old Testament prophecies of the Messiah. Christianity, therefore, was not a new religion but the logical fulfillment of Judaism.

Athenagoras of Athens (fl. 177). Athenagoras is best remembered for his *Plea on Behalf of the Christians*. Written to Marcus Aurelius, the *Plea* explained how Christians were loyal citizens and more moral than the followers of pagan religions. He explained that the charges of cannibalism, atheism, and incest were nothing more than pagan fabrications.

Theophilus of Antioch (late second century). Converted as an adult by the bishop of Antioch, Theophilus is best known for a series of books titled *To Autolycus* (ca. 182). In these works he attacked pagan idolatry and emperor worship and contrasted the morality of pagans with that of Christians. He also provided an allegorical interpretation of the book of Genesis. His chronology of the world demonstrated that Moses and the prophets predated Greek philosophy and thus were superior to it.

Tatian of Assyria (fl. 140–165). Tatian was the student of Justin Martyr. His surviving works are generally orthodox but were condemned by church fathers like Tertullian (160–220) and Irenaeus (140–202) because he fell into the Encratite heresy. (Encratites abstained from wine, animal meat, sexual intercourse, and marriage. Often they replaced wine in the Eucharist with water or milk.) Tatian despised the Roman Empire and may have been attracted to Christianity because it downplayed dedication to the emperor.

Widely read in Syria, Tatian's *Diatessaron* compiled the four Gospels into a biography of Jesus. *To the Greeks* was his great apologetic work. He defended Christianity against the charge of being a philosophy of barbarians, attacked the immorality of Greek religion, and argued that Moses and the Old Testament prophets were older and wiser than the Greek philosophers.

CHAPTER THREE

PROBLEMS FROM WITHIN

While the church was facing physical persecution and intellectual opposition from non-Christians, it was also dealing with doctrinal problems within its own ranks. The beliefs of some groups were deemed contrary to the Christian faith, and they were labeled heretics.

The five best-known heresies of the early church era were Gnosticism, Marcionism, Manichaeism, Monarchianism, and Montanism. Other doctrinal disagreements did not rise to the level of heresy but also led to schisms, some of which were permanent. The most important schisms of this era were those of the Novatianists and Donatists.

HERESIES

GNOSTICISM

The Gnostics (from the Greek word *gnosis*, meaning "knowledge") believed salvation came through attaining secret knowledge not available to all. With its emphasis on philosophy, Alexandria was a center of gnostic activity. Because the gnostics were a secret group, their origins are obscure. Claiming to have acquired knowledge that Jesus taught his disciples in private, they collected his

alleged sayings and interpreted them according to their own doctrine. As the first line of the gnostic *Gospel of Thomas* says, "These
are the secret sayings that the living Jesus spoke and Didymos Judas
Thomas recorded."[1]

Gnosticism syncretized elements of Platonic dualism, Persian
Zoroastrianism, Roman mystery religions, and Christianity.
Gnostics had some familiarity with Judaism as well. Justin Martyr
believed Simon Magus, the magician from Acts 8:9–24, was the
founder of Gnosticism.

Almost all that was known about the gnostics was provided by
their opponents until a large cache of their writings was uncovered
at Nag Hammadi, Egypt, in 1945.

Influential Gnostics included Cerinthus (ca. 100) in Ephesus,
Basilides (fl. 120–140) in Alexandria, Saturninus (fl. 150–160) in
Syria, and Valentinus (100–160) in Rome. Major gnostic writings
included the *Gospel of Truth*, the *Gospel of Thomas*, and the *Gospel of
Mary*. Gnostic churches were prominent in Gaul (modern southern
France), Syria, Rome, and North Africa.

There was no standard form of Gnosticism; there were many
gnostic systems, teachers, and beliefs. There were, however, several
shared characteristics among most gnostic systems. The hallmark of
Gnosticism was its belief in a secret knowledge that, once acquired,
led to salvation.

The gnostics taught that spirit and knowledge were good. Flesh
and physical substance were evil. As in Platonism, the body was seen
as the prison of the soul. In order not to create any more flesh, some
gnostics were celibate. Others gave themselves over to libertinism
since they believed the flesh was inconsequential.

The gnostic creation story was dualistic. Gnostics answered
the question, How could a good God create such a debased world?
by arguing that a good God did not create it. Since the world is
composed of substance, a good God could not have created it. An

inferior creator known as the demiurge and identified with Jehovah of the Old Testament created the physical world.

The Supreme Being or Father was the greater God. He placed a certain amount of divine substance or knowledge into each person. The *pneumatics* were said to have vast amounts of knowledge. The *psychics* had led less, but with the potential to gain more. The *hylics* had no divine substance and no potential to obtain it.

In order to achieve salvation, a person needed to be taught by a gnostic teacher who had already acquired the secret knowledge. As a person became aware of this knowledge, he climbed higher and higher through the heavenly realms until reaching *pleroma*, or fullness. The return of the gnostic soul to *pleroma* completed the salvation process.

For the gnostic Christian, Jesus was the avenue to secret knowledge. The *Gospel of Truth* states, "That is the gospel of him whom they seek, which he has revealed to the perfect through the mercies of the father as the hidden mystery, Jesus the anointed."[2] Jesus says in the *Gospel of Thomas*, "Whoever finds the interpretation of these sayings will not experience death."[3] Since the flesh was evil, the gnostics perceived Jesus as being pure spirit with no flesh. This teaching removed Christ's humanity and called into question the doctrines of his incarnation and crucifixion.

Obviously, the message of Gnosticism was opposed to the traditional Christian message. Orthodox Christianity taught that salvation was open to everyone. Gnosticism taught that salvation was only available to those who knew its secrets. As the *Gospel of Truth* stated, "If one has knowledge, he gets what belongs to him and draws it to himself."[4]

MARCIONISM

Born in Sinope in northern Asia Minor, Marcion (d. ca. 154) was a shipbuilder and the son of a bishop. He moved to Rome around 140 and gave a large amount of money (200,000 sesterces) to the church. This gift endeared him to the church, and he became influential. He then fell under the influence of Cerdo (ca. 138), a gnostic teacher. Marcion began to expound his new beliefs to the church in Rome around 144. His teachings were repudiated, and he was expelled from the church. The church even returned his money. He then founded his own church. Justin Martyr reported that, by 150, Marcionism had spread all over the empire.

Like Gnosticism, Marcionism taught a radical dualism: the spirit was good and the flesh was bad. There were also two gods: the demiurge, the Creator God of the Old Testament, and the God of love in the New Testament, revealed in Jesus. The demiurge was evil. He was strict, legalistic, and violent. He demanded an eye for an eye, allowed evil into the world, and required blood sacrifices. He was inferior to Jesus, who was forgiving and redemptive. Jesus came to declare a new way separate from the demiurge. Faith in Christ, not a secretive knowledge, was required for salvation. Jesus was not the Jewish Messiah of the Old Testament but a universal Savior. Jesus was not born but was rather a purely spiritual being.

Marcion was the first person to define a canon of New Testament writings that were considered authoritative. It included the Gospel of Luke and ten of Paul's letters. Marcion chose these books because he believed they were the least influenced by Judaism. Yet certain aspects of these books, he said, had been altered by Judaizers, Christians who still accepted Mosaic law. So he redacted these writings. For instance, Jesus' birth and genealogy were removed from the Gospel of Luke. Marcion believed that only the apostle Paul understood Jesus. The other disciples were teaching a modified Judaism. Marcion's canon gave much incentive for other Christians to begin to develop their own.

MANICHAEISM

Mani (216–277) was the founder of Manichaeism. Born in Persia, he was influenced by Zoroastrianism, ancient Babylonian religions, Judaism, and Christianity. In 240 Mani became convinced he was a prophet and began to teach his beliefs. Zoroastrians forced him to leave Persia, but when Sapor I (242–272) came to the throne in 242, he was allowed to return and resume teaching. Bahram I (273–276), a Zoroastrian, succeeded Sapor I and had Mani beaten to death in 276.

Similar to Gnosticism, Manichaeism taught a radical dualism between the god of light and the god of darkness. The god of darkness stole some of the light and used it to create the physical world. Some of the light was also trapped in men's souls. One achieved salvation when this light was freed. Jesus, Buddha, and others were sent to guide people to the light and purge the world of darkness. Followers of Manichaeism were divided into two classes. The *perfectaie* lived in perfect harmony with the light. They did not swear oaths, ate only vegetables, and were expected to remain celibate. The *hearers* heard the god of light's message but needed the help of the *perfectaie* to understand it. *Hearers* did not live by the *perfectaie* restrictions. The *perfectaie* dedicated their lives to preaching Manichaeism, and the *hearers* supported them financially.

In order not to create more fleshly prisons of the soul, Manichaeism stressed celibacy, though Augustine (354–430), who at one time was a Manichean hearer, doubted that anyone actually followed this stricture. The eating of meat was forbidden, and Manichees took part in a communal meal of fruit. Women could be *perfectaie* but could not hold leadership positions.

Manichaeism was present in the Mediterranean world until the sixth century and in central Asia until the thirteenth century. It may have influenced several medieval heretical groups such as the bogomils, cathars, and the Paulicians.

MONARCHIANISM

What is the relationship between God the Father and Jesus the Son? How did Jesus become divine? How can Christianity be monotheistic if it has more than one God? Monarchianism attempted to answer these questions and safeguard the unity of the Godhead.

There were two types of Monarchianism. Dynamic Monarchianism, or Adoptionism, was advocated by Theodoret (ca. 150); its goal was to protect the oneness of God. It taught that Jesus was not truly divine but a man adopted by God who became a point of divine activity. Paul of Samosata (ca. 200–275) taught that the *Logos* was infused into Jesus at his baptism. Jesus, therefore, was not the God-man but rather a man who became God. His task was to point people toward God.

Modalistic Monarchianism, or Patripassianism, was the belief that Christ and God the Father were one and the same. Sabellius of Rome (fl. ca. 215) was an advocate of this system. He taught that the Godhead was not three persons but one person who manifested himself in three different ways at different times: the Father in creation, the Son at redemption, and the Holy Spirit at sanctification. Sabellius supported his theory by appealing to John 10:30, "The Father and I are one." He was condemned by Tertullian and Hippolytus (170–235), and his arguments led to some of the earliest discussions of the Trinity.

Montanism

Montanus (fl. second century) was the founder of the montanist sect. He had been a priest of the Cybele in the Phrygian region of Asia Minor. This cult was based on supposedly divine, ecstatic utterances that were delivered in a frenzied state. Following his conversion to Christianity in 156, he began prophesying and claiming he was the spokesman for the Paraclete (Holy Spirit), if not the Paraclete himself. He declared that his prophecies were as authoritative as Scripture. Claiming to be under the influence of the Spirit, Montanus would appear to lose control and speak as if he were in ecstasy. His detractors argued that the biblical prophets were not removed from their faculties when prophesying. Detractors also took issue with Montanus's claim that his movement inaugurated a new age, characterized by a greater outpouring of the Holy Spirit and a more rigorous moral life among Christians. Two women named Priscilla and Maximilla accompanied him and were considered prophetesses.

Montanism was largely orthodox but overemphasized the role of the Holy Spirit. Montanists wanted to see the Spirit continue to act as he had in the New Testament era. They prophesied the imminent return of Christ, the new age of the Holy Spirit, and that the New Jerusalem would be in Phrygia. Montanists were also strict and legalistic. They held rigorous fasts, forbade widows and widowers to remarry, practiced extreme asceticism, and embraced the idea of martyrdom.

Montanism attracted followers because of its charismatic nature, its lack of reliance on the episcopal structure, and, since many viewed the church as morally permissive, its scrupulous principles. Tertullian of Carthage was attracted to Montanism because he agreed with its strict form of Christianity.

SCHISMS

NOVATIANISM

Novatianism was born out of the Decian persecution of 250–251, during which many Christians were martyred, others confessed Christ but survived, and others renounced their faith. Those who would not renounce Christ were known as confessors and were held in high esteem. Those who did renounce Christ were considered to have lapsed into apostasy.

When the persecution ended, those who apostatized (known as apostates) wanted to return to the church. Some Christians believed these apostates should be rejected. Others believed they could return but their leadership roles and participation in certain rites should be limited according to the gravity of their apostasy. Among the apostates, the *sacrificati* were those who willingly sacrificed to the Roman gods. The *libellatici* never sacrificed but had purchased false documents stating that they had. Some had sacrificed only under the duress of torture. Who could judge and forgive them? The confessors and the bishops both claimed this right.

The Decian persecutions had been harsh in North Africa, so the question of the lapsed was an important issue. The most prominent theologian who took part in the debates was Cyprian (d. 258), the bishop of Carthage. During the Decian persecutions, Cyprian left Carthage and directed the church from exile. When the persecution ended and Cyprian returned, he was appalled to learn that the confessors were forgiving most of the apostates. Such leniency jeopardized the purity of the church, he said. Moreover, Cyprian believed only the bishops, as successors of the apostles, were in a position to judge the lapsed.

Cyprian argued that if the lapsed were truly remorseful and made recompense for their sin as instructed by the bishop or his representative, a formal remission of sin could be given. The confessors could not forgive the lapsed. This was a major step in the development of the bishop's authority and the sacrament of penance.

In Rome an important leader named Novatian (ca. 200–258) saw the issue differently. Following the Decian persecution, he led the faction that did not want to taint the church by allowing the lapsed to return. When a moderate named Cornelius (251–253) became the bishop of Rome, Novatian's followers countered by naming him bishop of Rome as well. Novatian was removed from the church in Rome, but his followers had already founded churches throughout the empire.

Another question then arose. If a person was baptized in a Novatian church but wanted to join a Roman church, should the Roman church accept his baptism as legitimate? Cyprian and the North Africans said no. The Novatianist priests had turned their backs on the true church, and thus all their priestly functions were no longer valid. Bishop Stephen of Rome (254–257) took another position. He maintained that the performance of the rite mattered, not the person who performed it. In order to add weight to his position, Stephen made one of the earliest claims to the primacy of the Roman bishop. By appealing to Peter as Jesus' successor (Matt 16:18–19), Stephen concluded that all the churches should follow the lead of Peter's successor, the bishop of Rome.

DONATISM

The Donatist Schism was precipitated by the Great Persecution of Diocletian (303–311). Several of the North African bishops and pastors had turned over their copies of Scripture to the Romans for destruction. These clergymen were known as *traditores*, literally "those who handed over." When the persecution ended, they wanted to return to their former positions. Those who had remained firm did not want to allow the *traditores* to resume their offices.

The problem was complex. Three bishops who had not lapsed were required to perform the ordination of a new bishop. If one of the bishops who performed the ordination was later found to have lapsed, the ordination was considered invalid. This threatened the episcopal structure and thus the stability of the church, as in the case of Caecilian (d. before 343).

Caecilian had been ordained bishop of Carthage in 311. It was later determined that Felix of Aptungi, one of Caecilian's consecrators, had handed over Scriptures to the Romans. Caecilian had also encouraged Christians to flee rather than face martyrdom. An anti-Caecilian faction, who became known as Donatists, would not accept Caecilian as their bishop and named Majorinus (d. ca. 313–314) as a competing bishop of Carthage. The Donatists would not follow a bishop or priest who had fallen. They also maintained that if a sacrament had been administered by a member of the clergy who had lapsed, it was not valid. For instance, if a priest was found to be an apostate, no Eucharist he performed would have merit. This would be true for every sacrament he or someone he had ordained performed.

To settle the matter, Emperor Constantine (306–337) called for a council to be held at Arles (in France) in 314. The council determined that the sacrament itself was holy, not the priest. The anti-Caecilian position was declared heretical. The schism, however, did not end.

After the death of Majorinus, Donatus (d. 355) was selected by the anti-Caecilian faction as bishop of Carthage. The Donatists then set up their own churches. In order to enforce the decision of his council and put down the rival church, Constantine sent troops to North Africa in 317. Many Donatists had their property confiscated, and others were forced into exile.

An advocate of the Roman position, Augustine of Hippo frequently spoke out against Donatism. Based on the parable of the wheat and weeds (Matt 13:24–30), he said the church was never meant to be a pure body but rather a community of saints and sinners. God would perform the final separation at the end of time. The Donatists, therefore, were in error.

For Augustine, the church itself was holy; its people were not. Augustine argued that the Donatists placed too much emphasis on the priest and not enough on the grace of Jesus Christ. The value of the sacrament has nothing to do with the person who administers it, Augustine said. Jesus instituted it and guarantees its efficacy. In spite of persecution, Donatism remained strong in North Africa well into the seventh century.

CHAPTER FOUR

CHRISTIAN ORTHODOXY AND THE ANTE-NICENE FATHERS

The second-century heretics, Marcion in particular, forced the church to consider many theological issues. What was Jesus' message? Did any group have exclusive access to Christ's message? Was it legitimate for different groups to interpret Christ's message in different ways? The church refined its definition of orthodoxy as it answered these and other questions.

APOSTOLIC SUCCESSION

The office of bishop was the most important leadership position in the second- and third-century church, considered by Ignatius of Antioch to be the apex of ecclesiastical authority. The idea of apostolic succession implied an unbroken line of bishops that could be traced back to the apostles. The orthodoxy of the church could be protected, according to this line of reasoning, because each bishop received the teachings of Christ from the bishop before him. He then passed those teachings on to the bishop who followed him. The teachings of the church, therefore, would remain pure and consistent from the time of Christ and the apostles.

Irenaeus of Lyons (140–202) argued that apostolic succession was the best defense against Gnosticism. He insisted that the apostolic faith was preserved by a public succession of bishops that began with the apostles. Moreover, this faith was preached publically. Irenaeus believed this proved that the message remained the same. The gnostics on the other hand believed in secret knowledge that had not been preached consistently and publicly since the time of the apostles. Gnostics, Irenaeus said, could not demonstrate an unchanging line of doctrine traced back to Christ and his apostles. Apostolic succession, therefore, came to be viewed as a safeguard of consistency and truth.

The wealthiest cities became the most important sees, or homes of the bishops. In many cases a city asserted its importance by claiming that one of the apostles was its first bishop, had been martyred there, or performed some great service for the church there. Alexandria claimed Mark, Jerusalem was identified with James, and Ephesus aligned itself with John. Rome was associated with both Peter and Paul.

The elevation of the Roman bishop (later referred to as the pope) began as early as the late first century. There was already a tradition that Peter had been the first bishop of Rome and that Peter and Paul had both been martyred there. In the second century Irenaeus produced a list that traced the Roman bishops back to Peter. The tradition became so strong that around 165 a necropolis was erected on Vatican Hill on the supposed spot of Peter's crucifixion. Another was set up on the road to Ostia for the apostle Paul.

By the beginning of the third century, many viewed the church at Rome as the leading institution of the Christian world. There was no official recognition of Rome at this point, and many Christians were unwilling to follow its lead in doctrinal and practical matters. Still, there was little doubt about the Roman church's influence and importance.

Rule of Faith and the Apostles' Creed

The Rule of Faith was first mentioned by Irenaeus and Tertullian. It was not an actual document but a commonly accepted summary of Christian teaching that served as the norm for churches. Unlike the Apostles' Creed, whose wording was relatively fixed, the wording of the Rule of Faith varied. Yet its theological content was agreed upon and fixed. It was, in short, the apostolic message expressed in Scripture. It served as the basis for instructing catechumens and fighting heresy. A precursor to the Apostles' Creed, it focused on the virgin birth as well as Christ's death, resurrection, and return. Irenaeus defined the Rule of Faith as

> faith in one God, the Father Almighty, maker of heaven, and earth, and the sea, and all things that are in them; and in one Christ Jesus, the Son of God, who became incarnate for our salvation; and in the Holy Spirit, who proclaimed through the prophets the dispensations of God, and the advents, and the birth from a virgin, and the passion, and the resurrection from the dead, and the ascension into heaven in the flesh of the beloved Christ Jesus, our Lord, and his future manifestation from heaven in the glory of the Father "to gather all things in one," and to raise up anew all flesh of the whole human race.[1]

The earliest formal confessions of faith appeared in baptismal ceremonies, with the earliest known baptismal creed used by Hippolytus in the third century. In it the candidate was asked questions concerning the three persons of the Trinity. The Apostles' Creed used today dates from ca. 700. It is similar to the third-century Creed of Marcellus:

> I believe in God, All Governing; And in Christ Jesus His only begotten Son, our Lord, Who was begotten of the Holy Spirit and the Virgin Mary, Who was crucified under

Pontius Pilate and buried, Who rose from the dead on the third day, ascending to the heavens and taking His seat at the Father's right hand, whence He shall come to judge both living and dead; And [I believe] in the Holy Spirit, the holy Church for the forgiveness of sins, the resurrection of the body, life everlasting.[2]

DEVELOPMENT OF THE CANON

The thirty-nine books of the Old Testament were recognized officially by leading rabbis at the Council of Jamnia in AD 90, but they were already well established by the time of Jesus. Most early Christians accepted these books as authoritative for faith and practice but interpreted them differently from Judaism. Luke 24:44–45 stated that Jesus opened the eyes of the apostles so they could understand the Scripture's true meaning. The apostles then interpreted the Old Testament as pointing to Jesus, and the first Christians made the document their own.

The development of the New Testament canon was a more involved process. The term *canon* derives from a Greek word that means "rule" or "standard." At times New Testament authors refer to other New Testament writings as "Scripture"—the same word they used to refer to Old Testament writings. In 1 Timothy 5:18, quotations of Deuteronomy 25:4 and (a verbal match of) Luke 10:7 are identified as "Scripture." In 2 Peter 3:15–16, untaught and unstable people are said to "twist" Paul's letters "as they also do with the rest of the Scriptures." In their writings the early church fathers mentioned several criteria that a writing had to meet to be recognized as Scripture. It had to be written by or associated with an apostle (e.g., Mark was recognized as a close associate of Peter, and Luke, a traveling companion of Paul), follow the apostolic faith, be written during the apostolic era, and be widely accepted throughout the early church.

By the early second century, the church held a common under-standing of who wrote the four Gospels, and the authors' names were accepted as titles. According to third- and fourth-century historian Eusebius (260–339), Papias of Hierapolis (ca. 100) taught the following in the early second century:

> Mark became the interpreter of Peter and he wrote down accurately, but not in order, as much as he remem-bered of the sayings and doings of Christ. For he was not a hearer or follower of the Lord, but afterwards, as I said, of Peter, who adapted his teachings to the needs of the moment and did not make an ordered exposition of the sayings of the Lord. And so Mark made no mistake when he thus wrote down some things as he remembered them; for he made it his especial care to omit nothing of what he heard, and to make no false statement there-in. This is what Papias relates to Mark. Now concerning Matthew it is stated: "So then Matthew recorded the oracles in the Hebrew tongue, and interpreted them to the best of his ability."[3]

Justin Martyr accepted the Synoptic Gospels as Scripture, but his opinion of the Gospel of John is unclear. Tertullian accepted all four Gospels. He gave priority to Matthew and John because they had been written by apostles. Irenaeus believed that all four Gospels were authentic and believed it was important to include each of them in the canon since there were four corners and winds of the world. He also argued that these four testimonies provided a far more accurate picture of Christ than did Marcion, who only accepted the Gospel of Luke. By the end of the second century, the four Gospels, Acts, the thirteen letters attributed to Paul, and several other apostolic writings were accepted throughout most of Christendom.

Other books were more controversial. For instance, Christians in the East accepted the book of Hebrews, but those in the West initially did not. Christians in the West accepted the book of Revelation, but those in the East initially did not. Some Christian communities valued *First Clement*, Polycarp's *Letter to the Philippians*, the *Didache*, the *Shepherd of Hermas*, and other popular writings that were not included in the final canon.

The Muratorian Canon is a seventh- or eighth-century Latin reproduction of a Greek list of accepted texts that dates from the late second century. It lists the majority of books that are included in the modern Bible but excludes Hebrews, James, 1 and 2 Peter, and 3 John. It also includes the Wisdom of Solomon and the Apocalypse of Peter, both of which were excluded from the final canon. Eusebius of Caesarea listed the books he deemed canonical in 6.25 of his *Ecclesiastical History*. He acknowledged that some books were accepted by the church universally: the four Gospels, Acts, the letters of Paul (including Hebrews), 1 John, 1 Peter, and Revelation (though Eusebius personally considered Revelation spurious). Eusebius listed other books that were widely acknowledged as Scripture but disputed by some: James, Jude, 2 Peter, and 2 and 3 John. He also listed the books he deemed not canonical but valuable for Christian faith and practice: the *Acts of Paul*, the *Shepherd of Hermas*, the *Epistle of Barnabas*, and the *Didache*. Eusebius believed the *Gospel of Peter*, the *Gospel of Thomas*, the *Acts of Andrew*, and the *Acts of John* were heretical.

In his Easter Letter of 367, Athanasius of Alexandria (ca. 300–373) provided the first known list that corresponds exactly to the twenty-seven books of today's New Testament. These books were ratified as canonical by the Synod of Hippo in 393 and the Synod of Carthage in 397. Despite their authorization, some Christians still did not accept all twenty-seven books. Others continued to read books that had not been canonized.

THE ANTE-NICENE FATHERS

The church's leaders during this period are called the ante-Nicene fathers (a reference to the fact that they lived prior to the Council of Nicaea in 325). The following represent some of the most important ante-Nicene fathers.

IRENAEUS OF LYONS (CA. 125–200)

Irenaeus was a pupil of Polycarp, who in turn had been a student of the apostle John. He was a presbyter in Lyons (in France) who was sent to Rome in 177 with a letter from his bishop, Pothinus (ca. 87–177), concerning the Montanist controversy. While Irenaeus was in Rome, persecution of Christians broke out in Lyons, and Pothinus was killed. Upon his return Irenaeus was named bishop.

Irenaeus's most important work was *Against Heresies*. It warned Christians about the dangers of Gnosticism and Marcionism. To defeat these heresies, Irenaeus promoted apostolic succession as a safeguard of the Christian message. Irenaeus wrote:

> The Church, having received this preaching and this faith, although scattered throughout the whole world, yet, as if occupying but one house, carefully preserves it. She also believes these points of doctrine just as if she had but one soul, and one and the same heart, and she proclaims them, and teaches them, and hands them down, with perfect harmony, as if she possessed only one mouth. For, although the languages of the world are dissimilar, yet the import of the tradition is one and the same.[4]

Irenaeus insinuated that Rome was the most important see and that others should follow its lead. He called it "the very great, the very ancient, and the universally known Church founded and organized at Rome by the two most glorious apostles, Peter and Paul." The Roman church proclaimed "the faith preached to men, which comes down to our time by means of the succession of bishops." Irenaeus continued: "For it is a matter of necessity that every Church should agree with the [Roman] Church, on account of its preeminent authority, that is, the faithful everywhere, inasmuch as the apostolic tradition has been preserved continuously by those faithful men who exist everywhere."[5]

Irenaeus also wrote *The Demonstration of the Apostolic Preaching* to help a friend who was having difficulty choosing between Gnosticism, Judaism, and Christianity. This work became a guide for new converts.

Irenaeus's writings demonstrated his desire to defeat any form of what he considered to be heresy. His arguments were based on both the Old and New Testaments. He believed the Creator God and the Jesus-*Logos*, who was preexistent, were one and the same. Salvation was not a correction of creation but rather its fulfillment, which is found in Christ alone.

Irenaeus's Theory of Recapitulation was his most significant theological contribution. He based his theory on Romans 5:12 ("Therefore, just as sin entered the world through one man, and death through sin, in this way death spread to all men, because all sinned"), teaching that Jesus (*Logos*) was the new Adam. By not sinning, Jesus, who was fully man, reversed the effects of sin brought into the world by Adam. He wrote,

> For it was necessary that Adam should be summed up in Christ, that mortality might be swallowed up and overwhelmed by immortality; and Eve summed up in Mary, that a virgin should be a virgin's intercessor, and by a virgin's obedience undo and put away the disobedience of a virgin.[6]

With Jesus superseding Adam, disobedience was replaced with obedience. Jesus overcame Adam's mortality and death with immortality and life. Jesus was the new Adam who recovered all that was lost in the old Adam. In much the same way, the virgin

Mary overcame the sins of Eve. Irenaeus, therefore, was one of the first Christians to view Mary as playing a role in humanity's salvation alongside Jesus.

TERTULLIAN OF CARTHAGE (160–220)

A native of Carthage, Tertullian was the son of a Roman centurion. He received a good education and showed talent in rhetoric but despised philosophy, so he pursued law in Rome. After becoming a Christian around 192, he returned to Carthage. Tertullian said he had become a Christian because of the witness of the martyrs and a fear of hell. In fact, Carthage had faced so much persecution it was dubbed the "Church of the Martyrs." Tertullian's form of Christianity was legalistic and moralizing. His writings were often controversial. When arguing theology, he sought to win at all costs. Tertullian became an adherent of Montanism around 207. He may have been attracted to Montanists because his Christianity was strict like theirs.

Tertullian extolled martyrdom, but he did not run toward it. In fact, he wrote many Roman rulers to tell them that Christians were good citizens who did not deserve persecution. Tertullian believed women were responsible for original sin and perpetuated it through sex. Postbaptismal sin was to be feared. He insisted that Christians be totally dedicated to God. Therefore, they could not hold government office.

Tertullian was one of the first church fathers to use Latin in his theological treatises. He coined the terms *original sin, sacrament,* and *merit*. His description of the Trinity was one of the earliest and clearest: "one substance and three persons." Though later theologians fleshed out the meaning of this trinitarian formula, it became the definition of orthodoxy.

Tertullian viewed philosophy as a gateway to heresy. Christianity was based on apostolic teaching, not on philosophy. There was no reason to try to define difficult theological concepts in terms of philosophy. In many cases, Tertullian said, the truth of Christianity appeared ludicrous when evaluated by the standards of philosophy: "It is by all means to be believed, because it is absurd. And He was buried, and rose again; the fact is certain, because it is impossible."[7]

Tertullian is believed to be the author of thirty-one surviving writings. In his *Prescription Against the Heretics*, he claimed that the only true church is the visible church. It was not a secret society with secret knowledge as promoted by Gnosticism. He stated that only the true church, Catholic Christians, had the right to use the Scriptures. Apostolic tradition was the key to interpreting them correctly. In *Against Marcion*, Tertullian defended the oneness of Christ and the necessity of the Old Testament. In *Against Praxeas* he refuted modalism and provided an early explanation of the Trinity. *On the Flesh of Christ* was Tertullian's argument against the gnostic claim that all flesh is worthless and corrupt.

Cyprian of Carthage (200–258)

Cyprian was born into a rich pagan family in Carthage. He was converted at age forty-six. He then sold his possessions and gave the proceeds to the poor. Cyprian was elected bishop of Carthage in 249. When the Decian persecutions of 250 broke out in Carthage, he left the city and directed the church from exile. Because of this, many Carthaginian Christians accused him of being a deserter. His role in the readmittance of those who had apostatized or lapsed has already been discussed.

Cyprian was a clear spokesman for the developing monarchial episcopacy. He maintained that anyone who departed from the bishop departed from the church. He argued that one could not have God as Father if he did not have the church as mother.[8] His high view of the bishop was later used to promote Roman primacy, but Cyprian never held to Roman primacy himself. As one apostle was not superior to another, no church, including Rome, was superior to another, he said. Cyprian also introduced Old

Testament terminology into church life. He often referred to the bishop as "priest" and the Lord's Table as an "altar."

THE ALEXANDRIANS

Alexandria, Egypt, was home to a large Jewish population for several centuries prior to Christianity. These Jews had been influenced by the Septuagint. One prominent Alexandrian Jew named Philo (ca. 10 BC–ca. AD 45) allegorized the Old Testament and synthesized it with Greek philosophy. In fact, Philo claimed that Moses had been the tutor of the great Greek philosophers. Christianity was supposedly introduced to Alexandria by Mark, who may have written his Gospel there. Alexandria's Christians were more philosophical than believers in Rome or Carthage, and they used an allegorical method to interpret Scripture. In the first half of the second century, Gnosticism was popular in Alexandria, with gnostic leaders like Basilides (taught 117–138), Carpocrates (first half of the second century), and Valentinus frequently teaching there. In the latter half of the second century, orthodox Christianity strengthened. Its adherents soon developed their own catechetical school to educate Christians and battle the gnostics. Pantaenus (d. ca. 200) was the first known teacher in this school. Little is known about him. He is believed to have converted from Stoicism and hoped to reconcile Greek philosophy with Christianity. According to Eusebius, he became a missionary to India. Clement (ca. 150–215) and Origen (ca. 185–ca. 254) followed him and were Alexandria's greatest teachers and champions of orthodoxy.

CLEMENT OF ALEXANDRIA (CA. 150–215)

Born in Athens, Clement was converted after being convinced of Christianity's truths through philosophy. He relocated to Alexandria to study under Pantaenus. After Pantaenus left Alexandria, Clement became the primary teacher of the catechetical school.

His greatest student was Origen. After serving the school for many years, Clement left Alexandria during the 202 persecutions and was never heard from again.

He believed Greek philosophy pointed to and prepared people to hear the ultimate truth of the gospel. Just as the law had been given to the Jews, philosophy had been given to the Greeks: "Philosophy therefore is a preparation, making ready the way for him who is being perfected by Christ."[9] Whatever truth was gleaned from philosophy could be applied to the Scriptures and used by Christianity. He called this "plundering the Egyptians." Christianity was the last and greatest philosophy. For this reason Clement continued to wear his philosopher's robe.

Clement proposed a two-tiered system of understanding the Bible. Simple faith in the literal truth of Scripture was good and required of all, but it was not sufficient for one who wanted to mature in the Christian faith. The Bible should also be interpreted allegorically, using reason to build on foundational truths, he said, for such interpretation allowed one to discover principles of Platonic philosophy hidden in the biblical text. Those who were content to believe the Bible's literal meaning without ever moving on to allegorical interpretations were like children who were forever content with milk and refused to eat solid food, according to Clement. Wise people who reasoned their way to the Bible's deeper meaning he considered "true gnostics." Indeed, he regarded himself as a "true gnostic," leading others with similar desires for deeper truth.

Clement also emphasized the *Logos* doctrine. God was the loving Creator who revealed himself to humankind through the *Logos*. The *Logos* was the source of all truth and wisdom. Wherever there was truth, the *Logos* was present, displaying God's love. Thus, both the Greek philosophers and the biblical prophets received the truth they knew from the *Logos*. By refining their souls, the *Logos* helps Christians become more like Christ and follow his will. Only through the ministry of the *Logos* could a person become a true gnostic.

Clement was known for three great writings. *The Exhortation to the Greeks* was an apology that demonstrated the similarity of philosophy and Christianity. *The Instructor* portrayed Jesus as the divine *Logos*. *Miscellanies* showed how Christianity could resolve many intellectual concerns of the day.

ORIGEN (CA. 185–CA. 254)

Origen was born into a strong Christian family. Leonides (d. 202), his father, provided him with a basic Hellenistic education but also taught him the Christian Scriptures. Origen said that under his father's tutelage he memorized the entire New Testament and much of the Old.

When he was in his early twenties, he replaced Clement as the Alexandrian catechetical school's teacher. He also began to study Neoplatonism under Ammonius Saccas (175–242). He did this so he would be better equipped to combat the Greek philosophies that dominated Alexandria. This study, however, had the opposite effect. Neoplatonism had a deep impact on Origen and shaped his theology. Along with his teaching Origen visited Christian prisoners and attended their trials. He encouraged them to persevere even if it meant martyrdom. Demetrius (126–231), the bishop of Alexandria, became jealous of his fame and prevented him from visiting arrested Christians.

Origen taught during the day, and at night dedicated himself to study of the Scriptures. His study of Matthew 19:12, which references "eunuchs who have made themselves that way because of the kingdom of heaven," supposedly led him to castrate himself. The story of his castration might have been a fabrication of his jealous rivals though.

Origen visited Rome around 212. A few years later he traveled to Arabia at the governor's request to instruct him in the faith.

When persecution broke out in Rome in 214, Origen and his friend Ambrose went to Caesarea. At the request of the regional bishops, he preached and expounded the Scriptures. But Demetrius complained that a layman like Origen should not be permitted to preach and ordered him to return to Alexandria in 216. There he resumed his regimen of teaching, studying, and writing for the next fourteen years. In 230, Origen was sent on church business to Greece. On his way he stopped in Caesarea where his friends ordained him. Demetrius claimed the ordination was invalid because Origen's self-castration was against canonical law. Demetrius convened councils that revoked Origen's ordination.

Origen spent the last twenty years of his life in Caesarea teaching, studying, and writing. He was welcomed by the Christians of Caesarea, but Christians in Palestine were still facing sporadic persecutions. Emperor Trajan Decius blamed a plague that had raged throughout Rome on Christians who had refused to worship him as a god. Persecution followed and Origen was arrested, beaten, pilloried, and bound hand and foot. He would not apostatize and was eventually released. His death in 254, however, was certainly hastened by his torture.

Prior to Augustine, Origen was the most prolific theological writer in Christendom. His works have led some theologians to praise him as brilliant while others have denounced him as a heretic. Indeed his writings helped shape both what would become orthodoxy and what would become heresy.

Origin's *Hexapla* was an edition of the Old Testament with six versions placed side by side in six columns: the Hebrew Old Testament, a Greek transliteration of the Hebrew Old Testament, the Greek translation of Aquila of Sinope (fl. second century), the translation of Symmachus the Ebionite (fl. mid-second century [ca. 150]), the Septuagint, and the translation of Theodotion. There was probably only one complete copy of the *Hexapla*, and it was either lost or destroyed. Fragments of partial copies have been collected and published in various editions.

In *On First Principles*, Origen outlined his Tripartite Hermeneutic. He believed Scripture could be interpreted literally, morally, or spiritually (allegorically). Literal interpretation often was not possible, he said. The allegorical method allowed Christianity to explain away seemingly silly passages like those attributing human characteristics to God, according to Origen. (One would think that in his exegesis of Matthew 19:12, he would have chosen the allegorical approach.)

Origen perceived God as perfect and without a body. He is a purely spiritual mind. God is personal and has a relationship with the *Logos*, who is the first emanation of the Father. Origen affirmed the eternal generation of the *Logos* but still viewed it as subordinate to the Father. In turn, the Holy Spirit was inferior to the *Logos*. For this reason Arius (256–336) cited Origen as a source of his understanding of Jesus' subordination to the Father.

Origen understood the *Logos* as the wisdom of God, incarnate in the soul of Jesus Christ. God became comprehensible through Christ/the *Logos*. The *Logos* remained with the Father, but it also remained within Christ's human soul. Origen called this the hypostatic union. The *Logos* could be Christ the teacher and the source of redemption.

The *Logos* also spoke to Christians through the words of Scripture. Everything in Scripture points to Christ. Origen insisted that Old Testament passages that do not seem to be referring to Christ indeed do refer to him when read in a spiritual or allegorical sense.

Similar to Plato's concept of Forms, Origen believed in the preexistence and eternality of souls. He maintained that a person's soul existed prior to his physical state. Souls became embodied because of their sins in their purely spiritual existence.

Origin also held to the concept of *apocatastasis*, or universal salvation. He maintained that God was gradually purifying his creation. When this purification was complete, everything would be redeemed and placed back into God's order. As part of the created order, the Devil would be included in this redemption. Hell was not eternal but a place of learning.

Despite his departure from orthodoxy on the point of universal salvation, Origen's description of Christ's ultimate triumph is an apt illustration of the hope that drove all the ante-Nicene fathers.

> Seeing, then, that such is the end, when all enemies will be subdued to Christ, when death—the last enemy—shall be destroyed, and when the kingdom shall be delivered up by Christ (to whom all things are subject) to God the Father; let us, I say, from such an end as this, contemplate the beginnings of things. For the end is always like the beginning: and, therefore, as there is one end to all things, so ought we to understand that there was one beginning; and as there is one end to many things, so there spring from one beginning many differences and varieties, which again, through the goodness of God, and by subjection to Christ, and through the unity of the Holy Spirit, are recalled to one end, which is like unto the beginning.[10]

CHAPTER FIVE

WORSHIP IN THE
SECOND AND
THIRD CENTURIES

I n spite of its illegal status, Christianity continued to spread. By the end of the third century, there may have been as many as five million Christians. The largest concentrations were in Asia Minor, Egypt, North Africa, Syria, and central Italy.

In order to avoid the authorities, most second- and third-century Christians worshipped in small house churches. The oldest known surviving house church, dating to 232, was found in Dura-Europa on the banks of the Euphrates River in Iraq. In more populated areas Christians often worshipped and buried their dead in caves outside the city. They viewed these caves (*refrigariums*) as holding places where the dead slept until the return of Christ. Dating from approximately 150, the catacombs of Saint Callistus outside Rome are a prime example.

Second-century worship (liturgy) remained simple and largely unchanged from the previous century. By the beginning of the third century, however, the liturgy had become more structured, and distinct church offices were appearing, evidence of a developing episcopal system. The most important offices included bishop, presbyter or priest, and deacon. Minor offices also appeared, and personal devotional practices were abundant.

CHRISTIAN GATHERINGS

By worshipping on Sunday, Christians differentiated themselves from Jews. Christians believed Jesus had been resurrected on Sunday, so worship services on Sunday commemorated the resurrection. Important second-century patristic writers such as Irenaeus of Lyons, Justin Martyr, and Tertullian agreed that the Christian day of worship was Sunday.

The worship liturgy was a celebration of the new life and hope found in Christianity. Worship was a time to commune with Jesus. The services consisted of prayer, praise, thanksgiving, supplication, biblical readings, and a sermon. The service usually concluded with the Eucharist. Services would have also provided Christians with opportunities to share their experiences and needs with one another.

Justin Martyr was the first church father to describe the liturgical order of Sunday worship:

> And on the day which is dedicated to the sun, all those who live in cities or who dwell in the countryside gather in a common meeting, and for as long as there is time the Memoirs of the Apostles or the writings of the prophets are read, as long as time permits; then, when the reader has finished, the president verbally gives a warning and appeal for the imitation of these good things. Then we all rise together and offer prayers, and, as we before said, when our prayer is ended, bread is brought forth along with wine and water, and the president likewise gives thanks to the best of his ability, and the people call out their assent, saying the Amen. Then there is a distribution to each, and a participation in the Eucharist elements, which are also sent with deacons to those who are absent. Those who are wealthy and who wish to do so, contribute whatever they themselves care to give; and the collection is placed with the president, who aids the orphans and widows and those who through sickness

or any other cause, are in need, and those who are imprisoned and the strangers who are sojourning among us, and
in short, he takes care of all who are in need. The Day of the
Sun is the day on which we all gather in a common meeting, because it is the first day, the day on which God, changing darkness and matter, created the world; and it is the day
on which Jesus Christ our Savior rose from the dead. For
He was crucified on the day before that of Kronos; and on
that day after that of Kronos, which is the Day of the Sun,
He appeared to His apostles and disciples, and taught them
these things, which we have also submitted to you also for
your consideration.[1]

Christians also observed holy days. These gatherings were similar to the Jewish feasts and festivals recorded in the Old Testament.
The most important holy day was the Feast of Pascha, later known
as Easter, the Christian counterpart to the Jewish Passover. It commemorated the resurrection of Christ and served as the primary day
when catechumens were baptized. The date for Pascha was settled at
the Council of Nicaea in 325. The council determined that it would
be celebrated on the Sunday following the fourteenth paschal moon
after the spring equinox. Lent began forty days prior to Easter. It
was a time of preparation marked by fasting and penitence. Advent
was a time of expectation and preparation preceding the nativity of
Jesus that would be celebrated at Christmas. The Feast of Epiphany
was held on January 6. In the West it commemorated the arrival of
the magi, and in the East it marked Jesus' baptism. Observed fifty
days after Easter, Pentecost celebrated the descent of the Holy Spirit
upon the disciples in Acts. There were also feasts in honor of martyrs. These were localized commemorations held near each martyr's
tomb. When cathedrals were built, martyrs' bones were placed in
reliquaries, pilgrimages to them began, and the martyrs' cult grew.
Gradually more holy days were added, and a liturgical calendar took
shape.

Baptism

There are many possible antecedents for Christian baptism. One is the Jewish *mikvah*, a ritual bath that purified a person in preparation for worship. Christian baptism symbolized the washing away of sin and death and a rising to new life. The *Shepherd of Hermas* declared that "before a man bears the name of the Son of God he is dead; but when he receives the seal he puts mortality aside and again receives life. The seal, therefore, is the water. They go down into the water dead, and come out of it alive."[2]

Baptism marked a convert's entrance into the Christian community. The normal practice was total immersion, but sprinkling and pouring water also occurred. The *Didache* stated that the ceremony should be performed in running water. In some cases infants were baptized, but this did not occur without debate. Tertullian believed baptism should be reserved for those who knew and confessed Christ. Making reference to what would become known as original sin, Cyprian believed infant baptism was a defense against Adam's "disease of death."

In the second and third centuries, baptisms normally occurred only once or twice a year. Easter and Pentecost were the most common times. The rest of year was spent in instruction and preparation. Hippolytus of Rome (170–236) provided a detailed account of what occurred in the days leading up to a person's baptism. On Thursday the person took a bath. On Friday and Saturday he fasted as a sign of repentance. The baptism itself would occur early Sunday morning. Immediately prior to his baptism, the person would make a statement of faith and renounce Satan. Since the candidate was baptized in the nude, ceremonies were held separately for men and women. The mode was immersion, and it was often done three times in the name of the Father, the Son, and the Holy Spirit. The person would then be anointed with oil and, as a new member of the church, take the Eucharist.

The *Didache* described the baptism ceremony:

In regard to baptism, baptize thus: After the foregoing instructions, baptize in the name of the Father, and of the Son, and of the Holy Spirit, in living water. If you have no living water, then baptize in other water; and if you are not able in cold, then in warm. If you have neither, pour water three times on the head, in the name of Father, and of the Son, and of the Holy Spirit. Before the baptism, let the one baptizing and the one to be baptized fast, as also any others who are able. Command the one who is to be baptized, to fast beforehand for one or two days.[3]

EUCHARIST (LORD'S SUPPER)

The Lord's Supper was the central element of Christian worship and was performed every Sunday as a reminder of Christ's return. In many ways it mirrored the Jewish Passover. As the Passover celebrated Jewish freedom from Egyptian bondage, the Lord's Supper celebrated Christ's deliverance of Christians from the bondage of sin and death.

Though not formally defined until 1215, there appears to have been an early belief that Christ was truly present in the elements of the Eucharist. Justin Martyr's eucharistic liturgy noted:

This food is called among us the Eucharist of which no one is allowed to partake but the man who believes that the things which we teach are true, and who has been washed with the washing that is for the remission of sins, and unto regeneration, and who is so living as Christ has enjoined. For not as common bread and common drink do we receive these; but in like manner as Jesus Christ our Savior, having been made flesh by the Word of God, had both flesh and blood for our salvation, so likewise have we been taught that the food which is blessed by the prayer of

His word, and from which our blood and flesh by trans-
mutation are nourished, is the flesh and blood of that Jesus
who was made flesh. For the apostles, in the memoirs composed by them, which are called Gospels, have thus delivered unto us what was enjoined upon them; that Jesus took
bread, and when He had given thanks, said, "This do ye in
remembrance of Me, this is My body"; and that, after the
same manner, having taken the cup and given thanks, He
said, "This is My blood"; and gave it to them alone.[4]

AGAPE FEAST

Originally, the Agape Feast or "Love Feast" was an entire meal
surrounding the Eucharist (1 Cor 11:20–34). By the second century the Agape Feast and the Eucharist had become separate entities. The Agape Feast was often referred to as the Lord's Table, and
the Lord's Supper became known as the Eucharist. In some regions
the Agape Feast was held after the Eucharist. In other regions it was
entirely separate. Tertullian argued that the Agape Feast was a meal
meant for poor Christians:

> Our feast explains itself by its name. The Greeks call
> it *agape*, i.e., affection. Whatever it costs, our outlay in the
> name of piety is gain, since with the good things of the feast
> we benefit the needy; not as it is with you, do parasites
> aspire to the glory of satisfying their licentious propensities,
> selling themselves for a belly-feast to all disgraceful treat-
> ment,—but as it is with God himself, a peculiar respect is
> shown to the lowly.[5]

The Agape Feast was also time for Christians to fellowship as
they shared a meal. All were welcome, and no one was regarded as
superior to anyone else.

DEVOTIONAL PRACTICES

During the first three centuries of Christianity, there was no set pattern of prayer. The *Didache* (8) stated that Christians were to pray "Our Father" three times a day, but no specific times were given. Clement and Origen of Alexandria promoted a threefold pattern of morning, noon, and evening prayers. *The Apostolic Tradition* affirmed prayers at the third, sixth, and ninth hours (i.e., 9 a.m., noon, and 3 p.m.). By the fourth century Eusebius of Caesarea believed the pattern of prayer had been set. Concerning this pattern, later known as the cathedral or parochial office, he wrote,

> For it is surely no small sign of God's power that throughout the whole world in the churches of God at the morning risings of the sun and at the evening hours, hymns, praises, and truly divine delights are offered to God. God's delights are indeed the hymns sent up everywhere on earth in his Church at the times of mornings and evenings.[6]

Fasting was one of the most common devotional practices. Christ's forty-day fast in the wilderness served as the example. The *Didache* said that Christians fasted on Wednesdays and Fridays to distinguish themselves from the Jews, who fasted on Mondays and Thursdays.[7] The goal was to check fleshly desires in hope of attaining a higher level of spirituality. Fasting also reflected the suffering of Christ. As Christ suffered on the cross, Christians suffered in a small way through fasting.

Charity was another common practice. It was an opportunity to demonstrate Christian love by attending to the needs of others. With the development of the penitential system, priests would often assign some manner of giving to the poor as part of the reconciliation process.

ESCHATOLOGY

Second- and third-century Christians believed they were living in the end times. Several New Testament letters (e.g., 1 and 2 Corinthians and Revelation) and Roman persecution bolstered this conviction. They believed that when Christ returned, the righteous would receive their reward and God would punish those who had persecuted them. There were two schools of thought about what would happen at the "eschaton" or end of time. One view was that believers who had already died were waiting for Christ's return in the Hadean world, where the dead remained prior to the last judgment. When Christ returned, they would be resurrected. Others maintained that God's kingdom was heavenly, not earthly. Thus, the dead were already with Christ in heaven.

CHURCH OFFICES

BISHOPS

In the New Testament bishops/overseers (*episkopoi*) and presbyters or elders (*presbyteroi*) were identical (note how the terms are used interchangeably in Acts 20:17, 28 and in Titus 1:5–7). Their task was to care for the spiritual needs of the people. Soon after the biblical era, Ignatius separated the offices of bishop and presbyter, with the bishop being superior.

The bishop supervised all aspects of the church. He taught, preached, and administered the sacraments. He had total charge of the congregation, finances, and ordination of those in lower offices. The succession of bishops in a community demonstrated a continuity of teaching and practice. By virtue of the succession, the church's message remained constant.

Originally a bishop had authority only over one church. But as more churches began to appear in a region, the bishops of the individual churches often gathered and chose one of their own to oversee them all. It soon became common practice for regional bishops to be ordained by other regional bishops. This demonstrated that the bishop was not just an individual but part of the larger church.

A bishop's territory was known as a bishopric or see. Important bishoprics were Rome, Jerusalem, Antioch, Alexandria, and Ephesus. In times of relative security, bishops would gather to determine and standardize doctrine. Later this episcopal structure became an important source of church unity, particularly as it developed in the West.

PRESBYTERS

A presbyter served in one local church. He was ordained and appointed to that church by his bishop and served under his patronage. His task was to tend to the needs of his congregants, deliver sermons, visit the sick, and dispense the sacraments. The presbyter eventually became the local priest.

DEACONS

The office of deacon (servant) was derived from Acts 6, where seven men were selected to assist in the charitable work of the early church. Women did occasionally become deacons, but they only served other women. By the late second century, deacons were the bishop's assistants. They assisted at the Eucharist, distributed alms, and looked after widows and orphans. Cyprian of Carthage said deacons should report to the bishop regarding who was ill. Ignatius of Antioch charged his deacons with carrying letters. Eusebius of Caesarea described them as prison confessors and as those entrusted to bury martyrs. Based on the precedent of Acts 6, the number of deacons in a church was limited to seven until churches became larger and more deacons became a necessity.

Minor Orders

Four minor offices in the churches should also be noted: reader, acolyte, exorcist, and doorkeeper (*ostiarius*). During worship services the reader read liturgies or non-Gospel Scriptures to the church. Deacons read the Gospels. The acolytes were similar to the deacons. They delivered letters, distributed alms to the poor, and looked after widows. During worship services the acolyte lit the candles. The exorcist cast out demons from those believed to be possessed (as the Jewish exorcists did in Acts 19:13). The doorkeeper opened the doors of the church before services and closed them afterwards. He also warned the congregation of impending intruders.

Women

Although women outnumbered men in most churches, they were rarely permitted to hold church offices in the west. Tertullian argued that women should have no role in church ministry. He considered them to be temptresses, like Eve, and the gateway to evil. Their only contribution to Christianity was to bring their husbands to the faith and to be good wives and mothers. In the East the office of deaconess was somewhat widespread. The *Didascalia* (ca. 230) stated that men should perform most deacon functions, but some things that only a deaconess should do, such as visiting sick women and receiving baptized women.

Virginity was a popular choice for those who wanted to dedicate themselves to God. Widows also played an important ministerial role. Often they did not remarry in an effort to dedicate themselves fully to serving God. By the early third century, widows were perceived as prayer warriors and were often placed in charge of visiting sick women.

CHAPTER SIX

CONSTANTINE AND THE CONSOLIDATION OF CHRISTIANITY

As the fourth century began, the Roman Empire was in decline. Few of its emperors had died of natural causes. Most had been murdered by rivals. Barbarians were threatening the borders, and the Roman army was struggling to repel them. Taxes were high, and there was a constant shortage of food in the capital.

Times were difficult for Christians as well. Not only did they face the same problems as other Roman citizens, but they were also about to face their most relentless persecution to date. Out of these dark days, Christianity found an unlikely champion who propelled the faith to unprecedented heights.

DIOCLETIAN (285–305) AND THE GREAT PERSECUTION

With the support of his army, Diocletian became emperor in 285. He had witnessed the assassinations of his immediate predecessors at the hands of rivals and attempted to avoid their fate by creating the tetrarchy in 293. Instead of one emperor there would be four: an Eastern Augustus, an Eastern Caesar, a Western Augustus, and a Western Caesar. When an Augustus died, the Caesar would take his place. If a Caesar died, the Augustus would choose his replacement.

67

The first tetrarchy was composed of Diocletian (Eastern Augustus), Galerius (Eastern Caesar, 305–311), Maximian (Western Augustus, 286–305), and Constantius Chlorus (Western Caesar, 293–305). This political division between East and West contributed to the later division between the Eastern and Western churches.

Diocletian unleashed the Great Persecution in 303, catching Christians off guard because they had been left alone for almost forty years. (Interestingly, his wife Prisca [d. 315] and daughter Valeria [d. 315] were sympathetic to Christianity and may have been Christians.) No one knows precisely why Diocletian turned his wrath on Christianity, and some have theorized that Galerius instigated the Great Persecution. Regardless of who incited Diocletian though, his animus toward Christians was intense and his treatment of them cruel. There are several possible reasons for this.

Diocletian was having trouble with the Christians in his army. Not only did they refuse to kill, but they claimed their primary loyalty was to Christ, not the emperor. In retaliation he waged limited persecutions in 298. Diocletian was also a religious conservative, loyal to the old Roman religions. Many Romans feared that the spread of Christianity had decreased worship of the Roman gods that had always protected the empire. In 303 Diocletian visited the oracle of Apollo in the Maeander Valley of Asia Minor. The oracle allegedly told him that his soothsayers could not make accurate predictions because the empire was filled with false religions. Diocletian might have believed the oracle was referring to Christianity.

For whatever reason, Diocletian lashed out at Christians. Constantius Chlorus protected those in Gaul and England, but the remainder of the empire's Christians suffered. Diocletian ordered the destruction of all churches, the burning of Christian books, and attempted to force Christians to offer sacrifices to the traditional Roman gods. Confiscation of property, torture, and death awaited those who refused to comply. In his *Ecclesiastical History*, Eusebius wrote that Christians faced martyrdom with bravery. He told elaborate stories of how lions refused to eat Christians, how fires that intended to roast Christians alive would not ignite, and how soldiers' swords went dull while striking Christians. The lives of Christians who apostatized were spared, yet thousands died. When the Great Persecution ended, many of the apostates, bishops included, wanted to rejoin the church. Whether to receive them back and, if so, what manner of penance to require became important topics of debate.

Diocletian became ill and in 305 abdicated to Galerius (308–311). Maximinus Daia became the Eastern Caesar (305–308). Under Galerius's threat of invasion, Maximian abdicated, and Constantius Chlorus (305–306) was named the new Western Augustus. Garlerius appointed his colleague Severus (306–307) as the Western Caesar.

THE RISE OF CONSTANTINE (306–337)

Constantius Chlorus died in 306, and his soldiers refused to accept Galerius's plans. Instead they crowned Constantius Chlorus's illegitimate son, Constantine. His territory was Britain and Gaul. Shortly before his death in 311, Galerius stopped the persecution of Christians and asked them to pray for him. The tetrarchy at that time was Licinius (308–324), Maximinus Daia, Constantine, and Maxentius (306–312).

In 312 Constantine attacked Maxentius, whose capital was Rome. The night before the battle, according to Eusebius, Constantine had a vision of the Greek letters *chi* and *rho*. He asked his priests what the sign meant, but they could not tell him. A Christian priest named Hosius of Cordoba (ca. 257–359) told him it was the sign of Christ and he should fight under the banner of the cross. Eusebius writes:

> He said that about noon, when the day was already beginning to decline, he saw with his own eyes the trophy

of a cross of light in the heavens, above the sun, and bearing the inscription, CONQUER BY THIS. At this sight he himself was struck with amazement, and his whole army also, which followed him on this expedition, and witnessed the miracle.[1]

This vision was followed by an explanatory dream. In his sleep that night Christ allegedly appeared to him with the same sign he saw in the heavens and commanded him to make a likeness of it to use as a safeguard in all engagements with his enemies.[2] After having his soldiers paint the *chi-rho* on their shields, Constantine won the Battle of the Milvian Bridge on October 28, 312, and became sole emperor in the West. He credited the Christian God with the victory. Still it is debated whether his conversion occurred as Eusebius said, and some claim it was more a matter of political expedience than conviction.

Constantine certainly promoted Christianity, but he also participated in pagan rites after his supposed conversion, especially rites of the cult of Mithras, Christianity's strongest rival. Many of Constantine's actions imply either a confusion of Jesus with Mithras or a pragmatic attempt to appease the adherents of the empire's two largest religions. He kept Mithras on coins until approximately 321. He also retained the title *pontifex maximus* and presided over pagan rites such as lighting the Altar of Victory in the Senate. Moreover, he often failed to live by Christian moral principles, as when he executed his son and wife in 326 for fear they might usurp his power. Yet to credit his conversion entirely to pragmatism does not make sense. Christians were not a powerful segment of the population, with most belonging to the lower classes, and Constantine obviously believed Christ was powerful.

Whatever the reasons for his conversion, Constantine issued the Edict of Milan in 313. This document called for the end of all religious persecution. Christianity, however, was the only religion mentioned by name. Constantine defeated Licinius at Adrianople in 324 and became the sole ruler of the entire Roman Empire.

CONSTANTINE AND CHRISTIANITY

The reign of Constantine was a watershed in the history of Christianity. Whereas Christianity had been illegal, it was now tolerated and even favored. Constantine returned confiscated property to the church and gave the Lateran Palace to the bishop of Rome in 313. The cross was placed on Roman coins in 314. Constantine allowed Christian clergy to serve as judges in civil lawsuits and in 319 exempted them from paying taxes. He had churches built in Italy, Syria, North Africa, and Gaul. His mother Helena (ca. 250–330) was also a Christian, and while visiting the Holy Land, she authorized the building of the Church of the Holy Sepulcher in Jerusalem and the Church of the Nativity in Bethlehem. In 321 Constantine ordered that each Sunday would be a day of rest. In 330 he founded Constantinople (now Istanbul), making it his capital and the symbolic capital of Christianity. After Rome fell to the barbarians in 476, Constantinople remained a Christian stronghold for almost another thousand years.

Constantine brought the church under state control and believed he had a role to play in ecclesiastical affairs. According to Eusebius,

> Once, on the occasion of his entertaining a company of bishops, he let fall the expression, 'that he himself too was a bishop,' addressing them in my hearing in the following words: "You are bishops whose jurisdiction is within the Church: I also am a bishop, ordained by God to overlook whatever is external to the Church.[3]

What Constantine Meant to Christianity

Constantine left a profound mark on Christianity. By making it legal, he facilitated its spread all over the Roman Empire. Bishops were able to meet together to set doctrine without fear, and Christian morals began to affect society. One example was the ending of gladiatorial games in 325. In addition, Constantine saw the potential of Christianity, with its hierarchical episcopal system, to unify the empire.

Constantine's legacy was not entirely positive though. Before his reign people became Christians out of conviction. Now some joined the church to please the emperor. With the marriage of church and state, the clergy now had the right to persecute heretics, unbelievers, and Jews with the power of the state. Within a generation the persecuted had become the persecutors.

Thanks to Constantine, worldliness and spiritual laxity increased in the church. Pagan rites and buildings were assimilated into Christianity. Among the best examples of this were objects of adoration, saints, and the cult of relics. Some scholars speculate that Constantine postponed his baptism until his deathbed because he feared committing postbaptismal sin. Whether or not that was the case, others also postponed baptism and in consequence were not permitted to participate in the ordinances. Prior to Constantine the position of bishop did not bring wealth or imperial favor. After Constantine's reforms many bishops became more interested in money than in their pastoral duties. Opposition to these abuses helped give rise to monasticism.

Eusebius of Caesarea (260–339)

Eusebius was named bishop of Caesarea in 314. Caesarea was the home of Origen's library, and Eusebius adopted many of his beliefs. In addition, his teacher, Pamphilus (d. 309), was an Origenist. For this reason Eusebius's writings depict Christ as subordinate to the

Father. This belief, Arianism, was the greatest heresy of the early church (see discussion later in this chapter), and it led to Eusebius's excommunication. He later recanted and was accepted back into the orthodox community.

Eusebius was a better historian than he was a theologian. His two greatest works were *Ecclesiastical History* and *Life of Constantine*. In the former he collected all of the historical material on Christianity he could find. He provided a detailed account of Diocletian's persecution, quotes from church fathers, lists of bishops in important cities, and a list of martyrs in Palestine. If Eusebius had not chronicled this information, it may well have been lost and along with it much of the history of early Christianity.

In his *Life of Constantine*, Eusebius helped create much of the myth surrounding Constantine. He depicted him as a new King David, the servant of God, the rescuer of Christianity from persecution, and a man of constant prayer. According to Eusebius, Christianity owed its survival to Constantine.

ARIANISM

With Christians free from persecution, the clergy was able to discuss delicate theological matters, the most serious of which was Arianism. In comparison to Arianism, all other theological disagreements were minor.

Arianism was an attempt to describe the relationship among the three persons of the Godhead. What was the relationship between the Father and the Son? Was Jesus just another name for the Father, as the modalists proposed? Had Jesus been adopted, as the Dynamic Monarchianists believed? Arianism's answer was that the Son was the highest of all beings created by the Father.

Arius (250–336) was a presbyter in Alexandria. He studied under Lucian of Antioch (240–312), who stressed Jesus' inferiority to the Father. Lucian emphasized the human side of Christ over the divine. In fact, Christ was not even composed of the same substance as God, Lucian said. Arius argued that Scripture supported this position. For example, he cited John 14:28 where Jesus said, "The Father is greater than I" and Colossians 1:15 where Paul declared that Jesus "is . . . the firstborn over all creation."

The *Logos*, therefore, was a being created by God. There was a time when Jesus did not exist. As Arius wrote in a letter to Eusebius of Nicodemia, "The Son is not . . . in any way part of the unbegotten . . . before He was begotten, or created, or purposed, or established, He was not."[4] In developing his views, Arius drew from Origen, who taught that the Father eternally generated the *Logos*. As Arius saw it, there was no difference between generating and creating.

Debate intensified in 319, when Alexander, the bishop of Alexandria, delivered a sermon teaching that Christ was eternal and had always been with the Father. As evidence, he cited John 10:30: "The Father and I are one." Arius attacked Alexander's theology as modalistic, and soon all of Christianity was embroiled in the controversy. Alexander had Arius condemned in 321 along with Eusebius of Caesarea, who held similar views.

Constantine did not understand the intricacies of the debate, but he disliked its disruptive effect. Christianity was meant to unify the empire, not divide it. So Constantine sent Hosius of Cordoba to urge Alexander and Arius to settle their argument. The controversy, however, continued to rage. Hoping to bring it to an end, Constantine called the first ecumenical council of bishops to meet at Nicaea in 325.

THE COUNCIL OF NICAEA (325)

Constantine summoned 250 bishops from around the empire to attend the council in Nicaea (now Iznik, in Turkey) and lodged them in a palace. As the council met only twelve years after the Edict of Milan, many of the attendees bore the physical marks of the Diocletian persecution. The rapid transformation of the empire must have amazed them and made Constantine appear almost divine.

Constantine personally welcomed the bishops and attended the meetings of the council. He also made clear that he wanted the Arian controversy settled. His overriding concern was the unity of his empire, but he opposed the Arian position—a point that surely was not lost on the bishops in attendance.

The council condemned Arianism and defined the orthodox position. It spoke of the Father and Son as *homoousios*: composed of the same substance. The formula adopted by the council was amended in the years that followed and provided the basis for what came to be called the Nicene Creed:

> We believe in one God the Father Almighty, maker of things, visible and invisible; and in one Lord Jesus Christ, the Son of God, the only-begotten of his Father, of the substance of the Father, God of God, Light of Light, very God of very God, begotten, not made, being of one substance [*homoousios*] with the Father. By whom all things were made, both which be in heaven and earth. Who for us men and for our salvation came down from heaven and was incarnate and made man. He suffered and on the third day he rose again, and ascended into heaven. And he shall come again to judge both the quick and the dead, whose kingdom shall have no end. And we believe in the Holy Spirit. And whosoever shall say that there was a time when the Son of God was not, or that before he was begotten he was not, or that he was made of things that were not, or that he is of a different substance or essence from the Father or that he is a creature, or subject to change or conversion—all that to say, the Catholic and Apostolic Church anathematizes them.[5]

The formula declared God the "maker" of all things and said the Son was "not made," rejecting any claim that He was a creature. *Homoousios* was the most important word of the formula because it made explicit the divinity of the Son. At the same time the council preserved the biblical language of the Son's being the "only-begotten" of the Father, reflecting a distinction between the persons of the Trinity.

Eusebius of Caesarea probably did not agree with the Nicene Creed, but he knew Constantine supported it, and thus he signed it and was reinstated to the church. Eusebius of Nicodemia (d. 341), a strong proponent of Arianism, also signed the Nicene Creed but later attempted to modify it. As much as Constantine wanted the matter put to rest, debates and personal animosity between the factions continued.

Other items were settled at Nicaea. Rome, Antioch, Alexandria, and Jerusalem were now archbishoprics. The date for Easter was set. Twenty canon laws were passed, the most interesting of which was perhaps the first: forbidding self-castration—possibly intended as a denunciation of Origen.

The Council of Nicaea set several precedents for how the church would operate. First, the church and the state would work together. The church would pass canon law, and the state would enforce it. Second, councils would settle serious doctrinal questions. Third, creeds (*credo* in Latin, meaning "I believe") became the standard form of espousing the Christian faith. Those who did not or would not affirm the official creeds were considered to be outside the faith.

MONASTICISM

Many religions have groups of adherents who choose a solitary life in service to their gods. Christian men became monks for a variety of reasons. Some wanted to imitate Jesus and John the Baptist, neither of whom ever married or owned many possessions.

With the age of persecution gone, Christians could no longer demonstrate their mortification of the flesh through suffering and martyrdom. Some, therefore, attempted to demonstrate it by denying themselves food, water, sleep, human contact, and sexual pleasure, concentrating on prayer and spiritual warfare. Since Christ fasted and spent time in the desert after his baptism, the earliest monks decided the best place to practice their faith was in the desert. The deserts of Egypt were the home of many monks. Another motive for monasticism was a desire to escape the immorality, secularism, and laxity creeping into the church due to its close relationship with the state.

Because of their extreme gestures of piety, monks replaced martyrs as the new heroes of the church. Their biographies—though likely embellished to emphasize the monks' discipline and self-denial—became legendary, setting an example of piety that was admired for centuries.

Monasticism in the East developed much earlier than it did in the West. The Eastern monks were also stricter in their ascetic practices. The best known of these Eastern monks were Paul of Thebes (230–341), Antony (251–356), Simon Stylites (390–458), Pachomius (ca. 286–346), and Basil the Great (330–379). The most important Western monk in the patristic period was Benedict of Nursia (480–543). Other noteworthy monks were Martin of Tours (316–397), who was the father of monasticism in Gaul, and John Cassian (360–435), who brought monasticism to Marseille.

PAUL OF THEBES (230–341)

Paul of Thebes is credited with being the first Christian monk. His life was detailed in hagiographical fashion by Jerome (342–420) in *Vita Pauli*. During the Decian persecutions Paul fled Thebaid, Egypt, and took up residence in a cave. He spent the last seventy years of his life in constant prayer. Jerome reported that every day Paul was given half a loaf of bread by a raven. When Paul was visited

by the monk Saint Antony, the two spoke for a day and night and
then Antony left. When Antony returned, he found Paul dead.
Antony supposedly commanded two lions to dig Paul's grave.

Saint Antony (ca. 251–356)

Saint Antony is widely acknowledged as the father of Christian
monasticism. Most of the information known about him comes
from a book written by his friend Athanasius (295–373), *The Life
of Antony*.

Antony was born to wealthy Christian parents in Herakleopolis
Magna in Lower Egypt around 251. When they died, he inherited a
large fortune. However, after reading Matthew 19:21,[6] he decided to
give his possessions to the poor, placed his sister in the care of Christian virgins, and moved to the Egyptian desert near Nitra. Antony's
monastic regimen was harsh. He isolated himself from other people
and went without sleep, food, and physical exercise. Antony was
famous for struggling with demons that were said to have approached
him in the form of seductive women. Athanasius wrote:

> And the devil, unhappy one night even took upon him
> the shape of a woman and imitated all her acts simply to
> beguile Antony. But he, his mind filled with Christ and the
> nobility inspired by Him, and considering the spirituality
> of the soul, quenched the coal of the other's deceit.[7]

Antony overcame demons with prayer. One time the Devil
allegedly beat him unconscious. When admirers came to visit him,
they nursed him back to health.

Antony then moved further into the desert. His home for the
next twenty years was an abandoned Roman fort on a mountain by
the Nile called Pispir, now Del el Menun across from Crocodilopolis.
No one entered his cell. People who wanted to talk to him had to
listen through a crack in the wall. He was again said to have been

attacked by demons that came in the form of scorpions, snakes, and other animals. He rid himself of the demons by laughing at them.

During the harshest persecutions Antony was known to emerge from his cave to encourage the Christian community. At Athanasius's request he also spoke out against Arianism in 338. As his fame grew, more people began to visit him. He was reported to have healed the sick and cast out demons. To escape the crowds and continue his ascetic lifestyle, he retreated into the eastern desert of Egypt near an oasis where the Monastery of Saint Antony has been built. He died in 356 at age 105.

SIMON STYLITES (390–458)

Born in what is now Kozan, Turkey, Simon Stylites grew up in a devout Christian home. When he was thirteen, he began a regimen of fasting and sleep deprivation. At sixteen he joined a monastery in Antioch. While there, he adopted a form of Syrian monasticism that was so rigorous he nearly starved himself to death. While nursing him back to health, his fellow monks discovered that he had put on a tight girdle of palm fronds to constrict his organs and intensify his pain. After it was removed, he was asked to leave the monastery. He then moved into a hut where he lived for a year and a half without permitting himself to sit or lie down. After that he moved to a small cave at the top of what is now Sheik Barakat Mountain. Believing that he was a holy man, crowds began to visit him. To continue his ascetic life undisturbed, he decided to live on top of a pillar in 422. After years of additions, the pillar grew to sixty feet in height. He remained there until his death in 458. He supposedly never came down for any reason, and his followers sent food up in a bucket. From the top of his pillar, Simon was said to have cast out demons, healed the sick, and moved crowds to incredible acts of penance. He even persuaded the business leaders of Antioch to lower their interest rates. After his death many people attempted to emulate him; the sight of a man living atop a pillar, in a tree, or chained to a rock in fifth-century Syria was not uncommon.

PACHOMIUS (286–348)

Born to pagan parents in Thebes, Egypt, Pachomius was conscripted into the Roman army when he was twenty years old. He viewed his time in the army as a form of imprisonment, but prompted by the compassion of Christians who brought him food, he promised that when he got out, he would learn about their faith. He followed through on that promise and was baptized in 314. He then learned ascetic monasticism from a venerable monk called Elder Palaemon and reported hearing a voice that told him to build a home for hermits. In doing so, he became the founder of cenobitic or communal monasticism. Eventually he established nine monasteries and two convents. Within a generation of his death, the number of monks had grown to more than 7,000.

Pachomius was the first monk to set rules for monastic life. These rules included communal meals, group worship, and shared work. He was their leader and was called "abba" or father. The terms *abbot* and *abbey* were derived from *abba*. Pachomius was also a great orator. According to legend, when he preached, his words took on the physical form of jeweled birds, and listeners appeared to be drunk with the Holy Spirit. The popularity of Pachomius's communal monasticism helped it replace ascetic monasticism as the standard in both the East and the West.

BASIL THE GREAT (330–379)

Basil the Great was more famous as a theologian than as a monk. The importance of his work to define the Trinity cannot be exaggerated. But he was also known as the father of monasticism in Asia Minor. He visited Egypt in 357, where he observed cenobitic monasticism and brought it back to Asia Minor. The monks under his charge were expected to work, pray, study the Bible, and perform charitable deeds. For this reason Basil insisted that all mon-asteries be built near cities.

BENEDICT OF NURSIA (480–543)

The only surviving records of Benedict are Pope Gregory the Great's (590–604) hagiographical *Dialogues*. Born in Umbria in central Italy, Benedict's family was wealthy and made sure he was educated in Rome's finest schools. When he was twenty years old, he became disillusioned with education and moved to the small town of Enfide, forty miles from Rome. While traveling to Enfide, he met Romanus of Subiaco, a monk who lived in a monastery above a cave. Benedict decided to become a monk and lived alone in the cave below the monastery for three years. His asceticism became famous throughout the region.

Eventually Benedict was asked to become the abbot of a near-by monastery. He was familiar with its rules and knew the other monks would disagree with his rules, but he relented and became their abbot. It soon became apparent that the monks indeed did not agree with Benedict's stringent version of monasticism. They tried to poison his drink, but legend has it that after he prayed over the cup, it shattered. When his bread was poisoned, a raven supposed-ly flew into the room and took it away. Benedict eventually estab-lished thirteen monasteries and was abbot over all of them. The first and most famous was established in 529 at Monte Cassino, eighty miles south of Rome.

The Benedictine Rule governed life in his monasteries and established the authority of the abbot. The abbot was the father of the monastery, and the monks were his children. Thus, the abbot was to be obeyed without question. The Rule of Saint Benedict stressed poverty, chastity, agricultural work, and a minimum of speaking. Stability was also important. Monks were to remain permanently at the monastery they joined. The Benedictine Rule established a routine of prayer through the day and night: matins (night), lauds (prior to sunrise), vespers (just after sunset), and compline (before retiring to bed). The Rule of Saint Benedict has been influential in the development of virtually every Western European monastic order that followed.

CHAPTER SEVEN

FOURTH- AND FIFTH-CENTURY TRINITARIAN AND CHRISTOLOGICAL CONTROVERSIES

The dictums laid down at the Council of Nicaea did not end the Arian controversy. Indeed, it continued for much of the fourth century. Because the term *homoousios* ("same substance") could not be found in Scripture, several bishops rejected it. Plus, different groups defined *homoousios* in different ways. Now considered orthodox, the Nicenes maintained that Jesus and the Father were of the "same substance." Moderate Arians preferred the term *homoiousios* ("similar substance") because they believed this best preserved the distinction between the Persons of the Trinity. Extreme Arians such as the Anomoeans held that the Son was unlike the Father and that neither term was appropriate to describe their relationship. The great defenders of the Nicene position were Athanasius (295–373) and the Cappadocian Fathers: Basil of Caesarea (330–379), Gregory of Nyssa (331–395), and Gregory of Nazianzus (329–390).

As controversy raged on, attention turned to the person of Christ. Highlighting the differences between Alexandrian and Antiochene Christology, these debates were just as heated as those at the Council of Nicaea.

ATHANASIUS (295–373)

Prior to his attendance at the Council of Nicaea in 325, little is known about Athanasius. He studied under Peter the Martyr (300–311) and was ordained by his bishop, Alexander of Alexandria (313–328), in 319. He then served as Alexander's deacon and assistant at the Council of Nicaea. Upon Alexander's death in 328, Athanasius became the bishop of Alexandria and the great defender of Nicene theology.

Athanasius's most enduring treatise was *On the Incarnation of the Word*, which he wrote in 318. Athanasius maintained that the *Logos* became incarnate to save the world. Repentance in itself was not enough to save anyone, he said. Repentance meant that one stopped sinning; it did not compensate for sins that had already been committed. A repentant person was still corrupt. Only one who was not corrupt, the *Logos*, could remove this corruption by defeating death. Jesus paid the price for sin, and Satan lost his power over corrupt humans. Jesus had to be fully divine and fully human in order for human salvation to take place. Athanasius wrote:

> The Word takes on a body capable of death, in order that, by partaking in the Word that is above all, it might be worthy to die instead of all, and might remain incorruptible through the indwelling Word, and that for the future corruption should cease from all by the grace of the resurrection. . . . Hence he did away with death for all who are like him by the offering of a substitute. For it was reasonable that the Word, who is above all, in offering his own temple and bodily instrument as a substitute-life for all, fulfilled the liability in his death, and thus the incorruptible Son of God, being associated with all mankind by likeness to them, naturally clothed all with incorruption in the promise concerning the resurrection.[1]

Athanasius's interpretation of the incarnation led to his belief in the "deification" of Christians—the idea that believers partake of the divine nature and become like God. The term *deification* and the language Athanasius used can be somewhat misleading to modern readers, as when he wrote, "For He [God] was made man that we might be made God."[2] Athanasius was not arguing that Christians literally become God but that they reflect the one true God and become like him. The Cappadocian Fathers developed this concept further.

Athanasius's life was consumed by the Arian controversy. Though Constantine supported the Nicene position, not all of his successors did. And even Constantine believed Athanasius was a troublemaker because of his stubborn refusal to come to terms with the moderate Arians.

Consequently, Athanasius was exiled several times. His first exile occurred in 335. At the Council in Tyre, he was found guilty of not accepting the Council of Nicaea's position on the Melitian Schism. Like the Donatists, the Melitians refused to have communion with those who apostatized during the Great Persecution and then wanted to return to the church. The council conceded to the Melitians in the hopes of ending the schism. But Athanasius believed their penance should be harsh and treated those in his bishopric accordingly. Led by the Arian Eusebius of Nicodemia, Athanasius was exiled from Alexandria.

Just before his death in 337, Constantine was baptized by Eusebius of Nicodemia, to whom he entrusted the spiritual care of his sons. This action emboldened the Arians and severely weakened their Nicene opponents. Athanasius, however, was permitted to return to Alexandria where he was hailed as a hero.

After Constantine's death, the Roman Empire was divided up among his sons. Constantius II (337–361) received the East; Constans (337–350) and Constantine II (337–340) fought over the West, with Constans eventually winning. Constans was then usurped by Magnentius (350–353) and assassinated. Constantius defeated Magnentius in 350 and became the sole ruler of the Roman Empire.

Constantius espoused Arian Christology while Constans promoted the Nicene Faith. When Constantius granted amnesty to Arians in the East, Eusebius of Nicodemia rose in prominence. Eusebius then convinced Constantius to exile Athanasius in 339. Athanasius went to Rome under the jurisdiction of Constans, where he remained until 344. With the backing of the emperor, a pro-Arian council was held at Milan, Italy, in 355. Its purpose was to rescind the Nicene Creed and impose Arian beliefs. This led to an attempt to arrest Athanasius.in 356, but he escaped to the Egyptian desert where he was hidden by monks. At this time he met Antony the monk and wrote *The Life of Antony* along with many anti-Arian documents.

When Constantius died in 361, Julian I (361–363; aka Julian the Apostate) became emperor. He had studied Christianity but was more impressed with Neo-Platonism. Julian hoped to end Christianity, but he did not resort to overt persecution of Christians. Instead he rescinded the favored status of Christianity and promoted the pagan religions. Christians were neither permitted to attend schools nor to hold public office. Perhaps hoping the internal doctrinal feud among Christians would destroy Christianity, Julian allowed Athanasius to return to Alexandria in 361. Julian, however, was disappointed that Athanasius's return met with success and exiled him again in 362. After Julian died in 363, Athanasius returned.

Valens (364–368), a devout Arian, became the emperor in 364. Athanasius again was sent into exile, but because of his popularity and Valens's fear of an uprising, he was permitted to return. Athanasius died in 373, and the mantle of Nicene leadership passed to the Cappadocian Fathers.

THE CAPPADOCIAN FATHERS

The Cappadocian Fathers were Basil, bishop of Caesarea; his brother Gregory, bishop of Nyssa; and their friend Gregory, bishop of Nazianzus. All three were born in Cappadocia, a region in modern-day Turkey. Basil was born into a wealthy family in Caesarea. His first teacher was his grandmother, known as Macrina the Elder (270–340). Macrina had studied under Gregory of Thaumaturgus (213–270), who had been one of Origen's pupils. Basil, therefore, was imbued with a love of Origen from childhood. He began his formal education in Caesarea. While in Caesarea, he met Gregory of Nazianzus, and they became lifelong friends. He then studied briefly in Constantinople and finished his education by studying in Athens for six years. While in Athens, he studied with the future emperor Julian the Apostate. Upon Basil's return to Caesarea in 355, he taught rhetoric but was intrigued by Christian principles. He visited monastic sites in Egypt with Eustathius of Sebaste (357–377), a bishop and ascetic. When Basil returned in 356, he was baptized and started a small ascetic community on his father's property at Annesi in Pontus, where he was joined by Gregory of Nazianzus. Basil was ordained a deacon in 360 and then a presbyter by Eusebius of Caesarea (d. 370) in 362. When a financial crisis hit Caesarea, Basil liquidated much of his inheritance and gave it to the poor. He also convinced merchants not to take advantage of the situation. Because of Basil's efforts, Cappadocia was able to avoid an even more debilitating financial crisis.

After the death of Eusebius, Basil was elected bishop of Caesarea. His time as bishop was marked by opposition. As an advocate of asceticism, he often preached about the evils of wealth. The more affluent members in his church resented these sermons. He was also a strong supporter of Nicene orthodoxy though many of his subordinate clergy were Arian.

Gregory of Nyssa was Basil the Great's younger brother. He was not as well educated as Basil but still had a profound love of

Origenism. Basil appointed him bishop of Nyssa in 371. He was briefly deposed by the Arians but was reinstated two years later. In matters of Christology, Gregory insisted on the full divinity and full humanity of Christ. He became one of the most ardent proponents of Nicene theology at the Council of Constantinople in 381. Like Basil he believed in deification but not to the same degree. He maintained that Christians were able to participate in divinity through charity, prayer, chastity, and mercy. Through these acts Christians could rise to the likeness of God. Basil stated,

> Just as a sunbeam, falling on light and transparent bodies, makes them exceedingly bright and causes them to pour forth a brilliance from themselves, so too souls which bear the Spirit and which are illuminated by the Spirit of the future, understanding of the mysteries, discernment of what is hidden, sharing of good gifts, heavenly citizenship, a place in the choir of angels, joy without cease, abiding in God, likeness unto God, and that which is best of all, being made God.[3]

Gregory of Nazianzus was born in Nazianzus in the southwest region of Cappadocia. His family belonged to a Hellenized Jewish sect, but under the influence of his mother, Nonna (d. 374), they became Christians. When Gregory was a child, his father, Gregory the Elder (276–374), became the bishop of Nazianzus. Gregory the Younger was first educated by his uncle Amphylokhios (ca. 340–ca. 403) and then in Nazianzus. He then studied at Caesarea, where he met Basil, and Alexandria, where he developed a love of Origen. His final course of study was in Athens. On his journey to Athens, a storm threatened to sink the ship on which he was traveling. Gregory vowed that if Christ would save his life, he would dedicate himself to the church. He kept his promise.

While in Athens, he studied with Julian the Apostate. Julian must have been impressed with Gregory because when he became emperor and banned the teaching of Christianity, he made an exception for Gregory. Gregory subsequently joined Basil in Pontus where they practiced the ascetic life.

Gregory returned to Nazianzus in 361 and was ordained a presbyter by his father. Basil ordained him Bishop of Sasima in 372 to help in the Arian affair, but Gregory disliked his bishopric and made relatively little effort to administer it. In late 372 he returned to help his dying father with the church in Nazianzus. Upon his father's death Gregory refused to be named bishop. He accepted a preaching position in Constantinople in 378 and promoted Nicene theology in his sermons and lectures. As did Basil and Gregory of Nyssa, he maintained the full divinity and full humanity of Christ.

Gregory's greatest contribution to the trinitarian debates was his theology of the Holy Spirit. He maintained that the Spirit was as much God as the Father and the Son. Gregory's influence led to a fuller definition of the Holy Spirit at the Council of Constantinople in 381. His orations against the Arians were so successful that they attempted to kill him on at least one occasion.

The Emperor Theodosius (379–395) appointed Gregory bishop of Constantinople and president of the Council of Constantinople. But his enemies argued that, because he was already the bishop of another city, under canon law he could not occupy the bishopric of Constantinople. Despite his relative neglect of the bishopric of Sasima, he resigned the bishopric of Constantinople and his role of president of the council without an argument. He returned to Nazianzus, where he spent the last five years of his life writing. His most important writings were his *Theological Orations*, where he presented God's nature as unknowable but said God's presence could be felt throughout history, particularly in the incarnation of Christ.

The Cappadocian Fathers contributed significantly to an emerging trinitarian consensus. They believed the Father was in a sense the source and cause of the Son and Holy Spirit but the Son and Spirit were coequal with the Father. The Holy Spirit proceeded from the Father and the Son was begotten by the Father. The Trinity was defined as three distinct *hypostases* (modes of being) in one *ousia* (substance). Basil explained *hypostases* by employing Platonic categories. He gave the example that three people can be distinct but still share the essence of a human being. As with the three persons of the Godhead, there remains a distinction among the three people but also a unity. (Basil and the other Cappadocians recognized the weakness and limitations of the analogy. Nevertheless, they used it as an explanatory tool.) This formulation allowed for both unity and diversity in the Godhead.

Theodosius (379–395) convened the Council of Constantinople in an attempt to settle the trinitarian controversy. Indeed, Christians in the eastern portion of the empire still worried that the term *homoousios* obscured the threeness of the Godhead. The Western church on the other hand feared that those who would not accept the term *homoousios* subordinated the Son to the Father and embraced a form of Arianism. At the council the Cappadocian Fathers took the lead, and though not all bishops fully endorsed their Trinitarian formula, it was accepted as orthodoxy. The Council of Constantinople did not eradicate Arianism but precipitated its sharp decline.

Another theological problem discussed at Constantinople was Apollinarianism. Apollinaris (310–390) taught that Jesus had a human body but a purely divine mind. The *Logos*, Apollinaris said, took the place of his human intellect or soul. Apollinarianism was an overreaction to Arianism. To counter the Arians' downplaying of Christ's deity, Apollinarus denied his full humanity: "He is not a human being but is like a human being, since he is not coessential with humanity in his highest part."[4] In reaction to this teaching, Gregory of Nazianzus stated, "What was not assumed was not healed."[5] In other words, for humanity to be saved, Jesus had to take on humanity in every part of his being, mind and soul included.

Without naming Apollinaris, the Council of Constantinople condemned his teachings. It also proscribed Macedonianism, a heresy that denied the deity of the Holy Spirit.

Though Arianism was the major topic at Constantinople, several other significant issues demanded attention. Canon three, for example, affirmed that after Rome, Constantinople was the most important see. This sudden elevation of Constantinople began a rivalry between Rome and Constantinople that culminated in schism.

The Person and Nature of Christ

Following the Council of Constantinople, the great theological debates shifted from the Trinity to the person of Christ. Two leaders of this debate were Nestorius (386–451) of Antioch and Cyril (375–444) of Alexandria. An important backdrop to the Christological controversy was a longstanding theological divide between the church at Antioch and the church at Alexandria. Leaders in Antioch emphasized the humanity of Jesus while leaders in Alexandria emphasized his deity. But not all who adopted Antiochene Christology were from Antioch, and not all who adopted Alexandrian Christology were from Alexandria.

Born in Germanicia, Nestorius was named patriarch of Constantinople in 428. He had been a pupil of the great Antiochene bishop Theodore of Mopsuestia (350–428) and embraced much of his theology. In typical Antiochene fashion, Nestorius stressed the full humanity and suffering of Christ. He believed, however, that there was a distinction between Christ's humanity and his divinity. The flesh and the *Logos* did not constitute one entity. The humanity and divinity of Christ were partners that stood side by side. The *Logos*, therefore, did not suffer on the cross.

This belief led Nestorius to reject the term *Theotokos* (God bearer) for the virgin Mary. He stated:

Mary, my friend, did not give birth to the Godhead ("for what is born of flesh is flesh" [John 3:6]). A creation did not produce him who is uncreatable. The Father has just not recently generated God the *Logos* from the Virgin (for "in the beginning was the *Logos*," as John [John 1:1] says). A creature did not produce the Creator, rather she gave birth to the human being.[6]

Nestorius believed the term *Theotokos* implied a lack of humanity in Christ. In response he argued that Mary bore the manhood of Christ not the *Logos*. Within the womb of Mary, the Spirit "formed out of the Virgin a temple for God the *Logos*, a temple in which he dwelt."[7] For this reason Nestorius preferred the term *Christokos* (Christ bearer).

Nestorius's rejection of *Theotokos* was unacceptable to the Alexandrians. As bishop of Alexandria, Cyril was the obvious person to challenge it.

Born in Theodosiou, Egypt, Cyril was the nephew of Theophilus (358–412), the patriarch of Alexandria. Upon his uncle's death Cyril became patriarch. As a leader he clashed frequently with his opponents—Christians who differed with him, pagans, Jews, and the civil government. Cyril closed all the Novatianist churches, had many of the Jews removed from the city, and often used Nitrian monks to enforce his decrees.

In his debates with Nestorius, Cyril employed typical Alexandrian theology. In Jesus a divine nature and a human nature were united in one person, he said. The *Logos* existed without flesh prior to the incarnation. At the incarnation the *Logos* united with a human nature. While remaining God, the *Logos* took on humanity. Christ was fully God and fully man but one unified person. Cyril used the term "hypostatic union" to sum up his position—with Jesus there was a "union of hypostasis." The *Logos*, therefore, truly suffered on the cross. Thus, Cyril affirmed that Mary truly bore God and was the *Theotokos*.

The debate between Nestorius and Cyril grew so bitter that a council was called to settle the issue. The third ecumenical council took place in Ephesus in 431. Nestorius did not attend the council for fear of his life, and deliberations began before many of Nestorius's supporters arrived. Cyril's position was quickly upheld, and Nestorius and his followers condemned. When Nestorius and his supporters, led by John the Patriarch of Antioch (429–441), arrived, they convened their own council, condemned Cyril, and deposed him from his see. Emperor Theodosius II (402–450) finally intervened, arresting both Cyril and John and declaring actions of both councils void. Eventually John and Cyril agreed to a "formula of union" in 433, and it was decided that the condemnation of Nestorius by Cyril's council would stand. Nestorius spent the end of his life in exile in northern Egypt. Nestorianism, however, flourished and became the official doctrine of the Persian church. Nestorian missionaries reached China in the seventh century.

Eutychianism was the next Christological controversy that threatened to split the church. Eutyches (378–454) was the head of a large monastery in Constantinople. He pushed the Alexandrian interpretation of Christ to the extreme, teaching that Christ was "of one substance with the Father" but not "of one substance with humanity." The human and divine natures had blended in a way that allowed Jesus to be *homoousian* with the Father but not with man. This position became known as Monophysitism. He defined the relationship as a drop of humanity in an ocean of divinity. Eutyches, therefore, denied the full humanity of Christ.

Flavian (446–449), the patriarch of Constantinople, called a council in 448 that condemned Eutychus. Eutyches appealed to Dioscorus (444–451), the bishop of Alexandria, who called a competing council to meet in Ephesus in 449. Only the followers of Eutyches were allowed to attend. Even the legates of bishop Leo I (440–461) of Rome were turned away. For this reason it became known as the Robber's Synod and is not considered a legitimate

ecumenical council. At this council monks loyal to Eutyches and
Dioscorus attacked and killed Flavian. To finally settle the matter
and stop the bloodshed, a fourth ecumenical council was held at
Chalcedon near Constantinople in 451.

Called by the emperor Marcian (450–457), the Council of
Chalcedon began its deliberations on October 8, 451, with 500
bishops, mostly from the East, in attendance. The only Western
presence was the legates of Leo I.

The council determined that Dioscorus had abused his power,
and he was quickly deposed. Eutychianism and Nestorianism were
condemned. The council accepted as orthodox Leo's *Tome*, which
argued that the person of Christ was identical with the divine
Logos. The council determined that Christ was fully human and
fully divine. The natures were neither mixed nor separated. The
Antiochenes were pleased with this formula, as it preserved Christ's
humanity. The council's official statement became known as the
Definition of Chalcedon:

> Following, then, the holy fathers, we unite in teaching
> all men to confess the one and only Son, our Lord Jesus
> Christ. This selfsame one is perfect both in deity and also
> in human-ness; this selfsame one is also actually God and
> actually man, with a rational soul and a body. He is of the
> same reality as God as far as his deity is concerned and of
> the same reality as we are ourselves as far as his human-ness
> is concerned; thus like us in all respects, son only excepted.
> Before time began he was begotten of the Father, in respect
> of his deity, and now in these "last days" for us and on behalf
> of our salvation, this selfsame one was born of Mary the
> virgin, who is God-bearer in respect of his human-ness. We
> also teach that we apprehend this one and only Christ—
> Son, Lord, only-begotten—in two natures; and we do this
> without confusing the two natures, without transmuting
> one nature into the other, without dividing them into two

separate categories, without contrasting them according to area or function. The distinctiveness of each nature is not nullified by the union. Instead, the "properties" of each are conserved and both natures concur in one "person" and in one *hypostasis*. They are not divided or cut into to persons, but are together the one and only and only-begotten Logos of God, the Lord Jesus Christ. Thus have the prophets of old testified; thus the Lord Jesus Christ himself taught us; thus the Symbol of the Fathers has handed down to us.[8]

The Alexandrians who refused to accept this formula became known as Monophysites. Alexandrians, however, were pleased that the virgin Mary was determined to be the *Theotokos*. Canon 28 also proved to be important. It stated that Rome was the most honored see, but Constantinople was second. Rome accepted the findings of the council but would not affirm canon 28.

CHAPTER EIGHT

THEOLOGIANS OF THE FOURTH AND FIFTH CENTURIES

L ed by Alexandrian and Antiochene bishops, the theological debates of the fourth and fifth centuries focused on the Trinity and Christology. Theologians from other regions of Christendom also attempted to enforce Nicene orthodoxy and responded to pressing issues. What was the proper relationship between church and state? Should the church defer to the state or the state to the church? Was a person predestined to become a Christian? Does a person have free will? How should the New Testament be interpreted? How should the church deal with heresy? John of Chrysostom (347–407), Ambrose of Milan (339–397), Jerome (342–420), and Augustine of Hippo (354–430) attempted to answer these questions.

JOHN CHRYSOSTOM

Born in Antioch to the son of a military commander, John Chrysostom was known as the "Golden-mouthed" because of his excellent sermons and use of rhetoric. Chrysostom studied under the pagan rhetorician Libanius (ca. 314–ca. 394) in hopes of becoming a lawyer. Instead, after reading the Scriptures, he became a Christian. He was baptized in 368, studied under Melitius (d. 381), the bishop of Antioch, and dedicated himself to serving God. Chrysostom wanted to become a monk, but out of respect for his mother's wishes, he waited until she died in 373. Then he joined a Pachomian monastery near Tarsus. After two years he left the monastery because rigorous ascetic practices had damaged his health. He could no longer observe monasticism as intensely as he wished so he practiced a more moderate asceticism for the remainder of his life.

Chrysostom returned to Antioch in 378. He became a deacon in 381 and a priest in 385. While in Antioch he was shocked by the differences between the lives of his wealthy and poor parishioners. He believed the wealthy were not caring for the needs of people with less, and he was pained by the plight of the less fortunate. He was also convinced many of his wealthy congregants had come by their riches unjustly, an allegation he aired in his *Homily on Timothy*.

Chrysostom believed the church was becoming lax, bishops were corrupt, and government officials viewed themselves as exempt from Christian moral standards. These issues became the subjects of his most incendiary sermons. For example, in 387, after Emperor Theodosius (379–395) imposed new taxes, the citizens of Antioch rioted in protest. Chrysostom preached against the new taxes but told the citizens to stop their unchristian behavior. He also pointed out that many of them were protesting out of personal greed. At the urging of Chrysostom, Theodosius pardoned the city, and the citizens were spared his wrath.

In Antioch, Chrysostom perfected his preaching style. He viewed the entire Bible as the Word of God so he preached from each book. He was an excellent exegete, drawing the main points out of a biblical text and delivering them in an understandable way. His sermons were sincere and filled with practical application. On occasion Chrysostom's rhetoric was too acerbic and brought him into conflict with people of wealth and power.

Chrysostom was named patriarch of Constantinople in 398. Because of his conviction that the emperor was a member of the church and not its ruler and his controversial views on wealth, Chrysostom's time in the capital of the Eastern empire was not peaceful. His sermons against government corruption and opulence in the emperor's court were not well received. The wife of Emperor Arcadius (395–408), Eudoxia (d. 404), became his main antagonist. She resented the patriarch's veiled references to her as "Jezebel." And when she had a statue of herself placed in front of the church of Saint Sophia, Chrysostom referred to her in a sermon as "Herodias."

Chrysostom also experienced tension with fellow church leaders. As the patriarch of Constantinople, he was asked to participate in a synod in Ephesus that was investigating complaints lodged against Antoninus (ca. 380–400), the bishop of Ephesus. Chrysostom saw this as an opportunity to increase the influence of Constantinople over Ephesus and happily accepted the invitation. Antoninus, however, died before his arrival. To demonstrate his power in Ephesus, he and the council consecrated a new bishop and deposed six other bishops for simony. This action increased the friction between Constantinople and Ephesus.

Though not an active participant in the Alexandrian/Antiochene debates, Chrysostom aligned more closely with Antiochene theology. For this reason Theophilus (385–412), the bishop of Alexandria, considered him a threat. Theological differences aside, tension between Chrysostom and Theophilus was already high because Theophilus wanted to subordinate Constantinople to Alexandria.

Eventually the jealous Theophilus called a synod to investigate Chrysostom's theology. Three times Chrysostom was summoned to the Synod of Oak in 403. Each time he refused to attend. So the council condemned him in absentia and declared him removed from his see. Encouraged by Eudoxia, Arcadius accepted the council's decision and banished Chrysostom. Even though he enjoyed much popular support, Chrysostom left Constantinople without a fight. Shortly, however, the city was struck by an earthquake, and Eudoxia took it as a sign from God that Chrysostom should not have been removed. He returned and resumed his duties as patriarch, but his feud with Eudoxia continued. She had him exiled to Asia Minor in 404, then died later that year following a miscarriage. But Chrysostom still had many enemies in Constantinople. He was exiled to Cucusus in Lesser Armenia in 405. Yet, even at such a great distance, his letters reached Constantinople and raised the ire of his enemies. Finally he was exiled to an isolated village on the Black Sea. He was forced to walk to his new home and died from exhaustion on September 14, 407. His willingness to face exile and death rather than silence his prophetic voice to the monarchy bolstered the power of the church over the state.

He also spoke against Judaism and referred to Jews as the enemies of Christ. While in Antioch, Chrysostom wrote *Against Judaizing Christians*. He feared that Christians were being attracted to Judaism because of its celebratory feasts and festivals. He argued vehemently that Christians should not participate in Rosh Hashanah and Yom Kippur. His depiction of synagogues was inflammatory: "A place where a prostitute offers her wares is a house of prostitution. But the synagogue is not only a house of prostitution and a theater, it is also a hideout for thieves and a den of wild animals. . . . The synagogue is a temple of idolatry. Nevertheless, some go to these places as though they were sacred shrines."[1] His sermons against Judaism fueled medieval anti-Semitism.

Chrysostom's sermons and writings were his theological legacy. He wrote homilies on each book of the Bible, sermons celebrating saints' days, and treatises on the Christian life. His *On the Priesthood* is the first known book on the Christian ministry.

AMBROSE OF MILAN (339–397)

Ambrose was born into a Christian and aristocratic family. His father was a praetorian prefect in Gaul. In order to prepare him for a life in politics, his parents sent him to Rome to study law. Eventually he was named governor of Liguria and Amelia in Italy near Milan.

But Ambrose's career in politics came to a halt in 374. The Arian bishop of Milan died; and, as the governor of the region, Ambrose was responsible for maintaining order during the election of the new bishop. Supposedly a child yelled, "Ambrose for bishop," and the crowd took up the cry. Even though he had not been baptized, he reluctantly accepted their appeal. Within a week he was baptized, ordained, and consecrated bishop of Milan.

As bishop, Ambrose was dedicated to his pastoral duties, was staunchly Nicene, fought heresy, and managed to enforce his will on both Theodosius, the Eastern emperor, and Valentinian I (364–374), the Western emperor. Justina (364–375), the Arian mother of Valentinian, despised Ambrose. Ambrose first demonstrated his influence over Valentinian II (375–392) in 384 when a Roman prefect named Symmachus (345–402) wanted to restore the pagan Altar of Victory in the Senate. Ambrose said he would no longer support the emperor if the altar were returned. Valentinian relented, Symmachus was defeated, and Ambrose's power increased.

On several occasions his influence over secular rulers was evident. With permission from her son, Justina attempted to have the Portian basilica outside Milan rededicated for the Arians. Ambrose refused to comply and gathered his supporters. When ordered to obey the command of the emperor, he replied, "The tribute that belongs to Caesar is not to be denied. The Church, however, is God's, and it must not be pledged to Caesar; for God's temple cannot be a right of Caesar."[2] Justina was angered but had to acquiesce; the basilica remained orthodox.

In 386, Justina again attempted to promote Arianism in Milan by taking over the New Basilica. Ambrose was ordered to leave the city, but instead he retreated to his basilica and remained there for six months while his supporters gathered outside and sang hymns. During this period Ambrose declared, "The emperor is in the church not above it."[3] Again Justina was forced to give in. Indeed, Ambrose refused to allow the Arians to make inroads in his bishopric.

In 386, Christians rioted in Callinicum, Mesopotamia, and destroyed a synagogue. Theodosius demanded that the Christians responsible for its destruction pay to rebuild it. But Ambrose told Theodosius that even though the Christians had been wrong in their actions, they should not pay for a Jewish synagogue. Theodosius acquiesced to Ambrose.

In 390, citizens in Illyria assassinated their governor and a Roman official after the arrest of a popular charioteer. In retaliation Theodosius had 7,000 citizens executed. Ambrose immediately excommunicated the emperor and demanded that he do public penance before he would lift the order of excommunication. Once again the emperor capitulated.

Ambrose argued that Scripture had a threefold meaning: literal, moral, and allegorical. His interpretation of the Old Testament was typological. He also developed poetic liturgical hymns that could be easily understood. His sermons were laced with pithy statements, scriptural references, and frequent quotations from Cicero and Virgil. Later he came to be regarded as one of the four doctors of the Western church.

Ambrose had a vast legacy. He fought Arianism, promoted orthodoxy, and the excellence of his rhetoric had much to do with the conversion of Augustine. He was also among the first to advocate that monastic orders be under the control of the regional bishop. His *On the Duties of the Clergy* depicted the bishop as one who must not only guide the church but also chastise it, especially if greed needed to be curtailed.

Ambrose's legacy, however, was not entirely positive. His ability to force emperors to comply with his wishes fostered the belief that the church was above the state. Ambrose would serve as one of the church's examples of ecclesiastical superiority in the medieval period.

When he found what were believed to be the bones of two prominent martyrs in the Basilica of Ambrosiana in Milan, he extolled the power of relics to confer grace and aid in miraculous healings. He was one of the first bishops to place martyrs' bones under the altars of churches. This gave rise to the relic trade that eventually dominated the medieval period.

Ambrose also exaggerated the merits of female virginity. He believed the virgin Mary should be the supreme example for all women and helped establish worship of Mary in the church.

JEROME (CA. 342–420)

Born in Stridon near Dalmatia, Jerome was raised in a Christian home. He was baptized at age seventeen and went to Rome to study in 360. He remained in Rome for six years, where he became a master of Latin and Greek and amassed a large personal library. The hedonism of the clergy and Christians in Rome disgusted him. He later remarked that after the Roman emperors became Christians, the church "increased in influence and in wealth but decreased in Christian virtues."[4]

Jerome then moved to Aquileia, Gaul, where he entered the monastic life. The other monks were quickly offended by Jerome's overbearing personality. This led to his being sent to Chalcis, Syria, in 375. Though he wanted to continue in an undisturbed ascetic life, he was ordained a presbyter in Antioch in 377. He claimed to have left Chalcis because the desert was becoming crowded with hypocritical monks. He then settled in Constantinople in 379, where he remained for three years. He left for Rome in 382 because of conflict with Gregory of Nazianzus.

While in Rome he served as a secretary to Bishop Damasus (366–384). In that post, his most important task was biblical translation. Damasus asked Jerome to compile a revised Latin version of Psalms and the New Testament. He took his directions a step further and eventually translated the entire Bible into Latin. When translating the Old Testament, Jerome did not rely on the Septuagint as did the older Latin translations. He relied on the more accurate Hebrew text.

His rejection of the Septuagint also led to his personal skepticism about the canonical status of the Apocrypha, though he included it in his Latin translation. Known as the Vulgate, Jerome's work became the official Bible of the Catholic Church. He also translated into Latin *The Rule* of Pachomius and several biblical commentaries.

A vindictive man with an acerbic writing style, Jerome became embroiled in several controversies. The Helvidian and Jovian controversies concerned the ascetic life. Helvidius (fl. 380) argued that after giving birth to Christ, Mary enjoyed a normal sexual life. Marriage, therefore, was as virtuous as virginity. Jerome insisted that Mary remained a virgin for the entirety of her life. In *The Perpetual Virginity of Mary*, he wrote:

> We are to believe then that the same man who gave so much credit to a dream that he did not dare to touch his wife, yet afterwards, when he had learnt from the shepherds that the angel of the Lord had come from heaven and said to them, "Be not afraid; for behold I bring you good tidings of great joy which shall be to all people, for there is born to you this day in the city of David a Savior which is Christ the Lord"; . . . and when he had seen Anna the prophetess, the Magi, the Star, Herod, the angels; Helvidius, I say, would have us believe that Joseph, though well acquainted with such surprising wonders, dared to touch the temple of God, the abode of the Holy Ghost, the mother of his Lord?[5]

His arguments for the perpetual virginity of Mary contributed to the cult of Mary, which came to be known as Mariolatry.

Jovian (d. 405) had been a monk but changed his opinion of many ascetic practices. He taught that marriage pleased God as much as virginity or asceticism did. He based this on his belief that after baptism all believers are of equal worth. In *Against Jovian*, Jerome argued that if one does not deny the pleasures of the flesh, these pleasures will become lust. His primary example was King David whose lust for Bathsheba led to the murder of her husband. Moreover, who could believe that a marriage to God was inferior to a marriage with a spouse? In *Against Jovian*, Jerome wrote:

> She that is unmarried is careful for the things of the Lord, that she may be holy in both body and in spirit: but she that is married is careful for the things of the world, how she may please her husband [quoting 1 Cor 7:34]. . . . Is this sofa smooth? Is the pavement swept? Are the flowers in the cups? Is dinner ready? Tell me, pray, where amid all this is there room for the thought of God?[6]

Jerome's *Against Jovian* did much to promote female virginity in the medieval period.

The Vigilantian controversy was personal. Vigilantius (fl. ca. 400) was a presbyter in southwest Gaul. He visited Jerome's monastery near Bethlehem in 395 and was convinced Jerome was an Origenist. Perhaps Vigilantius had grounds for his suspicion. Jerome had translated Origen's *On First Principles* into Latin and made it available to a much larger audience. Whether founded or not, Vigilantius voiced his criticism to all who would listen.

In 406 Vigilantius attacked Jerome for his extreme asceticism. He told Jerome that during a heated argument he should not cross himself. Jerome told him to mind his own business. Vigilantius also claimed that martyr worship, the power of relics, and self-mortification had little or no value. Jerome defended ascetic practices in *Against Vigilantius*:

Tell us more clearly (that there may be no restraint on your blasphemy) what you mean by the phrase "a bit of powder wrapped up in a costly cloth in a tiny vessel." It is nothing less than the relics of martyrs which he is vexed to see covered with a costly veil, and not bound up with rags or hair-cloth, or thrown on the midden, so that Vigilantius alone in his drunken stupor may be worshipped. Are we, therefore, guilty of sacrilege when we enter the basilica of the Apostles? Was the Emperor Constantine guilty of sacrilege when he transferred the sacred relics of Andrew, Luke, and Timothy to Constantinople?[7]

Thanks in part to Jerome's efforts, the worship of relics and martyr veneration increased.

AUGUSTINE OF HIPPO (354–430)

Augustine was born in Thagaste, Roman Africa (modern Algeria), in 354. His father, Patricius, was a moral pagan and his mother, Monica (331–387), a devout Christian. She would be a strong influence in his life. Augustine wrote a great deal about his early life in *Confessions*. When reading *Confessions* though, one must remember that Augustine was attempting to demonstrate how sinful he had been in his youth and how God had saved him from himself. *Confessions* was written in his maturity.

His parents wanted him to teach rhetoric and saw that he received a fine education. Augustine was sent to Carthage to study in 371. However, he did not like to study, despised Greek, had a bad temper, and claimed he often stole. He also enjoyed sex and came to believe that his desire for sex was his thorn in the flesh, and he assumed that if something was a problem for him, it must be a problem for everyone else. He had a mistress for thirteen years, but he never mentioned her name in the *Confessions*. Together they had a son named Adeodatus.

While in Carthage he read Cicero's *Hortensius*, fell in love with learning, and dedicated his life to seeking wisdom. In Carthage he also became a Manichean. Manicheanism promised answers to questions about salvation and the universe. In particular, he was attracted to Manicheanism's answer to the question of sin and evil: The good, supreme God created humans as spiritual beings. An evil demiurge tied humanity's spirit to the material world. For a time this answer satisfied Augustine.

The leaders of Manicheanism were known as "perfectae," and the novices were called "hearers." The perfectae did not swear, did not work, and were chaste. The hearers swore, worked, and were allowed to engage in sex. Augustine seems to have been content to remain a hearer. He moved to Thagaste to teach grammar and literature in 375 but found his time there unfulfilling and the students too unruly.

Upon his return to Carthage, Augustine began to express doubts about Manicheanism. He did not believe the perfectae were as pure as they claimed. He also had reservations about the Manichean explanation of evil. He was told that when the great Manichee guru Faustus arrived, all his questions would be answered. After meeting Faustus though, Augustine was unimpressed and concluded that Manicheanism held no answers. Still, the dualism of Manicheanism may have influenced him toward Neoplatonism and the teachings of Plotinus (ca. 204–270).

He moved to Rome in 382, where he taught rhetoric for three years, and left for Milan in 385 after his students refused to pay him. Through influential friends, including several Manichees, he became a professor of rhetoric at the court of Valentinian II. His career was now on the rise, and he needed to marry a woman of standing, so he sent his mistress back to Africa. He was soon betrothed to an heiress, but his life would change before he could marry her.

Augustine heard that Ambrose was a strong rhetorician and began to attend his sermons. Augustine was not particularly interested in the content of his messages but rather his oratory and use of rhetoric. The content, however, gradually began to affect him. Ambrose's sermons, which synthesized Neoplatonism and Christianity, appealed to Augustine's intellectual nature. He also read a commentary on the apostle Paul by Marius Victorinus (ca. 300– ca. 365), who had been a Neoplatonist. He learned that Christianity was reasonable and gave mental assent to some of its doctrines. His libertinism, however, delayed his true conversion. His final surrender to Christianity came in 386 while he was in a garden agonizing over his moral failings. He heard a child's voice telling him to "pick up and read." So he picked up a Bible that was sitting on a bench next to him. The text he happened upon was Romans 13:13–14: "Let us walk with decency, as in the daylight: not in carousing and drunkenness; not in sexual impurity and promiscuity; not in quarreling and jealousy. But put on the Lord Jesus Christ, and make no plans to satisfy the fleshly desires." This passage confronted Augustine as if it were written only for him. He surrendered to Christ, was converted, and was baptized by Ambrose on Easter Eve in 387.

Along with his mother, his son, and his friend Nebridius, Augustine planned to move to Thagaste and take up the monastic life. They spent the next two years in Cassiciacum near Milan in preparation for their move. Then Monica died.

Augustine returned to North Africa in 393 and began looking for a location to set up his monastery. While exploring the region around the town of Hippo Regius (ca. 390), he was ordained a priest by popular acclaim. He assisted Valerius, the elderly bishop of Hippo, for two years. Valerius retired in 395, and Augustine was named his successor in 396. He held this bishopric for the rest of his life.

While bishop of Hippo, Augustine was extremely active. He participated in debates, developed his theology, and wrote voluminously. His theology was heavily dependent on the apostle Paul's letters, and often he employed it in combatting what he perceived to be heresies.

Donatists were still prevalent in North Africa. In fact, in Hippo they outnumbered the Catholic Christians. The Donatists refused to accept clergy members who had apostatized by handing Scriptures over to their persecutors. Furthermore, clergy who had been ordained by an apostate bishop were not true ministers and could not administer the sacraments, the Donatists said. Augustine believed the Donatists put too much stress on the purity of the individual administering the sacraments. The most important reality, he said, was that the sovereign God had endowed his church corporately with authority to administer the sacraments. In sacramental matters it did not matter if a priest had apostatized. Augustine contended that the holiness of God was not reflected primarily in the individual clergy members but in the church. He argued for the concept of *ex opere operato* (Latin for "from the work done"), which stressed that the efficacy of a sacrament stemmed from the sacramental action itself. The administrator has little to do with the accomplishment of the task. The Donatists, therefore, were outside the true church, according to Augustine.

Augustine also believed the church was composed of true believers and unbelievers. He cited the parable of the wheat and the tares or weeds (Matt 13:24–30) as a metaphor for the body of Christ. Just as the tares would be separated from the wheat on judgment day, the true Christians would be separated from the false Christians. The Donatists, therefore, placed too much emphasis on purifying the church.

Citing Luke 14:23 ("Then the master told the slave, 'Go out into the highways and lanes and make them come in, so that my house may be filled.'"), Augustine argued that civil government was to enforce proper worship of God and belief in correct doctrine. He stated:

> It is indeed better (as no one could ever deny) that men should be led to worship God by teaching, than that they should be driven to it by fear of punishment or pain; but

it does not follow that because the former course produces the better man, therefore those who do not yield to it
should be neglected. For many have found advantage (as we
have proved, and are daily proving by actual experiment), in
being first compelled by fear or pain, so that they might
afterwards be influenced by teaching, or might follow out
in act what they had already learned in word.[8]

With Augustine's support, the Donatists were persecuted by
the church, forced to give up their churches, and levied heavy fines.

A great deal of Augustine's theology came to light in the
Pelagian controversy. Pelagius (ca. 350) was a British monk who
came to Rome in 390. He taught that Adam and Eve were created
sinless. When they first sinned, it only affected them. He believed
they were mortal and would have died even without the fall. Babies
were born in the same state as Adam prior to the fall and therefore
were sinless. All guilt was incurred from actual sins and not inherited from Adam. Pelagius wrote, "Everything good and everything
evil, in respect of which we are either worthy of praise or of blame
is done by us, not born with us."[9] Living a life without sin was a possibility, but highly unlikely. Salvation was achieved by using one's
freedom to lead a life of obedience. Grace was simply the opportunity God granted humans to live obediently, according to Pelagius.

Augustine disagreed with Pelagius and his even more troublesome disciple Celestius (ca. 360–370). Augustine claimed that no
person could achieve salvation on his own. That was the task of
the sovereign God. Because of the fall, Augustine taught, man lost
his free will, that is, his ability to live a perfectly obedient life.
Augustine believed original sin was passed on generation to generation through the sexual act. Through the action of procreation,
everyone is born with guilt and a proclivity toward sin. Infant baptism, he said, plays a role in removing the taint of original sin.

In response to Pelagius, Augustine emphasized predestination
and divine control. Augustine described predestination as God's

gracious gift. All deserve death and hell, and all will rebel against God if left to their own devices. But God chose to elect some to salvation, sovereignly overcoming their sinful wills and giving them a desire to follow Him. As God is no respecter of man, a person's election or nonelection was not based on God's foreknowledge. God's election was permanent. Nothing could change it. Man was totally depraved. He could make no move toward God. In *On Grace,* Augustine stated:

> A man's free choice avails only to lead him to sin, if the way of truth be hidden from him. And when it is plain to him what he should do and to what he should aspire, even then, unless he feel delight and love therein; he does not perform his duty, nor undertake it, nor attain to the good life. But to the end that we may feel this affection "the love of God is shed abroad in our hearts" not through the free choice which springs from ourselves, but "through the Holy Spirit which has been given to us" (Romans v. 5).[10]

Developing a theology of history was another of Augustine's important contributions. In his day many believed Rome was God's city. When Alaric the Goth (395–410) sacked Rome in 410, some Christians feared its destruction would lead to the end of Christianity. In his *City of God,* Augustine argued the Christians simultaneously were citizens of two cities: the city of God and the city of man. They had obligations in both human society and God's kingdom, he said, but their ultimate citizenship was in heaven. There was no need for despair at the fall of Rome, for it was not the object of a Christian's ultimate allegiance or the hope of his ultimate salvation. In effect, he provided Roman Christians with reassurance. Rome was just a city of man. He believed the city of God was heavenly and eternal.

> When the two cities began to run their course by a series of deaths and births, the citizen of the world was

the first-born, and after him the stranger in this world, the citizen of the city of God, predestined by grace, elected by grace, by grace a stranger below, and by grace a citizen above. . . . For the city of the saints is above, although here below it begets citizens, in whom it sojourns till the time of its reign arrives, when it shall gather together all in the day of the resurrection; and then shall the promised kingdom be given to them, in which they shall reign with their Prince, the King of the ages, time without end.[11]

Augustine was the most influential Latin theologian of the early church. His writings and theology affected the medieval theologians much more than those of any other church father. His concept of original sin tied grace closely to the sacraments and made the church the dispenser of this grace. Augustine also influenced the Protestant Reformation. Martin Luther (1483–1546) quoted him on hundreds of occasions, and John Calvin's (1509–1564) teachings on predestination and election reflected a dependence on Augustine's arguments.

CHAPTER NINE

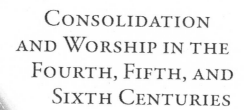

CONSOLIDATION AND WORSHIP IN THE FOURTH, FIFTH, AND SIXTH CENTURIES

U nder Constantine, Christianity and the Roman Empire became virtually indistinguishable. As Christianity consolidated, Constantine's successors, with the exception of Julian the Apostate, passed edicts that placed it in a privileged position over other religions. In Rome, Constantius II banned all pagan sacrifices in 341 and temporarily closed all pagan temples in 356. Pagan shrines and idols were destroyed. Many of the temples that were not torn down were reconsecrated and made into Christian churches. For instance, in 608 the Pantheon in Rome was rededicated to the memory of all Christian martyrs. Julian the Apostate allowed pagan temples to reopen in 361, but his reign was brief and so was the pagan revival. Gratian (367–383) gave up the title *pontifex maximus*, confiscated revenue from pagan priests, and removed the Altar of Victory from the Senate. Theodosius made Christianity the official religion of the empire in 380 and issued a series of decrees to combat paganism. In 399, he struck a final blow to the last vestiges of paganism, decreeing: "If there should be any temples in the country districts, they shall be torn down without disturbance or tumult. For when they are torn down and removed, the material basis for all superstition will be destroyed."[1] Where the empire remained strong, Christianity, in a legal sense, was victorious.

By the fourth and fifth centuries Christianity had a firm foundation in Asia Minor, much of Italy, Palestine, and North Africa. Some of these regions may have had Arian inclinations, but Nicene Christianity was dominant. Other regions of the empire were slower to embrace the faith. Because of traditional religions and barbarian dissent, Gaul and Britain were slow to accept Christianity.

Monks who served as missionaries were largely responsible for the conversion of Gaul and Britain. Martin of Tours (316–397) set up a parochial system in the countryside around Tours in what is now central France. The Arians proved to be strong missionaries in much of Gaul. The Arian Ulfilas (ca. 311–383) made strong evangelistic inroads with the Goths in the East. When the Goths migrated west, they brought Arianism with them. Ulfilas translated much of the Bible into their language. Because of their inclination to war, he left out the bloodiest parts of 1 and 2 Kings, not wanting the Gauls to use these passages as precedent for waging war.

After promising his wife Clotilda (475–545) that he would convert to Christianity if he won a battle, Clovis (466–511), the king of the Franks, kept his word and was baptized along with 3,000 of his solders on Christmas Day in 496. The Franks soon followed suit. The faith of many Gauls, however, remained Arian.

In Ireland, Saint Patrick (ca. 390–460) did much missionary work. He was not the first bishop in Ireland, though. That honor belonged to Bishop Palladius (fl. 408–431), who was consecrated to the task in 430. Patrick was captured by pirates when he was fifteen years old and sold into slavery in Ireland. After spending six years as a slave, he managed to escape to Gaul. He returned to his native Britain in 411. He then supposedly had a dream of one of his former captors begging him to return to Ireland and bring the people Christianity. The British clergy consecrated him bishop of Ireland in 432. In Ireland he converted pagan chieftains, established monasteries, and set up an episcopacy. His work centered on the region of Ulster and Connaught. Patrick's success made him one of the most celebrated figures in Irish history and many legends developed around him. There is no evidence, for instance, that he was responsible for running all the snakes out of Ireland.

Armenia, Georgia, and Persia were difficult to convert. All Romans, including monks, were suspected of being spies. Gregory the Illuminator (240–332) evangelized in Armenia but suffered under Persian persecution. The Bible, however, was translated into Armenian. According to legend, Nino (fl. ca. 330) led many to the Christian faith in Georgia. She was credited with numerous miraculous healings and the conversion of the Georgian king and queen. But after the Persian invasions, Christianity had little influence in Georgia for nearly fifty years. Persia was dominated by Zoroastrianism, and the Zoroastrians persecuted Christians in 340 and 372. By 410, persecution ceased and Christianity began to flourish. The Persian churches then embraced the Nicene faith.

Development of Papal Supremacy

Since the earliest days of Christianity, Rome had been held in esteem. Early church fathers such as Cyprian, Tertullian, Irenaeus, and Augustine asserted that Rome was the most important see and all others should follow its lead. The leading bishoprics such as Alexandria, Constantinople, Antioch, and Jerusalem acknowledged its prestige as the home of Peter and Paul but gave it no precedence over their own sees. Rome's authority, however, began to increase.

Several bishops of Rome attempted to impose their will on other bishoprics. Bishop Damasus (366–384) referred frequently to Rome as the Apostolic See, and Emperor Theodosius proclaimed that Christianity in the form professed by Damasus was the official standard of the empire. Damasus proclaimed Latin the official language of the church and endorsed Jerome's Vulgate. In 380, he took a bold step by appointing Acholius (d. 383) bishop of Thessalonica, a city that had long been considered part of Constantinople's

domain. Damasus also founded the Vatican library, built several
churches in Rome, and reopened the catacombs for pilgrims.

Leo the Great (440–461) claimed that as the bishop of Rome,
he was the successor of Peter, the chief apostle. Rome's bishop,
therefore, was superior to all others. He stated:

> But the Lord desired that the sacrament of this gift should
> pertain to all the Apostles. And he wanted his gifts to flow
> into the body from Peter himself, as from the head, in such
> a way that anyone who dared separate himself from the sol-
> idarity of Peter would realize that he was himself no longer
> a sharer in the divine mystery.[2]

During Leo's time as bishop, three significant events added to
Rome's prestige. At the Council of Chalcedon in 451, his *Tome* was
read and accepted by the bishops in attendance. The bishops reportedly chanted, "Peter wills it." The acceptance of the *Tome* effectively gave Leo the last word in the Christological debates. Christ had
two natures, without confusion or change. As Chalcedon was in the
bishopric of Constantinople, the *Tome*'s acceptance was even more
significant.

Second, Leo met Attila the Hun (406–453) outside Rome in
452 and kept him from destroying the city. It was reported that
Attila had a vision of Peter and Paul accompanying Leo, and the
vision kept Attila from sacking the city. Other reports claim he was
persuaded to spare the city by a cartload of gold given by Leo. In
455, Leo similarly met with the Vandal Gaiseric (389–477) outside
of Rome and convinced him to show a measure of mercy to the city.
The third event came in 445, when Emperor Valentinian III (423–
455) declared the primacy of Rome's bishop:

> Therefore, inasmuch as the preeminence of the Apos-
> tolic See is assured by the merit of Saint Peter, the first of
> the bishops, by the leading position of the city of Rome
> and also by the authority of the Holy Synod, let not

presumption strive to attempt anything contrary to the authority of that See. For the peace of the churches will only then be everywhere preserved when the whole body acknowledges its ruler.[3]

Bishop Gelasius (492–496) proposed the theory of the two swords. One sword belonged to God and the other to the emperor. The sword of God wielded by the bishop of Rome, however, was superior to that of the emperor. In a letter to Emperor Anastasius (491–518), Gelasius wrote:

> There are two powers, august Emperor, by which this world is ruled from the beginning: the consecrated authority of the bishops and the royal power. In these matters the priests bear the heavier burden because they will render account, even for rulers of men, at the divine judgment. Besides, most gracious son, you are aware that, although you in your office are the ruler of the human race, nevertheless you devoutly bow your head before those who are leaders in things divine and look to them for the means of your salvation; and in the reception of proper administration of the heavenly sacraments you know that you ought to submit to Christian order rather than take the lead, and in those matters follow their judgment without wanting to subject them to your will.[4]

Baptism and the Eucharist

Baptism in the late patristic period had a multifaceted meaning. Most importantly, it brought the convert into the church. Baptism was believed to wash away both original and actual sin and seal the recipient with the Holy Spirit. For this reason the candidate for baptism put on white clothing after the sacrament was concluded. Baptism also symbolized the death, burial, and resurrection of Christ.

Finally, often it was perceived as an exorcism. For an infant, baptism was said to remove original sin, replacing it with God's grace.

As in the first two centuries, Pascha or Easter was the most popular date for baptism. During Lent candidates were given instructions on the Christian life. The baptismal service began on Easter Sunday morning with an exorcism and the candidate verbally renouncing Satan. The priest then blessed the water, and the candidate stood in the water and answered questions to demonstrate that he or she understood what was occurring and was freely accepting baptism. The candidate was then baptized three times in the name of the Father, the Son, and the Holy Spirit.

The Eucharist was the most important element in the liturgy. By the middle of the fourth century, many Christians believed that when the priest consecrated the elements, Jesus himself descended into the bread and wine, which were transformed into his body and blood, although they still had the appearance of bread and wine. In this regard Ambrose of Milan stated:

> You may perhaps say: "My bread is ordinary." But that bread is bread before the words of the Sacraments; where the consecration has entered in, the bread becomes the flesh of Christ. And let us add this: how can what is bread be the Body of Christ? By the consecration. The consecration takes place by certain words; but whose words? Those of the Lord Jesus. Like all the rest of the things said beforehand, they are said by the priests; praises are referred to God, prayer of petition is offered for the people, for kings, for other persons; but when the time comes for the confection of the venerable Sacrament, then the priest uses not his own words but the words of Christ. Therefore, it is the word of Christ that confects the Sacrament.[5]

CHURCH CALENDAR

As the church continued to grow and gain stature, its calendar expanded. Pascha remained the most sacred holiday, but because of the influence of the pagan spring fertility rites in northern Europe, new elements were added to the celebration. In particular, rabbits and eggs, which were symbols of fertility, became a part of Pascha. Some scholars believe the name Easter was an adaptation of Eostre, the Anglo-Saxon goddess of spring. By the mid-330s and after many calculations, the celebration of Christ's birth was placed on December 25. This date was chosen to draw pagans away from the December 25 celebration of the birth of Sol Invictus. By the fifth century, Christ alone claimed this date. By 600, many Christians were fasting during Lent in preparation for Easter. The calendar was also filled with dates commemorating martyrs and saints.

CHRISTIAN DEVOTIONAL PRACTICES

In their prayer lives, Christians in this era attempted to emulate monks. Their desire was for pure prayer that was not polluted by any thoughts of things other than God. Devout Christians, like monks, prayed five times a day at designated times. With the adoption of personal saints, intercessory prayers in a saint's name became common practice. As the *Theotokos*, Mary was the most popular intercessor.

Christians also began to venerate the remains of martyrs and saints. The first known veneration was by the followers of Polycarp, who said his relics were "more precious than costly gems and finer than gold."[6] The influence of a martyr or saint survived in his or her relics. Saints and martyrs were perceived as friends of God. If one could be in their company, it was hoped that their holiness would spread. For this reason, in the second and third centuries the Eucharist was often celebrated at the grave of a martyr or in Rome in the catacombs. Cyprian wrote, "Take note of their days on which they depart, that we may celebrate their commemoration among the memorials of the martyrs. . . . There are celebrated here by us oblations and sacrifices for their commemorations."[7]

Many Christians believed the bodies of martyrs were a special dwelling place of the Holy Spirit. This belief had much to do with placing martyrs' bones beneath the altar in a cathedral. Augustine compared relics to family heirlooms that helped Christians remember the dedication of a saint or martyr. He stated,

> For if the dress or the ring or anything of the sort belonging to parents is the more dear to their offspring as their affection for them was the greater, certainly then the bodies themselves are not to be scorned, which are much closer and more intimately joined to us than anything we wear.[8]

As the veneration of relics increased, Jerome reminded the church, "For we may not serve the creature rather than the creator, who is blessed forever. Still we honor the relics of the martyrs, that we may adore Him whose martyrs they are."[9]

Many believed that a relic of a saint or martyr could cure disease, produce miracles, and protect a person from evil. For this reason many chapels and churches were built on what were thought to be the graves of martyrs and saints. For instance, Saint Peter's Basilica was built over what was believed to be Peter's grave on Vatican Hill in Rome. In other instances relics were taken from their original locations and placed in cathedrals. The entire body was not needed. A bone from a finger, hand, arm, or even an article of clothing would suffice. The saints or martyrs who were important enough to have their relics venerated also had a feast day or a festival. On those days it was believed that penitents who visited the relics were more likely to have their prayers answered. This created a thriving business for local churches that provided access to the relics for a small offering. Because of the fiduciary opportunities, the stealing of relics became a chronic problem. Belief in the power of relics also led to pilgrimages to the Holy Land where relics were numerous. While in the Holy Land the penitent tourist would often buy a souvenir and add to a local church's treasury. One of the first people to procure relics was Helena, the mother of Constantine who claimed to have brought several items back to Rome, including a piece of the cross.

After the acceptance of the *Theotokos* at the Council of Ephesus in 431, Marian veneration increased exponentially. Mary became the greatest intercessor. Miracles were associated with her all over the Mediterranean. By the fifth century apocryphal stories of Mary's life appeared, her relics were valued over all others except for Christ's, and churches, such as Saint Mary Maggiore in Rome, were dedicated to her.

WORSHIP AND ARCHITECTURE

Before the Roman Empire's adoption of Christianity, most churches were small; many were rooms in the homes of Christians. When Constantine became emperor, Christian churches benefited and came into the open. He donated the Lateran Palace to the bishop of Rome and built Saint Peter's basilica for his use. Constantine financed the construction of churches all over the empire, including the Church of the Holy Sepulcher in Jerusalem and the Church of the Nativity in Bethlehem. Churches were now lavish and reflected the new stature of Christianity in the empire.

For larger churches the basilica layout was popular. The church was long and rectangular with one central aisle (nave) and two or more other aisles. The altar was always the focal point. It stood at the center in front of the congregation. The eucharistic elements were placed on the altar with the relics of martyrs frequently placed below the altar. Scripture was read from a desk or lectern in front of the altar. After the Scripture was read, it would be removed. The bishop's chair (*cathedra*) was placed at the center of the apse (the rounded area where the altar was). Presbyters sat on benches on either side of the *cathedra*. Deacons normally sat on benches around the altar. The western portico was often reserved for those who had not yet been baptized. Even if married, women sat separate from men. Statues and paintings also began to appear. Art depicted scenes from the Bible that the illiterate and those who did not understand Latin could comprehend. This would have been the majority of the congregation.

CHAPTER TEN

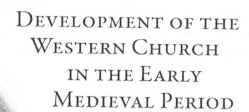

DEVELOPMENT OF THE WESTERN CHURCH IN THE EARLY MEDIEVAL PERIOD

B y the close of the sixth century, the vast territory that had been the Western Roman Empire was in turmoil. For the previous two centuries, one military defeat after another weakened the once formidable empire into a mere shadow of its former self. The defeat of Valens (364–378) at the battle of Adrianople in 378 marked the beginning of Rome's final decline. Rome was then sacked by Alaric the Visigoth (370–410) in 410, Vandals conquered North Africa in 429, and the Vandal Gaiseric (389–477) rampaged through Rome in 455. France was soon settled by Franks, and Anglo-Saxons moved into the former Roman provinces in Britain. Huns, Franks, Lombards, and Vandals built their own kingdoms in what had been the western provinces of the Roman Empire. Little did European Christians know that these defeats would prove minor in comparison to a new challenge that would soon emerge in Arabia.

A plethora of internal problems contributed to the military defeats and ultimate collapse of the Roman Empire. There was no orderly imperial succession but rather constant internal fighting for the Western throne. The armies often were called home from the frontier to carry out or prevent coups. There was a lack of agricultural production, a failure of industry, and a population in decline. An air of superstition in Europe led to a disregard for education. European society had changed a great deal in two centuries. Barbarians now lived in former Roman provinces and saw themselves as Roman citizens. They had adopted Roman customs and culture but had retained their traditional clothing and languages. Latin gave way to various Germanic dialects.

The Western church held European society together. Almost all matters of education, public services, and law fell to the church. For this reason, its power continued to grow. However, the Eastern Roman Empire, based in Constantinople, did not fall until 1453. It became the guardian of Roman thought, classical Greek, and other traditions. From its creation in 330, Constantinople regarded itself as the true capital of the empire; and with the fall of Rome, its claim gained credence.

GREGORY THE GREAT

Gregory the Great (590–604), bishop of Rome, brought Christianity into the medieval period. Though other bishops of Rome claimed Peter's keys and Rome's primacy as the apostolic see, Gregory increased the papacy's power to new levels.

Gregory was born into a wealthy Italian family with deep Christian roots; his great-grandfather Felix II (483–492) and another relative, Agapetus I (535–536), both had been bishops of Rome. Trained as a lawyer, Gregory began a promising career in civil administration, rising to become prefect of Rome in 573. The following year, however, he abandoned his political career and became a monk at Saint Andrews in Rome, one of seven monasteries he had built with his inheritance. He then served as the bishop of Rome's *apocrisarius* or diplomatic representative to Constantinople from 578 to 585. Upon his return he became abbot of Saint Andrews monastery. Gregory's administrative abilities and dedication to monasticism soon caught the attention of the church in Rome.

In 590 Gregory was the first monk to be elected pope. He was abundantly qualified for the position: a devout churchman, a capable administrator, and an excellent theologian. Gregory believed that the wealth of the church belonged to the poor. He used church funds to start farms and rebuilt many aqueducts that had fallen into disrepair. On several occasions he personally passed out food to the hungry in Rome. In political matters he demonstrated a strong allegiance to the Eastern emperor and negotiated peace with the invading Lombards. Gregory clearly saw his office as not only spiritual but also as political.

As pope, Gregory exercised spiritual care over Gaul, England, Spain, and Italy. He appointed missionaries and bishops to these regions who were loyal to him first and to their monarch second. To demonstrate their loyalty to Rome, they were given the official Roman pallium or scarf. Many of the people in these regions wanted a connection with Roman civilization, and the church gave them one. These bishops brought Roman law, order, and civilization to remote regions. In many ways the church was the bearer of civilization.

One of his most important acts was sending missionaries to England. After the Roman army's departure, England and its church were in disarray. Paganism prevailed amid elements of an Irish Christianity. Gregory appointed a monk named Augustine (d. 604) as bishop to England in 597. Bede (672–735) wrote:

> It was here that God's servant Augustine landed with companions, who are said to have been forty in number. At the direction of blessed Pope Gregory, they had brought interpreters from among the Franks, and they sent these to Ethelbert, saying that they came from Rome bearing very glad news, which infallibly assured all who would receive

it of eternal joy in heaven and an everlasting kingdom with the living and true God.[1]

Augustine reorganized the church, built monasteries, converted the king of Kent, and made Canterbury the primary see of England. Though he died years before it occurred, the Synod of Whitby in 664 was the culmination of Augustine's work, signifying England's acceptance of the Roman faith. The Synod was called by Oswy (642–670), king of the Northumbrians, to settle a debate over the date of Easter. The Celtic and Catholic Christians were celebrating on different days, and the local kings wanted them to adopt the same date for the holiday. The Synod decided to stand with Rome, an act that increased the Catholic Church's dominance over the Celtic church.

The monks of England also sent missionaries to Germany, perhaps the most famous of which was Wynfrith, better known as Boniface (675–755). Boniface was instrumental in the removal of paganism from Germany and its replacement by Catholicism. He was known for his bold manner of evangelism. In one instance he cut down the Mighty Oak of Thor at Geismar in Hesse (a sacred tree worshipped by thousands of German pagans). When he asked why Thor had not punished him, the people had no answer. He then used the wood from the tree to build a chapel dedicated to Saint Peter. Boniface also set up many bishoprics and built monasteries throughout Germany. For these reasons he is considered the father of Catholic Christianity in Germany.

As Gregory continued to consolidate Roman power and send out missionaries, he clashed with the patriarch of Constantinople, John IV (582–595). John claimed he was the ecumenical patriarch of all Christianity. Gregory rejected that claim, and a dispute arose over which see was supreme. In reality, although Rome was under the official jurisdiction of the court at Constantinople, each bishop was supreme in his own domain.

Gregory is remembered for many other accomplishments beyond his papal administration. He is often designated the father of monotone Gregorian chants and the originator of the term "seven deadly sins": pride, envy, gluttony, lust, anger, greed, and sloth. In an effort to ameliorate Augustine of Hippo's theology, he argued that grace is resistible and softened the doctrine of predestination. He believed that at the fall only goodness was lost, not free will.

Gregory also advanced the idea of purgatory. He stated:

> Everyone is presented in judgment just as he is when he departs this life. But nevertheless, it must be believed that there is, for the sake of certain lesser faults, a purgatorial fire before the judgment, in view of the fact that truth does say that if anyone speak blasphemy against the Holy Spirit it will be forgiven him neither in this world nor in that to come. In this statement we are given to understand that some faults can be forgiven in this world and some in the world to come. For if something is denied to one in particular, the intellect logically infers that it is granted for some others. But as I said before, this must be believed to be a possible disposition for some small and lesser sins.[2]

The Pastoral Rule was his most influential work. In it he exhorted pastors to be shepherds of the congregation. He also penned *Moralia* (a commentary on Job), a biography of Benedict of Nursia, and more than 800 letters that have survived. His *Dialogues* were accounts of supposed miracles performed by saints. His emphasis on divine power and the imminent presence of God encouraged a strong expectation of miracles and contributed to the superstitions that dominated the Middle Ages. One example of superstition developed during a plague. Gregory told the people of Rome that if they said, "God bless you," after they sneezed, God would protect them from the plague. Gregory is one of the four doctors of the Catholic Church.

The Carolingian Dynasty

With the end of the Roman Empire, the barbarian kings of Gaul and Germany supplanted Roman government as the protectors of the Catholic Church. Their support was needed as a bulwark for Roman primacy and to protect the city of Rome from invaders. For this reason popes would bestow titles and honors on their barbarian patrons.

Reliance on secular monarchs weakened the papacy over time. In principle, if not in reality, the papacy was under the jurisdiction and protection of Constantinople and the Byzantine emperor. But in an attempt to force the Frankish monarchs to bow to the wishes of the papacy, the *Donation of Constantine* was written, a forged document claiming that Bishop Sylvester I of Rome (314–335) had cured Constantine of leprosy and been granted in return oversight over all other bishops and dioceses. Moreover, the document claimed that Constantine had given the bishop of Rome rights to the entire western half of the empire. It also said the state was not to interfere with the church and the state depended on the church for its legitimacy. Throughout the medieval period, the *Donation of Constantine* was cited by popes as a basis for their ultimate supremacy. In 1431 Lorenzo Valla (1407–1457) demonstrated definitively that the *Donation* was a forgery.

At any rate a family of rulers known as the Merovingian Dynasty were the first Frankish monarchs to provide the papacy with military support. Prior to his death Clovis divided his kingdom among his sons, who proved incapable of holding the kingdom together. A new, powerful family of rulers stepped into the breach: the Carolingians.

Pepin III (752–768) was the first Carolingian ruler. Pope Zacharias (741–752) gave Pepin permission to depose the last of the Merovingians, Childeric III (743–752), and be named king of the Franks. Pope Stephen (752–757) came to Paris in 754 and anointed Pepin at the Basilica of Saint Denis. Stephen then named Pepin *Patricus Romanorum*, "Faith Protector of the Romans."

Stephen called on Pepin to repay the favor in 754. He needed help against the Lombards, who had replaced the Byzantine Empire in Italy and were threatening Rome. Pepin defeated them and granted the papacy land from Ravenna to Rome. Much of this area eventually became known as the Papal States.

After Pepin died, his kingdom was split between his two sons. After the death of Carolman in 771, Charles the Great or "Charlemagne" (Holy Roman emperor 800–814) became the ruler of the Franks and most of Western Europe. Charlemagne was an imposing man. He was reported to have been nearly seven feet tall, broad shouldered, and warlike. At the request of the papacy, he had destroyed the Lombards in northern Italy by 777. He also conquered the Saxons of Eastern Europe by 780 and was almost constantly at war with the Spanish Moors from 797 to 812.

Charlemagne believed the relationship between church and state should be complementary. The church was the soul and the state was the body. He promoted missions, enforced the Benedictine Rule for monks, attacked enemies of the state, and often gave pagans (the Saxons for instance) the choice between accepting Christianity or death. All Saxon children were to be baptized before they were a year old. If they were not baptized, their parents could be put to death. All people in Charlemagne's conquered territories were required to accept the authority of the pope.

Charlemagne was loyal to the pope but believed the church was subordinate to the state. In 799, a faction in Rome sought to depose Pope Leo III (795–816) for perjury and adultery. He appealed to Charlemagne's court for aid. Charlemagne went to Rome, helped dismiss the charges against Leo III, and placed him back on Saint Peter's throne. On Christmas Day 800, Leo crowned Charlemagne emperor of the Romans, thus creating the Holy Roman Empire. The importance of the event was not lost on Charlemagne. If the pope had the right to crown a king, then the pope also had the authority to dethrone one. Leo III's masterful political move gave the papacy an important precedent in the quest to control the future monarchs of Europe. (A millennium later Napoleon Bonaparte [1769–1821] avoided this situation by taking the crown from the hands of Pope Pius VII [1800–1823] and crowning himself emperor of France.)

While unlettered himself (as were most Europeans of his age), Charlemagne made possible a renaissance of learning that affected Europe for several generations. One of his first actions was to bring Alcuin of York (735–804) to his court in Aachen as tutor to the king's children and those of other influential nobles. Charlemagne hoped to reconcile Christianity with secular learning and opened cathedral and palace schools. These schools were the precursors to the great medieval universities and developed the basic framework for university curriculums: the *trivium* (grammar, rhetoric, dialects) and *quadrivium* (astronomy, music, arithmetic, and geometry). Once these liberal arts were mastered, a student could study the Bible. To make Christian writings more available, Charlemagne assigned the monks the task of copying the Vulgate, the lives of the saints, and other Christian books. This facilitated education and continuation of the Latin language.

FEUDALISM

After the death of Charlemagne, his empire began to crumble. His three grandsons divided the empire, making its collapse complete. Almost all semblance of a centralized government disappeared. His descendants were unable to protect the people from a new menace: the Scandinavian Vikings. The Vikings constantly pillaged the seaside communities of England. Since they were not Christians, monasteries and churches were not safe. The Viking problem was equally serious on the continent. Anywhere near a river a Viking attack was a distinct possibility. The Vikings left an indelible mark on Europe. The Normans who conquered England in 1066 and the founders of the Russian nation were Vikings.

Until the rise of the nation-states in the late Middle Ages, feudalism proved to be the best source of security. Nobles and mounted knights were given land (fiefs) by the king in exchange for their loyalty.[3] The king would charge them rent for the land, and, if necessary, they would fight for him. Feudal lords lived in manors. A manor was the basic land unit that could support mounted, armored knights. They would become his vassals. The nobles and knights would then give land to freemen who would swear loyalty to them. These freemen would then provide land to peasants who would live and work on it. This lowest class was known as serfs. They were bound to the land and, in actuality, were nothing more than slaves. In the feudal system every person was a vassal to the person above him. The king was the only exception.

Many of the larger feudal estates had their own clergy. The clergy's salary was paid by the lord of the manor. These family churches were known as *eigenkirche*. There were also *reichskirche* or imperial churches that were maintained by the emperor. Often this caused problems. To whom did these feudal clergy members owe ultimately loyalty: the papacy or their temporal lord? Many people gave large tracts of land to the church. This made many clergy members prosperous, more interested in wealth than in spiritual issues, and more loyal to their patron than the church.

ISLAM

Into this milieu, Islam (meaning "submission" or "surrender") was born. The founder of Islam was a camel driver named Muhammad (570–632). From 605 to 610, he began to search for illumination on matters of religion. In 610, he claimed to have visions that recurred throughout his life in which recitations were given to him by the angel Gabriel. The angel supposedly commanded him to preach that there was no god but Allah and those who did not accept him would be bound for eternal damnation. Those who did accept Allah would enjoy eternal paradise.

The teachings of Muhammad were codified in the Qur'an. Highly dependent on Judaism and Christianity, the Qur'an is roughly two-thirds the length of the Christian New Testament and composed of 114 chapters. It taught that prominent Old and New Testament characters such as Jesus, Abraham, and Moses were prophets. Jesus was born of a virgin but was not divine and did not die on the cross. Muhammad was the greatest and last of the prophets.

The Qur'an promoted monotheism with Allah as the only God. Developed from the teachings of the Qur'an, the Five Pillars of Islam are the foundation of Muslim life: declaring that there is no God but Allah and Muhammad is his prophet, praying five times a day facing Mecca, giving alms to the poor, fasting during the daylight hours of Ramadan, and, if one is physically able, making at least one pilgrimage to Mecca.

After the death of Muhammad, Islam began to expand rapidly. Its greatest gains occurred between 632 and 732. Jerusalem fell in 638, and the second-holiest Islamic location, the Dome of the Rock, was built on the site of the Temple Mount. Syria fell to Islam in 640, Persia in 650; and if not for Charles Martel (688–741) at the Battle of Tours in 732, all of France and possibly Europe would have been lost. Within 200 years, much of what had been the eastern Roman Empire became a part of the ever-expanding Islamic Empire.

Islam affected Christianity in the East more than the West. Most Christians viewed Muslims as infidels and considered Islam a false religion. The Eastern emperors attempted to negotiate and pay tribute to the Islamic leaders, but every decade Byzantium became smaller and smaller. Because of its unique location, Constantinople was able to remain in the hands of Christians until 1453. The city was then conquered by the Turks and renamed Istanbul.

CHAPTER ELEVEN

CHRISTIANITY
IN
THE EAST

As early as the third century, the Roman Empire and Christianity were divided between east and west. Diocletian's creation of the tetrarchy created eastern and western halves of the empire politically. Rome, located in the west, was the ancient capital of the empire. Constantine, however, created Constantinople in the east on the Straits of the Bosporus in Asia Minor in 330 and made it the new capital. From that date the two cities battled for dominance of the church. The rivalry intensified when Emperor Theodosius separated the administration of the two sees in 395 and in effect created two different churches. As a result of the Council of Chalcedon in 451 and Constantinople's corresponding elevation in status, the rivalry intensified again. When Rome fell in 476, Constantinople remained and its case for precedence strengthened.

There were many differences in the traditions and beliefs of the two regions. The West used Latin as its primary language; the East used Greek. The West emphasized the act of sacrifice in the Eucharist; the East stressed the divine presence. The West was more practical in its theology; the East was more philosophical. Clergy in the West could not marry, but in the East anyone below the rank of bishop could marry. During Lent the West permitted eating cheese and milk; the East forbade it. In the East, bishops gathered at synods to hammer out theological questions and set doctrine, with the patriarch of Constantinople considered "first among equals." In the West, questions of theology and doctrine were settled by the pope. In the East, the emperor played a more significant role in church affairs than in the West—a practice known as *caesaropapism*. According to the East, the Byzantine emperor was God's vice-regent on earth, a living representative of Christ. Following Justinian's (527–565) removal of the barbarians from Italy in the Gothic Wars (535–554), the patriarchs of Constantinople became more assertive. In the West there was no emperor. Though Rome was supposedly under the authority of the emperor in Constantinople, it was too far away for him to call the pope to task. Often the West was under barbarian rule, and the pope acted as he if were an emperor.

Though the two sees were bitter rivals, East and West both owe a debt of gratitude to Byzantium. When Rome fell, Constantinople became the custodian of Roman culture. When Islam arose and began to push further west, the Byzantine Empire held it back.

JUSTINIAN (527–565)

Succeeding his uncle Justin (518–527) in 527, Justinian I became emperor of the Roman Empire (in actuality just the eastern half) and continued to hold court in Constantinople. Educated in theology and law, he gained experience as prefect of Constantinople. Though there were numerous insurrections during his early years as emperor, Justinian, with the aid of his beautiful and cunning wife Theodora (527–548), had firm control of the throne by 537.

Justinian's greatest desire was to unify the Eastern and Western empires under his leadership. He defeated the Vandals in North Africa in 534, which led to the conversion of Ethiopia. When he defeated the Goths in Italy in 555, he appeared to be well on his way to reunification, for his conquest of Italy gave him power, though temporary, over Rome and the papacy. The Lombards took Italy in

556, and his grip on the papacy weakened. Justinian's military conquests drained the royal treasury, and his successors were unable to retain the territories he had gained.

Justinian placed his stamp firmly on the Eastern church through edicts. He produced the *Codex Junis Civilis* (issued from 529 to 534), which combined Roman law and church law. Under these laws the emperor had full responsibility for the defense of the church. He believed the "prosperity of the realm [would] be secured if the Holy Canons of the Apostles, preserved and explained by the Holy Fathers, [were] universally obeyed."[1]

Justinian was harsh to those he perceived as heretics and pagans. He closed the Sophist schools in Athens in 529, including the Academy, and persecuted the Montanists nearly to extinction. He restricted the rights of Jews and barred them from civic offices. Regarding the Jews, Justinian stated:

> If any among them seek to introduce impious vanities denying the resurrection or the judgment, or the work of God, or that angels are part of creation, we require them everywhere to be expelled forthwith; that no backslider raise his impious voice to contradict the evident purpose of God. Those who utter such sentiments shall be put to death, and thereby the Jewish people shall be purged of the errors which they introduce.[2]

In 543, he condemned nine points of Origen's *On First Principles* and attempted to destroy all of Origen's works. When reconciliation with the Monophysites failed, he persecuted them relentlessly.

Justinian's buildings were known for their beautiful frescos and elaborate icons. He built the Hagia Sophia in Constantinople in 538. Its dome was more than 180 feet tall and appeared to float in the air. Its windows allowed light to enter the basilica in a way that made its golden altar, mosaics, and tapestries appear to glow. Procopius (500–565) described the basilica's magnificence:

St. Sophia is distinguished by indescribable beauty, excelling both in its size, and in the harmony of its measures, having no part excessive and none deficient; being more magnificent than ordinary buildings, and much more elegant than those which are not of so just a proportion. The church is singularly full of light and sunshine; you would declare that the place is not lighted by the sun from without, but that the rays are produced within its self, such an abundance of light is poured into this church.[3]

After the Hagia Sophia was completed, Justinian reportedly said, "Solomon, I have surpassed you." During the mass dedicating the Hagia Sophia, Justinian served the Eucharist to the patriarch and clergy. He also built orphanages, hospitals, and monasteries. He set a precedent in matters of building and architecture that was followed by succeeding Byzantine emperors.

CHURCH OF THE SEVEN COUNCILS

The Eastern church is often called the Church of the Seven Councils because it accepted as authoritative seven councils between 325 and 787. These ecumenical councils defined the nature of the Trinity, the person of Jesus, and the correct use of icons.

The Eastern church accepted the findings of the Council of Nicaea (325) and its interpretation of Christ being one with the Father (*homoousios*). It also recognized Constantinople I (381) and its statement on the Holy Spirit's equality with the Son and the Father. At the Council of Ephesus (431), the Eastern church affirmed Mary as the *Theotokos* and Christ as both human and divine. Most Christians in the East, though not all, acknowledged the Definition of Chalcedon (451), which affirmed Christ's two natures in one person and that neither nature was destroyed. The Monophysites, who were prominent in Egypt and Syria, did not accept Chalcedon. Their theological position appeared under different names at future ecumenical councils. As the Alexandrians placed more emphasis on Christ's divinity than on his humanity, they were particularly pleased with Constantinople II (553), which condemned Theodore of Mopsuestia (350–428) and the Antiochene position that placed a greater stress on Christ's humanity. By siding with the Alexandrian position, the council also mollified the Monophysites.

The Eastern church took the lead in Constantinople III (680–681). This sixth ecumenical council was called by Constantine IV (652–685) to settle the Monothelite controversy. Similar to Monophysites, the Monothelites believed Christ had two natures but only one will. The divine will superseded the human will. After early support by Emperor Heraclius (610–641) of Constantinople, who wanted to pacify the many Monophysites in his domain, the Monothelite position began to lose favor. Under guidance and pressure from the Eastern church and Constantine IV (668–685), the sixth ecumenical council determined that Christ had both a human and a divine nature and a human and a divine will, all in harmony and never in conflict:

> This we preach in accordance with the teaching of the holy Fathers. And two natural wills, not contrary (God forbid), as the impious heretics assert, but the human will following his divine and omnipotent will, not resisting it nor striving against it, but rather subject to it.[4]

Pope Agatho (678–681) affirmed this statement. It was a reaffirmation of Chalcedon but with different terminology.

Pope Honorius I (625–638) of Rome was deemed a Monothelite after he affirmed in 634 that Christ had one will. Popes such as Severinus (640), John IV (640–642), and Theodore I (642–649) condemned the Monothelites and declared Honorius a heretic. Under this precedent Constantinople III anathematized

Honorius I. The Protestant Reformers later used the condemnation of Honorius I to demonstrate that the pope was not beyond
reproach.

Nicaea II (787)—the Icono-
clastic Controversy

An icon is a visible representation of a person or event deemed
important to Christianity. Like relics, icons were thought to be capable of intercession, of conferring grace, and of expelling demons. By
reflecting on an icon, believers thought they could commune with
the person it depicted. The most common icons were of Jesus, Mary,
the apostles, and saints. Sometimes they depicted biblical scenes or
Christian legends. In the Eastern church an icon was usually a flat
panel made of cloth, wood, or metal. Frescos, paintings, and statues
were considered icons by the Western church. Making an icon was
considered an act of worship, and every step in the process had a
corresponding prayer.

Icons became increasingly popular in Eastern Christian life and
worship. Some church leaders who opposed the use of icons became
known as Iconoclasts. They argued that veneration of icons was the
worship of graven images. They found icons depicting Christ particularly reprehensible. Iconodules disagreed. They argued that since
Christ came in the flesh, a visible representation of him should not
be considered idolatry.

The emperor of the east, Leo III (717–741), forbade kneeling to pictures or images in 726 and in 730 had all images but the
cross removed from churches. He blamed his military defeats at the
hands of Muslims on Christian idolatry. Islam prohibited images of
Muhammad, and he wanted to rebut Muslim and Jewish charges
that Christians were idolatrous. Moreover Leo wanted to curb the
growing power of monks who made a steady income from selling
icons.

When Leo destroyed an image of Christ that stood above one of the entrances to the palace at Constantinople and replaced it with a cross, the citizens, instigated by monks, killed the man who had been in charge of the removal. Constantine V (741–775) attempted to destroy all icons and persecuted those who supported their use in worship. The Empress Irene (752–803), who served as regent for her son Constantine VI (780–797), however, believed icons to be an important part of Christian worship and wanted destroyed icons to be replaced.

At the urging of Irene, the seventh ecumenical council met at Nicaea in 787 with the explicit purpose of restoring the use of icons. With her support the council decided in favor of the Iconodules. Since Christ took on human form, forbidding icons was tantamount to denying his humanity, the council said. An icon could be venerated but not adored or worshipped. Worship and adoration were reserved for God alone.

JOHN OF DAMASCUS (CA. 655–CA. 750)

Born in Damascus and educated in Greek, Arabic, law, and philosophy, John of Damascus was the last and greatest of the Eastern Orthodox fathers and was later named a doctor of the church. He may have served as a high-level court official for the Muslim caliph of Damascus. Eventually he joined the monastery of Saint Sabas near Jerusalem, where he became a priest.

John's most influential book, *The Fount of Knowledge*, is a standard theological work of the Eastern Orthodox Church. The text was divided into three sections, which some theologians treat as separate books. The first section was philosophical, based on Aristotle's ontology, and was meant to prepare the reader for the doctrinal sections that followed. The second section described Christian heresies and concluded with a treatment of Islam. The third section, "The Orthodox Faith," synthesized Nicene and post-Nicene theology, explained Mary's sinlessness and assumption into heaven, modified the doctrine of predestination, and explained the Trinity. John also composed many hymns.

John believed in the veneration of icons. By taking on flesh, Jesus made all matter, such as bread and wine, a fitting way to communicate God's grace, he said. Matter, therefore, was not evil. In *On the Worship of Images*, he wrote, "Is not the blessed table matter which gives us the Bread of Life?"[5] He reminded the opponents of icons that Iconodules were not worshipping the image and described to them the purpose of images:

> It certainly happens frequently that at times when we do not have the Lord's Passion in mind, we may see the image of His crucifixion and, being thus reminded of His saving Passion, fall down and adore. But it is not the material we adore, but that which is represented; just as we do not adore the material of the Gospel or that of the cross, but that which they typify.[6]

MYSTICISM

DEIFICATION

Prominent in Eastern Orthodoxy, deification or divinization concerns the transforming work of Christ in the believer's life. In a literal sense it means "becoming God," but that is misleading. Eastern Christians did not believe humans could become gods but rather that they could partake of the divine nature. Two biblical texts supported this notion. The first text is 2 Peter 1:4: "So that through them you may share in the divine nature." The second text is John 14:17: "But you do know Him, because He remains with you and will be in you."

Deification or participation began with Christ's incarnation. The union of the two natures in Christ helped unify believers and

God. As the God-man, Christ brought reconciliation between man and God through his sinless life. Union with Christ purifies man and allows God to share himself with man through Christ in holiness and righteousness but not essence. This unity enables man to have a true vision of God. Through this grace, man can overcome the effects of the fall and truly participate in God.

Participation has its roots in the patristic era writings of Clement and Cyril of Alexandria. The most prominent patristic advocate of participation, however, was Athanasius of Alexandria, who wrote that "He [God] became man so that we might be made God."[7] In the Middle Ages, Pseudo-Dionysius, Maximus the Confessor (580–662), and John of Damascus were advocates of deification.

HESYCHASM

Also known as "quietude," Hesychasm was a form of mystical prayer and contemplation practiced in Eastern Orthodoxy. It was begun by tenth-century monks of Mount Athos in the Macedonian region of Greece. The goal of Hesychasm was to produce an inner harmony that was beyond language and images. It is based on Matthew 6:5–6:

> Whenever you pray, you must not be like the hypocrites, because they love to pray standing in the synagogues and on the street corners to be seen by people. I assure you: They've got their reward! But when you pray, go into your private room, shut your door, and pray to your Father who is in secret. And your Father who sees in secret will reward you.

Hesychasm involved inner focus, blocking out all sensory perception, controlled breathing, placing one's head on the chest in order to fix the eyes on the heart, and chanting the Jesus prayer: "Lord Jesus Christ, Son of God, have mercy on me, a sinner." If done properly, the penitent supposedly would achieve a union of the mind and heart and have a vision of divine light as expressed at the transfiguration. This light was not God but his divine energies as displayed in his actions.

In an attempt to defend themselves from attack and tie their practice to the early church, advocates of Hesychasm cited Gregory of Nyssa, John Chrysostom, and the desert fathers as practicing a form of quietude. In the late Middle Ages and after considerable controversy, Hesychasm was established as an accepted part of Eastern Orthodoxy.

THE VIRGIN MARY

Following the Council of Ephesus in 431, the virgin Mary was venerated increasingly. By the mid-fifth century hymns and poetry were dedicated to her. She was invoked in prayer, icons of her were produced, and Marian holidays were added to the church calendar.

The noncanonical *Protoevangelium of James* (ca. 160) was an important document in the development of Eastern Mariolatry. It described Mary's consecration as a virgin at age three, the grace given to her by God at the temple, how she was fed by angels until she was twelve, and how she was instructed to marry an older widower named Joseph. The *Protoevangelium* depicted Joseph as having several children by a previous marriage. This explained the biblical depiction of Jesus having brothers and sisters although Mary remained a virgin.

John of Damascus promoted the idea of the "Assumption of Mary" into heaven. He wrote:

> And just as the all holy body of God's Son, which was taken from her, rose from the dead on the third day, it followed that she should be snatched from the tomb, that the mother should be united to her Son; and as He had come down to her, so she should be raised up to Him, into the more perfect dwelling-place, heaven itself. It was right that

she, who had sheltered God the Word in her own womb, should inhabit the tabernacles of her Son.[8]

John of Damascus also believed her to be the ultimate mediator between Christ and man:

> In a word, she grieves over every sin, and is glad at all goodness as if it were her own. If we turn away from our former sins in all earnestness and love goodness with all our hearts, and make it our constant companion, she will frequently visit her servants, bringing all blessings with her, Christ her Son, the King and Lord who reigns in our hearts.[9]

THE SLAVIC TERRITORIES

The Slavic people populated much of Central and Eastern Europe. Unlike the Franks who desired all things Roman and accepted Latin as the only language of Christianity, the Slavs wanted to worship in their native tongues. Prince Ratislav (846–870) of Moravia requested that Constantinople send missionaries to preach, teach, pray, and lead services in Slavic languages. In reply Michael III (840–867), the Byzantine emperor, sent brothers Cyril (826–869) and Methodius (815–885) to Moravia in 863. They were so successful that they became known as the "Apostles to the Slavs." Citing the example of Pentecost, they taught that a person could praise God in any language. They were reported to have converted and baptized thousands. The brothers were also credited with developing a system of letters known as Glagolitic script, which allowed the translation of the Bible into the language now known as Old Church Slavonic. Cyril and Methodius also ministered in the Slavic territories of Bulgaria and Pannonia.

RUSSIA

Eastern Orthodoxy's first contact with Russia came through the migration of Slavic tribes to areas surrounding Kiev. The first definitive mention of official contact between the see of Constantinople and Russia was in 867. In that year, Patriarch Photius (858–867 and 877–886) mentioned in an encyclical letter that the "Rus" had been converted.

The first convert from Russian nobility was Queen Olga (945–ca. 963) of Kiev. In the tenth century Olga's grandson, Vladimir (979–1015), the Grand Duke of Kiev, decided to abandon paganism because of its hedonism. Several human sacrifices had been reported from Kiev, and he believed a change in religion might curb these atrocities. To find the best form of monotheism, he sent envoys to converse with Catholic and Eastern Orthodox Christians, Jews, and Muslims. The envoys were most impressed with Constantinople and Eastern Orthodoxy. They enjoyed the Byzantine liturgy and were overwhelmed with the beauty of the Hagia Sophia. Vladimir adopted Eastern Orthodoxy as the official religion of Russia and was baptized on January 6, 988, where Saint Vladimir's Cathedral now stands. Many of the citizens of Kiev followed suit and were baptized in the Dnieper River a few months later. Vladimir built churches and monasteries and destroyed pagan temples, statues, and shrines throughout his territories. He did not acknowledge any authority outside Russia, but his grandson Yaroslav the Wise (1019–1054) acknowledged the supremacy of Constantinople. He is credited as being the father of Russian Orthodoxy.

ISLAM'S EFFECT ON THE EAST

While Constantinople managed to withstand Islamic conquest until 1453, the other major Eastern sees were not as fortunate. Islam claimed Jerusalem in 636, Antioch in 638, and Alexandria in 641. Entire regions that once belonged to the Eastern empire and church became part of the Islamic Empire. Armenia fell in 654, Georgia voluntarily submitted to Islam, and by 709 all of North Africa was under Muslim rule. Not all of these territories, however, saw the arrival of Islam as a terrible event. The Monophysites of Egypt and Syria believed Islam was more loyal to monotheism than was Byzantium. As Islam became more militant, the belief that Muslims were liberators quickly dissipated.

By the dawn of the new millennium, the Byzantine Empire lost most of its territory and population. It was confined to Asia Minor, the Balkans, and a tiny section of southern Italy. The Mediterranean never again would belong exclusively to Christianity.

THE FINAL STRAWS—THE SCHISM OF 1054

Since the establishment of Constantinople in 330, the rivalry between Rome and Constantinople had grown. By the ninth century an official break between the two sees appeared likely. The argument over the *Filioque* clause and the Photian Schism were the final straws.

Both East and West believed the Holy Spirit was fully divine and a member of the Trinity. But there were differences in their articulations of the relationship between the Spirit and the other two persons of the Trinity. The Eastern churches stringently maintained the Nicene-Constantinopolitan Creed, which said the Holy Spirit proceeded from the Father. The West believed the Holy Spirit proceeded not only from the Father but also from the Son (the Latin word *Filioque* means "and the Son"). The Catholic Church would officially add the *Filioque* clause to the Western creed in the eleventh century. The Eastern church insisted that the Catholic Church did not have the right to alter the Nicene-Constantinopolitan Creed. In an attempt to gain support from other sees, Patriarch Photius I of Constantinople wrote:

They have attempted to adulterate the sacred and holy creed, which has been approved by the vote of all the ecumenical synods and has unconquerable strength, with spurious arguments, interpolated words, and rash exaggerations. They are preaching a novel doctrine: that the Holy Spirit proceeds not from Father alone, but from the Son as well.[10]

This episode increased the estrangement between the two supreme sees.

The Photian Schism began in 863 when Pope Nicholas I (858–867) opposed Byzantine Emperor Michael III's (842–867) appointment of Photius I as patriarch of Constantinople. Photius had been ordained by a bishop who was suspended by Ignatius, the former patriarch of Constantinople. Followers of Ignatius (847–858 and 867–877) declared Photius ineligible to serve as patriarch and excommunicated him. Pope Nicholas sent legates to investigate the situation and eventually declared Photius deprived of office— influenced no doubt by Photius's criticism of Western doctrine and his complaints that Roman missionaries were encroaching on the East. When Basil the Macedonian (867–886) took the throne from Michael, he sided with the papacy and reinstated Ignatius. Before he was removed from office, Photius condemned Rome in an encyclical for meddling in affairs outside its jurisdiction and its use of the *Filioque* clause. Later that same year a council in Constantinople excommunicated Pope Nicholas. The schism over Photius was only temporary though, and he became patriarch of Constantinople again in 877.

The struggle between East and West continued in 1054, when the patriarch of Constantinople, Michael Cerularius (1043–1058), condemned the West for using unleavened bread in the Mass. For Cerularius, the use of unleavened bread was too close to Judaism. In reply Pope Leo IX (1048–1054) sent legates to Constantinople to settle the controversy. The legates excommunicated Cerularius on July 16, 1054, placing the Bull of Excommunication on the altar of the Saint Sophia Cathedral. Cerularius responded in kind by excommunicating the papal legates and their supporters. Though there had been tension before, these excommunications marked a decisive split between the Eastern and Western churches that has never healed.

The Schism of 1054 damaged the Orthodox Church much more than it did the Catholic Church. The schism coupled with the Muslim invasion separated Byzantium and its church from Europe. The Catholic Church became strong thanks to the rise of nation-states that swore loyalty to Peter's Church. It became the owner of large parcels of land throughout Europe and became wealthy. The Eastern Orthodox Church could not accumulate land or wealth because of Islam. Later, Catholicism benefited from the Renaissance and regained some of its spiritual vitality by correcting the abuses Protestants brought to light. The Orthodox Church just sought to survive and as a result declined in size, stature, and viability.

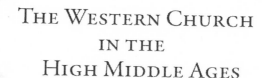

CHAPTER TWELVE

THE WESTERN CHURCH
IN THE
HIGH MIDDLE AGES

In the Middle Ages the Catholic Church became the most power-ful entity in Europe. It was one of the largest landowners, asserted its right to crown and dethrone kings, and claimed ownership of the only set of keys to heaven. With great power and wealth, however, came a succession of popes who wanted their share of both. The papacy was plagued by corruption, and no fewer than thirty-five popes served between 882 and 998. Piety took a backseat to power and influence.

Popes of the Middle Ages believed ultimate Christian power and leadership belonged to them. This belief was tested on many occasions as they contended with the rise of nation-states and their powerful kings. The passing of the Carolingian dynasty ended the days of the Frankish kingdom and made way for the kingdoms of Germany, France, England, and Spain.

The Kingdom of Germany[1] began to take shape in 919 when its tribal dukes elected Henry the Fowler (919–936), the Duke of Saxony, as king. He was succeeded by his son Otto I (936–973), who defeat-ed the powerful Magyars in 955. Otto became Holy Roman Emper-or in 962, and the Kingdom of Germany became part of the empire. He made the German dukes his vassals and interfered in church affairs by selecting abbots and bishops without papal permission. To strengthen his position against the pope and the powerful German dukes, Otto created bishoprics in Brandenburg (948), Magdeburg (968), and Prague (973).

With the selection of Hugh Capet (987–996), Duke of France and Count of Paris, as king in 987, the nation of France began to emerge from a patchwork of Frankish tribes. The French kings had many dealings with the papacy and, for a period, housed the popes at Avignon.

Though Aethelstan (925–939) reigned over the various small kingdoms that encompassed England in the tenth century, William the Conqueror (1066–1087) made England a viable nation-state. He set up the *curia regis* (Latin for "royal council"), a royal advisory group comprised of feudal lords. Because of England's distance from Rome, the English monarch often attempted to impose his will in ecclesiastical matters. This led to several bitter clashes with the papacy.

Spain became a nation-state in 1469 when Ferdinand of Aragon (1479–1516) and Isabella of Castile (1451–1504) married, uniting the largest and most powerful regions of Spain. The monarchs then were able to bring nobles under their royal patronage. With papal permission the Spanish monarchs expelled all Jews and Moors who refused to convert to Christianity. Whereas Charlemagne had a strong relationship with the pope, the papacy's relationship with kings of Germany, France, and England was often less than amicable. Spain, however, was always loyal to the see of Rome.

In several instances popes tried to reform the church and return spirituality to the forefront. The major abuses addressed during these efforts were clerical marriage and simony (buying and selling access to the sacraments, including ordination to church offices). Reform efforts often led to tension with kings and nobles and competing factions within the church. Simony was a difficult sin to correct. Many of the clergy purchased their offices, and several monarchs sold key bishoprics to the highest bidders.

Popes became increasingly concerned with preserving their power. Monarchs and church leaders attempted to balance the power of the pope with that of ecclesiastical councils and secular rulers, but the papacy remained dominant. A series of popes was so powerful that their reigns became known as the "Papal Monarchy." Their call for the Crusades demonstrated their power, as monarchs, nobles, and peasants answered the summons to fight.

The Crusades were an attempt to wipe out not only Islam but all heresies. At least one heretical group, the Cathars, was brought to the brink of extinction.

Papal Decline

Prior to becoming pope, Formosus (891–896) was bishop of Portus and led diplomatic missions for several popes. After being accused of plotting against the Roman see, attempting to acquire the Bulgarian archbishopric, and plundering the monasteries of Rome, he was excommunicated in 872. His excommunication was rescinded in 878 under the condition that he never return to Rome or administer the sacraments. Pope Marinus I (882–884) permitted Formosus to return to his bishopric in Portus in 883 and resume his priestly duties. Formosus was then elected pope in 891.

His papacy was filled with scheming and political posturing. He crowned Guy III (d. 894) of Spoleto in Italy as Holy Roman emperor in 891. He then persuaded Arnulf of Carinthia (850–899) to invade Italy in 894. When Guy died, Formosus crowned Guy's young son Lambert II (880–898). Arnulf finished his conquest of Italy in 896 and Formosus crowned him Holy Roman emperor.

Formosus's successors refused to let him rest in peace. In 897 Pope Stephen VI (896–897) had his skeleton dug up, placed in the papal chair, interrogated,[2] and condemned. His first two fingers, which he used in the papal blessing, were cut off and his vestments removed. The corpse was dragged through the streets of Rome and finally thrown into the Tiber River. A monk retrieved the body and, after the death of Stephen VI, had it buried at Saint Peter's. Pope Sergius III (904–911) had the bones of Formosus removed from his grave and again put on trial. Once more the dead pope was found guilty, and this time he was beheaded.

Many popes were murdered during this era. Pope Stephen VI (896–897) was thrown in jail and strangled. Leo V (903) met the same fate. John X (914–928) was suffocated with a pillow. Antipope John XVI (997–998) had his eyes gouged out, his tongue cut out, and his nose, lips, and hands cut off. He was then dragged through the streets of Rome but somehow managed to survive.

The Tusculum Popes

The Tusculum popes were either descendants of or aligned with the powerful aristocrat Theophylact (ca. 864–925) and his family from Latium near Rome. Theophylact's descendants were so powerful in tenth-century Italy that they were known as the "pope makers." Through the sexual exploits of Theophylact's daughters, Theodora (d. ca. 928) and Marozia (890–936), the family controlled the papacy for much of the tenth century. They were just as successful in the first half of the eleventh century.

Because of these women, this era has been called the "Pornocracy." Marozia was married to the powerful Count Alberic of Spoleto (Alberic I, d. 925). After her husband's death, she married Margrave Guido of Tuscany and saw to the selection of her son John as Pope John XI (931–935). Alberic II (912–954), her son by Alberic I, then deposed his mother and ruled Rome.

On his deathbed Alberic II saw to it that his seventeen-year-old son, Octavian, would become the next pope. Octavian was selected the following year and took the name John XII (955–964). He reportedly turned the Vatican into a brothel. Some claim he took money to have a ten-year-old boy named bishop of Todi, committed incest with his nieces, and defiled nuns. He was said to have even blinded his confessor, castrated a cardinal, and toasted the devil.

Gregory (d. 1012), the Count of Tusculum, arranged to have his son, who took the name Benedict VIII (1012–1024), elected pope in 1012. After Benedict's death his brother was elected pope and became known as John XIX (1024–1032).

Alberic III (d. 1044) purchased the papacy for his son, Benedict IX (1032–1044). One of the worst popes in the 2,000-year history of the church, Benedict was only eighteen years old when elected. He was reported to have committed sodomy, rape, and bestiality. These charges led to his removal from Rome in 1036 and 1044, but with military aid from the Germans he regained the papacy. In 1045, Benedict sold the office of pope to his uncle who took the title Gregory VI (1045–1046). Soon afterwards, Benedict regretted this action and claimed he was still the legitimate Pope. Gregory VI, however, was recognized as the true pope. Benedict took the papacy by force and took up residence in the Lateran palace. Benedict was finally excommunicated in 1049, left Rome, and disappeared from history.

PAPAL REFORM

Following Formosus and the Tusculum popes, the Catholic Church desperately needed reform. Though subsequent popes sought to eliminate ecclesiastical abuses, they still viewed themselves as the chief representatives of Christ on earth and would not share power with earthly monarchs. They also pressured European monarchs to obey them or face excommunication or even have interdicts[3] placed on their countries.

Leo IX (1048–1054), a German, was the first pope to make a concerted effort to correct his predecessors' abuses, reforming the church along the lines of Cluniac monasticism. The Cluniac standard repudiated all simony and nepotism and demanded clerical celibacy. Leo held a synod in Rome in 1049 that condemned simony. That same year he convened a synod in Reims, which stated that bishops and abbots would be chosen by the clergy rather than feudal lords. He also led an army against the Normans in south Italy. Leo did much to correct the course of the Catholic Church, but it was his legates who excommunicated the patriarch of Constantinople, precipitating the Schism of 1054.

The bishop of Florence, Nicholas II (1059–1061), was elected pope over strong opposition. The Tusculums supported Benedict X (d. 1080), who had been elected pope in 1058. He was deposed later that year after having been found guilty of bribing cardinals to vote for him. After much bloodshed Nicholas became pope. Like his predecessors Nicholas claimed superiority to all earthly monarchs. He stressed the papacy's independence from all European rulers, yet he argued that the pope legitimized the reigns of secular rulers. Nicholas II's greatest achievement was the reform of papal elections. At the Lateran Council of 1059, he placed the task of electing popes in the hands of the cardinals. In effect, this ended the Roman aristocracy's ability to select the pope and liberated the church from outside influence. Moreover, it helped eliminate rival claims to the papacy.

Gregory VII

With the election of Gregory VII (1073–1085), formerly Hildebrand of Tuscany, the papacy reached an unprecedented level of power. Hildebrand had been a constant presence at the papal court, serving as secretary to five popes. At the funeral of Alexander II (1061–1073) the people demanded that Hildebrand be pope. In response he took the papal throne and claimed the papacy for himself. Despite the irregularity of his actions, the cardinals affirmed him. King Henry IV of Germany (1056–1105), however, resented that the cardinals did not consult him. Later, when Henry was Holy

Roman emperor, he used the unusual circumstances of Hildebrand's selection against him in a power struggle.

Hildebrand was interested in reform but unwilling to give up papal power to accomplish it. He attacked simony, immorality within the church, deeding of church property to the clergy's children, and pressed for clerical celibacy. Many of the German nobility and clergy, however, paid for clerical positions and opposed Hildebrand. Furthermore, he made papal election by the cardinals official canon law, which Henry took as a personal affront.

The hallmark of Hildebrand's reign was the Investiture Controversy. The debate concerned whether the pope or the monarch had the right to appoint bishops in a kingdom. Henry IV of Germany believed this privilege was reserved for the king. After all, the king was divinely appointed by God. This position became known as lay investiture. The king would bestow the symbols of the bishop's office on all those who served in his kingdom. Hildebrand maintained that the right belonged to the church and specifically to the pope. Only the Roman church owed its foundation to God; its pontiff alone was universal; princes should kiss the pope's feet; and the pope could depose emperors. Both the king and the pope understood the importance of the debate. Whoever appointed a bishop or abbot earned his loyalty.

The Investiture Controversy came to a head when Henry (Holy Roman emperor 1084–1105), wanted to appoint the new archbishop of Milan. Hildebrand tired of Henry's interference and denounced him. At the Diet of Worms in 1076, Henry declared that Hildebrand had been elected pope illegally. With the strong support of the German bishops, Henry sent the pope a letter demanding his abdication. Hildebrand retaliated by excommunicating Henry and deposing him as emperor. Henry's subjects were no longer bound to obey him, and the legitimacy of his reign was in question.

Henry was the first to give in. While Hildebrand was in Germany to discuss with nobles the selection of a new king, his entourage stopped to rest at a castle in northern Italy. Henry appeared at the gate dressed in sackcloth and ashes and begged Hildebrand for forgiveness. Hildebrand forced Henry to stand barefoot in the snow for three days as an act of penance. He then lifted the order of excommunication. The German nobility, who had no love for Henry, used his absence to elect a new king. A civil war erupted, and Hildebrand called an assembly in 1080 to decide who should rule. Henry believed Hildebrand would back his opponent, Rudolph Duke of Swabia (1057–1079), so he tried to keep the council from convening. Hildebrand, in turn, excommunicated him again. With the majority of the German bishops behind him, Henry invaded Rome, removed and exiled Hildebrand, and installed Guibert of Ravenna, who became the anti-pope Clement III (1080–1100). Clement then gave Henry the imperial crown of Germany.

Hildebrand's position, however, was ratified by the Concordat of Worms in 1122. It was determined that the church would bestow the ring and staff (symbols of ecclesiastical office), and the monarch would give the regalia (symbols of temporal authority). The actual appointment, however, remained in the hands of the church. Though he died in exile, Hildebrand defied the king of Germany and won. The pope was the most powerful monarch in Europe.

THE PAPAL MONARCHY

Alexander III (1159–1181) rose from deacon cardinal to priest cardinal, to papal chancellor, and finally to pope. Soon after his election he began to experience conflict with Germany. Alexander opposed the campaigns of the German Holy Roman Emperor Frederick Barbarossa (1152–1190) against the free cities in northern Italy. When Barbarossa ignored Alexander's command to cease the campaigns, Alexander excommunicated him. In retaliation, Barbarossa took Rome and replaced Alexander with three successive anti-popes: Victor IV (1159–1164), Paschal III (1164–1168), and Calixtus III (1168–1178). Alexander gave his support to the Lombard League of southern Italy, which defeated Barbarossa at the Battle of Legnano in 1176. With his position weakened, Barbarossa signed the Peace of Venice. He threw himself at the pope's feet and begged forgiveness. Once again a pope had brought an emperor to his knees.

Alexander was also known for his feud with Henry II of England (1154–1189). Henry wanted more autonomy for England in religious affairs. He passed the Clarendon Code in 1164, which placed the election of clergy under his jurisdiction and said that clergy had to be tried in civil rather than ecclesiastical courts. The archbishop of Canterbury, Thomas Becket (1118–1170), would not support Henry's actions and in 1170 convinced Alexander to excommunicate the king. Becket was then murdered by four of the king's knights in Canterbury Cathedral in 1170. Alexander hailed Becket as a martyr and canonized him in 1173. Because of Becket's popularity, Henry performed penance and humbled himself before his grave. Alexander had strengthened the papacy's influence in England.

Elected when he was thirty-seven years old, Innocent III (1198–1216) was one of the most powerful popes in history. He was well connected to powerful Roman families and was the first pope to claim the title *vicarius Christi* or "vicar of Christ." He asserted the pope's power over the state and convened the Fourth Lateran Council in 1215.

Innocent maintained that the pope was under God and over all men. All kings and princes, therefore, owed their authority to him. In a famous statement known as "The Sun and the Moon," Innocent said:

> The creator of the universe set up two great luminaries in the firmament of heaven; the greater light to rule the day, the lesser light to rule the night. In the same way for the firmament of the universal church, which is spoken of

as heaven, he appointed two great dignities; the greater to bear rule over souls (these being, as it were, days), the lesser to bear rule over bodies (those being, as it were, nights). The dignities are the pontifical authority and the royal power. Furthermore, the moon derives her light from the sun, and is in truth inferior to the sun in both size and quality, in position as well as effect. In the same way the royal power derives its dignity from the pontifical authority: and the more closely it cleaves to the sphere of that authority the less is the light with which it is adorned; the further it is removed, the more it increases in splendor.[4]

Innocent's position was put to the test by European monarchs on two occasions. The first surrounded the divorce of King Philip Augustus (1180–1223) of France. Philip had been married to Ingeborg of Denmark (1175–1236) for one day when he decided that he had made a poor choice. He forced the French bishops to grant his divorce, married Agnes of Merania (1196–1201), and placed Ingeborg in a convent. Ingeborg appealed to the pope. Innocent told Philip that Ingeborg was his true wife and that he must put away Agnes. When Philip would not comply, the pope placed an interdict on France. The French people were so distraught that it appeared they might revolt against Philip. He had no choice but to capitulate.

The second event was similar. When King John of England (1199–1216) attempted to name the archbishop of Canterbury, Innocent placed an interdict on England that lasted for five years. John replied by seizing monasteries and churches. The king was forced to acquiesce when Innocent created an alliance with France and prepared for an invasion. As a result, England became a vassal of the papacy in 1213.

Innocent III also endorsed the Franciscan and Dominican Orders, advocated celibacy, fought simony, and made church officials regularly visit monasteries and convents. Under his leadership the Fourth Lateran Council affirmed transubstantiation, determined that the laity would receive only the bread but not the cup during mass, and said that mass was the means by which the laity received grace. The council's decree stated:

> There is one universal Church of the faithful, beyond which no one at all is saved. In it Jesus himself is both priest and sacrifice, whose body and blood are truly contained in the sacrament of the altar under the species of bread and wine by the transubstantiation of bread into body and wine into blood through divine power: that through the perfecting of the mystery of unity we receive of him from himself, that which he received from us.[5]

Everyone was required to take mass at least once a year, punishments for lax clergy were defined, and rules were enacted that governed admission to the priesthood. The council also insisted that the clergy use its energies to preach, offer mass, and hear confessions. Regarding simony, the council was unequivocal:

> As we have certainly learnt, shameful and wicked exactions and extortions are levied in many places by many persons, who are like the sellers of doves in the temple for the consecration of bishops, the blessing of Abbots and the ordination of clerics. There is fixed how much is to be paid for this or that and yet another thing. Some even stride to defend this disgrace and wickedness on the grounds of long-established custom, thereby heaping up for themselves still further damnation. Wishing therefore to abolish so great an abuse, we altogether reject such a custom which should rather be termed a corruption. We firmly decree that nobody shall dare to demand or extort anything under any pretext for the conferring of such things or for their having been conferred. Otherwise both he who receives

and he who gives such an absolutely condemned payment shall be condemned with Gehazi and Simon.[6]

In addition, the council required bishops to seek out heretics in their domains. Jews and Muslims were forced to wear readily identifiable clothing. This set a precedent for the Inquisition.

The Crusades

The rationale for the Crusades was political, religious, and economic. There were nine major Crusades and several other minor ones.[7]

The first reason for the Crusades was the rise of the Seljuk Turks, Sunni Muslims whose empire encompassed the Holy Land and most of Asia Minor by the end of the eleventh century. They were not as tolerant of Christian pilgrims as their predecessors had been. Islamic conquests well into Europe were now a distinct possibility. With the rise of powerful Normans, the papacy hoped it had a fighting force strong enough to stop their progress.

The second reason for the Crusades was to unite feudal lords in fighting a common enemy so they would stop fighting one another. Indeed, feudal lords were frequently at war with one another, and a culture of violence developed. To curb the violence, the papacy created the "Peace of God" and the "Truce of God." The Peace of God required that no unarmed people be attacked, prohibited unnecessary violence, and protected sacred places and churches from destruction. The Truce of God stated that no feudal warfare could occur between Wednesday and Sunday, during church festivals, or on holy days. When all of these days were removed, the feudal lords were left with fewer than 100 days each year to fight one another. These restrictions, however, did not stop the fighting. Christian Europe needed a common enemy to unite it. Islam proved to be the answer. In Pope Urban II's (1088–1099) call for the First Crusade at the Council of Clermont, he stated, "Let those who have formerly been accustomed to contend wickedly in private warfare against the faithful, fight against the infidel and bring to a victorious end the war which ought long since to have been begun."[8]

Preserving the ability of Christians to make pilgrimages to the Middle East also fueled the Crusades. Since the fourth century, Christians had made pilgrimages to the Holy Land to visit sites mentioned in the Bible. By the tenth century, a system developed that required pilgrims to visit certain sites. As Holy Land venues were now cut off, the church lost the revenue pilgrims brought.

Many individuals fought in the Crusades because the church claimed participation would shorten their time in purgatory. By the tenth century, the Catholic Church's penitential system of contrition, confession, and works of satisfaction was well established. The works of satisfaction could be completed in this life or in purgatory. If a person died in a state of grace but still had unconfessed sins, those sins would have to be purged before they could enter the kingdom of heaven. Purgatory was where this purging took place. The church could shorten a soul's time in purgatory if certain criteria were met. The most common ways to remove years were through prayers, almsgiving, and indulgences. The normal process for indulgences was to visit a holy site or shrine, pay a fee, and receive a writ of indulgence that removed years that would otherwise be spent in purgatory. Participating in a Crusade became another way to reduce time in purgatory. Many people had such a fear of purgatory that they were willing to risk their lives far away from home to avoid its flames.

There were also economic and penal motives to fight. Much of the European population was comprised of peasants who hoped that going on a Crusade would alleviate their daily struggles. They believed that as part of a papal army, they would receive food, money, and be permitted to settle on the land they conquered. Others saw an opportunity to gain wealth through plundering because the crusaders were allowed, if not given outright permission, to rob

Muslims. The church, of course, expected to receive its share of the revenue. Others went on Crusades to get out of prison. A person could end his prison term and receive a spiritual blessing by going on a Crusade. These reasons led to armies composed of zealous, almost fanatical Christians, those looking to get rich through plunder, others hoping to acquire their own land, and criminals.

From the time of Pope Sylvester II (999–1003), Catholics sought to remove the Turks from the Holy Land. Hildebrand wanted to go on Crusade, but his difficulties with Henry IV prevented him. The impetus for the First Crusade (1095–1099) was Byzantine emperor Alexius I's (1081–1118) call for help against the Seljuk Turks who were encroaching on Constantinople. Hoping to gain influence in the East, Pope Urban II (1088–1099) told crowds at the Council of Clermont to retake the Holy Land so pilgrimages could occur. Since this was a pious work, he said violence was acceptable and offered remission of penalties for sin to all who fought. Urban proclaimed, "The sins of those who set out thither, if they lose their lives on the journey, by land or sea, or in fighting against the heathen, shall be remitted in that hour; this I grant to all who go, through the power of God vested in me."[9] The crowd began to yell "Deus le volt" or "God wills it!" The crusaders were instructed to place a red cross on the back of their clothing on their way to the Holy Land and on the front on their return. Urban hoped that only the nobility and knights would take up the cross, but this was not to be the case. His speech caused a religious frenzy among many of Europe's religious peasants.

The first wave of the initial Crusade was composed almost exclusively of peasants. A fiery monk known as Peter the Hermit (d. 1115) echoed Urban's call throughout Germany, Hungary, and the Balkans in 1096. Soon 40,000 peasants marched to the Holy Land but without provisions. While traveling, they robbed cities for food, pillaged, and killed thousands of Jews. Cities fought back, and only about 16,000 troops arrived at Constantinople. Alexius

I was horrified at the rabble he saw outside his walls. He quickly had them loaded into boats and sent to the Holy Land. Since they received no military training, they were decimated by the Turks near Nicaea.

The second wave of the First Crusade was different. The mission included as many as 700,000 men. Its leaders were Hugo of Vermandois (1053–1101) from France, Godfrey of Bouillon (1060–1100) from Belgium, and Robert of Normandy (1054–1134). The Crusaders took several cities in Asia Minor and, at great cost, Jerusalem on June 15, 1099. They were brutal, killing Muslim and Jewish defenders of the city along with women and children. With Jerusalem in their hands, the crusaders set up a kingdom which became known as the "Latin States." This did not please Alexius, who thought he was asking his Christian brothers for help without promising to give up traditional Byzantine territory. The Islamic forces initially were plagued by internal arguments and could not expel the crusaders. After uniting, the Islamic forces retook Edessa in 1144.

The purpose of the Second Crusade (1146–1149) was to retake Edessa for the Christians. In an almost ecstatic manner, Bernard of Clairvaux (1090–1153) challenged men to join the Crusade and reminded them that their predecessors gained remission of sin by doing so. The leaders of this Crusade were Conrad III of Germany (1137–1152) and Louis VII (1137–1180) of France. The crusaders accomplished nothing, and Edessa remained in Muslim hands. In the West, however, crusaders removed the Muslims from Lisbon, Portugal. Adding to the humiliation, Bernard condemned many of the crusaders for atrocities against the Jews of Germany.

The Third Crusade (1188–1192) was a response to the great Muslim general Saladin's (1138–1193) retaking of Jerusalem in 1187. Unlike the crusaders a century earlier, Saladin did not mercilessly kill everyone in the city. Instead, he held them for ransom. If ransoms were not paid, they were sold into slavery.

The participants in this Crusade were some of the greatest leaders in Europe: Frederick Barbarossa of Germany, Philip Augustus of France, and Richard I (1189–1199) "the Lionhearted" of England. The Crusade, however, did not achieve the success one would expect from this leadership. Barbarossa drowned on the way to the Holy Land, and Augustus argued with Richard and returned to France. Richard and his crusaders achieved a few minor victories and convinced Saladin to allow pilgrims to enter Jerusalem. While returning to England, Richard shipwrecked and was captured by his enemy, Duke Leopold V (1177–1192) of Germany. Leopold gave Richard to Henry VI (1191–1197) of the Holy Roman Empire who held him for ransom. The ransom was paid and Richard was eventually released.

Instigated by Innocent III, the Fourth Crusade (1200–1204) sought to recapture Egypt. Instead, the crusaders captured Constantinople in 1204 and placed it under control of the pope, where it remained until 1261. Constantinople's riches, relics, and even the bones of martyrs and saints were either sent to Rome or ended up in private collections throughout Europe. The Hagia Sophia was plundered.

Innocent denounced the atrocities committed in the taking of Constantinople but did not hesitate to place the city under papal control. There had been hope that the Eastern and Western branches of Christianity might reconcile. But the sacking of Constantinople, coupled with the creation of the Latin States, ended this dream.

The so-called Children's Crusade followed in 1212. Innocent said the adults of Europe were unworthy of the task, so a boy in France, Stephen of Cloyes, supposedly called for children to take up the cross. An eloquent speaker, he was reputed to have gathered close to 30,000 children. In Germany, Nicholas of Cologne gathered about 7,000 more.[10] The average age of Stephen and Nicholas's army was twelve, according to some reports. Stephen and Nicholas found no sympathy with the monarchs or the pope though. In fact, they were told to go home but to no avail. They were determined to go on Crusade. None of the children made it to the Holy Land. They went home, died of hunger, or were captured by Islamic forces and sold into slavery. Some scholars maintain the Children's Crusade is fiction.

The Fifth Crusade (1217–1221) captured Damietta, but the army was defeated at Cairo, Egypt, and forced to surrender. During this Crusade, Saint Francis of Assisi (1181 or 1182–1226) crossed the lines at Damietta and attempted to convert the Islamic Sultan Al-Kamil (1180–1238). The sultan was impressed with Francis but did not convert to Christianity. He let Francis return safely to the crusader encampment.

The Sixth Crusade (1228–1229) was led by Frederick II (1220–1250) of the Holy Roman Empire. By means of a treaty, Christians were given access to Jerusalem, Bethlehem, and Nazareth. The Seventh Crusade (1248–1254) was instigated by the Knights Templar and ended in their defeat. The Eight Crusade (1270) was led by Louis IX (1226–1270) of France, who wanted to free Syria from Islamic control. Louis died of sickness in Tunisia, and the Crusaders never reached Syria. The Ninth Crusade (1271–1272) was carried out by an unlikely alliance of crusaders and Mongols. They recorded a few victories but were eventually defeated. Antioch (1268), Tripoli (1289), and Acre (1291) fell, and Islamic forces expelled Christians from the Holy Land.

RESULTS OF THE CRUSADES

The Crusades did not achieve their primary objective. Some cities in the Holy Land were conquered, but they were eventually retaken by Islam. The atrocities of the Crusades continue to be a black eye on Catholicism in particular and Christianity in general. The violence unleashed on the Jews of Europe fueled anti-Semitism that continued for centuries. The needless killing of the noncombatant Islamic and Jewish citizens of Jerusalem, Richard the Lionhearted's slaughter of citizens in Acre, and other crusader atrocities against Muslims bred mistrust and violence that has lasted into the twenty-first century.

The Crusades also affected Catholicism. If in need of military force, the pope could now call upon the kings of Europe. The sale of indulgences advanced. The cult of relics grew as crusaders brought every sort of relic back from Jerusalem. Thorns from the crown of Christ, pieces of the cross, and even the seamless garment worn by Christ at his crucifixion were reported to have made their way to Europe. When Islam retook the Holy Land, the influx of relics ceased, and the value of those that had already made their way to Europe increased. The birth of militant monastic orders such as the Knights Templar and Hospitalars led to clerics who preferred fighting for the faith over ministering to the masses. The sacking of Constantinople and the establishment of the Latin States irreparably damaged relations between the Eastern and Western churches.

The Crusades weakened European feudalism. When knights and nobles left their manors to go on Crusade, the king often stayed in his country. To raise money for their Crusade, many nobles sold their property to the newly arising middle class. Others died on Crusade, and members of the middle class purchased their land. With the aid of the new middle class and the removal of troublesome nobility, kings centralized nations under their control. In turn, the rise of nation-states led to strong feelings of national loyalty that competed with, and often eclipsed, loyalty to the papacy.

Positively, the Crusades stopped feudal warfare among the Christian lords and helped unify much of Europe. With Venice taking the lead, trade and commerce increased. There was a renewed interest in the Arabic, Greek, and Hebrew languages, and many Islamic advances in medicine and mathematics were adopted by European society. This influx of learning paved the way for the Renaissance.

CRUSADES AGAINST THE HERETICS

The church also fought heretics at home. Pope Innocent III called for a Crusade against the Albigenses or "Cathars" of France and Italy in 1209. In many ways the Cathars were similar to the gnostics of the early church. They believed in a radical dualism and taught that the spirit was superior to the flesh. Marriage and sex, therefore, were forbidden. Jesus was an angel who never died on the cross. The Cathars were massacred by the pope's forces and finally defeated at the battle of Montségur in 1244. Those who would not surrender and repent were thrown into a fire. By the fifteenth century the Cathar movement ceased to exist.

Founded by Peter Waldo (d. 1218) in 1177 in Lyons, France, the Waldenses, or as they preferred to be called "the Poor of Christ," were another group the Catholic Church decided to eliminate. Unlike the Cathars, who were true heretics, the Waldenses were heretical only in a Catholic sense, but many of their teachings would be embraced by Protestantism. The Waldenses believed the schisms in the Catholic Church had corrupted it. They sought to return the church to Jesus' teachings, particularly the Sermon on the Mount, and New Testament principles. They taught that oaths to anyone but God were forbidden, that sacraments administered by an unworthy priest were worthless, that any devout layperson could administer the sacraments, and that poverty was virtuous. They also rejected purgatory, masses for the dead, relics, icons, images, and the veneration of saints. In 1179 Pope Alexander III (1159–1181) forbade them to preach, teach, or exegete Scripture. They disobeyed and were declared heretical in 1215. For the next 400 years the Waldenses faced the wrath of the Catholic Inquisition and were forced to worship in secret. Pope Innocent VIII (1484–1492) ordered their extermination in 1487. Later that same year a Crusade was organized in the provinces of Dauphine and Piedmont that led to the deaths of thousands of Waldenses. A similar Crusade occurred in Provence in 1545. Unlike the Cathars, who were virtually eliminated, the Waldenses fled to southern Italy and later to South America, where they survived and in many cases thrived. Needless to say, they welcomed the Protestant Reformation.

CHAPTER THIRTEEN

MONASTICISM, SCHOLASTICISM, AND THE FINAL CONQUEST OF EUROPE

Church-state struggles and the Crusades dominated the period from 900 to 1300, but other important events also took place. New monastic orders such as the Cluniacs, Cistercians, Dominicans, and Franciscans added spiritual vitality to the church in an otherwise dry era. Higher education thrived. Scholasticism, with its emphasis on Aristotelian philosophy, transformed European universities. There was, however, a reaction to the academic nature of scholasticism. Many Christians wanted a more personal, intuitive relationship with God than scholasticism offered. They turned to mysticism.

MONASTICISM

The first monastery in eastern France was organized in Cluny by William I, the Duke of Aquitaine (875–918), with Berno (850–927) serving as the first abbot. Under Odo (927–942), the second abbot, Cluny grew in stature. It claimed that it was subject only to the pope, not local nobility or bishops. In order to serve God, the Cluniacs believed their independence was necessary. All the Cluniac monasteries were under the authority of the abbot of Cluny. They followed the Benedictine Rule but added more strictures to assure

169

their piety. Monks were not permitted to relocate; they remained celibate; and they were staunch opponents of simony. Other reform-minded clerics emulated their ethical standards and spiritual regimen. The monks of Cluny were responsible for the addition of All Souls Day (November 2) to the church calendar. They were also advocates of the "Peace of God" and helped ensure that warring feudal lords honored it. In this regard the Cluniacs helped protect noncombatants, pilgrims, women, and church property.

Cluniac monasteries were wealthy. Though the monks took vows of poverty, their altars were adorned with jeweled cups, and the candelabras were made of gold and silver. When offering mass, the Cluniacs wore only the finest linen robes. The monks also ate well. Roasted chicken and wines from their own vineyard were staples. These excesses eventually contributed to the decline of the order.

The Cistercians were founded by Robert of Molesme (1028–1111) at Cîteaux, Burgundy, in 1098. Their true spiritual father, however, was their third abbot, the Englishman Stephen Harding (d. 1134). Because of their white robes, they were known as the "White Monks." In order to preserve autonomy, each Cistercian monastery was under the charge of its founder. Cistercians were stricter than Cluniacs in their interpretation of the Rule of Benedict. They did not adorn their churches, were silent except when necessary, and stressed manual labor. To assist contemplation, Cistercian monasteries were located in remote regions. Cistercians were also devoted to veneration of the virgin Mary and increased her stature in the church in the late Middle Ages. By 1300, Cistercian monasticism had spread throughout France. Cistercian convents were established all over England and France.

Bernard of Clairvaux (1090–1153) was the most famous Cistercian in the first half of the twelfth century. His fiery preaching and charisma led to the establishment of several monasteries, including his own in Clairvaux, France. Bernard was so influential that popes often sought his support. He helped settle papal elections, chastised kings, and rebuked clerics. He was also the leading proponent of the Second Crusade. His preaching on the sufferings of pilgrims visiting Palestine and the desecration of holy sites led thousands to enlist in the armies of the Crusades. Bernard did not care for scholasticism and was largely responsible for the condemnation of the scholastic Peter Abelard (1079–1142) ca. 1140. He was also one of the few medieval churchmen to speak out against the persecution of Jews.

The Crusades created the monks of war. These monks took the customary vows of chastity, obedience, and poverty but also took up arms in defense of the faith. Initially the Hospitalars cared for sick pilgrims en route to the Holy Land but later developed a military component to their activities. The Order of the Knights Templar was founded in 1118. Originally created to protect pilgrims visiting the Holy Land, it later became a powerful fighting force against Islam. The Knights were famous for their skill at warfare, and Muslim armies feared them. When the Crusades ended, the Templars became Europe's first bankers. To avoid paying a large debt he owed them, King Philip IV (1285–1314) of France arrested the Templars on Friday, October 13, 1307, accused them of heresies, and executed most of them. The superstition about Friday the thirteenth may have its roots in this event.

The Mendicants

Known as "begging brothers" because they lived off the gifts people gave them, Mendicants were different from other monks. They did not own property, took a vow of absolute poverty, preached to the poor, and sought to convert Muslims and heretics. They labored in the world rather than secluding themselves in cloisters. They were not priests and thus not members of the clergy. For this reason they were known as friars (brothers) rather than fathers. The Mendicants recognized only the pope's authority. The most prominent Mendicant orders were the Dominicans and the Franciscans.

Founded by Dominic Guzman (1172–1221), the Dominicans or "Black Friars" initially defined their calling as preaching orthodoxy to the heretical Albigenses and Waldenses. Through their argumentation and example of piety, Guzman and his companions brought several Albigensian women back to the Catholic faith and opened a convent for them at Prouille, France, in 1206. Guzman then founded his first monastery in Toulouse, France, in 1214. In 1216, he received permission from Pope Honorius III (1216–1227) to found the "Order of Preachers." They were to preach, evangelize, and bring heretics back to the true church. The Dominicans evangelized in Europe, Asia, and Africa and accompanied the explorers and conquistadors to the New World.

Because of their thirst for knowledge, Dominicans attended the best universities in Europe. Thomas Aquinas (1225–1274) was perhaps the most influential Dominican intellectual. Dominicans' emphasis of the mystical aspects of Christianity provided a framework for the philosophies of Meister Eckhart (1260–1327) and Saint Catherine of Siena (1347–1380).

Because of their Catholic orthodoxy and loyalty to the papacy, the Dominicans played a prominent role in the Inquisition. In 1184, Pope Lucius III (1181–1185) required bishops to root out heretics and Jews. In 1224, Emperor Frederick II (1220–1250) ordered the burning of unrepentant heretics, and in 1231 Pope Gregory IX (1227–1241) continued the practice. The Dominicans often served as the inquisitors.

Most activities of the Inquisition centered in Spain, Portugal, and the German states. Its most likely victims were converts from Judaism or Islam because the sincerity of their conversions often was questioned. The most horrific of the Inquisitions began in Spain in 1484 and did not officially end until 1834. One of the most infamous Spanish inquisitors was the Dominican Tomás de Torquemada (1420–1498). He was believed to have condemned 2,000 heretics and Jews to the flames.

The inquisitor, often a Dominican, frequently arrived in a community unannounced and encouraged the residents to anonymously report suspected heretics. The accused rarely knew the charges against them, but they were required to prove their innocence. All the accused were assumed to be guilty. With the approval of Innocent IV (1243–1254), interrogations of the accused were accompanied by torture, which often produced false confessions. If a person admitted guilt, he or she was normally permitted to perform penance and released. Those who refused to renounce their beliefs were frequently burned alive. Sometimes dozens of heretics were burned at once. The Inquisition not only rooted out heretics, but it also added to the church's coffers. If a person was found to be a heretic, the church confiscated his property. Much of the legacy of the Dominicans was defined by their role in the Inquisition.

The Franciscans were founded by Francis of Assisi (1182–1226). Francis came from a wealthy family and enjoyed a life of privilege. He served in the Assisi military, was captured by the Perguians in 1201, and spent a year as a prisoner of war. After his release he returned to Assisi and was ill for a year. When he recovered, he lost all desire for his former life. One day while praying in the church of Saint Damian, near Assisi, he believed he heard Christ ask him to repair his "falling house." Francis took it mean that he was to repair a local church. He sold some of his father's holdings and rebuilt the church. He then undertook a pilgrimage to Rome where he was moved to give his clothes to a beggar outside Saint Peter's. Upon his return Francis gave away his belongings and dedicated his life to the service of God, like Anthony the monk. Unlike Anthony, however, who lived in solitude, Francis gathered eleven followers who were to preach to the masses. Francis was renowned for his gentle spirit, his preaching to the birds, and his popularization of the Christmas crèche. He loved the goodness of the world into which Christ was born and wrote songs in praise of nature. Catholic tradition maintains that Francis was the first person to receive the stigmata—wounds on the hands and feet that resembled those of Jesus at the crucifixion.

Much like their founder, the Franciscans were dedicated to preaching, poverty, displaying Christ's love, and obedience to the papacy. All traveling was done barefoot, and they slept wherever they could. They always greeted people with the phrase, "The Lord give you peace." Unlike the Dominicans, the Franciscans emphasized service to the Christian community over education. Franciscans could be found preaching and working in Europe, Muslim Asia, and North Africa. Pope Innocent III approved the Franciscan order in 1209 and granted the Franciscans permission to start a women's order in 1212. Named after their founder, Clare of Assisi (1194–1253), the order was known as the Poor Clares. Francis created a third order in 1221. Called the "Brothers and Sisters of Penance," they kept the principles of Franciscan life but were permitted to marry.

SCHOLASTICISM

The cathedral schools of the early Middle Ages emphasized the liberal arts. Their teaching included the *trivium* (grammar, logic, and rhetoric), the *quadrivium* (arithmetic, geometry, music, and astronomy), and advanced studies in theology. Around 1100, theological education began to divide into two camps. The monastic schools emphasized a literal biblical perspective and the teachings of the church fathers, while the cathedral schools used philosophy to complement theology. The cathedral emphasis led to development of scholasticism. These cathedral schools soon gave way to the great medieval universities, such as those at Bologna, Paris, Oxford, and Cambridge. Scholasticism dominated their pedagogy from approximately 1050 to 1350.

Scholasticism derived its name from the "schoolmen" who taught it. The scholastics sought to protect and strengthen Catholic theology by reconciling the Bible, the works of the church fathers, and the Greek and Latin classics. They were confident sound reason would illuminate the truths of the Bible and contribute to a more vibrant spirituality.

In the first millennium, Plato was the preferred philosopher of Christian theologians. Augustine accepted the Neoplatonism of Plotinus (204–270) and applied it to Christianity. Neoplatonism employed deductive reasoning that analyzed a problem by working from specific facts and discovering general principles. The Platonic concept of the spirit's superiority to the body was believed by most scholastics to be consistent with Christian teachings.

In the twelfth century Aristotle's writings made their way to Spain with the Arabic philosopher Averroes (1126–1198). The Byzantine Empire also preserved and transmitted some of Aristotle's works. His philosophy was inductive. It began by taking a general truth, applying it to a particular instance, and then comparing the general to the particular to derive new truth.

Aristotle's four types of causes (material, formal, instrumental, final) challenged the medieval mind. The material cause referenced what an object was made of. The formal cause referenced its shape or appearance. The instrumental cause referenced outside forces that changed or moved it. The final cause was its purpose, end, or aim. For the Christian scholastic, God's plan was the final cause. Despite the new interest in Aristotle, a scholastic could be either Platonic or Aristotelian. The most important scholastics were Anselm of Canterbury (1033–1109), Peter Abelard (1079–1142), Thomas Aquinas (1225–1274), John Duns Scotus (1265–1308), and William of Ockham (1280–1349).

The scholastic method entailed questioning and evaluating the pros and cons of earlier authorities' arguments. Within scholasticism there were two competing systems of thought: realism and nominalism. Realists held that universal categories (like colors, shapes, and sizes) existed in the mind of God prior to and independent of the creation. Moderate realists were more inclined to Aristotle than to Plato. Nominalism maintained that abstract concepts or universals were created by the human mind and had no independent existence. Universals were mere verbal constructs rather than metaphysical realities, according to nominalists. Nominalists also insisted that individuals were superior to institutions. Martin Luther incorporated this belief into his arguments against the Catholic Church.

Born in northern Italy and educated at the Abbey of Bec, Anselm became the archbishop of Canterbury in 1093. He was a realist and the first true scholastic. Much of his thought was based on Platonism. Anselm taught that reason could improve one's understanding of the world but that faith in God's revealed truth was required before one could begin to reason properly. His motto was "faith seeking understanding." He maintained that there were many things man could not know without revelation—the way of salvation, for instance.

In the *Monologion* (1076) Anselm proved the existence of God by arguing from cause to effect. The good things man enjoyed were reflections of the one supreme good from which all things derived. This supreme good was God. In the *Proslogion* (1077–1078), Anselm used inductive argumentation to develop his ontological argument for the existence of God:

> It is quite conceivable that there is something whose non-existence is inconceivable, and this must be greater than that whose non-existence is conceivable. Wherefore, if that thing than which no greater thing is conceivable can be conceived as non-existent; then, that very thing than which a greater is inconceivable is not that than which a greater is inconceivable; which is a contradiction. So true is it that there exists something than which a greater is inconceivable, that its non-existence is inconceivable: and this thing are Thou, O Lord our God![1]

In *Cur Deus Homo (Why the God-Man)*, Anselm applied scholastic principles to sin and redemption. He said sin offended God's righteousness and man could not be saved until God's righteousness was satisfied. As all men were sinful and unrighteous, God sent Jesus to satisfy God's righteous demands through his death and open the door for man's salvation. This became known as the satisfaction theory of the atonement and was one of Anselm's greatest contributions to Christianity. The Eastern churches rejected Anselm's theory. He was named a doctor of the church in 1720.

The French theologian Peter Abelard (1079–1142) believed Christianity was dependent on both faith and reason. He was a moderate realist, meaning that he believed in a middle ground between nominalism and realism. (Many scholars consider him a nominalist though.) Abelard rejected the idea that universals existed outside the mind, but he claimed they were not mere verbal constructs. They had real existence in the mind, he said. Universals were derived by sense perception and referenced similarities among particular things, identifying a pattern in God's mind by which he created them. This theory became known as conceptualism.

Abelard also believed in the philosophy of doubt:

> It is perhaps difficult to speak confidently in matters of this sort unless they have been investigated. Indeed, to doubt in special cases will not be without advantage. For through doubting we come to inquiry and through inquiry we come to truth. And the Truth Himself says: "Seek and ye shall find, knock and it shall be opened unto you."[2]

He applied his philosophy of doubt in his most influential writing, *Sic et Non*. In this work he listed 158 propositions along with the teachings of the church fathers on each (which often were contradictory). He hoped that by pointing out these contradictions he would stimulate scholarly discussion that would result in new answers to the questions.

Many of Abelard's detractors, however, accused him of challenging the teachings of the church. His main critic, Bernard of
Clairvaux, claimed that Abelard's ideas led to false interpretations
of the Trinity, the atonement, and original sin. The Council of Sens
condemned sixteen of Abelard's propositions ca. 1141. The event
broke him, and he retired to a monastery where he died a year later.
Abelard is remembered today less for his philosophy than for his
tragic love affair with his student Heloise (ca. 1101–1164).

Educated at Monte Cassino and the University of Naples,
Thomas Aquinas was a Dominican monk, a moderate realist, and
the greatest of the scholastic philosophers. Aquinas sought to inte-
grate theology with Aristotelianism, believing it was possible to use
both to prove the existence of God. He taught that each human soul
was immortal and unique. Human knowledge was based on sensory
experience but functioned in conjunction with the mind's innate
capacity. Revelation was the mind's primary source of information.
Natural revelation had great value, but it could not produce a full
disclosure of God and the way of salvation. Special revelation came
from God by means of the Bible, the church fathers, and councils.
It allowed man to understand theological concepts such as sin, the
incarnation, and the Trinity. For Aquinas, the Greek philosophers
were valuable but insufficient for attaining full knowledge of spiritual realities because they did not have knowledge of Christ or the
Bible.

Aquinas believed reason and revelation were each sufficient to
demonstrate God's existence. He made five famous arguments for
the existence of God known as the Five Ways:

1. Some things are in motion, and nothing can move itself.
There cannot be an infinite regression of movers, so there must be a
Prime Mover (God).

2. Some things are caused, and nothing can cause itself. There
cannot be an infinite regression of causes. Therefore, there must a
first cause (God).

3. It is possible for the things we observe in the universe not to exist, and they have not always existed. That is, they are contingent beings. If everything in the universe were a contingent being, there would have been a time when nothing existed. But if there were such a time, nothing would exist now because there would not have been anything to bring it into existence. That is obviously absurd, so there must be one necessary being who has always existed and is not dependent on any other being for his existence (God).

4. The world has varying degrees of goodness and beauty in it. This implies that an ultimate standard of perfection exists (God).

5. Natural objects act toward ends. This is characteristic of intelligence, but these objects have no intelligence. There must be an intelligent being who guides all natural objects toward their ends (God).

Summa Theologica was Aquinas's most influential book and the ultimate exposition of his system. In this massive text he explained in intricate detail the nature of God, the Trinity, and man's desire to advance toward God. In the final section, he applied moderate realism to the seven sacraments and demonstrated how they were channels through which God infused grace into humanity. The recipients of that grace were then capable of love, and God was activated within their lives. The *Summa Theologica* was a theological masterpiece and has been hailed as the definitive exposition of the Catholic faith.

Aquinas also developed the theory of the "Treasury of Merit." When a saint died, he or she was believed to have more merit than necessary to escape purgatory. This extra merit was placed into the Treasury of Merit. The church could then draw from the treasury and apply merit to those who lacked it. The Treasury of Merit concept fueled the indulgence system and thus contributed to the Protestant Reformation.

John Duns Scotus was the greatest of the Franciscan theologians. He believed reason and faith (Aristotelianism and Augustinianism)

were related but distinct. He taught that humans could know metaphysical and theological principles by natural reasoning, though
divine revelation made men certain of them. Scotus believed God
guided men, but humans could reject God's guidance. Though
humans had an inclination to love God, they did not have to do so,
he said. Scotus was a favorite target of the Renaissance humanists,
who ridiculed his followers for adhering to theories they thought
to be outdated. The term "dunce cap" derived from the name Duns
Scotus.

A student and later professor at Oxford University, William of
Ockham was a Franciscan and a nominalist. He believed that faith
and reason were often incompatible and maintained that men could
not prove the truths of theology. Because theology was derived from
the Bible, however, it had to be accepted as true. Ockham eliminated from his philosophy the idea of universals, which he viewed
as mere mental constructs. One of his theories, which came to be
known as "Ockham's Razor," stated that simpler theories were better unless complexity resulted in greater explanatory power.

MYSTICISM

By the late Middle Ages, the Catholic liturgy had become
extremely ritualized. Apart from the Eucharist, there were few
opportunities for a Christian to commune with God. Mysticism
resolved this dilemma for many. Its adherents sought a more inti-
mate encounter with God. Furthermore, mysticism did not require
a church. It could be practiced alone.

In most cases the mystical process consisted of three stages. In
the first stage, purgation, the soul was cleansed. In the second stage,
illumination, the believer acquired a fresh appreciation of the truths
of the church and Scripture. The final stage was oneness with God
that often resulted in ecstasy. Mystical experiences took the forms

of trances, miracles, and visions. The ecstasy was temporary, but it often affected the believer for the remainder of his or her life.

Mysticism was not new. Many of the early church fathers such as the Pseudo-Dionysius[3] (late fifth century) spoke of mystical ways to reach God. In his influential works *Ecclesiastical Hierarchy, The Celestial Hierarchy*, and *On Divine Names*, he taught that the goal of the Christian life was for the soul to climb to God.

Fourteenth-century mystics often followed the example of Saint Bonaventure (1217–1274). He maintained that all human knowledge was nothing compared to God's infinite knowledge. The highest degree of spiritual knowledge could be achieved only when God provided supernatural illumination, making possible the perception of Christian truths. The most important fourteenth-century mystics were Meister Eckhart (1260–1327), John Tauler (1300–1361), Thomas à Kempis (1380–1471), Catherine of Siena (1347–1380), and Julian of Norwich (1342–1417).

A German Dominican, Meister Eckhart taught at Paris and held influential ministerial positions in Erfurt, Strasbourg, and Cologne. Eckhart was greatly influenced by Neoplatonism. He maintained that God was the source of all being and that man should seek to be fused with the Godhead. In order to reach God, one had to break away from the flesh to unite with the *Logos*. This would allow a fusion between the essence of man and God that resulted in spiritual ecstasy. His dependence on Neoplatonism, however, led to charges that he was a heretic and a pantheist.

A Dominican and member of the "Friends of God," John Tauler was influenced by Eckhart. The Friends of God was a popular movement in the German Rhineland whose adherents rejected the elaborate worship of the Catholic Church in favor of seeking an inner, mystical transformation. Tauler believed the rituals of the Catholic Church had little value and thought an inner experience with God better served the soul. Such an experience allowed a person subsequently to serve God with his outer life. Tauler's sermons emphasized charity and humility.

From the Netherlands, Thomas à Kempis advocated a reform movement known as the *Devotio Moderna*, which was associated with the Brethren of the Common Life. The Brethren did not take monastic vows and were encouraged to continue their secular occupations. They were known for their lofty spiritual goals. The Brethren believed intense meditation on the crucifixion would bring them into communication with God. In his *Imitation of Christ*, Thomas taught that the love of Christ and spiritual devotion would lead a person to serve him in humble yet practical ways:

> Having left all things behind, he must also leave himself—totally abandon himself—keeping nothing of his self, self-centered ways. And when he has done all that he knows must be done, then let him believe that he has done nothing. Let him not be deluded when others praise him, but let him admit in all honesty that he is only a humble servant of God. As Truth himself has said: "When you have done all that is asked of you, say to yourselves, we are unworthy servants." Then he will be truly poor and naked in spirit, and he may say with the Prophet: "I am alone and poor." Yet, no one is richer, no one more powerful, no one more free than the person who can give his whole life to God and freely serve others with deep humility and love.[4]

A lay Dominican, Catherine of Siena was famous for her visions. She claimed that when she was six years old she had her first vision, in which Jesus smiled at her. At seven she had a second vision in which she was told to take a vow of virginity. Hoping she would one day marry, her parents were not pleased with her vow and required her to remain in their home. During her childhood she fasted and mortified her flesh and remained obedient to her parents. They permitted her to join the Dominican Order of Penance when she was sixteen. At twenty Catherine claimed to receive a vision in which she was instructed to take care of survivors of the plague. Her *Dialogues* included 400 of her letters and prayers.

An English mystic, Julian of Norwich lived outside the walls of the Norwich Church. At age thirty, during a serious bout with illness, she claimed to have visions of the Passion of Christ and the virgin Mary, which she described in her *Short Text*. In her *Sixteen Revelations of Divine Love* (ca. 1393),[5] she said God's love could be seen everywhere and in everything. Realizing this would lead a person to complete joy.

Julian perceived God as both masculine and feminine. One of her most famous statements was that Jesus was a mother who nourished the faithful through the Eucharist: "A mother can give her child milk to suck, but our precious mother, Jesus, can feed us with himself. He does so courteously and most tenderly, with the Blessed Sacrament, which is the precious food of true life."[6]

CONVERTING THE REMAINDER OF EUROPE

Despite many popes with less than holy ambitions, Christianity continued to grow. Following the conversion of King Harold Bluetooth in 965 (958–ca. 986), Denmark began to accept Christianity. Under King Sweyn (985–1014) and Cunute the Great (r. 1014–1035), Christianity became the favored religion in Denmark, eclipsing paganism. Christianity spread in Norway with the conversion of King Olaf Haraldson (1016–1030), who became the country's patron saint. Olaf forcibly converted pagans and developed the rudiments of a state church. Norway soon became known for its "stave" or wooden churches.

German missionaries and monks introduced Christianity to Bohemia and Poland. At the beginning of the tenth century, Wenceslaus I, Duke of Bohemia (907–935), advanced Christianity throughout his territories. "Good King Wenceslaus" was martyred in 935 and became the patron saint of Bohemia. Legends claimed he frequently gave alms to the poor and widows and walked barefoot through snow as an act of piety. In Poland, Prince Mieczyslaw I (ca. 930–992) advanced Christianity. He was baptized in 966 and made his country a vassal state of Rome.

CHAPTER FOURTEEN

PAPAL DECLINE
AND
THE RENAISSANCE

Between 1300 and 1517 the Western world turned upside down. Trapped by its own vices, the papacy's tight grip on Europe loosened dramatically. At one point, two rival popes each claimed to be the true spiritual heir of Peter. Later three popes all claimed headship of the Catholic Church. In addition, the black plague of the mid-fourteenth century ravaged central Europe. Out of these dark days, however, arose a rebirth of learning, an appreciation of the arts, a spirit of individualism, and the groundwork for a new brand of Christianity.

PAPAL DECLINE

The idea of a European Christian empire modeled after Charlemagne's kingdom faded with the rise of nation-states, each with its own identity, customs, and beliefs. The people and the clergy were often more loyal to their kings than to the pope. Boniface VIII's (1294–1303) papacy marked the beginning of the end of papal dominance in Europe.

His papacy did not begin well. The board of cardinals was divided, and it took two years for him to be elected. Then he became embroiled in controversy with King Philip IV (1285–1314) of

France. Needing money to fight Britain, Philip believed the monarchy had the right to tax the clergy. Boniface threatened to excommunicate Philip with the papal bull Clericis Laicos, in which he argued that no secular power had the right to seize church property or tax church officials.

Despite these threats Boniface was unable to intimidate Philip, who challenged the right of the pope to issue dictums concerning French bishops and cut off the supply of money from France to Rome in retaliation. Over half of the French clergy sided with the monarch against the pope. To strengthen his position, Philip created a parliament that supported him as well. Boniface was forced to capitulate.

Boniface's *Unam Sanctam* of 1302 precipitated another confrontation. Despite the decline of papal power, this bull declared that the church was still superior to the state. If earthly powers did not uphold their office, they could be held accountable by the church. No one, not even a king, could be a true Christian and defy the pope's authority at the same time:

> Thus, concerning the Church and her power is the prophecy of Jeremiah fulfilled, "See, I have this day set thee over the nations and over the kingdoms," etc. If, therefore, the earthly power errs, it shall be judged by the spiritual power; and if a lesser power err, it shall be judged by a greater. But if the supreme power err, it can only be judged by God, not by man; for the testimony of the apostle is "The spiritual man judgeth all things, yet he himself is judged of no man." For this authority, although given to a man and exercised by a man, is not human, but rather divine, given at God's mouth to Peter and established on a rock for him and his successors in Him whom he confessed, the Lord saying to Peter himself, "Whatsoever thou shall bind," etc. Whosoever therefore resists this power thus ordained of God, resists the ordinance of God. . . . Furthermore, we

declare, state, define and pronounce that it is altogether necessary to salvation for every human creature to be subject to the Roman pontiff.[1]

Critics of Catholicism viewed this dictum as the papacy's attempt to control political life. In the United States, the legacy of *Unam Sanctam* played a role in the defeat of the presidential candidate Al Smith (1873–1944) in 1928. Another Catholic and presidential candidate, John F. Kennedy (1917–1963), narrowly escaped a similar fate in 1960.

In order to ensure his election, some believe that Gui Faucoi, the future Clement V (1305–1314), bound himself to Philip IV of France, who promised to instruct the French cardinals to vote for him. With the French cardinals' support, he was elected but encountered resistance from the Italian clerics. Therefore, he relocated the papacy from Rome to Poitiers, France, in 1305 and from there to Avignon in 1309, where it remained until 1377. Francesco Petrarch (1304–1374) termed this era the "Babylonian Captivity of the Church."

Even more so than in Rome, the Avignon popes lived in ostentatious luxury. Nepotism and simony were rampant. Clement had four Franciscan leaders burned for insisting that since Christ had no possessions, neither should his church. Petrarch described what he saw at Avignon:

> Instead of holy solitude we find a criminal host and crowds of the most infamous satellites; instead of soberness, licentious banquets; instead of pious pilgrimages, preternatural and foul sloth; instead of the bare feet of the apostles, the snowy coursers of brigands fly past us, the horses decked in gold and fed on gold, soon to be shod in gold, if the Lord does not check this slavish luxury. In short, we seem to be among the kings of the Persians or Parthians,

before whom we must fall down and worship, and who we cannot be approached except presents be offered.[2]

Clement also suppressed the Knights Templar, cancelling the debt Philip IV owed them. By capitulating in every way to Philip and the French interest, Clement diminished the stature of the papacy in the eyes of other monarchs, clergy, and the faithful.

The Western Schism (1378–1417)

At the urging of Catherine of Siena, Gregory XI (1370–1378) returned the papacy to Rome in 1377. Upon Gregory's death in 1378, Urban VI (1378–1389) was elected pope. He announced that he was going to reform the College of Cardinals to make the church leadership more representative of the Roman laity. The French cardinals protested and demanded the return of the papacy to Avignon. Urban then threatened to excommunicate the French cardinals if they did not obey him. They returned to Avignon and declared Urban's pontificate void. Those French cardinals who had elected Urban VI then disavowed his election and elected Clement VII (1378–1394). Known for treachery, simony, and extortion, Clement ruled from Avignon.

The Avignon papacy was supported by France, Scotland, Navarre, Castile, Aragon, Cyprus, and Naples. The Roman papacy held sway with England, Scandinavia, northern Italy, Ireland, the Holy Roman Empire, and Portugal.

The Council of Pisa in 1409 attempted to end what had become known as the Western Schism. The council was called by the cardinals of Avignon and Rome. Both Benedict XIII (1394–1423), the Avignon pope, and Gregory XII (1406–1415), the Roman pope, refused to attend. The council of more than 500 members of the clergy deposed both popes and chose Alexander V (1409–1410) as the true pontiff. Alexander V was succeeded by John XXIII

(1410–1415) in 1410. There were now three popes, each of whom claimed to be the only legitimate one.

Tiring of the schism, Sigismund, King of Bohemia and Germany and future Holy Roman emperor (1433–1437), and John XXIII called the Council of Constance (1414–1418). The council was attended by twenty-nine cardinals, 100 doctors of law and divinity, 134 abbots, and 183 bishops and archbishops. To make sure the large contingent of Italian cardinals would not dominate the election, the council determined that Germany, France, Italy, and England would each have one vote. In order for an act to be binding, all four powers had to vote in favor of it. Gregory XII resigned under suspicion of fornication and murder. In exchange, he was named bishop of Tusculum. The council deposed Benedict XIII and John XIII and elected Martin V (1417–1431).

The council both ended the Western Schism and demonstrated the viability of conciliarism, a growing movement that asserted the authority of councils to make decisions for the church in times of crisis without the pope's input. The decree of the council made this point clear:

> This holy Council of Constance . . . declares, first that it is lawfully assembled in the Holy Spirit, that it constitutes a General Council, representing the Catholic Church, and that therefore it has it authority immediately from Christ; and that all men, of every rank and condition, including the Pope himself, is bound to obey it in matters concerning the Faith, the abolition of the schism, and the reformation of the Church of God in its head and its members.[3]

The Council of Constance also dealt with heresy. It ordered that the bones of John Wycliffe (1329–1384) be disinterred and thrown into the Swift River near Lutterworth, England, and that his books be burned. His legacy and works, however, survived. A student and then professor at Oxford University, Wycliffe was influenced by William of Ockham, employing Ockham's razor when necessary.

Wycliffe desired to return the church to its spiritual mission and to promote English nationalism. He insisted that money should not be given to a papacy that was under the control of a country, France, with which England was constantly at war. This money could be put to better use in England. Wycliffe found many advocates in the English middle class. In *Of Civil Dominion,* he called for a moral church leadership. In order to do this, he believed all immoral clergy should be removed from office with their church property confiscated and given to the state. He also said Christians were not bound to obey an immoral pope. He singled out the Avignon popes for their greed and ambition. He was not concerned with the threat of excommunication or even an interdict on all of England. Since he believed the visible, Roman Church was not necessarily composed of true Christians, Wycliffe stressed the invisible church of true believers. Rome, therefore, was not necessary, and excommunication was a worthless threat.

Wycliffe opposed relics, the cult of saints, and pilgrimages. He despised indulgences as empty promises. In terms Luther reiterated, he stated,

> I confess that the indulgences of the pope, if they are what they are said to be, are a manifest blasphemy, inasmuch as he claims a power to save men almost without limit, and not only to mitigate the penalties of those who have sinned, by granting them the aid of absolution and indulgences, that they may never come to purgatory, but to give command to the holy angels, that when the soul is separated from the body, they may carry it without delay to its everlasting rest. . . . They suppose, in the first place, that there is an infinite number of supererogatory merits, belonging to the saints, laid up in heaven, and above all, the merit of our Lord Jesus Christ, which would be sufficient

to save an infinite number of other worlds, and that, over all this treasure, Christ hath sent the pope. Secondly, that it is his pleasure to distribute it, and, accordingly, he may distribute there from to an infinite extent, since the remainder will be infinite. Against this rude blasphemy I have elsewhere inveighed. . . . This doctrine is a manifold blasphemy against Christ, inasmuch as the pope is extolled above his humanity and deity, and so above all that is called God—pretensions which, according to the declarations of the apostle, agree with the character of the Antichrist; for he possesses Caesarean power above Christ, who had not where to lay his head.[4]

In 1379 Wycliffe denounced the doctrine of transubstantiation, contending that Christ was spiritually but not physically present in the Eucharist. Speaking against transubstantiation cost him the support of the nobles who had been his benefactors.

Wycliffe's greatest contribution to the church was his translation of the Bible into English. He believed Scripture was the only authority for Christians. The Catholic Church declared that only it could interpret the Bible, and Wycliffe assumed official Catholic interpretations were slanted to protect the church's interests. For this reason he decided to supervise the translation of the Bible into English. The translators completed the New Testament in 1382, and Nicholas of Hereford (fl. 1380–1390) finished the Old Testament in 1384. Wycliffe's team translated from Latin, though, not the original Greek and Hebrew.

With waning support from the middle class and nobles, in 1382 Wycliffe was confined to the rectory at Lutterworth. His work, however, was continued by his followers, who became known as Lollards. After Richard II (1377–1399) married Anne of Bohemia (1366–1394), Bohemian students began to study at English universities, where they encountered Wycliffe's teachings. When they returned to Bohemia, they took Wycliffe's doctrine with them, and it became popular. Jan Hus (1373–1415) was influenced by the Lollards; he was also condemned at the Council of Constance.

A former student and later rector at the University of Prague, Hus hoped to reform the church of Bohemia along the same lines as Wycliffe. In his sermons and writings, Hus refuted transubstantiation and indulgences and said the Catholic Church was no older than Constantine. He also stated that a Christian's only authority was the Scriptures. In 1412, his *De absolutione a pena et culpa* argued that no one, not even the pope, had the right to command anyone else take up the sword in the name of the church. In *De ecclesia* (1413), he denied that the pope was the head of the church; this honor was Christ's alone. Hus was offered safe passage to the Council of Constance to defend his beliefs. Once there he was arrested and ordered to recant. He refused and was burned at the stake on July 6, 1415. His teachings, however, resonated with Martin Luther, who called himself a Hussite.

Hus's followers became known as Taborites. The Taborites refused to accept any church doctrine or teaching that could not be found in the Bible. Many of the Taborites took up arms against the papacy in the Hussite Wars of the fifteenth century. The Ultraquists were a branch of the Taborites. They stressed that any aspect of worship not found in the Bible should be eliminated and that communion should be served in both kinds (i.e., both bread and wine).

THE BLACK DEATH

The Black Death was named for the black spots that appeared on the bodies of its victims. Carried by fleas on rats aboard merchant ships from the Middle East, the Black Death appeared in Europe in 1347 and finally abated in 1351. It killed as much as one-third of Europe's population. In England almost half of the population died. Because so many priests died and others were scared of contracting the plague, Christians often died without last rites. Biblical prophecy coupled with the superstitious nature of European Christians led many to believe the apocalypse had come. This resulted in a panic that led to religious excess. The flagellants, for example, appeared in Germany. They walked the streets beating themselves with whips in hopes of ending the plague by emulating the suffering of Christ. These processionals often lasted thirty-three days, one day for each year of Christ's life. A contemporary observer described the sight:

> Among others, the people of Germany began to go through the country on the main roads in companies, carrying crucifixes, standards and great banners, as in processions; they went through the streets, two by two, singing loudly hymns to God and our Lady, rhymed and with music; then they assembled together and stripped to their chemises twice a day and beat themselves as hard as they could with knotted lashes embedded with needles, so that the blood flowed down from their shoulders on all sides.[5]

Other Christians sought to emulate Christ by caring for people who contracted the disease. At great threat to her own life, Catherine of Genoa (1447–1510) stayed with the ill and opened a hospital for them. Such altruism, however, was rare.

The Jews were often blamed for the plague and at times massacred in retaliation. According to one account, a Jew was tortured until he "confessed" that he had been instructed by a rabbi to poison Venice's wells. The poisoning of wells was a common charge against Jews, and many were burned at the stake across Europe. One safe haven was Avignon, where the pope protected them.

THE RENAISSANCE, 1300–1517

By about 1300, the Middle Ages gave way to a period known as the Renaissance. In many ways the Renaissance was the opposite of all the Middle Ages represented. The feudal system that dominated the Middle Ages began to weaken, and an upwardly mobile middle class emerged. Commerce shifted from agriculture to trade, and more people in the trading cities—particularly Genoa, Pisa, and Venice—became wealthy. Previously forbidden as usury, the loaning of money at interest led to the rise of banking and the powerful Medicis of Florence. Centralized governments began to appear and threaten Constantine's church-state synthesis. The laity continued to follow church law, but it no longer held as much influence in their personal lives and belief systems. Among the educated, a new interest developed in classical Greek and Latin literature and oratory. This led to the rejection of scholastic writings. With the invention of the printing press in 1450, books became more available, literacy increased, and new ideas were spread. Perhaps most importantly, the value of the individual was elevated.

The Italian Renaissance was concerned with a fresh examination of ancient Greek and Latin texts. In Italy, the Renaissance humanists valued individuals over institutions. They trusted the ability of the human mind to solve problems and appreciated the beauty of the human body. They also hoped for fame, praise, and to be remembered by history. Instead of showing a medieval preoccupation with the life to come, Renaissance humanists wanted to enjoy their time on earth.

The start of the Italian Renaissance dates approximately to the mid-fourteenth century. The home of Francesco Petrarch (1304–1374) and Dante Alighieri (1265–1321), who share the title of "the first modern man," Italy spawned a rebirth of interest in the arts, literature, and humanist philosophy.

Petrarch has been called "the father of humanism." Like other Italian humanists, he was less concerned with religion than with human values, capacities, and worth. Petrarch was renowned for his love of nature, books, Cicero, Seneca, and beauty. He also had an overwhelming fear of death. He spent much of his time writing poems in the Italian vernacular. Petrarch set the standard for the Italian Renaissance humanists who followed him.

In his *Divine Comedy*, Dante Alighieri communicated medieval theology and philosophy in the Italian language, helping to establish it as the language of literature. In *Canto V* of *Paradiso*, Dante wrote, "The greatest gift that God in His bounty made in creation, and the most conformable to His goodness, and that which He prizes the most, was the freedom of will, with which the creatures with intelligence, they all and they alone, were and are endowed."[6]

The Italian Renaissance was a time of artistic achievement. Under Lorenzo de Medici (1449–1492), Florence became the great patron city of the arts. Sandro Botticelli (1445–1510), Leonardo Da Vinci (1452–1519), and Michelangelo (1475–1564) at one time all called Florence home. The study of human anatomy gave rise to artistic realism, which depicted the human body with all of its imperfections. Realism became popular among Renaissance painters and sculptors and stood in stark contrast to the dark, distorted figures depicted in medieval art. Bright colors now appeared in paintings. In literature, Niccolo Machiavelli (1469–1527) wrote *The Prince,* in which he claimed amorality in a monarch was acceptable if not necessary. In architecture, the cathedral dome reappeared. Filippo Brunelleschi (1377–1446) designed the dome of the Basilica di Santa Maria del Fiore in Florence.

Exploration was a part of the Italian Renaissance. The journeys of Henry the Navigator (1394–1460), Christopher Columbus (1451–1506), Vasco da Gama (1460–1524), Ferdinand Magellan (1480–1521), and Amerigo Vespucci (1454–1512) opened up a new world on earth. Meanwhile, Nicolaus Copernicus (1473–1543) and Galileo Galilei (1564–1642) explored the heavens.

North of the Alps, the hallmark of the Renaissance was religious humanism, which extolled the dignity, beauty, and potential of the individual. It emphasized the Bible in its Greek and Hebrew form as the primary Christian authority.

The best-known figures in religious humanism were Johannes Reuchlin (1455–1522) and Erasmus (1456–1536). Reuchlin had a strong interest in Hebrew. In 1506, he published his *Rudiments of Hebrew*, which helped students better understand the Old Testament. Because of his interest in Hebrew and the Cabalà, Reuchlin was often accused of being a secret Jew.

In *In Praise of Folly* (1509), Erasmus threw countless barbs at the debauchery of clerics and the silly arguments of the Scholastics. His most cutting remarks were reserved for monks:

> The whole tribe is so universally loathed that even a chance meeting is thought to be ill-omened—and yet they are gloriously self-satisfied. In the first place, they believe it's the highest form of piety to be so uneducated that they can't even read. Then when they bray like donkeys in church, repeating by rote the psalms they haven't understood, they imagine they are charming the ears of their heavenly audience with finite delight. Many of them too make a good living out of their squalor and beggary, bellowing for bread from door to door, and indeed making a nuisance of themselves in every inn, carriage or boat, to the great loss of all other beggars. This is the way in which these smooth individuals, in all their filth and ignorance, their boorish and shameless behavior, claim to bring back the apostles into our midst![7]

Erasmus depicted his main character, Folly, as praising indulgences, pilgrimages, and herself. His satirical description of transubstantiation and the Trinity, however, enraged many clerics.

The *Enchiridion* (1501) was Erasmus's attempt to synthesize humanism and Christianity. It stressed the importance of personal prayer and knowledge of the Scriptures. His most influential work was his 1516 edition of the Greek New Testament, which allowed humanists to compare the original New Testament text to the Vulgate. The differences were noticeable. Several passages of the Vulgate appeared to have been adapted to fit Catholic tradition. At first it appeared that Erasmus would align with Luther in his attempts to reform the church, but Erasmus believed more good could come from reforming the church from within than by tearing it apart. He also insisted on human free will against Luther's belief in divine predestination.

Even the papacy fell under the sway of the Renaissance. Popes were among the greatest patrons of the arts, almost to the exclusion of religious concerns. Nicholas V (1447–1455) was the first of the Renaissance popes. His interest in humanism led him to repair the churches of Rome. He also began razing the oldest parts of the Vatican so that new sections could be built. He constructed several of Rome's famous fountains and repaired one of Rome's most important aqueducts. To raise the money for these projects, he declared 1450 a jubilee year and invited thousands of pilgrims to Rome. While there, they filled the papal coffers by purchasing indulgences.

Nicholas donated 5,000 of his own books to what became the Vatican Library. He also commissioned Lorenzo Valla (1407–1457) to translate ancient Greek texts into Latin and placed them in the Vatican Library. Nicholas was responsible for moving the pope's residence from the dilapidated Lateran Palace to the more comfortable Vatican.

Callistus III (1455–1458), a member of the notorious Borgia family, was obsessed with advancing the interest of his family and retaking Constantinople from the Turks. The Borgias dominated the Catholic Church for nearly fifty years. Callistus appointed two of his nephews as cardinals, one of whom became Pope Alexander VI (1492–1503). A crusade to reclaim Constantinople for Christendom, however, never came to fruition.

Sixtus IV (1471–1484) was a Franciscan whose papacy was steeped in intrigue. He surpassed Callistus III in nepotism by appointing two of his nephews and thirty of his friends as cardinals.

In addition, he sold benefices and church offices. Sixtus was involved in a family feud with the Medicis of Florence, and many suspected he was complicit in an assassination attempt on Lorenzo de Medici. More admirably, he repaired bridges, restored aqueducts, and rebuilt the Hospital of the Holy Spirit. He also refurbished or rebuilt thirty of Rome's rundown churches, including San Vitale (1475). In addition, he erected seven new churches in Rome. Sixtus was also responsible for financing the Sistine Chapel, which bears his name. To adorn the walls, he hired Florence's most eminent artists: Botticelli (1445–1510), Perugino (1446–1523), and Pinturicchio (1454–1513). Sixtus donated several Roman sculptures that became the foundation for collections in the Capitoline Museum.

Alexander VI's (1492–1503) election was secured by bribes to cardinals. As pope, he granted divorces and dispensations in exchange for money and political alliances to advance his family's fortunes. He supported the Spanish Inquisition, attempted to exterminate the Waldenses, and was responsible for dividing the New World between Spain and Portugal. Alexander had the Florentine Reformer Girolamo Savonarola (1452–1498), who denounced his excesses, burned at the stake.[8] Alexander flaunted his several mistresses and fathered a large number of illegitimate children. He named one of his sons, Cesare Borgia (1475–1507), a cardinal. Cesare was so ruthless in the advancement of his father's ambitions that many believed he was the model for Machiavelli's infamous prince. Alexander rebuilt Rome's Borgo district, expanded the Vatican's Borgia apartments, and had Pinturicchio decorate them with frescos. He served as patron to Bramante (1444–1514), Raphael (1483–1520), and Michelangelo (1475–1564).

Julius II (1503–1513) was the "Warrior Pope," who switched his allegiances as necessary. His contributions to the Renaissance, however, were significant. He hired Bramante to rebuild Saint Peter's Basilica and commissioned Michelangelo to paint the ceiling of the Sistine Chapel. He had Raphael decorate the rooms in the Vatican Palace that are now known as the *Stanze* of Raphael. After conquering Bologna, he commissioned Michelangelo to make a bronze statue of him. To demonstrate their distaste for Julius II, the citizens of the city removed it from above the church of San Petronio, melted it down, and made a cannon out of it. Erasmus was so dismayed at the sight of Julius leading the papal army into Bologna that he wrote *Julius II exclusus* to express his feelings. In the story, when Julius approaches Saint Peter at the gates of heaven, Peter does not recognize his armor-wearing successor.

Leo X (1513–1521) was the son of Lorenzo de Medici. In the Florentine manner he made the papal court a home for artists. He commissioned Raphael to add frescos to the Vatican and Michelangelo to paint his portrait. Leo, however, will always be remembered as the pope who clashed with Martin Luther.

CHAPTER FIFTEEN

WORSHIP
IN THE
MIDDLE AGES

Catholic liturgies in the Middle Ages combined patristic-era tradition with new elements from scholasticism. In this era the seven sacraments were defined, incorporated into church doctrine, and became the Christian's path to heaven. As life for most people was difficult, short, and had few prospects for improvement, hopes focused on the afterlife. To ensure direct entry to heaven and avoid purgatory, penance assumed new prominence. Two of the most popular avenues of penance were indulgences and pilgrimages. The veneration of saints, the virgin Mary, shrines, and relics became increasingly popular among the laity. A vestige of pagan worship, sacramentals, was introduced into Catholic life, and the Renaissance influenced church architecture, replacing the Romanesque cathedrals of the early Middle Ages with Gothic cathedrals.

THE SACRAMENTS

In his *Four Books of Sentences* (ca. 1150), Peter Lombard (1100–1160) listed the seven sacraments (baptism, confirmation, Eucharist, penance, marriage, holy orders, and extreme unction). Lombard and other medieval theologians described the administration of the sacraments throughout the life of a Christian, beginning with baptism and ending with the last rites, or extreme unction. Baptism, confirmation, and holy orders were only given once. Penance and the Eucharist were to be received regularly. Last rites were reserved for those near death but could be administered again if a dying person recovered. Marriage was to occur only once, though exceptions were possible. According to Lombard:

> A sacrament bears a likeness to the thing of which it is a sign. "For if the sacraments did not have a likeness of the things whose sacraments they are, they would not properly be called sacraments" (Augustine). . . . Something can properly be called a sacrament if it is a sign of the grace of God and a form of invisible grace, so that it bears the image and exists as its cause. Sacraments were threefold instituted for the sake of sanctifying, as well as signifying. . . . Those things which were instituted for the purpose of signifying alone are nothing more than signs, and are not sacraments, as in the case of physical sacrifices and ceremonial observance of the Law, which were never able to make those who offered them righteous.[1]

The seven sacraments of the Catholic Church were adopted by the Fourth Lateran Council of 1215. Following Lombard, the Council ruled that the sacraments were channels of grace in which God was uniquely active. Using Aristotelian categories, the council spoke of the physical materials involved in sacraments (e.g., bread, wine, water) as matter and the words of consecration as the form. Moreover, a sacrament resembled the thing it signified, making it tangible by symbolic words and gestures. *Ex opere operato* assured that the sacrament achieved its purpose through Christ, not through the priest who administered it. As Augustine employed this phrase against the Donatists, the Catholic Church in the Middle Ages used it to combat the notion that sacraments administered by immoral clergy were invalid.

The sacraments of baptism and confirmation worked in conjunction. For an infant to be baptized, the parents had to agree to raise their child in the church. The infant was then baptized by immersion or effusion in the name of the Trinity and anointed with the chrism (ceremonial oil). The infant then supposedly received the Holy Spirit and grace that removed the stain of original sin. For adults the sacrament of confirmation involved a similar ceremony, only without water, and the person spoke for himself.

The sacrament of confirmation can be traced to Tertullian and Hippolytus in the late second century. As infant baptism became more common, confirmation became important. After a child reached the age of seven and received instruction in the faith, a member of the clergy gauged his dedication to Christianity and asked him to reaffirm the commitment of faith given by his godparents at baptism. The cleric then laid hands on the child and anointed his forehead with oil. This act represented the infusion of the Holy Spirit. The child would then be permitted to take Communion. According to Thomas Aquinas:

> The sacraments of the New Law are instituted to produce special effects of grace. Accordingly, where a special occasion occurs, there a special sacrament is provided. Things of sense bear the likeness of things of mind, and turning points in the life of the body have their equivalents in the life of the spirit. Coming of age ends a definitive period; after that a man is capable of acting for himself. . . . By the process of being born we receive bodily life, by the process of growing up we become adult. So it is in the life of the spirit. Born by baptism, we reach our full stature by confirmation.[2]

Confirmation is the Catholic version of the Jewish bar/bat mitzvah. For adults, it involved anointing with the chrism immediately following baptism. It was a visible way to demonstrate the putting on of the Holy Spirit. The initiate now had full membership in the church.

Transubstantiation was defined and declared the official eucharistic doctrine of the Catholic Church at the Fourth Lateran Council in 1215. Drawing from Aristotelian metaphysics, the council said the substance of the elements changed into the body and blood of Christ, but the senses still perceived the elements as wine and bread. The Eucharist was a sacrifice, and Christ's presence in the elements was real. After the twelfth century, Catholics withheld the cup from the laity for fear they would spill Christ's blood. According to the principle of concomitance, the body and blood of Christ were both present in both elements, so the wine was not necessary.

The sacrament of penance involved four phases: contrition, confession, absolution, and satisfaction. The penitent had to be contrite and remorseful for his sins. A priest would then hear his confession. If he believed the penitent was truly remorseful, he would assign some manner of penance. If the penitent promised to perform the penance, the priest would offer absolution or forgiveness.

In the Middle Ages penance often involved giving alms, abstinence from sex, or prayer. In some cases penitents with means considered the penalties too heavy, so other avenues of penance were created. In this regard a reforming monk named Peter Damian (1007–1072) wrote,

> When priests impose a penance of many years on certain sinners, they sometimes indicate the sum of money necessary for remission of the annual stint, so that those who dread long fasts may redeem their misdeeds by alms. This money payment is not found in the ancient canons of the Fathers, but is not therefore to be judged absurd or frivolous.[3]

Absolution was given only for sins that were confessed. If sins were not confessed or if the penitent forgot them, they were not absolved, and the person had to spend time in purgatory to expunge them.

As the Middle Ages progressed, the fear of purgatory increased. Families often worried about deceased loved ones whose unconfessed sins relegated them to purgatory. The bereaved were encouraged to purchase indulgences from itinerant preachers who had been granted special permission by the church to sell them. Indulgences supposedly conferred extra merit on the deceased, drawn from the saints, and abolished or shortened their time in purgatory. A person could also purchase indulgences for himself. A plenary indulgence pardoned all sins a person had committed or would commit. Everyone who went on the First Crusade received a plenary indulgence. This manner of indulgence also paid for the construction of Saint Peter's Basilica. The abuses of indulgences and pilgrimages for monetary gain were foundational reasons for Martin Luther's desire to reform the church.

Marriage was a consensual sacrament shared by two Christians, a representation of the love between Christ and the church. Vows were exchanged before a priest who served as the representative of Christ. The early church fathers who extolled female virginity and who often expressed hostility to marriage paid little attention to this sacrament. Augustine, however, believed it was good because it promoted monogamy, produced children, provided mutual support, and created an indissoluble union between the husband and the wife. A Christian was forbidden to marry a pagan or a Jew.

Ordination into the priesthood, or holy orders, conferred God's grace on men who served as bishops, presbyters, and deacons. For them it replaced the sacrament of marriage. The priest married Christ and dedicated his life to church service. When the minister laid hands on the ordination candidate, he was endowed with the power of the Holy Spirit to administer the sacraments. A priest could not leave the ministry for any reason other than death. Gregory of Nyssa was an early advocate of ordination as a sacrament.

The sacrament of extreme unction was the anointing of a sick or dying person with oil, based on James 5:14–15: "Is anyone among you sick? He should call for the elders of the church, and they should pray over him after anointing him with olive oil in the name of the Lord. The prayer of faith will save the sick person, and the Lord will restore him to health; if he has committed sins, he will be forgiven."

The priest laid his hands on the person's head and anointed him with oil. It was a way for a Christian to be given spiritual health and comfort, be physically healed, or if near death, to have his remaining sins forgiven. In combination, anointing of the sick, confession, and taking the Eucharist constituted the last rites.

SACRAMENTALS, SHRINES, AND RELICS

Sacramentals were objects or actions blessed by the clergy as sources of merit. For example, blessings were bestowed on wells, animals, and crops. These sacramentals became popular in the agricultural areas of medieval Europe. The best-known sacramentals were holy water, making the sign of the cross, wedding rings, saying grace, genuflecting, and wearing crucifixes and medallions. The use of sacramentals was believed to ward off evil and was a vestige of the pagan religion in Germany and the Slavic regions. There were special sacramentals associated with the virgin Mary, the most popular of which were the rosary and medals.

As mentioned in earlier chapters, relics were bones or possessions thought to have belonged to Christ, the apostles, Mary, martyrs, saints, and other holy people. Relics were believed to have power to protect and heal those who venerated them. Churches often collected relics and dedicated a shrine to them. In the hope of being blessed, pilgrims visited the shrine. Most shrines and relics were in the Holy Land. Some of most popular shrines in Europe were in Rome (at the supposed graves of Peter and Paul), Canterbury (at Thomas Becket's grave), and Venice (at Mark's supposed grave). Relics often were placed in vaults, reliquaries, or, if they were of someone prominent, beneath the altar. In the words of Abbot Suger (1081–1151) of Saint Denis:

> Since it seemed proper to place the most sacred bodies of our Patron Saints in the upper vault as nobly as we could, and since one of the side-tablets of their most sacred sarcophagus has been torn off on some unknown occasion, we put back fifteen marks of gold and took pains to have gilded its rear side and its superstructure throughout, both below and above, with about forty ounces. Further we caused the actual receptacles of the holy bodies to be enclosed with gilded panels of cast copper and with polished stones, fixed close to the inner stone vaults, and also with continuous gates to hold off disturbances by crowds; in such a manner, however, that reverend persons, as was fitting might be able to see them with great devotion and a flood of tears.[4]

Churches often charged a fee to see relics and in doing so became wealthy. It was believed that saints were most willing to help pilgrims on their feast days. Churches, therefore, held lengthy celebrations in honor of their saints. At these celebrations pilgrims viewed relics such as sweat alleged to have come from Christ's brow, splinters of the cross, and milk from the virgin Mary's breasts. Because relics and shrines were a lucrative source of income, churches sought the relics in greatest demand, made false claims about the authenticity of relics, and even stole relics from one another. During the Fourth Crusade, which resulted in the sacking of Constantinople, Crusaders stole Byzantine relics and brought them back to Europe. Many of these relics ended up in the Vatican.

Veneration of the virgin Mary played a major role in the Middle Ages. France was particularly dedicated to the virgin. In twelfth- and thirteenth-century France, eighty cathedrals and churches were dedicated to her. Building on her early church designation of *Theotokos* and virgin, Mary became known as the mother of all humanity. As the mother of Christ, Christians believed they could have access to Christ through her. The twelfth-century book *Miracles of the Virgin* was a collection of stories about how she served as an advocate for those who venerated her. Alleged apparitions of Mary and pilgrimages to sites that held her relics became commonplace. Built between 1193 and 1250, Chartres Cathedral outside of Paris was one of the most popular sites for Marian pilgrimages; it ostensibly had the "Sacred Tunic" she wore when she gave birth to Christ.

The idea of the immaculate conception became widespread in the Middle Ages. Advocated by John Duns Scotus, it was the principle that Mary was conceived without the stain of original sin (not to be confused with the virgin conception of Jesus). This led many to believe that Mary played a role in salvation and could even be considered *coredemptrix* with Christ. The immaculate conception became official doctrine in 1854.

The assumption was another popular Middle Ages belief. It held that at the end of her life, Mary was taken to heaven in body and soul. The assumption of Mary became official doctrine in 1950. (Catholics differ on whether or not Mary died. The 1950 papal declaration is intentionally ambiguous on this point, stating that Mary was assumed into heaven "having completed the course of her earthly life.")

Prayers were dedicated to Mary. Tradition maintained that the virgin Mary appeared to Saint Dominic (1170–1221) in 1214 and gave him the rosary—a string of beads, each of which corresponded to a particular prayer. One prayer associated with the rosary was known as the Hail Mary: "Hail Mary, full of grace, the Lord is with thee; blessed art thou amongst women, and blessed is the fruit of thy womb, Jesus. Holy Mary, Mother of God, pray for us sinners, now and at the hour of our death. Amen." Regarding the Hail Mary, Thomas Aquinas said:

> [Mary] was so full of grace that it overflows on to all mankind. It is indeed, a great thing that any one saint has so much

grace that it conduces the salvation of all mankind; and thus it is in Christ and in the Blessed Virgin. Thus in every danger thou canst find a refuge in the same glorious virgin.[5]

Because of her supposed sinless conception, role as intercessor, assumption, and the intense devotion dedicated to her, Mary's popularity rivaled that of Christ.

ARCHITECTURE

Romanesque architecture dominated the first half of the Middle Ages. Cathedrals had heavy, rounded arches and a cruciform shape. The roof was usually shaped like a cylinder and called a barrel vault. Because of the weight of the barrel vault, the supporting walls had to be strong. The Romanesque cathedral, therefore, had few windows and looked like a fortress. It evoked a sense of solitude and solemnity. The cathedral was decorated with tapestries, chalices, and jewels; and a relic, often of its patron saint, was placed underneath the altar. Charlemagne's Palatine Chapel in Aachen (805), Durham Cathedral in England (1093), and the Cathedral of Lisbon (1147) are prime examples of Romanesque style.

The Gothic or French style was more prevalent in the second half of the Middle Ages (ca. 1150–1550). Gothic cathedrals were particularly popular in university cities. They followed the cruciform plan but used pointed instead of arched ridges and had vertical lines that drew the gaze heavenward. To distribute the weight of the ceiling, these cathedrals had flying buttresses. As a result, they were taller and had thinner walls and more windows. Gothic cathedrals, therefore, were filled with light. The rose window behind the altar was the largest window. The other windows depicted religious scenes. The Gothic cathedrals were famous for their spires that were visible from miles away.

Begun in 1137 and completed in 1144, the Cathedral of Saint Denis in Paris was the first true Gothic cathedral and a model for similar churches across Europe. The most famous Gothic cathedral is Notre Dame in Paris (founded in 1163 and completed in 1345).

CHAPTER SIXTEEN

THE DAWN
OF THE
REFORMATION

At the beginning of the sixteenth century, many factors led to a reshaping of Christianity. Nation-states were growing in strength and becoming more concerned with their own affairs than with Rome's. Rulers of nation-states coveted the vast tracts of land owned by the church. Even the most staunchly Catholic states often wanted a papal blessing without having to submit to papal authority. The decline of the Catholic Church's domination was accelerating.

Economic factors also contributed to the situation. Commerce increased, resulting in capitalism[1] and the decline of agriculture. This led to a shortage of food and high rates of inflation. Many peasants could not afford food. Commerce also threatened the traditional feudal system. For the lord of the manor, it was now more economical to hire peasants to work the land than to feed and house serfs.

These changes altered the social hierarchy. A person was no longer bound to a class but could elevate himself by accumulating wealth. A peasant now had the ability to increase his personal worth, and many peasants migrated to urban areas in an attempt to do just that. A new middle class emerged. Still, the church continued to demand its tithes, and the fear of purgatory caused many to spend their earnings on indulgences. This led to resentment of the Catholic Church.

The Renaissance also paved the way for the Reformation. In Germany humanism took root, including its emphasis on *ad fontes*, a Latin phrase meaning "to the sources" that humanists used to encourage study of ancient texts. This emphasis not only led to increased study of Greek and Latin classics but also to increased study of the Bible and a consequent challenge of traditional Catholic teachings. Erasmus's Greek New Testament contributed to this challenge as did the Renaissance belief in the importance of individuals over institutions. People began to question the sincerity of the church's commitment to caring for their souls. To many it appeared that the institutional church was more concerned with taking care of itself and its pontiff. After all, a succession of popes lived in luxury while most believers lived in poverty.

Not all Catholic priests and nuns craved power and wealth. But noble clerics normally served in lowly positions within the hierarchy. Their more visible superiors had less pious motives and understandably drew criticism.

All of these factors paved the way for the Reformation, but someone had to take the first step. That someone was an Augustinian monk from the state of Saxony in Germany.

Martin Luther (1483–1546)

Born in Eisleben, Saxony, Martin Luther and his family moved to Mansfeld soon after his birth. His family descended from the peasantry, but through the efforts of his father Hans (ca. 1459–1530), they eventually owned six copper mines. Luther's family had high aspirations for their son, whom they expected to take over the family business. His education began in 1497 at the cathedral school of Magdeburg run by members of the Brethren of Common Life. After completing his studies at Magdeburg, he attended the university in Eisenach to study law. He earned his bachelor of arts from Erfurt University in 1502 and his master's in 1505. While at

Erfurt, he studied the nominalism of William Ockham and developed a distrust of Thomas Aquinas and scholasticism.

Shortly after Luther began studying at Erfurt, he started to worry about the state of his soul and how to achieve salvation. This concern may have been prompted by the deaths of two friends and his own brush with death after accidentally severing an artery in his leg. Luther perceived God as distant, unapproachable, and harsh. Christ was equally strict. He concluded that one of the few ways to escape God's wrath was to become a monk.

On July 2, 1505, Luther found the final motivation needed to take the cowl. While returning to Erfurt through a field, he found himself in the middle of a storm. After almost being struck by lightning, Luther swore to Saint Anne, the patron saint of miners, that if he were spared, he would become a monk.

Against the wishes of his father, Luther kept his promise and entered an Augustinian monastery in 1505, where he was trained in theology. He received his own copy of the Vulgate and Gabriel Biel's (1420–1495) *Canon of the Mass.* He became a priest in 1507.

Even as a priest, he spent hours in the confessional, wrestled with his thoughts at night, sought the merits of the saints, and practiced self-denial—all in an effort to find salvation and rest for his soul. These practices only gave him momentary solace. Luther remained concerned over the sins he had not confessed. His studies only raised more questions and concerns, for God was still a stern father. Monasticism brought him no relief. Years later Luther recalled, "If anyone could have gained heaven as a monk, then I would indeed have been among them."[2]

Luther's confessor and vicar-general of the Augustinian Order in Germany, John von Staupitz (1460–1524), sent him to Wittenberg University in 1508, where he received three degrees and later joined the faculty. He remained at Wittenberg for the remainder of his life.

Academics, however, gave him no relief. His mind still dwelled on his sinful state. Hoping that visiting Rome would bolster his faith, Staupitz sent him there on business in 1510. Luther visited the shrines, climbed the holy stairs on his knees,[3] and purchased indulgences for family members; but he soon became dismayed by the debauchery of Rome. The pope was more warlike than spiritual, members of the clergy frequented prostitutes, and indulgences were being sold for every imaginable sin to people who were not contrite.

When he returned from Rome, he was more preoccupied with his sin than ever. He clung to the belief that God would grant grace to those who did all they could, but he wondered if he was doing enough. To take his mind off of his worries, Staupitz had Luther begin a doctorate in theology at Wittenberg.

During his studies Luther began a lifelong love affair with the books of Psalms, Galatians, and Romans. When he received his doctorate in 1512, at Staupitz's urging he accepted an appointment as professor of theology at Wittenberg. In 1514 he was also named preacher of Saint Mary's Church.

Luther's early lectures were on Psalms, Galatians, Romans, and Hebrews. Around 1515 these lectures led to his theological break-through or what he termed his "Tower Experience." It came while studying Romans 1:17: "For in it God's righteousness is revealed from faith to faith, just as it is written: 'The righteous will live by faith.'"[4] He then read Romans 1:17 in conjunction with Romans 3:24: "They are justified freely by His grace through the redemption that is in Christ Jesus." His thoughts then became clear. He understood that right standing before God is a gift of grace one cannot earn and has to be accepted freely. People are saved by what God has done for them in Christ. God provided everything a person needs to be justified, including faith. Luther maintained that faith was a positive response to the Word and a gift from God. In this regard Luther used the term "Word" to signify the eternal *Logos*. Faith was trust that united the believer to Christ. God was not an unjust lawgiver but gracious and loving. In recalling his Tower Experience, Luther wrote:

Though I lived as a monk without reproach, I felt that
I was a sinner before God with an extremely disturbed conscience. . . . I did not love, yes, I hated the righteous God
who punishes sinners, and secretly . . . I was angry with
God. . . . Thus I raged with a fierce and troubled conscience.
Nevertheless, I beat importunately upon Paul at that place
[Romans 1.17], most ardently desiring to know what St.
Paul wanted. . . . At last, by the mercy of God, meditating
day and night, I gave heed to the context of the word, namely, "In it the righteousness of God is revealed, as it is written, 'He who through faith is righteous shall live.'" There I
began to understand that the righteousness of God is that
by which the righteous lives by a grace of God, namely by
faith. And this is the meaning: the righteousness of God
is revealed by the gospel, namely, the passive righteousness
with which the merciful God justifies us by faith.[5]

Known as justification by faith or, in Luther's words, "passive
righteousness," this revival of the Pauline doctrine became the heart
of Luther's theology. Luther's doctrine, however, placed him at odds
with a Catholic penitential system that was based more than ever on
the purchase of indulgences.

In 1514, the margrave of Brandenburg and archbishop of
Magdeburg, Albert of Brandenburg (1490–1545), borrowed
21,000 ducats from Jacob Fugger (1459–1525) so he could buy the
archbishopric of Mainz from Pope Leo X (1513–1521).[6] To repay
the loan, Leo gave Albert permission to sell indulgences. Half of
the money went to rebuilding Saint Peter's, and the other half went
to Albert. A Dominican indulgence salesman named John Tetzel
(ca. 1469–1524) was in charge of raising the money. Tetzel told his
customers that all they needed to do to free someone from purgatory was to buy an indulgence. It did not matter if the purchaser
was in a state of grace or not. To purchase an indulgence, contrition
for sin was not necessary. Tetzel persuaded prospective customers

to purchase indulgences by deliberately burning his hand to show how the souls of loved ones were tormented in purgatory. The tune he supposedly sung while selling indulgences became legendary: "When a coin in the coffer rings, a soul from purgatory springs."

People in Wittenberg heard of Tetzel's amazing indulgences and went to purchase them. Luther became incensed when he heard Tetzel was belittling the sacrament of penance by making it a financial transaction. Absolution could not be acquired by purchasing it. Luther insisted that true contrition was required to gain forgiveness.

To stimulate an academic debate on the veracity of indulgences, Luther nailed his *Ninety-Five Theses on the Power and Efficacy of Indulgence* to the Wittenberg castle church door on October 31, 1517. He also sent a copy to Archbishop Albert of Mainz and Brandenburg, who forwarded it to Pope Leo X. In this text Luther questioned the validity of indulgences, the pope's power to forgive sin, and the existence of the Treasury of Merit. Point 82 challenged the pope's reason for selling indulgences: "Why does not the pope empty purgatory for the sake of holy love and the dire needs of souls that are there if he redeems an infinite number of souls for the sake of miserable money with which to build a church? The former reasons would be most just; the latter is most trivial."[7]

The *Ninety-Five Theses* caused an immediate sensation. They were translated from Latin into German and, thanks to the printing press, disseminated across Germany. As early as 1519 the *Ninety-Five Theses* and several of Luther's other writings could be found as far away as France, Italy, and England. Many agreed with Luther's assertions, and the sale of indulgences in Germany plunged.

Luther had no intention of breaking from the Catholic Church. He had no idea that one of his colleagues would translate the theses into German and have them circulated beyond Wittenberg, sparking the Reformation.

Luther continued to attack indulgences and began to teach justification by faith in his classroom and from the pulpit. His ideas became popular. Leo X initially paid little attention to Luther. A fellow Augustinian, Leo told the general of the Augustinian Order to discipline the monk. Rather than punishment though, Luther found support from his brethren and became more emboldened.

Finally, Leo summoned Luther to Rome to force him to recant and apologize for the charges he levied in his *Ninety-Five Theses.* Frederick (1463–1525), the Elector of Saxony, believed if Luther traveled to Rome, his life would be in danger and asked that the trial be held in Augsburg in October 1518, where the Imperial Diet was scheduled to occur (a diet was an official meeting of the electors of the Holy Roman Empire of the German Nation). Because of Frederick's power and influence, Augsburg became the location of the trial. The pope sent Cardinal Tommaso de Vio Gaetani Cajetan (1480–1547) to Augsburg as his representative. Most observers expected Luther to recant and beg forgiveness, but he refused. He asserted that the pope could and had made mistakes, that a general council was superior to the pope, and that if a person without faith took a sacrament, the sacrament was worthless. Luther then declared that the Bible was the only Christian authority. Cajetan replied that the Bible had to be interpreted and only the pope could do so. Luther then denied that the pope was above the Scriptures and even accused Leo of abusing them. Luther had made himself an enemy of the pope. Cajetan was to arrest Luther if he did not recant, but as Luther had the people of Augsburg behind him, Cajetan decided against this. Luther's friends found him a horse and helped him flee the city under cover of darkness.

In June 1519 one of Luther's supporters, Andreas Karlstadt (1486–1541) and a renowned Catholic theologian named Johan Eck (1486–1543) held a public debate at Leipzig. Luther was invited to speak. Luther denied papal primacy, the doctrine that the pope has authority over all other bishops and the church in general. The Bible was the only authority he recognized. Eck did, however, trap Luther into saying he approved of the doctrines of Jan Hus.

Luther dedicated much of 1520 to writing. In his *Address to the Christian Nobility of the German Nation*, he advocated that the Christian magistrates be involved in reshaping the church. He denied that the state was subservient to Rome. In fact, he maintained that the visible church was a material entity in a prince or magistrate's territory and should be under the authority of the state. The papacy's arguments regarding its own authority were invalid, he said.

> First, when pressed by the temporal power, they have made decrees and said that the temporal power has no jurisdiction over them, but, on the other hand, that the spiritual power is above the temporal power. Second, when the attempt is made to reprove them out of the Scriptures, they raise the objection that the interpretation of Scriptures belongs to no one except the pope. Third, if threatened with a council, they answer with the fable that no one can call a council but the pope.[8]

The task of ministers, according to Luther, was to administer the sacraments and preach the true message of Christ. In addition, all true believers had access to God (a doctrine known as the priesthood of all believers), could interpret Scripture for themselves, and could choose their own ministers. The government was to ensure the purity of the church.

Luther realized that for the Reformation to succeed, he needed the backing of the civil magistrates. By writing against the Catholic Church's authority in Germany, he hoped to gain support for his reforms.

In the *Address to the Christian Nobility of the German Nation*, Luther also denied the validity of monasticism, the necessity of clerical celibacy, and the pope's right to convene an ecumenical council. Because wealth interfered with its task of caring for souls, Luther, echoing Wycliffe, advocated that the church not have numerous possessions.

In *On the Babylonian Captivity of the Church* (1520), Luther attacked the sacramental system. He called for the elimination of four of the seven sacraments, keeping only baptism, the Eucharist, and penance. (Later he dropped penance as a sacrament.) Luther insisted that the Eucharist be served in both kinds and that it was not a repeated sacrifice of Christ.

In *The Freedom of the Christian* (1520), Luther argued that works could not produce faith. Faith in God alone justified and united one's soul to Christ. No outward works could do this. Christians, therefore, were no longer bound to keep the law but rather had the freedom to serve God and their neighbors.

On June 15, 1520, Leo X sent Luther the papal bull *Exsurge Domine* that gave him sixty days to recant the *Ninety-Five Theses* and his other writings or suffer excommunication. When the bull arrived, Luther promptly burned it along with his books of church law and scholastic theology. Leo excommunicated Luther on January 3, 1521. Luther's separation from the Catholic Church was complete.

With Luther protected by Frederick and the citizens of Saxony, Charles V (1519–1556), the newly elected Holy Roman emperor from Spain and a devout Catholic, convened the Diet of Worms on April 17, 1521, where the general estates of the empire were to judge Luther. Only after Frederick gained him safe passage to and from Worms did Luther consent to attend. He was refused the opportunity to debate or discuss his views. Instead, his books were placed on a table and he was asked if he had written them. After affirming that they were his, Luther was asked if he would renounce them. After asking for a day to consider the matter, he returned and refused to repudiate them:

> Unless I am convinced by the testimony of the Scrip-
> tures or by clear reason (for I do not trust either in the pope
> or in councils alone, since it is well known that they have
> often erred and contradicted themselves), I am bound by
> the Scriptures I have quoted and my conscience is captive

to the Word of God. I cannot and will not recant anything, since it is neither safe nor right to go against conscience. May God help me. Amen.[9]

Luther then left Worms and began to make his way back to Wittenberg. On May 25, before the Diet concluded, Holy Roman Emperor Charles V (1519–1556) had Luther declared an outlaw and a heretic. Anyone who gave Luther food or shelter would be considered a criminal. Luther could be killed without any consequence, and those who killed him would be considered friends of the church. Luther's journey home would be perilous.

Frederick realized the danger of Luther's situation and had his men intercept him and stage it as a kidnapping. Luther was taken to the safety of the Wartburg Castle near Eisenach. He wore the vestments of a knight, grew a beard, and was addressed as Sir George. For all intents and purposes, Luther appeared to have been captured and killed. He remained in Wartburg Castle for ten months.

While sequestered, Luther dedicated himself to producing the *September Bible* (1522), a translation of the New Testament into German.[10] He believed the Scriptures should be in the hands of the people in a language they could understand. The *September Bible* not only accomplished this, but it also had a major influence on the development of the modern German language. Luther, however, was not beyond altering the text to advance his theology. For example Romans 3:28 reads, "For we conclude that a man is justified by faith apart from the works of the law." After "justified by faith," Luther added the word "alone."

Since many believed Luther was either dead or would never return, Wittenberg fell into chaos. Wanting to capitalize on Luther's popularity and possible martyrdom, Karlstadt sought to push the Reformation forward. He celebrated the Christmas Mass of 1521 without his clerical robes, the Lord's Supper was served in both kinds, and much of the liturgy was performed in German. Karlstadt also promoted the destruction of statues and images in the churches and became a champion of social equality. These events disturbed the magistrates and nobles who had supported Luther.

Two days after Karlstadt's Christmas Mass, the Zwickau Prophets,[11] a group of radicals inspired by Luther's teachings on the priesthood of all believers, arrived in Wittenberg. They preached that their revelations were superior to Scripture, that the church should be free from the state, and that the apocalypse was imminent. They likely won over Karlstadt.

To restore order, Luther emerged from seclusion, chastised Karlstadt, and, after delivering eight fiery sermons, ran off the Zwickau Prophets. Luther was not completely against Karlstadt's changes but rather the speed at which they were enacted. For Luther, the Reformation had to be done in a calm and peaceful manner with the interests of the magistrates and nobles kept in mind.

Charles V spent most of his time and resources from 1521 to 1529 fighting the French on his western border and the Turks to his east. Luther used this time to continue the Reformation.

When nine nuns who had hidden among fish barrels to escape their convent arrived at Wittenberg, Luther gave them sanctuary and found husbands for eight of them. The ninth was Katherine von Bora (1499–1552), who married Luther on June 13, 1525. He said he married her to give her a name, please his parents, and to spite the pope. By all accounts Luther and Katie were in love.

Erasmus wrote *On the Freedom of the Will* in 1524. The book argued that all humans had the ability to respond to God's offer of grace. The doctrine of divine predestination to salvation, Erasmus said, was unbiblical. Luther responded in 1525 with *On the Bondage of the Will*. He argued that sin perverted the human will and made it incapable of choosing to follow God of its own accord. Salvation was a unilateral act of God by grace alone, in which he transformed the will so that it desired to follow him. Humans could do nothing to bring themselves to God. Any hopes of an alliance between Luther and Erasmus were dashed.

Believing Luther supported their push for social and political reform, thousands of German peasants revolted against the princes in protest of economic turmoil and widespread poverty. Behind radicals such as Thomas Müntzer (1489–1525), who had been inspired by the Zwickau Prophets, the peasant revolt of 1524–1525 had strong millenarian overtones. For Luther though, the Reformation aimed at correcting the church, not the German social order. In April 1525 he wrote *An Admonition to Peace*, in which he told the peasants to be patient and peaceful and the German princes to address some of the peasants' grievances. When it became clear that the peasants had turned to violence, Luther penned *Against the Robbing and Murdering Hordes of Peasants* in May 1525. In vitriolic fashion he told the princes they could "smite, slay, and stab, secretly or openly, remembering that nothing can be more poisonous, hurtful, or devilish than a rebel. It is just as when one must kill a mad dog; if you do not strike him, he will strike you, and a whole land with you."[12]

On May 15, 1525, German nobles destroyed the peasant army at the Battle of Frankenhausen. The prince's reprisals were brutal, and many of the surviving peasants fled eastward. Luther appeared to have turned his back on the peasants, and many of them returned to the Catholic Church.

The Diet of Speyer was convened by the German princes in 1526. With Charles preoccupied with his war against the French and Turks, the Lutheran princes gained a temporary reprieve of the Edict of Worms, which condemned Luther to death. A national council was to be held that would settle the church question. Until this council convened, there was to be a truce between the factions. This action gave the Lutheran princes the ability, though briefly, to advance Lutheranism within their domains.

After Charles's armies halted the Turks at Vienna in 1529, he again turned his attention to Luther. The Second Diet of Speyer convened in March 1529. It condemned Luther and mandated that all territories return to Catholic worship. Lutheranism would be tolerated only in regions where squelching it required violence. A significant minority of princes and magistrates protested these decisions and came to be known as Protestants.

Luther's reforms galvanized others. One such person was Ulrich Zwingli (1484–1531) of Zurich. At the request of Philip I of Hesse (1504–1567), who hoped to unite their movements, Luther and Zwingli met at the Marburg Colloquy in 1529. Although they agreed on fourteen of fifteen articles of faith, their disagreement on the fifteenth made unity impossible. Luther insisted on the principle of consubstantiation—the idea that the body and blood of Christ were truly present in the bread and wine of the Eucharist, although the elements were not transformed into flesh and blood as transubstantiation held. Zwingli argued that the Eucharist was merely a memorial of what Christ had done at the cross for believers. The heart of the disagreement was over the person of Christ. According to Luther, Christ had one nature, which was present in all places. Christ, therefore, was present in the bread and wine. Zwingli emphasized the distinction of Christ's two natures. His divine nature was present in all places, but his humanity could only be in one place at a time, and that was at the right hand of the Father. Christ, therefore, could not be physically present in the bread and wine.

Charles V convened the Diet of Augsburg in 1530. As an outlaw, Luther could not attend. He had Philip Melanchthon (1497–1560) draw up what became known as the Augsburg Confession to express his positions. The Lutherans appeared to be winning the day, so Charles demanded that all Protestant territories return to Catholicism and dismissed the Diet. The Protestant princes were convinced Charles would move against them, so they formed the Schmalkaldic League as a defensive measure.

To pressure Charles to stop persecuting Lutherans, the German princes aligned with the French. To hold his empire together, Charles held a meeting at Augsburg in 1555 with his dissident princes. Under the terms of a settlement known as the Peace of Augsburg, *cuius regio, eius religio* (whose realm, his religion) would be the determining principle of a region's religion. Each prince could determine whether his territory would be Lutheran or Catholic. In "free" cities, Lutherans and Catholics would live together and have equal rights. It was also decided that people could immigrate to cities of their religious choice without forfeiting their holdings. With this freedom most of northern Germany was Lutheran by 1540. Lutheranism found adherents among German settlers in Hungary, Poland, Denmark, and Sweden.

LUTHER'S CONTRIBUTIONS

First, Luther maintained that Scripture was the authority for the church's life. It was more trustworthy than tradition, scholastic theologians, or the papacy. By appealing to the Scriptures and not to the church hierarchy, Luther hoped to demonstrate that many traditions of the Catholic Church were unbiblical.

Luther believed the Bible was the means by which God made himself known to the world. Moreover, he believed the Scriptures did not belong to the church but rather to all Christians in their own language.

Second, Luther saw the importance of congregational singing as a way to teach theology and Scripture. He wrote several hymns, but his most famous was "A Mighty Fortress Is Our God." Using Psalm 46 as his reference, the last verse said a great deal about his ordeals and trust in God:

> That word above all earthly powers,
> no thanks to them, abideth;
> the Spirit and the gifts are ours,
> thru him who with us sideth.
> Let goods and kindred go,
> this mortal life also;

the body they may kill;
God's truth abideth still;
his kingdom is forever.[13]

Third, Luther's revival of the Pauline doctrine of justification by faith was his greatest theological contribution to the Reformation. Because humans were unable to keep the law, Luther taught that they were separated from God. In his Tower Experience, he determined that only a God-given grace could provide justification. The presence of Christ in a person's life provided faith, transformed the heart, and promoted a desire to serve Christ. The belief that humanity could earn salvation through piety and good works was baseless.

Fourth, Luther held that the church was both visible and invisible. The Catholic Church was not a true church. A true, visible church was defined by the truthful preaching of the Word and observance of only baptism and the Eucharist as the sacraments. The invisible church had always existed and was comprised of all true believers, according to Luther, including those within the Catholic Church.

Luther's reforms sought to return the church to apostolic teachings and practices, not split it. Instead, his reforms were so profound that an irreversible split occurred between Protestants and Catholics. Moreover, because of Luther, other Protestant denominations soon came into existence.

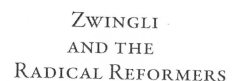

CHAPTER SEVENTEEN

ZWINGLI
AND THE
RADICAL REFORMERS

After Luther took the daring first step and inaugurated the Protestant Reformation, other religious leaders began to follow suit. Along with parts of Germany, the Swiss Confederation was receptive to the Reformation. In fact, Switzerland was the home of three great Reformation movements, led by Ulrich Zwingli (1484–1531), the Anabaptists, and John Calvin (1509–1564). Since Zwingli was the first prominent Swiss Reformer and the earliest Radical Reformers were his former students, they will be discussed together in this chapter. John Calvin will be discussed in a separate chapter.

Though Zwingli and Luther failed to reach agreement at the Marburg Colloquy, Luther had a strong influence on Zwingli, Zurich, and other Swiss cantons. Like Luther in Saxony, Zwingli sought to reform Zurich with the aid of the government. Some of his followers, however, desired a complete separation of the church from the civil government. These people became known as the Anabaptists (rebaptizers).

The Swiss Situation

In the early sixteenth century, the Holy Roman Empire claimed modern Switzerland as part of its domain. The Swiss, however, did not accept the sovereignty of the empire and announced their independence in 1499. The country now known as Switzerland was composed of sixteen independent city-states, or cantons. Though independent, the cantons formed a defensive league to protect themselves from their more aggressive neighbors. When determining matters that would affect all the cantons, each canton had one vote. The smaller cantons, therefore, could combine their votes against the larger ones. The southern cantons were known for providing mercenaries to European monarchs and the papacy.

Each canton could pick its own religion. The smaller, more rural cantons tended to remain loyal to the Catholic Church. Beginning in 1471, these cantons supplied many of the Vatican's Swiss Guards. The larger cantons, such as Zurich, Basel, and Geneva, became havens for humanists and were more inclined to support reform.

Ulrich Zwingli

Born in Wildhaus in the canton of Saint Gall, Zwingli attended the University of Vienna and, in 1502, the University of Basel. At Basel he excelled in music, received a humanist education, and studied under the noted antischolastic and humanist Thomas Wyttenbach (1472–1526). He earned his bachelor of arts in 1504 and his master of arts in 1506. He was then ordained to the priesthood.

In 1506, he was appointed to his first pastorate in the canton of Glarus. He remained in that position for ten years. When not performing his ecclesiastical services, he taught himself Greek and Hebrew, memorized the Pauline Epistles, and read all of Erasmus's available work.

In 1513 and again in 1515, Zwingli served as chaplain to the Swiss mercenaries who were hired to fight for the Old Swiss

Confederacy against France. After seeing many young Swiss men die at the Battle of Marignano on September 13–14, 1515, he began to oppose the mercenary trade, even in service of the pope. Because he served as a chaplain in a war against the hated French, he received a papal benefice.

In 1516 Zwingli was named pastor of Einsiedeln, a city famous for its healing shrine of the Black Virgin. Taking advantage of the shrine's popularity, the Catholic Church financially abused pilgrims and sold a vast number of indulgences. Like Luther, Zwingli feared that people were putting their faith in indulgences rather than in God.

In 1518 Zwingli was named preacher of the Grossmünster, one of the major churches in Zurich. He held this influential position for the remainder of his life. He was appalled by the sale of indulgences in his new canton. In particular he despised the indulgence salesman Bernardini Sanson (fl. 1518) and convinced the papacy to have him removed from his jurisdiction.

In Zurich, Zwingli began his reform movement. Like Luther, he worked with elected officials to advance his reforms. More so than Luther though, he was influenced by humanism, and it drove many of his efforts. He was so enamored with humanism that he believed the great pagan philosophers, especially Plato, would be welcomed into heaven.

Zwingli preached his first sermon at the Grossmünster on January 1, 1519. Rather than follow the Catholic prescriptions for preaching, he decided to preach only from the Bible. He started with the book of Matthew, then moved to the other Gospels, the remainder of the New Testament, and the Old Testament. His sermons were delivered in the local dialect and laced with disparaging comments about purgatory, monasticism, and indulgences. He also preached that unbaptized infants were not damned.

Zwingli began to hold "Prophecy Meetings" in 1519. These meetings were attended by young men who wanted to receive a humanist education and read the Greek classics. The most erudite and outspoken attendees were Conrad Grebel (1498–1526) and Felix Manz (1498–1527). Their studies soon moved beyond Greek and Hebrew to Zwingli's ideas of reform. Gradually they became Zwingli's most ardent disciples.

In April 1522, Zwingli published a tract in which he advocated his canton's freedom from the papacy. Moreover, in defiance of his vows, he secretly married Anna Reinhart (1484–1538).

An event later dubbed the "sausage incident" occurred on Ash Wednesday in 1522. One of Zwingli's followers, Christopher Froshauer (1490–1564), was attempting to finish a printing of the Pauline Epistles to be distributed after Easter. His workers became hungry, and he wanted to treat them to sausage. Since it was Ash Wednesday, they were not permitted to eat sausage. Basing his position on Acts 10:10–16,[1] Zwingli told Froshauer that Lent was not biblical and that they could eat sausage. The men ate, but Zwingli abstained, not wanting to confuse less mature Christians. He defended their actions in his *Of Freedom of Choice in the Selection of Food* (April 1522):

> If the spirit of your belief teaches you thus, then fast, but grant also your neighbor the privilege of Christian liberty, and fear God greatly, if you have transgressed his laws, nor make what man has invented greater before God than what God himself has commanded. . . . You should neither scorn nor approve anyone for any reason connected with food or with feast days whether observed or not (an exception is always to be made of Sunday until after hearing the Word of God and partaking of the Lord's Supper).[2]

Though this seems like a trivial incident, the Catholic Church viewed it as an act of open hostility and sent representatives to investigate. The city council and the Grossmünster were admonished by the bishop of Constance on May 24.

On January 29, 1523, the bishop of Constance sent Johann Faber (1478–1541), the vicar-general, to debate Zwingli before an audience of 600, an event that became known as the First Zurich Disputation. The city council would determine the winner, and the city would adopt his position. As he had in his *Sixty-Seven Theses* (1523), Zwingli argued not only against Lent but also against the authority of the pope and clerical celibacy. He said the mass was not a resacrifice of Christ but a commemoration of his once-for-all sacrifice on the cross. Zwingli said the Bible was the Christian's sole source of authority and salvation was by faith. The city council decided in Zwingli's favor and vowed to protect him from Catholic authorities, as Prince Frederick protected Luther. To maintain that protection, Zwingli always worked through the city council, followed its determinations, and required his followers to do the same.

The Second Disputation of Zurich took place October 26–28, 1523. The first day's topic was images; the second day's, the Mass (Lord's Supper); and the third day's, purgatory.

The discussion of images stemmed from the actions of Leo Jud (1482–1542), one of Zwingli's friends and the pastor of Saint Peterskirche. Jud preached against images, and several pictures in his church and in the neighboring Church of Our Lady were destroyed. Even the wooden cross that stood above the city's Oberdorf Gate was removed by the iconoclasts (ones who destroyed religious images). Although Zwingli agreed that images had no place in churches, he was not an iconoclast.

The disputation was held in front of 900 people, but not one spoke in favor of images. An Anabaptist leader and early ally of Zwingli, Balthasar Hubmaier (ca. 1480–1528), stated that only things explicitly mentioned in Scripture should be allowed in worship. Therefore, images were idolatrous and should be eliminated. At that point the discussion ended with the anti-image party carrying the day. But the city council gave no direction on how to enforce the ban on images.

The second day of the disputation was dedicated to discussion of the mass. Zwingli contended that transubstantiation was an invention of scholastic theologians that had been imposed on the biblical text. Later he presented this view more fully in *Commentary on True and False Religion* (1525). In that text he claimed that as Christ was in heaven, he could not be present physically in the elements. The mass, or Lord's Supper, was merely a memorial to him.

A majority of attendees at the disputation condemned the notion that the mass was a sacrifice. Grebel stated that unless some instruction was given about the mass, the disputation had been for nothing. Zwingli announced that the High Council of Zurich would give such instructions. At that point Zwingli was interrupted by Simon Strumpf (fl. 1517–1527), the priest at Honng, who told him that the real presence of Christ in the Mass was decreed by the Spirit of God and was not up for discussion. Zwingli reminded the assembled that they had been convened to judge whether the Mass was a sacrifice. The High Council would determine what changes to make in the Mass, he said.

The disputation reconvened on October 28. The discussion of purgatory was put aside, and the Mass once again assumed center stage. Hubmaier argued that the Lord's Supper should be held in the simple apostolic manner, given in both kinds, and performed in the vernacular. Zwingli agreed with him in principle but believed the political cost of enacting all those changes at once was too high. The Mass was still revered by many. Some people sympathetic to Zwingli's reform effort were willing to alter it but not to eliminate it. Moving too quickly might divide Zwingli's supporters. As a compromise Zwingli suggested that the Lord's Supper be investigated more fully prior to any decision.

The Catholic Mass, however, was removed from Zurich in April 1525. It became a simple memorial and was administered in German. Zwingli's other reforms, such as clerical marriage and the removal of images, and his vision of a theocratic Zurich were also implemented. Soon the cantons of Gall, Basel, and Bern eliminated the Mass and adopted many of his other reforms.

Zwingli's theology arose from humanism and conviction. He believed in the authority of the Scriptures alone. If something was not mentioned in the Bible, it had no place in worship. This led him to remove stained-glass windows from churches, eliminate organ music, and remove all statues from churches and cathedrals. His teachings often led to iconoclasm.

In matters of church polity, Zwingli maintained that the civil government had the final word. He held that the true church of believers was invisible. In the visible church only God knew who the true Christians were.

The Swiss cantons were loyal either to the Catholic Church or to the Reformation. They narrowly avoided a war of religion in early 1529. But in the Second Kappel War (1529–1531), the forest cantons attacked and defeated Zurich on October 9, 1531. Zwingli was killed in the battle, and his body was captured. His enemies had it quartered, mixed with dung, and burned.

After Zwingli's death Heinrich Bullinger (1504–1575) took the mantle of leadership in Zurich. John Calvin, however, emerged as the leader of the Reformed churches.

Despite widespread support for Zwingli in Zurich, not all of its residents agreed with him. His marriage of church and state as well as his belief in infant baptism alienated his prophecy students. By September 1524, they began to meet in a home directly behind the Grossmünster.

On January 17, 1525, Grebel and the "brethren," as they called themselves, debated Zwingli on infant baptism. Initially Zwingli agreed it could not be found in Scripture. But he connected it with the Old Testament ritual of circumcision. It was not salvific but brought the infant into the visible community of the church. For Grebel believer's baptism was the only biblical practice. He insisted that unbaptized infants were saved by Christ's grace. Grebel and his companions were labeled "Anabaptists" or rebaptizers. They believed Zwingli stopped before the task of reformation was complete. The Grebel group questioned the city council's right to govern religious affairs and wanted a radical break of the city's churches from the magistrates' control. As expected, the council disagreed with their views and determined that parents who refused to have their children baptized must leave the city. Zwingli's break with his former students was complete.

Zwingli realized the political implications of infant baptism. The entire city council had been baptized as infants, so the renunciation of infant baptism would in effect remove them from church membership. Moreover, baptism into the Zurich church made a person a citizen of the canton. Nullifying infant baptism would destroy social unity. His former students did not accept the council's verdict. They began to perform believer's baptism in 1525.

The popularity of Grebel and his followers made them dangerous. On March 7, 1526, the Zurich city council ruled that rebaptism was a crime punishable by death. To keep the favor of the magistrates, Zwingli turned on his former students. Grebel was imprisoned, and on January 5, 1527 Manz, was executed by drowning in the Limmat River. He was one of the first Anabaptists to be executed.

THE RADICAL REFORMERS

Many Anabaptist groups existed, each with its particular theological beliefs. Their roots were in Switzerland, but they quickly spread throughout Germany and the Netherlands. The majority were peasants or craftsmen who were dissatisfied with their impoverished socioeconomic situation. Luther and Zwingli's protests raised hopes for an egalitarian society, but eventually these Reformers disappointed the Anabaptists.

Anabaptist church membership was comprised of people who freely came together. No king, reformer, or pope had forced them to join. This concept was known as voluntarism. Parents could not speak for their infant children. To join the church, a person had to make his or her own confession of faith in Christ.

The majority of Anabaptists opposed any participation in government. They did not hold office or take oaths of loyalty. They believed civil government was necessary but claimed that true Christians should not be involved in it because God set it up to guide and discipline non-Christians. Congregations should discipline Christians, according to Anabaptists.

Anabaptists such as the Swiss Brethren were biblicists and peaceful. They contrasted with other groups of Radical Reformers. These groups included the South Germans, the Millenarian Revolutionaries, the Spiritualists or Inspirationalists, and the Anti-Trinitarians.

THE SWISS BRETHREN

The Swiss Brethren emerged as the first Anabaptist group. Its members, strict biblicists, were Ulrich Zwingli's former followers at Zurich. Its leaders were Conrad Grebel and Felix Manz. When a break with Zwingli appeared imminent, Grebel began to contact radicals in Germany. In spite of Grebel's pacifism, he attempted to correspond and associate with Thomas Müntzer (1489–1525), who was an Anabaptist but also a political revolutionary. Events in Zurich, however, came to a head before any relationships with other radicals were established.

In January 1525, Grebel and George Blaurock (1492–1529) baptized each other and the rest of the student group. Their new church was based on scriptural authority and a New Testament pattern of organization.

Zwingli persecuted the Anabaptists. Since they believed in adult baptism, their enemies saw execution by drowning as particularly fitting. Grebel, after his imprisonment, died of the plague in 1526.

Much later, Jacob Amman (1644–1711) led some of the Swiss Brethren to adapt plain clothes, foot washing, frequent Lord's

Suppers, and the shunning of excommunicated brethren. His followers became known as the Amish.

The remaining Swiss Brethren exported their movement. Blaurock and William Reublin (1484–1559) started congregations and baptized believers in Switzerland, the upper Rhine River Valley, and Tyrol. These Brethren were forced into hiding or to more hospitable regions to the east in Austria and Moravia due to persecution by the Catholic Hapsburg rulers.

THE SCHLEITHEIM CONFESSION

The Schleitheim Confession was the earliest statement of faith by a group of Anabaptists and summarized their convictions. It was penned by Michael Sattler (1490–1527) and approved by a conference of Anabaptists at Schleitheim, on the German side of the Rhine River, in 1527. It consisted of seven articles.

First, baptism was for believers only:

> Baptism shall be given to all those who have learned repentance and amendment of life, and who believe truly that their sins are taken away by Christ, and to all those who walk in the resurrection of Jesus Christ, and wish to be buried with him in death, so that they may be resurrected with him, and to all those who with this significance request it [baptism] of us and demand it for themselves. This excludes all infant baptism, the highest and chief abomination of the pope. In this you have the foundation and testimony of the apostles. Mt. 28, Mk. 16, Acts 2, 8, 16, 19. This we wish to hold simply, yet firmly and with assurance.[3]

Second, if a person was not perceived to be living a Christian life, he was placed under "the ban." No one, not even a spouse, was to speak or have contact with someone who had been banned. Third, the breaking of bread or Lord's Supper was for baptized believers. Fourth, believers were to separate themselves from evil.

They were to have no contact with anyone who was ungodly. Fifth, pastors were to be of good repute, teach, exhort, and be supported by the church.

Sixth, believers were never to take up the sword, not even in self-defense. For this reason they should not hold office or join the military. The confession stated:

> It will be observed that it is not appropriate for a Christian to serve in the magistrate because of these points: The government's magistracy is according to the flesh, but the Christians' is according to the Spirit; their houses and dwellings remain in this world, but the Christians' citizenship is in heaven; the weapons of their conflict are war and carnal and against the flesh only, but the Christians' weapons are spiritual, against the fornication of the devil. The worldlings are armed with steel and iron, but the Christians are armed with the armor of God, with truth, righteousness, peace, faith, salvation and the Word of God. In brief, as is the mind of Christ toward us, so shall the mind of the members of the body of Christ be through Him in all things, that there may be no schism in the body through which it would be destroyed.[4]

Seventh, oaths were prohibited based on Jesus' statement in Matthew 5:37, "Let your word 'yes' be 'yes,' and your 'no' be 'no.' Anything more than this is from the evil one."

THE SOUTH GERMANS

Balthasar Hubmaier received his doctorate in theology at Ingolstadt in Bavaria and then joined the faculty. He became preacher at Regensburg Cathedral in 1516 and in 1523 in Waldshut, Austria. While in Waldshut he became an evangelical believer, breaking with Rome.

He met with Zwingli in 1523 and participated in the Second Zurich Disputation. He later spoke out against infant baptism and made an enemy of Zwingli. He accepted believer's baptism in 1525, helped the peasants during the war of 1525, and on December 6, 1525, fled Waldshut. In *Concerning Heretics and Those Who Burn Them* (1525), he insisted that magistrates did not have the authority to persecute the church. He also called for religious freedom and the separation of church and state. However, he differed with the majority of pacifist Anabaptists because he believed Christians could use the sword to punish criminals and defend one's city.

Hubmaier believed he would find shelter when he and his fellow refuges arrived at Zurich. Instead, Zwingli had him arrested and forced him to recant his opposition to infant baptism.

Hubmaier finally relocated to Nikolsburg, Moravia, where the teachings of Jan Hus continued to influence the Czech and German populace. According to some reports, he baptized about 6,000 people while there. He insisted on scriptural authority alone, preached in the local vernacular, and reaffirmed his belief in adult baptism: "The meaning of this sign and symbol (baptism) is the pledge of faith until death, in hope of the resurrection of life to come, is to be considered more than a sign. This meaning has nothing to do with babes, therefore infant baptism is without validity. In baptism one pledges himself to God, in the Supper to his neighbor."[5]

Ferdinand, Archduke of Austria (1521–1564) and future Holy Roman Emperor (1558–1564), arrested Hubmaier and had him burned at the stake on March 10, 1528, in Vienna. Three days later his wife was executed by drowning in the Danube River. Hubmaier influenced Anabaptist congregations that developed from Strasburg to Moravia.

Pilgrim Marpeck (d. 1556) was one of the most important Anabaptist pastors and church organizers in South Germany. His greatest strength was his exposition of the Scriptures. Untrained in any exegetical tradition, he interpreted the Scriptures in a practical and pastoral manner. His interpretations allowed him to explain concepts such as the church, eschatology, the gospel, and the Trinity in a way his congregants could grasp. Marpeck saw a great difference between the Old and New Testaments and held that since Christ was the center of the New Testament, it must be superior to the Old. He believed the Catholic Church, Luther, and Zwingli failed to make this distinction. Marpeck helped lay the foundation of the believers' church in South Germany.

Jacob Hutter (ca. 1500–1536) trained in Prague as a hatmaker. He gravitated to Anabaptism in Klagenfurt, Austria, in 1529 and began to preach in Tyrol in Western Austria. He fled to Moravia in 1533. He brought several Anabaptist communal settlements together as the Hutterite Brethren, a group that taught pacifism and the sharing of goods. When the Moravian government moved against the Anabaptists in 1535, they fled to surrounding countries. Hutter went to Tyrol, where he was arrested and ordered to recant. He refused and was burned at the stake on February 25, 1536.

Menno Simons (1496–1561) was a parish priest in Friesland. But he became disenchanted with the doctrine of Catholicism, accepted evangelical views, and left the Catholic Church in 1536. After meeting six Anabaptist refugees, he became convinced that infant baptism was wrong, received believer's baptism, and joined the Anabaptists. He described his decision:

> Then I, without constraint, of a sudden, renounced all my worldly reputation, name and fame, my unchristian abominations, my masses, infant baptism, and my easy life, and I willingly submitted to distress and poverty under the heavy cross of Christ. In my weakness I feared God; I sought out the pious and though they were few in number I found some who were zealous and maintained the truth.[6]

As an Anabaptist, Simons stressed pacifism and the strict use of excommunication. He believed Christians should obey the government unless it interfered with their faith. One could serve the state but not in ways that might require violence, he said. He was declared a heretic in 1537 and spent the remaining twenty-four years of his life evading persecution. His followers founded the Mennonite Church.

The Millenarian Revolutionaries

Some Anabaptists promoted a radical millenarianism. The upheaval and religious persecution caused by the Reformation convinced them they were living in the end times described in the book of Revelation. Some groups became violent. They wanted to hurry the end along by attacking their opponents or, as they put it, "separating the wheat from the chaff."

Melchior Hoffman (1490–1543), Jan Matthys (d. 1534), and John of Leiden (1510–1536) were influenced by both Luther's teachings and the Zwickau Prophets. As a lay preacher in Wolmar, Dorpat, and Revel, Hoffman became active in iconoclasm. He then traveled to Wittenberg where he sought Luther's advice. Luther told him to abstain from iconoclasm. He was forced to relocate to Stockholm in 1526 but was soon expelled for iconoclastic preaching. Luther was also disturbed by Hoffman's support for the Zwinglian form of the Lord's Supper, his belief that the government should not interfere with the church, and his belief that each congregation should govern itself. Hoffman briefly lived in Denmark and was expelled from Kiel, Germany.

He relocated to the more tolerant city of Strasbourg in 1530 and joined the Anabaptists there. In Strasbourg he began to promote the idea that Christ did not receive his human flesh from Mary but had heavenly or celestial flesh. This belief became known as Melchiorite Christology and was adopted by many Anabaptist groups in Northern Germany and the Netherlands.

Hoffman announced that Christ's millennial reign would begin in 1533 at Strasbourg, which he called the "New Jerusalem." He instructed his followers to arm themselves for the imminent apocalypse, then traveled to Denmark to gain more followers. His most important disciple was Matthys, a baker. When Hoffman returned to Strasbourg, he arranged to have himself arrested; he died in prison ten years later. After 1533 passed, Matthys announced that he was the biblical Enoch and assumed leadership of the Hoffmanite Anabaptist movement.

Because of Bernhard Rothmann's (1495–1535) preaching in 1533, the city of Münster in Northwest Germany embraced an evangelical and Anabaptist reform movement. Persecuted Anabaptists began to pour into the city. Consequently, Matthys relocated to Münster, announced that it was the New Jerusalem, and called all true believers to gather there. Matthys announced that citizens had to prepare the city for the coming of God by taking up the sword and killing the ungodly. In 1534 the radicals took control of the city, abolished all private holdings, instituted communalism, and required that everyone receive believer's baptism or leave the city. More than a thousand people were baptized, but many of the citizens left and were replaced by even more radical refugees. The Catholic bishop of Münster, Franz von Waldeck (1491–1552), was expelled. He soon returned with an army and laid siege to the city.

After his prophesied date of the Lord's return passed, Matthys and thirty of his followers attacked the bishop's forces. They were all killed. Matthys's head was cut off and displayed on a pole for all the citizens of Münster to see.

John of Leiden became the next leader of the apocalyptic Anabaptists of Münster. He declared that he was King David. He sat on a golden throne, had a harem, and lived in opulence while his followers starved. He had his opponents executed.

The siege ended in June 1535 with the storming of the city. Leiden was captured, tortured, and executed on January 22, 1536. His corpse and those of two of his followers were left to rot in cages hanging from the steeple of St. Lambert's Church. Because of the Münster Rebellion, the Anabaptists acquired a reputation of being traitors and insurrectionists. As a result, they were persecuted relentlessly and banned from many countries. In many parts of twenty-first-century Europe, people still equate advocates of believer's baptism with Münsterites.

THE SPIRITUALISTS OR INSPIRATIONALISTS

Some Radical Reformers believed they had a mystical encounter with the Holy Spirit. Kaspar Schwenckfeld (1499–1542) and Sebastian Franck (1499–1542), for example, held that the Holy Spirit took precedence over all authorities, including the Scriptures.

Franck was a priest who left the Catholic Church after being influenced by Erasmus and Luther. He joined the Protestant movement in 1525 and accepted a pastoral position in Nuremburg. By 1529, he moved away from the Magisterial Reformers and began to advocate evangelical spiritualism. He lived in Strasbourg from 1530 to 1532 and in Ulm from 1533 to 1539. Echoing the medieval mystic John Tauler in many ways, Franck believed God communicated with man through a divine essence or Spirit that resided in each person. He taught that nothing, not even the Bible, superseded or should be permitted to interfere with the direct guidance of the Spirit.

THE ANTI-TRINITARIANS

A Spaniard and former medical student at the University of Paris, Michael Servetus (1509–1553) was the most famous anti-Trinitarian author. He was a renowned physician credited with discovering the pulmonary circulation of blood. His preoccupation, however, was theology. Starting in 1531 with *Errors about the Trinity*, Servetus published several books in which he questioned orthodox views of the Trinity. He believed the names for God in the Old Testament were nothing more than different ways in which God introduced himself to the Hebrew people. This continued into the New Testament with the addition of Jesus and the Holy Spirit. Servetus's perception of the Trinity was modalistic. In 1553 he published *Restitution of Christianity*. In this text he added gnostic cosmology to his views. He made contact with John Calvin in 1545 through a bookseller and asked the Genevan Reformer questions about the Trinity. Calvin responded by sending him a copy of his *Institutes of Christian Religion*. Servetus wrote glosses in the margins where he believed Calvin erred and sent it back to him. Calvin was insulted.

For several years Servetus lived under a false identity near Lyon, but then the Catholic authorities, perhaps with Calvin's help, became aware of his presence and sought to arrest him. While fleeing Lyon, Servetus made the mistake of traveling through Geneva, where he was captured. He was condemned by Calvin, placed on trial, and burned at the stake on the orders of the city council on October 27, 1553.

An Italian humanist, Leo Sozzini (1525–1562) observed the Servetus trial and later led a group with similar beliefs in Poland. He taught that Christ was a man who became divine because God's Spirit came upon him. The obedience of Christ at the cross should be emulated by all of his followers. Sozzini denied original sin, the Trinity, and predestination. His nephew Faustus Socinus (1539–1604) published these views in the *Racovian Catechism*. Today Unitarian churches consider these men the founders of their movement.

CHAPTER EIGHTEEN

JOHN CALVIN

John Calvin (1509–1564) was a Magisterial Reformer in the ilk of Martin Luther and Ulrich Zwingli. Working primarily in Geneva, Switzerland, Calvin was among the most brilliant theologians of the Reformation era. Calvin's theological system, presented in his book *Institutes of the Christian Religion*, continues to have a profound influence on many Protestant denominations.

GENEVA

In the early sixteenth century, the Swiss cantons of Geneva and Zurich were under constant threat from their more powerful neighbors. Geneva was in the path of the ever-encroaching nation of France. The city was also on the main trade route across the Alps and, since the fourteenth century, had been a center of artisan trade and commerce.

Politically and religiously, Geneva was under the patronage of the Catholic duke of Savoy and had been ruled by the city's bishop for centuries. Though this patronage remained in place, the duke of Savoy granted the residents permission to govern their city in 1387. They established a general assembly, which elected four syndics that governed the city along with the bishop. The city broke with the

Catholic Church in 1526 and sought an alliance with Protestant Bern, rejecting its long-standing ties with Savoy. In June 1527 all Catholic priests in Geneva were expelled for fear that they were pro-Savoy. The bishop fled the city in August. Over the next eight years Geneva withstood several Savoy threats but was not drawn back into the Catholic fold. When Calvin arrived in 1536, the city was a virtual republic administered by the Little Council, the Council of Sixty, and the Council of Two Hundred.

Bern supplied Geneva's first Protestant preachers. The most important was Guillaume Farel (1489–1565) whose efforts led to the acceptance of Protestantism by the city's general assembly on May 31, 1536. Farel's most important legacy in the city was recruiting John Calvin to be its clerical leader.

JOHN CALVIN

Born in Noyon, France, sixty miles northeast of Paris, John Calvin was raised in a staunchly Catholic family. His father, Gerard (d. 1531), was secretary of the bishop of Noyon. John was educated at the University of Paris and supported financially by a benefice from the bishop of Noyon.

The direction of John's life changed when Gerard was accused of misappropriating the bishopric's funds. He resigned from his job in Noyon[1] and transferred his son to the University of Orleans to study law in 1528. The following year Calvin enrolled at the University of Bourges and received his law degree there in 1532.

While at Orleans, Calvin became acquainted with Melchior Wolmar (1497–1561), a man with Lutheran leanings, who taught him Greek and encouraged him to study the New Testament. Calvin was well on his way to the acceptance of Protestantism.

During this time (1528–1532) Calvin had a sudden religious conversion, which he described in his *Commentary on Psalms*:

He [God] tamed to teachableness a mind too stubborn for its years—for I was so strongly devoted to the Papacy that nothing less could draw me from such depths of mire. And so this mere taste of true godliness that I received set me on fire with such a desire to progress that I pursued the rest of my studies more coolly, though I did not give them up altogether.[2]

After the death of his father in 1531, Calvin returned to Paris to study theology and humanism at the College Royal. He was pushed toward Protestantism by his cousin Pierre Robert Olivétan[3] (1506–1538) and the writings of Jacques Lefèvre d'Étaples (1455–1536). In April he published his first work, a commentary on Seneca's *Treatise on Clemency*. The book was a veiled attempt to encourage Francis I of France (1515–1547) to be more tolerant of Protestantism.

In Paris Calvin found humanism in vogue, Protestantism on the rise, and the faculty of the College Royal embroiled in controversy with several members of the faculty of the University of Paris. The younger faculty members at the College Royal were advocates of humanism, and the older University of Paris faculty was devoted to scholasticism. At this time Calvin began to associate with a group of reform-minded scholars; the most influential was his old friend Nicolas Cop (ca. 1501–1540), a Protestant. On November 1, 1533, as the new rector of the University of Paris, Cop spoke of the need for reform within the Catholic Church. His speech was laced with references to Erasmus and Luther. His audience was not receptive, and he incited an anti-Protestant backlash.

Because of his ties to Cop, Calvin went into hiding for a year in Noyon and Orleans. While at Noyon he resigned his benefice and spent a brief time in prison for his Protestant views. Following a mass Protestant protest known as the Affair of the Placards[4] in 1534, King Francis viewed Protestants as anarchists, imprisoned hundreds of them, and executed thirty-five. Calvin fled to Basel in 1535, where he joined Cop.

In Basel, Calvin completed his first edition of the *Institutes of the Christian Religion* (1536) and dedicated it to Francis. In the *Institutes* he responded to the false accusations levied against the French Protestants. Following Luther's *Small Catechism*, it began with an exposition of God's law, the Apostles' Creed, the Lord's Prayer, the two sacraments, and Christian liberty. Between its first edition and its final edition in 1559, the *Institutes* grew from six to eighty chapters and became the first complete systematic theology of Protestantism.

In early 1536 Calvin traveled to Ferrara, Italy, to visit Princess Reneé of France (1510–1574). In June he returned to Paris to settle his father's affairs. He then determined to go to Strasbourg. On his journey he traveled through Geneva, where he met Farel. Farel told him God would be displeased if he did not assist him in Geneva. Believing God was speaking through Farel, Calvin changed his plans.

Calvin and Farel brought to the city's Little Council their *Articles on the Organization of the Church and Its Worship at Geneva.* The council adopted the document. In it the Reformers laid out their plans for congregational singing, the mandatory observance of the Lord's Supper at least once a month,[5] church discipline, and excommunication. To protect the sanctity of the Lord's Supper, they reserved the right to deny it to those deemed unworthy. They proposed that all citizens be required to sign a confession of faith affirming Protestant beliefs.

A new city council elected in 1538, however, did not believe the church had a right to impose social morality. The council believed such issues fell to them. Within a year, Calvin and Farel fell out of favor. Many citizens believed they were trying to hand Geneva over to France. Further complicating matters, Bern was attempting to impose Zwinglian views on Geneva with the acquiescence of the council.

In 1538, the Council of Two Hundred mandated that the Lord's Supper be given to all citizens and that the Bern model of using unleavened bread be followed. The Reformers did not care if unleavened bread was used but refused to allow everyone in the city to take the Lord's Supper. To them it appeared that the Council of Two Hundred was attempting to remove church discipline from the ministers and place it in their own hands. In defiance, on Easter Sunday 1538 the Reformers refused to serve the Lord's Supper. They were immediately asked to leave Geneva and did so on April 23.

Farel relocated to the Swiss canton of Neuchâtel, and Calvin accepted an invitation from Martin Bucer (1491–1551) to come to Strasbourg. While in Strasbourg, Calvin married Idelette de Bure (d. 1549). He remained in Strasbourg for three years (1538–1541), pastoring a congregation of nearly 500, most of whom were displaced French Protestants. During this time he expanded the *Institutes* to seventeen chapters, making it a theological textbook for ministers. In his 1540 *Commentary on Romans*, Calvin used Greek texts and provided a detailed exposition. He also participated in theological discussions in Worms, Frankfurt, and Hagenau. While in Worms, he met Philip Melanchthon, who was so impressed with Calvin that he nicknamed him "the theologian."

By 1540, the political and religious situation in Geneva changed. Those who pushed for Calvin's removal lost power in 1539, and many were perceived as traitors. Geneva's relationship with Bern was strained, and Cardinal Sadoleto (1477–1547), the bishop of Carpentras, attempted to bring Geneva back into the Catholic fold. In a letter Sadoleto informed the citizens of Geneva that they had moved away from the true faith and should return to the one true church. Geneva did not want to return to Catholicism but did not have anyone who could rebut Sadoleto's arguments. Calvin was asked to write the reply. In his *Reply to Sadoleto*, Calvin argued:

> You teach that all which has been approved for fifteen hundred years or more, by the uniform consent of

the faithful, is, by our headstrong rashness, torn up and destroyed. . . . But our agreement with antiquity is far closer than yours; all we have attempted has been to renew the ancient form of the Church which, at first distorted and stained by illiterate men of indifferent character, was afterwards criminally mangled and almost destroyed by the Roman pontiff and his faction.[6]

For this refutation of Sadoleto, Calvin was viewed as hero and invited to return to Geneva. Arriving on September 13, 1541, he was named pastor of the cathedral of Saint Pierre and given a generous salary. He immediately pressed forward with his *Ecclesiastical Ordinances*, which the city council accepted on November 20, 1541. The *Ordinances* outlined the church offices of pastor, teacher, and elder. (All pastors were elders, but not all elders were pastors.) A church court known as the Consistory was composed of Geneva's ministers, two members of the Small Council, four from the Council of Sixty, and six from the Council of Two Hundred. The Consistory's makeup demonstrated the close collaboration of church and state in Geneva. Calvin and the Consistory instituted a wide range of ecclesiastical laws and judged cases of blasphemy, adultery, poor church attendance, and other disciplinary issues. In short, the Consistory was to monitor the citizens' conduct to ensure they were living as God's people. It would counsel and finally excommunicate the unrepentant. No one was to speak against the Consistory or Calvin. Everyone was to be watched. Members of the Consistory "should be elected in such a manner that there will be some of them in each quarter of the city, so that their eyes will be everywhere."[7]

An early example of stifling the freedom to disagree with Calvin occurred in 1544. Sebastián Castellion (1515–1563) was exiled from Geneva for disagreeing with Calvin's interpretation of Christ's descent into hell and for believing that the *Song of Songs* was not canonical. Another citizen, Jacques Gruet (d. 1547), protested that Calvin ruled Geneva as an autocrat, the citizens had no freedom, and in trials Calvin served as both judge and jury. Gruet was accused of leaving an acrimonious and threatening letter addressed to Calvin on the Saint Pierre pulpit. Gruet was arrested, tortured, and, after being forced to confess to a myriad of heresies, beheaded on July 26, 1547. Calvin silenced Jerome Bolsec (d. 1584) for daring to challenge his teaching on predestination and convinced the city council to banish him in 1551.

Calvin had several enemies who believed he had instituted his own Inquisition. Since a large number of French refugees extremely devoted to Calvin came to Geneva from 1548 to 1555, the native-born feared that Calvin would become a tyrant or deliver Geneva to the French. In February 1553 Calvin's enemies were elected to several important positions, and it appeared his exile was imminent. The arrival of the anti-Trinitarian Michael Servetus (1511–1553) and his execution proved to be Calvin's saving grace. Though the execution of Servetus marred Calvin's legacy, it caused citizens of Geneva to view him as the defender of orthodoxy. The next elections in 1554 turned out in Calvin's favor, and the Consistory regained power in all ecclesiastical affairs. By 1559, Calvin was the virtual ruler of Geneva. After suffering from declining health for several years, John Calvin died on May 27, 1564.

Calvin's Theology

Based largely on the Pauline letters and Augustine's theological interpretations, Calvin's theological system was defined in his 1559 *Institutes* and elaborated on in his *Commentaries on the New Testament*.[8] Similar to Augustine's thought, the *Institutes* assert the centrality of the Bible, the sovereignty of God, the bondage of the human will because of sin, and justification by grace through faith. For Calvin, Scripture was the paramount authority, and his entire system was based on it. Church tradition was a secondary authority.

Calvin began the *Institutes* by discussing what man could know about God and himself. Calvin maintained that nature revealed

God and made everyone responsible for knowing him. No one, therefore, could claim ignorance of God, and all were guilty of sin. Saving knowledge, however, came only from the Scriptures. The Scriptures taught that all good comes from God. But the Scriptures could only be understood by those who were enlightened by the Holy Spirit. The Old Testament had a more important place in Calvin's system than in Luther's. It served as a moral guide for the Christian life. Unlike Luther, who accepted practices that were not explicitly forbidden in the Bible, Calvin agreed with Zwingli and disallowed anything not explicitly sanctioned in the Bible. He rejected all feasts, festivals, icons, images, and even the celebration of Christmas.

As Calvin's system rested on God's complete sovereignty, predestination had a role. In Book Three of the *Institutes*, he defined *predestination* as

> the eternal decree of God, by which he determined with himself whatever he wished to happen with regard to every man. All are not created on equal terms, but some are preordained to eternal life, others to eternal damnation; and, accordingly, as each has been created for one or other of these ends, we say that he has been predestined to life or to death.[9]

The concept of double predestination (specific election to either heaven or hell) disturbed many Christians. Calvin, however, meant it to provide comfort for the elect. His successor in Geneva and chief disciple, Theodore Beza (1519–1605), reinforced this belief to assure believers that God's gracious purpose in their lives could not be thwarted. There were signs that could give evidence of saving faith and thus election. If one were of the elect, his life would manifest good works. These fruits would provide the person with assurance that he was numbered among God's people.

The elect were to transform the world to conform to Christ's rule as much as they were able. Everyone was called to an occupation to be performed for the glory of God. This gave Calvinists the reputation of being hard workers and honest. In *The Protestant Ethic and the Spirit of Capitalism* (1904), Max Weber (1864–1920) argued that this Reformed work ethic promoted economic success.

In matters of ecclesiology, Calvin maintained that the church was led by pastors and teachers, as well as lay elders and deacons. The task of the pastor was to preach, serve the sacraments, and provide leadership. Teachers were to give instruction in religion and doctrine. Elders were to oversee morality. Deacons were to dispense charity.

Baptism and the Lord's Supper were the only sacraments. Calvin insisted on infant baptism, arguing that like circumcision under the old covenant, it brought the children of believers into God's covenant people. Elect infants could be regenerated in infancy, he said, and cited John the Baptist as an example. The sacrament of baptism showed God's forgiveness. For Calvin, election and infant baptism complemented each other. He rejected the physical or bodily presence of Christ in the Lord's Supper. Instead, he believed in the spiritual presence of Christ in the Supper. Communion served as a reminder of Christ's sacrifice and a symbol of unity among Christians. The Holy Spirit ministered to believers through the Lord's Supper in a unique way, he said. Calvin wrote:

> That sacred communication of his own flesh and blood by which Christ pours his life into us, just as if he were to penetrate into the marrow of our bones, he witnesses and attests in the Supper. And he does not by putting before us a vain or empty sign, but offering there the efficacy of his Spirit, by which he fulfills his promise. And in truth he offers and displays the thing there signaled to all who share that spiritual feast; though only by the faithful it is perceived and its fruits enjoyed. . . . If it is true that the visible

sign is offered to us to attest the granting of the invisible reality, then, on receiving the symbol of the body, we may be confident that the body is no less given to us.[10]

The preaching of the word was the heart of Christian worship and should be understood by all, according to Calvin. Sermons, therefore, were delivered in the vernacular and in a simple manner. The Holy Spirit would use the sermon to aid the elect to understand and apply Scripture to life.

Christians were encouraged to participate in the government as long as it did not interfere with their faith.

EXPANSION OF THE REFORMED FAITH

Calvin's theological system was by no means exclusive to Geneva. In 1549, the *Consensus Tigurinus* defined the Lord's Supper in a manner that was acceptable to both Calvin and Zurich's Zwinglians. With their unification the northern Swiss cantons became staunchly Reformed.

The Reformed movement spread to France, the Low Countries, and Scotland for three reasons. First, as a clear exposition of the Reformed faith, the *Institutes* provided a doctrinal standard. Second, Calvin and Beza sent out hundreds of ministers from Geneva's Academy. Third, Geneva became a refuge for exiled Protestants. When they arrived in Geneva, they were impressed with Calvin's theocracy and the way it appeared to spawn godliness. When they returned home, they tried to model their churches and countries after Geneva. The great Reformer of Scotland, John Knox (1514–1572), proclaimed that Geneva was "the most perfect school of Christ that ever was on earth since the days of the Apostles."[11]

As Geneva was just across the border, France was one of the first places in which Calvin's system took root. More than 150 ministers poured into France, planted forty-nine congregations, and made a large number of converts among the middle class. In 1549 a national synod was held in Paris, and the Gallican Confession of Faith, prepared by Calvin himself, was adopted. The French Calvinists became known as Huguenots.[12] In two years the number of Huguenot congregations grew to 2,150.

France, however, had strong ties to the papacy. The French monarchy persecuted Huguenots, and there was widespread conflict between Protestants and loyal Catholics from 1532 to 1562. With ten-year-old Charles IX (1550–1574) on the throne, his mother Catherine de Medici (1519–1589) pursued warfare until a truce was declared in 1570. On August 18, 1572, the Huguenot Henry IV of Navarre (1553–1610) married the Catholic Margaret of Valois (1553–1615) to promote peace.

But on August 24, Catherine sent assassins to kill the Huguenot leaders. In what became known as the Saint Bartholomew's Day Massacre, more than 2,000 Huguenots in Paris and from 7,000 to 8,000 in the surrounding provinces were murdered. This led to renewed warfare between Catholics and Huguenots. After great difficulty Henry of Navarre gained the French throne in 1589 as Henry IV; he took control of the Paris area in 1593, following his conversion to Catholicism. He reportedly said, "Paris is worth a mass." After five years of persecuting Protestants, Henry IV issued the Edict of Nantes in 1598, which granted toleration to Huguenots.

The Edict remained in force until 1685, when Louis XIV (1643–1715) revoked it. Many of the Huguenots then migrated to Germany, Switzerland, the Netherlands, South Africa, and England. Others settled in colonial North America, where their Calvinism flourished.

The spread of the Reformed faith in the Low Countries (Belgium, Netherlands, and Luxembourg) was aided by popular hatred of the Catholic Hapsburg rulers. The Catholic Church was guilty by association. As devout "papists," the Spanish authorities outlawed all but Catholic worship in the Low Countries. King Charles V (1516–1556) persecuted and martyred thousands of Anabaptists and Lutherans throughout the Low Countries.

Prior to the arrival of Reformed ministers in the early 1550s, the majority of Protestants in the Low Countries were Anabaptists. They stressed pacifism, which kept many from taking up arms against the Spanish. The Reformed, though, had no reservations about taking up arms against oppressive rulers.

The Reformed population grew to such a degree that a national synod was held in 1559 to form the Dutch Reformed Church. It adopted the Belgic Confession in 1566. The confession unified the citizens and promoted a sense of nationalism. Flush with confidence, the Protestants rebelled in 1566 and destroyed images of saints throughout the region. The Protestants claimed that if they were wrong in doing so, God would protect the Catholic Church's sacred images. Spanish king Philip II (1556–1598) sent 10,000 troops to the Low Countries in 1569. They executed 2,000 Protestants and forced thousands more to flee. The Dutch, however, refused to surrender. The Netherlands declared independence in 1581 with its established Reformed Church. In the south, the Spanish Netherlands (later renamed Belgium) remained Catholic.

From November 13, 1618, to May 9, 1619, a synod was held at Dordrecht (Dordt) in the Netherlands to determine the proper interpretation of the Reformed faith. The synod was called in response to the teachings of Jacob Arminius (1560–1609). A professor at Leiden, Arminius was a Calvinist who studied under Theodore Beza in Geneva. Arminius determined that predestination was based on God's foreknowledge, atonement was not limited, grace could be resisted, and one could fall away from the faith. Arminius's teachings became popular, and his followers became known as Remonstrants.

The Synod of Dordrecht drew Reformed participants from other European lands and condemned the position of Arminius and the Remonstrants. It adopted what became known as the Canons of Dordt. The canons stressed that all people were depraved. Because of the fall of Adam and the corruption it introduced, man could do nothing to save himself. Election was not due to God's foreknowledge. It was God's sovereign choice. Humans were morally incapable of believing in Christ before the Holy Spirit regenerated them. Christ's atonement for sin was limited to the elect. He died only for them. If a person was chosen by God, he or she could not fully and finally resist the call of the Holy Spirit. The elect would persevere and could not fall from grace or lose salvation. These Canons became known as the "Five Points" of Calvinism.

A minister in the Church of England, chaplain to King Edward VI, and former Catholic priest, John Knox, "the Thundering Scot," brought Reformed theology to Scotland. During the reign of the Catholic Queen Mary Tudor (1553–1558), Knox found refuge in Geneva. There he became acquainted with and accepted Calvin's Reformed theology and embraced Presbyterian church polity. After Mary's death in 1558, he returned to Scotland with his newly acquired Reformed theology in tow. A powerful preacher, Knox became the most influential minister in his homeland and helped to create the Presbyterian Church of Scotland in 1560.

Knox also played a prominent role in the birth of English Puritanism. While in exile, he was briefly pastor to fellow exiles in Frankfurt (September 24, 1554–March 26, 1555). Almost immediately upon his arrival, a disagreement erupted in the congregation. One group desired a strict interpretation of the second *Book of Common Prayer* (1552). They were tied to the Church of England. Knox identified with the second group, which sought to modify the second *Book of Common Prayer* and adopt a more Reformed liturgy. Among this second group were the first Puritans. The disagreement became so vitriolic that Knox left Frankfurt and returned to Geneva. This event marked the end of his days in the Church of England. However, he continued to criticize it for retaining too many Roman Catholic practices and using the second *Book of Common Prayer*.

Upon becoming queen, Mary Tudor immediately began to persecute Protestants. Along with Knox, English Protestants found refuge in Geneva. They adopted the Reformed system, and after the Protestant Queen Elizabeth (1558–1603) took the throne, they returned to England. Like Knox, they wanted to purify the Church of England of all remnants of Catholicism. For this reason they became known as Puritans. Some Puritans remained in the Church of England. Others separated from it and were persecuted by Elizabeth and her successors James I (1603–1625) and Charles I (1625–1649). Many Puritans fled to New England where they shaped both church and state according to Calvinist principles.

CHAPTER NINETEEN

THE ENGLISH REFORMATION, PURITANISM, AND SEPARATISM

According to the Venerable Bede's *Ecclesiastical History of the English People*, England became a Catholic nation in 597. The English people, however, had a long history of resisting papal decrees that they believed were not in their national interest. As early as 1066, William the Conqueror (1028–1087) refused to swear allegiance to Pope Gregory VII (1073–1085). Other monarchs clashed with the papacy over lay investiture and papal taxation. During the Avignon papacy, the monarchs and citizens of England agreed that money donated to the English church should remain in England. The attempted reforms of John Wycliffe and the Lollards were popular. Erasmian humanism was making inroads at Oxford and Cambridge universities. Martin Luther's writings were beginning to find their way into England. Moreover, William Tyndale's (1492–1536)[1] English translation of the Bible introduced his countrymen to the evangelical faith.

THE KING'S GREAT MATTER

The Reformation on the continent had little in common with the religious changes that occurred in England. The Reformation of Luther, Calvin, and Zwingli was based on religious principles.

The Reformation in England was based on politics in the guise of religion.

The English Reformation had its roots in King Henry VII's (1485–1509) attempt to strengthen the Tudors' hold on the English throne.[2] One of his first acts was to form an alliance with Spain through marriage. Henry's oldest son and heir, Arthur (1486–1502), married Catherine of Aragon (1485–1536), the oldest daughter of King Ferdinand (1479–1516) and Queen Isabella (1474–1504) of Spain. Arthur, however, died six months later.

Henry VII died in 1509, and his son, Henry VIII (1509–1547), was crowned king of England. Henry then married Catherine, and his famous quest for an heir began. The Tudors had recently won the crown in the War of the Roses, and Henry realized he needed a male heir to ensure the dynasty. Other than the uncertain reign of Matilda (1107–1167) in the twelfth century, England had never been ruled by a female monarch. Only a son would guarantee the perpetuation of the Tudor line.

When Catherine became pregnant in 1515, Henry and all of England hoped that she would bear a son. Their hopes were dashed on February 18, 1516, when a daughter, Mary (1516–1558), was born. Further efforts to produce a male heir ended in disappointment. Mary was their only child to live to adulthood. Since Henry fathered at least one illegitimate son, he began to believe the problem was with Catherine. Moreover, Henry became infatuated with Anne Boleyn (1501–1536), whom he believed would provide him with a son.

Henry and his advisors decided in 1527 to seek an annulment of his marriage to Catherine. For this he needed permission from Pope Clement VII (1523–1534). As grounds for the annulment, Henry claimed Catherine and Arthur had consummated their marriage. He then cited Leviticus 20:21,[3] which forbade a man to marry his brother's wife. Henry apparently believed that God was punishing him for breaking this scriptural law. Since Henry had been named

"Defender of the Faith" by Pope Leo X (1513–1521) for writing *In Defense of the Seven Sacraments* (1521) against Martin Luther, he expected the annulment to be granted quickly. Henry's most trusted minister, Cardinal Woolsey (1473–1530), was charged with securing it.

Controversy, however, was unavoidable. Pope Julius II (1503–1513) granted a papal dispensation for Henry to marry Catherine, and no pope wanted to repeal a dictum issued by a predecessor. In addition, Catherine was the aunt of Charles V, Holy Roman emperor (1519–1556) and king of Spain (1516–1556). Charles had recently campaigned in Italy and held the pope prisoner. Charles did not want to see his aunt humiliated. Moreover, if Henry and Catherine did not have a male heir, Charles would have a claim to the English throne. Because he was unable to secure the annulment, Cardinal Woolsey lost favor with Henry. Woolsey later died of an illness on his way to London to be tried for treason.

After being denied by Rome, Henry began to seek opinions on his "great matter" from dons of the great European universities. Though not all supported his position, the majority held that England was an independent nation and the king held sovereign authority. Therefore, he could not be denied an annulment.

With the aid of Thomas Cranmer (1489–1556) and the skilled jurist Thomas Cromwell (1485–1540), Henry decided to sever ties with Rome. His first step was to force the English Convocations, official assemblies of clergy members, to bow to his will. In 1530, he accused the English clergy of sending money to Rome to destabilize his reign, a serious crime. He also condemned the clerics for approving Woolsey as a papal legate without his consent. The Convocations were terrified of how Henry might punish them, named him Supreme Head of the English Church and Clergy, and paid a hefty fine to ensure his forgiveness. He appointed Thomas Cranmer as archbishop of Canterbury in 1532 and began to confiscate church properties. In 1533 Parliament passed the Act of Restraint of

Appeals, stating that all ecclesiastical judgments would be rendered in England without consulting Rome. Cranmer then annulled the king's marriage to Catherine, and he married the already pregnant Anne Boleyn in 1533.

Parliament passed the Act of Supremacy on November 3, 1534. The act stated:

> Albeit the king's majesty justly and rightfully is and ought to be the supreme head of the church of England, and so is recognized by the clergy of this realm in the Convocations, yet nevertheless for corroboration and confirmation thereof, and for increase of virtue in Christ's religion within the realm of England, and to repress and extirp [destroy] all errors, heresies, and other enormities and abuses heretofore used in the same; be it enacted by authority of this present Parliament, that the king our sovereign lord, his heirs and successors, kings of this realm, shall be taken, accepted, and reputed the only supreme head in earth of the Church of England, called the *Anglican Ecclesia*.[4]

This Act of Supremacy created a Church of England separate from Rome and made the ruling monarch its head. The clergy were required to give their first loyalty to the king. Anyone who rejected this act was executed for treason. Henry's friend and former tutor Thomas More (1478–1535) and a number of Carthusian monks were among the more prominent victims to be executed under this act. In 1534, the Restraint of Annates, denying the papacy any income from English churches, was enacted. Pope Paul II (1534–1549) then began the process of excommunicating Henry. In August 1535, Paul sent a letter warning Henry that if he did not stop usurping Rome's authority, he would be excommunicated.

In 1536, Henry replied by confiscating property and money from the Catholic Church in England. Based on an investigation by Cromwell that accused monks of living irreverent lives, Henry dissolved 376 monasteries and seized the lands. By 1540, the number of dissolved monasteries had grown to 800. This action intensified the loyalty of many citizens to Henry, but many to the north found it reprehensible. The result was the Pilgrimage of Grace, in which thousands from York and the surrounding territories marched south to protest the suppression of the Catholic Church and the dissolution of monasteries.[5] By making promises that he had no intention of keeping, Henry persuaded the participants to disband. The leaders and more than 200 participants were executed within a year.

Henry's second marriage ended after Anne bore only a daughter, Elizabeth (1558–1603). Because of court rumors that Anne was unfaithful and unable to provide a male heir, Henry soon became dissatisfied with his second queen. He divorced her and saw to her execution in 1536. In hope of producing a male heir, he married four more times.

Henry broke with Rome but not with the Catholic faith. Aside from the refusal to recognize the authority of the pope, the Church of England differed little in practice from the Catholic Church. Henry issued the Church of England's first articles of faith in 1536. These Ten Articles affirmed the sacraments of baptism, penance, and the Eucharist. Images were retained but not to be worshipped.

To affirm his Catholic faith, Henry issued and saw to the approval of Six Articles in 1539. These Articles affirmed transubstantiation, private masses, celibacy for all clergy, and that in the Eucharist only the bread would be offered. Under the influence of Cranmer, one of Henry's few contributions to true reform was his allowance of an English Bible, known as the Great Bible, to be placed in all parish churches in 1538.

After Henry's death in 1547, Edward VI (1547–1553), his son by Jane Seymour (1508–1537) and only legitimate male heir, came to the throne. Edward was educated by Protestant tutors appointed by Henry. As Edward was only nine years old at his coronation, his uncle Edward Seymour (1506–1552), the Duke of Somerset, served as his first protector, ruling on his behalf while he was a child. Under Seymour's tutelage Edward embraced Protestantism. The Six Articles and many heresy laws were repealed, the cup was given to the laity, images were removed from churches, and priests were permitted to marry. Written by Thomas Cranmer in 1549, the *Book of Common Prayer* became the Church of England's official guide for worship. It also contained its doctrinal standards. In an attempt at a *via media*, the *Book of Common Prayer* tried to depict the sacraments in a manner that was acceptable to both Protestants and Catholics. It outlined how prayers were to be said, the hours of church services, the administration of the sacraments, and an episcopal form of church government. To appease Catholics, the Church of England retained several Catholic practices such as prayer for the dead and the wearing of vestments. Protestants who desired a less Catholic Church of England were not pleased and pressed for a more complete break.

The Duke of Northumberland, devout Protestant John Dudley (1504–1553), replaced Seymour as Edward's primary advisor in 1550 but chose the term *regent* rather than *protector*. Dudley's religious inclinations were apparent in the 1552 revision of the *Book of Common Prayer*. Prayers for the dead, exorcism, and all references to the Mass were removed. A declaration at the end known as the Black Rubric required laity to kneel at Communion but not to adore the host.

The Forty-Two Articles were issued by Royal Mandate in 1553. All members of the clergy, university professors, and students were required to subscribe to them. The articles denounced the pope and transubstantiation. Soon afterwards, all images associated with Catholicism, such as crosses, statues, and altars, were removed from churches. Ministers were permitted to marry and the laity received Communion in both kinds. During Edward's reign the Church of England temporarily became much more Protestant. Yet he was sickly from birth and died in 1553. Dudley attempted to place Lady

Jane Grey (1536–1554), his daughter-in-law, on the throne, but after a brief reign she was removed.

With no male heirs remaining, Henry's eldest daughter, Mary (1553–1558) became queen of England. Like her mother Catherine, Mary was a staunch Catholic. In order to be accepted as the legitimate queen, she reestablished the Catholic Church and in 1554 had Parliament declare her mother's marriage to Henry valid. Mary rescinded the *Book of Common Prayer*, the Forty-Two Articles, and all religious laws passed by Henry VIII and Edward VI. She removed all Protestants from political office. Mary especially wanted to ensure that children were brought up in the Catholic faith. The Royal Injunctions, passed on March 4, 1554, stated in Article Seventeen:

> That they examine all schoolmasters and teachers of children, and finding them suspect in any wise, to remove them and place Catholic men in their rooms, with a special commandment to instruct their children, so as they may be able to answer the priest at the Mass and so help the priest to Mass as has been accustomed.[6]

More than 800 Protestants, known as "Marian exiles," fled to the continent. Of those remaining in England, "Bloody Mary" put 300 to death. Vacillating between returning to the Catholic fold to save his life and remaining a Protestant, Thomas Cranmer chose to die a Protestant martyr. To cement her ties to the papacy and to ensure that England would remain Catholic, the queen married Phillip II (1556–1598), the future king of Spain, in 1554. Phillip stayed in England until September 1555 and then returned to Spain. Like her brother Edward, Mary was frail and died childless in 1558.

Mary's half-sister Elizabeth, Henry VIII's daughter by Anne Boleyn, became queen. (Mary had imprisoned her in the Tower of London to prevent the Protestants from crowning her.) For the same reason that Mary feared Protestantism, Elizabeth feared

Catholicism. If the Catholic Church were in power, Elizabeth would be regarded as illegitimate. To remedy this potential problem, Elizabeth immediately reinstated the Church of England, the *Book of Common Prayer*, and the Act of Supremacy. She also instituted the Thirty-Nine Articles, a revision of the Forty-Two Articles, which explained the differences between the Anglican and Catholic Churches. Any remaining Catholic clergy were sent into exile.

Even though she reasserted the religious policies of Henry VIII, the early years of Elizabeth's reign were marked by attempts to mollify English Catholics and unify the country. Nevertheless, she was excommunicated by the pope in 1570. When Catholic plots and assassination attempts began in 1585, her position changed. She began to persecute Catholics and send military aid to Protestants in Scotland and France. Elizabeth also sent soldiers to aid the Protestants of the Netherlands in their bid for independence from Spain. This made war with Spain inevitable. In 1587, Elizabeth executed her cousin Queen Mary of Scots (1542–1587), who was found guilty of attempting to overthrow her. In 1588, Spain gained papal permission and attempted to invade England in order to return it to Catholicism. The English defeated the Spanish Armada on July 12, and the threat was averted.

With a Protestant queen on the throne, the Marian exiles returned to England. They compared Elizabeth to the biblical character Deborah and declared her able to preside over a godly nation. These exiles, particularly those who found a home in Geneva, had changed theologically. Many embraced Calvinism and hoped to model England after Geneva. Their first goal was to purify the Church of England of any remnants of Catholicism. For this reason they became known as Puritans. Elizabeth, however, proved to be a great disappointment to them. She retained many traditional Catholic practices the Puritans argued did not have a scriptural basis. They believed practices without precedent in the Bible should be banned from worship. For this reason they despised the 1559

Book of Common Prayer, which emphasized genuflecting, the office of bishop, kneeling at Communion, and liturgies. Regarding the Communion rite, the wording implied both a real presence and a symbolic one. Elizabeth hoped both Protestants and Catholics would find the *Book of Common Prayer* accommodating. In 1563, she declared that it had to be used at all parish churches. Harsh penalties were imposed on those who refused to comply.

To appease the Protestants, the Thirty-Nine Articles denied that the virgin Mary was sinless (15) and the Mass was a sacrifice (31) and declared that all ministers could marry (32). Transubstantiation was repudiated in harsh terms (28): "Transubstantiation, or the change of the substance of the bread and wine into the substance of Christ's body and blood in the supper of the Lord, cannot be proved by Holy Writ, but is repugnant to the plain words of Scripture, overthroweth the nature of a sacrament, and hath given occasion to many superstitions."[7] These measures became known as the Elizabethan Settlement. Though slanted toward Protestantism, they were an attempt to form a *via media* between traditional Catholicism and Protestantism that would allow all to find a home in the Church of England. The settlement provided the Protestants with an official break from Rome and transubstantiation, but it retained many familiar liturgies and ceremonies for former Catholics.

Puritans rejected the Elizabethan Settlement and considered the *Book of Common Prayer* too Catholic. Some pressed for reform while remaining in the Church of England. Others chose to worship in their own congregations and agitate for reform in public. Elizabeth did not like her authority being challenged, so in 1593 she passed An Act for Retaining the Queen's Subjects in Due Obedience. This act made it illegal to be absent from Church of England services. Those who disregarded the law were imprisoned, and their property was confiscated. Upon release, if they still would not bend to Elizabeth's will, they were given the choice of exile or death. Many of those of who were exiled found homes in the Netherlands and later in America. After one of the longest and most successful reigns in British history, Elizabeth died in 1603.

With Elizabeth's death, the crown went to the Stuart family of Scotland. The great-great grandson of Henry VII, James I (1603–1625), became the new king of England. He was already King of Scots (1567–1625). Since Scotland was Presbyterian, the Puritans hoped for changes in the Church of England. They believed James would allow them to purify the church and remove the *Book of Common Prayer*. In 1603, they presented him with the Millenary Petition with nearly a thousand signatures, asking him to remove all Catholic practices from the Church of England. James refused. On January 14, 1604, at the Hampton Court Conference the Puritans asked him again to bring the church more in line with Reformed theology and practice. The president of Corpus Christi College, Oxford, John Reynolds (1549–1607), presented the Puritan requests. After listening to Reynolds's argument, James declared that the Church of England would not be altered. He said if the Puritans' desires were granted, "then Jack, and Tom, and Will, and Dick shall meet, and at their pleasure censure me and my council and all our proceedings."[8] James made clear that if the Puritans did not conform, he would remove them from England. As a result, 300 Puritan clergy went into exile. James's only concession was permission to prepare a new translation of the Bible. Published in 1611, it became known as the Authorized Version (AV) or the King James Version (KJV).

Charles I (1625–1649) discovered the intensity of Puritan commitment. His problems began when he took a Catholic queen and ruled without convening Parliament. The archbishop of Canterbury, William Laud (1633–1645), persecuted many Puritans in his infamous church court, Star Chamber. When Charles and Laud attempted to force Anglicanism on the Presbyterian Church of Scotland, the Scots rebelled and invaded northern England. In order to raise money for an army to put down the rebellion, Charles was forced to convene Parliament. As soon as Parliament was in session though, the members sought to limit Charles's power. The king sent soldiers to arrest several members in 1642, but the London militia stopped them.

With Civil War looming, the Puritans in Parliament realized they might receive aid from the Presbyterians of Scotland. They convoked the Westminster Assembly, which met from 1643 to 1649 and produced the Westminster Confession (1646). The Westminster Confession, a Calvinistic document that promoted a Presbyterian manner of church government, was adopted by Parliament for the Church of England in 1646. When the monarchy was restored in 1660, Charles II (1660–1685) repealed the confession, and traditional Anglicanism was reestablished. The Westminster Confession, however, remained the doctrinal standard for the Church of Scotland and became the cornerstone of the Presbyterian Church. It also had a substantial influence on English Particular Baptists, whose subsequent confessions of faith drew heavily from it.

The English Civil War broke out in 1642. Under the leadership of Oliver Cromwell (1599–1658), the Parliamentary Army defeated the Royalists in 1646. Cromwell had King Charles and Laud executed. Later he rid Parliament of Presbyterians, leaving his supporters in control. After defeating the Irish and Scots, Cromwell became Lord Protector of England in 1653 and held the title until his death in 1658. In reality, he was a military dictator. Cromwell, however, did provide religious toleration to all Protestant sects.

After Cromwell's death no leader could hold the new government together. Finally Parliament invited Charles I's son, Charles II (1660–1685), to return from exile in France and become king. Upon his return Charles reestablished the Anglican Church and repealed Cromwell's toleration of dissenters from the state church, barring them from holding religious services. On his deathbed Charles shocked England when he said he had always been a Catholic.

Charles II's brother James II (1685–1688) was crowned king and sought to return England to the Catholic Church. Parliament reacted by inviting the rulers of the Netherlands, William (1688–1702) and his wife Mary (1688–1694), James II's daughter, to England. With the Glorious Revolution of 1688 came the Act of Toleration in 1689 that encompassed all forms of Christianity except Catholicism and Unitarianism.

Separatism

After James I refused to meet any of the Puritan requests, many Puritans concluded that the Church of England was beyond purification. Rather than worship in what they saw as a false church, they separated and formed their own illegal congregations. Initially, Elizabeth and then James did not allow their royal authority to be challenged and persecuted these Separatists. Many fled to the Protestant Netherlands. Other Separatist leaders such as John Greenwood (1559–1593), Henry Barrowe (1550–1593), and John Penry (1559–1593) were executed. The most prominent Separatists were Robert Browne (1550–1633), Francis Johnson (1562–1617), and John Robinson (1575–1625).

Robert Browne was the earliest architect of the Separatist movement in England. He started a Separatist church in Norwich governed by congregational polity. In *A Treatise of Reformation, Without Tarrying for Anie* (1582), Browne taught that a church's membership should be based on a covenant of true believers. The Church of England began to pressure Browne's congregation, and they fled to the safety of the Netherlands. While there, Browne had difficulties with his church and returned to England. He was then reconciled with the Church of England and ordained by it. Browne, however, continued to critique the state church. He was excommunicated in 1631 and executed in 1633. He was a pioneer in the development of congregational polity, inspired others to leave the Church of England, and made the Netherlands a popular location for persecuted Separatists.

Like Browne, Francis Johnson was educated at Cambridge University where he became a Puritan. After graduating, he became a fellow at Cambridge. His most famous student was John Smyth (1570–1612), who became the first Baptist. Johnson was dismissed from Cambridge in 1589 after promoting a Presbyterian system of church polity rather than the episcopal system of the Church of England. After five months in jail, he was permitted to relocate to Middleburg, Holland, where he ministered to a Puritan congregation. At first Johnson opposed Separatism. For this reason the British government asked him to destroy the Separatist writings of Henry Barrowe and John Greenwood. He destroyed all the copies he could find except for one. After reading *A Plaine Refutation of the Claims of the Establishment* (ca. 1590), he went to London and met with its imprisoned authors. Instead of refuting them, Johnson agreed with them and became a Separatist and pastor of the Ancient Church in London in 1592. As a result, he was imprisoned for five years. The Ancient Church relocated to Amsterdam, Holland, in 1593 and was led by Henry Ainsworth (1571–1622). After being released from prison in 1597, Johnson joined them and resumed his pastoral duties. The congregation drafted the *True Confession* and influenced the shape of Separatist churches in both England and America.

The Netherlands also became a haven for John Smyth and Thomas Helwys (1550–ca. 1615). Smyth became a Puritan at Cambridge under Johnson's influence. Smyth soon became dissatisfied with Puritanism though and became a Separatist. He formed churches in Gainsborough and Scrooby Manor. The best-known member of the Gainsborough group was Thomas Helwys. The Scrooby Manor church was led by John Robinson, William Brewster (1560–1643), and William Bradford (1590–1657). To avoid persecution, the two groups relocated. Smyth's group in Gainsborough went to Amsterdam in 1607, and Robinson's group went to Leyden in 1607–1608.

Several members of this "Pilgrim" church boarded the *Mayflower* and landed at Plymouth in New England in 1620.

Under the leadership of Smyth, Helwys and the Gainsborough congregation adopted believers' baptism (though perhaps not by immersion). Smyth baptized himself, then Helwys, and then the remainder of the congregation. In doing so, they became the first English Baptist church. Smyth wanted the church to join the Dutch Anabaptist fellowship. Helwys objected and the two parted ways. After Smyth's death his congregation merged into the Waterlander Mennonite congregation.

Helwys wrote the first English Baptist confession of faith. It was Arminian in soteriology, congregational in polity, and insisted on complete religious freedom. Baptists of this ilk became known as General Baptists. Helwys led his congregation back to England in 1612. At Spitalfields outside the walls of London, they became the first Baptist church in England. Helwys's most important contribution to the Baptist cause was his *Short Declaration of the Mystery of Iniquity* (ca. 1611). Dedicated to King James, this text was the first English plea for complete religious liberty. Helwys stated, "Let them be heretics, Turks, Jews, or whatsoever, it does not appertain to the earthly power to punish them in the least measure."[9] James did not agree, and Helwys was thrown into Newgate Prison, where he died around 1615. In spite of persecution by the king, the General Baptists grew to seven congregations by 1625.

The Baptists with the most lasting influence in England were the Particular Baptists, who held Calvin's view on election. Particular Baptists trace their origin to a schism in a Separatist church in London led by Henry Jessey (1603–1633). In 1638, John Spilsbury (1593–1668) led a group to separate and form a church that embraced believers' baptism. Other Puritan and Separatist churches soon followed its lead and became Particular Baptists. Particular Baptists had a strong influence on the development of Baptists in America.

CHAPTER TWENTY

CATHOLIC REACTION AND RESPONSE TO THE PROTESTANT REFORMATION

Luther, Calvin, and Zwingli were not the only ones in Europe pressing for reformation. Forces within the church also attempted moral and spiritual reforms—beginning well before the Protestant Reformation. When Protestantism arose, Catholic reformers continued their quest, calling for the renewal of Roman Catholicism while simultaneously denouncing those they viewed as schismatic.

PRE-REFORMATION ATTEMPTS AT INTERNAL REFORM

To ensure Spain's allegiance to Catholicism, Ferdinand and Isabella set up the Spanish Inquisition in 1480. Under the direction of Tomás de Torquemada (1420–1498), thousands of perceived heretics, Muslims, and Jews were tossed into the flames or beheaded. Spain was indeed dedicated to Catholicism. The church's pastoral and spiritual functions, however, were largely abandoned.

The revitalization of Spanish spirituality was initiated by a Franciscan friar named Francisco Ximénez de Cisneros (1436–1517). After studying at the University of Salamanca, he was consumed with a desire for discipline and complete devotion to Christ.

273

He left the priesthood and became an Observantine Franciscan in 1484, entering the convent of San Juan de los Reyes in Toledo. Committed to asceticism, he slept on the floor, wore a haircloth shirt, fasted often, and followed the Franciscan rule of poverty. Ximénez was appointed as Isabella's personal confessor in 1492. In this role he had tremendous influence over the queen. Isabella had him named minister provincial of the Franciscan Order of Spain in 1494 and, in spite of his wishes, archbishop of Toledo in 1495. An ascetic at heart, Ximénez attempted to flee, but Isabella's soldiers brought him back and forced him to take the position. In 1502 he became cardinal and inquisitor of Castile and León.

From these positions of power, Ximénez dedicated himself to reforming the Franciscan Order. He ordered all monks who had wives or concubines to leave them, to live at their parish, attend confession, and preach outside the confines of the monastery. Recalcitrant monasteries were dissolved and their monies given to orphanages and hospitals. Under Ximénez, the University of Alcalá became a center of humanist biblical scholarship. His most influential writing was the *Complutensian Polyglot Bible* (1520). In this text he printed the Old Testament in Hebrew, Greek, and Latin, and the Targum[1] (a Jewish commentary on the Old Testament) in parallel columns. In the New Testament he followed the same format. He used his own Greek translation[2] as well as the *Vulgate*. Next to the passages he added his own commentary. When the *Polyglot Bible* was translated into Spanish, the Inquisition burned it, fearing that laity who could read the Bible in Spanish would question the Vulgate and the traditional teachings of the church. Fears about the *Polyglot Bible* may have played a role in the Council of Trent's decision to name the Vulgate the only true and authoritative Bible.

Ximénez ordered all remaining Moors and Jews to become Christians or leave Spain. All Arabic religious writings were destroyed, and mosques were demolished or converted to Christian churches. Jews and Muslims who converted to Christianity were closely watched and often tortured to ensure the sincerity of their conversions. In 1500, he reported to Ferdinand and Isabella that there were no remaining mosques or Moors in their former stronghold of Grenada. Not content with his victories in Spain, he personally led an invasion of Moorish North Africa in 1509. Ximénez, therefore, has been remembered by some as a hero but by others as a tyrant.

A Dominican friar and humanist in Florence, Girolamo Savonarola (1452–1498) claimed to have visions and direct communication with God. Beginning around 1490, he delivered apocalyptic messages informing congregants that they were living in the last days. A plague and a war with France made his claims seem credible. Savonarola preached that the excesses of the ruling de Medici family, humanism, and the corruption of Pope Alexander VI (1492–1503) brought the Florentines under God's judgment. Savonarola declared:

> All of Italy must be turned upside down, Rome as well, and then the Church must be renewed. But you do not believe! You should believe, however, for God has said it to you rather than I. . . . Therefore, when you see that God permits the heads of Church to be weighed down by evils and simonies, say that the flagellation of the people is near. . . . Go, see what is done for the churches of God and what devotion is there, for the worship of God seems and is today lost. You will say: "Oh, there are so many religious and so many prelates, more than there have ever been!" Would that there were fewer of them! O tonsured ones, tonsured ones! . . . You are the cause of this evil! And nowadays everyone thinks he is holy, if he has a priest in his house; and I say to you that that time will come when it will be said: "Blessed is the house that does not have a shaved head!"[3]

France conquered Florence in 1492, and the de Medici family was removed from power. Now unimpeded, Savonarola began to preach against Florentine immorality and excesses. He condemned many Florentine businesses and had them shut down. Homosexuality was declared a capital offense, and in 1497 he orchestrated the "Bonfire of the Vanities." His followers went door-to-door collecting cosmetics, pagan books, immoral statues, and ancient poetry and had them burned in the Piazza della Signoria.

Believing that Savonarola was a false prophet, a Franciscan monk challenged him to trial by fire. Savonarola declined and his influence began to wane. Open rebellion against Savonarola began in late 1497, and Pope Alexander VI excommunicated him in 1498. After a struggle in which several of his followers were killed, he was arrested, tortured, and confessed to crimes and immoralities he most certainly did not commit. He was then taken to the Piazza della Signoria and cast into the flames. Due to his unbending personality, alienation of local merchants, and strong-arm tactics, Savonarola's efforts at reform were a failure.

Catholic Developments in the Reformation Era

A desire for change in the church manifested itself in the birth of new monastic orders and the reform of older ones. Catherine of Genoa (1447–1510) founded the oratory of Divine Love in 1497. It was composed of both high-ranking laity and clergy who were deeply involved in charitable works, moral development, and spiritual growth. They frequently attended mass and were diligent in caring for the sick.

The Roman branch of the oratory was born in 1517. Its goal was to reform the church. Several future leaders of the Catholic Church belonged to the Oratory of Divine Love. The most influential were Gaetano dei Conti di Thiene, known as Cajetan (1480–1547),

Giovanni Pietro Caraffa (1476–1559), who became Pope Paul IV, and Gasparo Contarini·(1483–1542).

The Oratory of Divine Love spawned the Theatine Order. It was founded in 1524 by Cardinal Cajetan, from whom the Order took its name, and Caraffa. The order was committed to poverty, working with the laity, charity, obedience, and the end of clerical abuses.

The Capuchins were organized by Matteo da Bascio (1495–1552) in 1528. The name derived from the pointed cowl worn by the order's founder. A Franciscan monk, Matteo hoped to return the Franciscans to their roots of poverty, order, and service of the laity. The Capuchins were known for their persuasive scriptural preaching, which made them effective adversaries of the Protestants. Their strong dedication to and study of the Bible, however, resulted in some leaving the Catholic faith. In one instance the superior of the Capuchin Order, Bernardino Ochino (1487–1564), became convinced of justification by faith and turned to Protestantism. His conversion resulted in the near dissolution of the order.

Angela Merici (1474–1540) founded the Ursulines at Brescia in 1535. Dedicated to Saint Ursula and for women only, the Ursulines initially did not take religious vows. They worshipped in parish churches and dedicated themselves to the education of girls, obedience, and charity. In light of their popularity and growth, they became an official order in 1546.

A Spanish nobleman and soldier, Ignatius of Loyola (1491–1556) founded the Society of Jesus, or Jesuits. After his leg was shattered by a cannon ball while fighting against the French in 1521, he spent several months convalescing. During that time Ignatius read books on the lives of the saints, Ludolph the Carthusian's (d. 1378) *Life of Christ*, and other devotional materials. Soon afterward, he reported having a vision of Jesus and the virgin Mary. He then dedicated himself to spiritual discipline, becoming a soldier for Christ and the virgin Mary, and serving the Catholic Church. He symbolically hung up his sword at the altar of Mary at Montserrat

in Barcelona and traded clothes with a beggar. His spiritual journey continued with the reading of Thomas à Kempis's *Imitation of
Christ*. These experiences became the foundation of his most influential work, *Spiritual Exercises*.

Loyola made a pilgrimage to the Holy Land in 1523. His journey convinced him that he should dedicate his life to the evangelization of Muslims. After attending the University of Bologna and
the University of Paris (1524–1535), Loyola and six of his friends,
the most notable being Francis Xavier (1506–1552), set out for
Jerusalem in 1534. Because of a war with the Turks, they were not
permitted to go beyond Venice. While in Venice he impressed
Cardinals Caraffa and Contarini, who introduced him to Pope Paul
III (1534–1549). The pope approved a new order under his direction on September 27, 1540. The Jesuits were dedicated to working with the laity, evangelism, and education. Their first allegiance,
however, was to the papacy. The order's constitution declared that
its members

> with the utmost pains strain every nerve of our strength
> to exhibit this virtue of obedience, firstly to the Highest
> Pontiff, then to the Superiors of the Society; so that in all
> things, to which obedience can be extended with charity,
> we may be most ready to obey his voice, as if it were issued
> from Christ our Lord.[4]

In the Jesuits, the papacy found its most ardent and dedicated
defenders.

Published in 1548, Loyola's *Spiritual Exercises* was the Jesuit
handbook for the preparation of new members. By means of meditation and prayer, *Spiritual Exercises* took an individual through a
monthlong exercise that taught him to surrender to God. The exercises offered instruction on how to meditate in a way that produced
powerful visions. It also placed strong emphasis on obedience to
one's superior and above all to the pope. In section 2 of *Spiritual*

Exercises, Loyola wrote, "Always be ready to obey with mind and heart, setting aside all judgment of one's own, the true spouse of Jesus Christ, our holy mother, our infallible and orthodox mistress, the Catholic Church, whose authority is exercised over us by the hierarchy."[5]

The Jesuits were not founded to combat the Protestants, but their belief in education and loyalty to the papacy made them perfect for this role. Their greatest successes in Catholic apologetics occurred in southern Germany, Austria, Lithuania, and Poland, where many were won back to the Catholic faith.

Because of their fervent evangelism, they became effective missionaries in Brazil, India, and China. In South America, the Jesuits set up missions and villages and fought the slave trade. Francis Xavier was one of the most famous Jesuit missionaries. He worked in India and Japan for ten years and was reported to have been responsible for as many as 700,000 conversions. Matteo Ricci (1562–1610) was the most prominent Jesuit missionary in China. He brought telescopes to China and gave clocks to the emperor. His ability to work with the Chinese and to understand their culture opened an avenue for evangelism. He was believed to have converted 6,000 Chinese. By 1700, the Jesuits claimed 200,000 conversions in China. In what is now California, Junípero Serra (1713–1784) set up missions along the coast. These missions taught natives the rudiments of Catholicism, educated them, and protected them from other hostile tribes.

Because of their intense loyalty to the papacy, Jesuits were suspected of doing the pope's bidding by meddling in state affairs. They also served as inquisitors and were accused of being hired assassins for the pope. For these reasons the Jesuits were removed from Portugal in 1759, France in 1764, and Spain in 1767. Pope Clement XIV (1769–1774) suppressed the order in 1770. In spite of their suppression, they remained a powerful force in Germany, Austria, and the British colony of Maryland in America. They were restored as a religious order in 1814 by Pius VII (1800–1823). In the twenty-first century, the Jesuits serve primarily as educators and parish priests. Francis I of Argentina, elected in 2013, is the first pope from the Jesuit order.

THE HUMANISTS

In his writing, Desiderius Erasmus (1466–1536) helped pave the way for the Protestant Reformation, though he surprised many by refusing to join the Protestants. Instead, he sought to preserve the unity of the Catholic Church and promote its reform from within. Erasmus advocated charity, good works, and piety rather than the mere repetition of dogma. In his *In Praise of Folly*, he attributed many of the Catholic Church's ills to poorly trained priests who did not understand the basic teachings of Christianity. He believed the scholasticism taught at universities contributed to the problem.

Erasmus, the "Prince of Humanism," appeared too Protestant for many Catholics, and Protestants were disappointed that he did not join them. Although he found few avenues through which to institute his reforms, his efforts left an imprint on both Catholicism and Protestantism.

In England, Lord Chancellor Thomas More (1466–1536) was the leading humanist. His work *Utopia* (1516) described an ideal community living by a religion based on natural law and reason. His love of humanism played a large role in introducing Greek language study to the University of Oxford. More was a dedicated Catholic and advocate of papal authority. He wrote against Protestant ideas and Tyndale's translation of the Bible, and he may have been the author of Henry VIII's tome against Luther. Though he had a close relationship with Henry, he did not support England's break with Rome. This stance led to his arrest, imprisonment, and martyrdom.

THE MYSTICS AND QUIETISM

Mysticism was another spiritual expression that played a role in Catholic reform efforts. It arose from the desire for intense personal experience with God and allowed Catholics to develop a vibrant faith while remaining true to the sacraments and church dogma.

Teresa of Ávila (1515–1582) was the most famous sixteenth-century mystic. She was born into an affluent Spanish family that converted from Judaism. Against her family's wishes, Teresa entered a Carmelite convent when she was twenty years old. But she became disenchanted with the convent's moral laxity. To aid her spiritual pilgrimage, she began to read devotional materials and immersed herself in prayer. When Teresa was forty, she began reporting visions of Christ, speaking in tongues, and experiencing ecstasy while supposedly united with Christ. She claimed that these events led her to discover the "way of perfection," the title of a book she wrote.

Teresa's extraordinary claims attracted many followers who wanted to have similar spiritual experiences. For this reason she founded the Convent of Saint Joseph at Ávila in 1562. Because they did not wear shoes, the nuns were known as Discalced Carmelites or Barefoot Carmelites. They remained cloistered, accepted no money or endowments, and dedicated themselves to pursuing perfect lives, with Teresa's *Way of Perfection* as their guide. Her other important works were *Foundations* and the *Interior Castle*. In these works she described the ascent of the soul to Christ and different states of prayer. In 1572, Teresa claimed that her life of perfection resulted in a spiritual marriage with Christ.

Teresa of Avila made a strong impression on Juan de Yepes Álvarez, better known as John of the Cross (1542–1591). Disillusioned with their laxity, he wanted to reform the Carmelites along the lines of Teresa's Discalced nuns. After being imprisoned and escaping, in 1579 he founded the Order of Discalced Carmelites for men. John was named the prior of Granada in 1582 and Segovia in 1588. However, because of his strictness, he fell out of favor with the order's vicar-general and was exiled to Andalusia until his death.

John's greatest contributions to Catholic mysticism were his writings. In his *Spiritual Canticle* he used an allegory to describe the traditional three-step process of mystics: purgation of the soul from sin, illumination, and unification with Christ. His *Ascent of Mount Carmel* and *Dark Night of the Soul* described how a soul could become detached from the distractions of the physical senses and listen to God's instructions. In *Living Flame* he described how God united with man in pure love. His writings were popular in the sixteenth century and continue to be widely read today.

A Spaniard, Miguel de Molinos (1628–1696) founded quietism, a spiritual system that condemned all reliance on human effort. His writings were similar to those of Teresa of Ávila. They described his states of ecstasy, mystical experiences, and visions. Molinos, however, went further than Teresa. He taught that in order to be perfect, a person had to give up the entirety of his will, avoid activity, and shun responsibility. One was merely to rest in the presence of God. Even thoughts and concern about salvation had to be given up. When a person achieved the state of perfection or union with God, he or she was unable to sin. People living in the state of perfection could commit acts considered sins in the physical world without having them count as sins. Molinos was condemned as a heretic in 1687 and spent the remainder of his life in prison.

THE ROLE OF THE PAPACY

Initially, the papacy reacted slowly to Protestantism. If Leo X had taken immediate action against Luther, the Reformation might have ended before it took root. But Leo was too involved in papal politics and building the Vatican to bother with a German monk.

A native of the Burgundian Netherlands, Hadrian VI (1522–1523) blamed the sins of the Catholic Church for the birth of

Protestantism. He attempted to reform the bureaucracy of the papal court and by doing so stem the spread of Protestantism. But he died before any major attempts at reform could occur.

Clement VII (1523–1534) made no attempts to win back the Protestants. Instead he accused them of heresy. His attempt to broker the conflict between France's Francis I and Holy Roman Emperor Charles V dominated much of his papacy.

Paul III (1534–1549) was the first pope to respond to the grievances raised by Protestants. He believed in reform and wanted to correct abuses by appointing an investigative committee to assess the health of the church and recommend reforms. The committee was composed of cardinals who were in favor of limited reform, including Giovanni Caraffa, who became Pope Paul IV (1555–1559), Jacob Sadoleto (1477–1547), Reginald Pole (1500–1588), and Gasparo Contarini (1483–1542). The committee reported that nepotism and simony were rampant. The committee stated:

> The city and Church of Rome is the mother and teacher of other churches; thus divine worship and virtuous customs should be especially conspicuous here. For this reason, most Holy Father, all strangers are scandalized who enter St. Peter's basilica, where slovenly and ignorant priests celebrate mass, dressed in vestments and attire with which they could not really appear even in a squalid house. . . . In this city courtesans go about or ride on mules like honest women. In broad daylight they are followed by men of noble families who are members of households of cardinals, and by clerics. In no other city do we see such corruption save in this [one], which should be an example to all others.[6]

The committee also determined that money, power, and territorial ambitions dominated the affairs of the Holy See to the detriment of its pastoral role.

The Roman Inquisition

Modeled after the highly effective Spanish campaign, a Roman Inquisition was instituted in 1542. The accused were guilty until proven innocent and did not have the right to confront their accusers. Torture was used to force confessions. Nearly all of the Protestants and any remnants of dissent were eliminated in Italy.

The Council of Trent

Pope Paul III called for the nineteenth ecumenical council in 1535, but it did not take place until 1545. Emperor Charles V wanted the council to be held in Germany while the pope wanted it in Rome. Moreover, Charles wanted the Catholic Church to compromise with Protestants to end the chaos that divided the empire. Paul wanted the meeting to be doctrinal and to highlight the differences between the Catholic Church and Protestants. Located in the Alps northwest of Venice, Trent was chosen as the site. The city was in Hapsburg territory but easily accessible from the Vatican.

The council did not adjourn until 1563. In its eighteen years of periodic sessions, it scrutinized all aspects of the Catholic Church. Although some Protestants were invited, only a few attended since they realized their arguments would be rejected. The Council of Trent was the Catholic Church's official attempt to define its theology in contrast to Protestantism. Its canons and decrees became known as Tridentine Catholicism.

The council was held in three major blocks of sessions, each with a separate agenda and each convened by a different pope. The first sessions were held from 1545 to 1547. Each bishop was given one vote, and the majority of attendees were Italians.[7] In effect, the pope controlled the council. These meetings generally reaffirmed the traditional Catholic faith. The Nicene-Constantinopolitan Creed and the seven sacraments were upheld with no alterations. Transubstantiation was reaffirmed and Aquinas's theology was declared normative. Against Luther's declaration of *sola scriptura*, both Scripture and the traditions of the Church were upheld as the sources of doctrinal authority. The Council also determined that justification was by both faith and good works. Canon nine, which assumed a notion of infused grace, stated: "If anyone says that the sinner is justified by faith alone, meaning that nothing else is required to cooperate in order to obtain the grace of justification, and that it is not in any way necessary that he be prepared and disposed by the action of his own will, let him be anathema."[8] Despite the anti-Protestant findings of the Council, several Catholic leaders hoped for reconciliation with Protestants.

After a four-year hiatus, Pope Julius III (1550–1555) reconvened the council. Some Protestant leaders attended in 1551 but stayed only briefly. The major topics were the Eucharist and penance. The Lutheran and Reformed interpretations of Christ's presence in the Supper were rejected. Prayers for the dead were retained.

After Pope Paul IV refused to reconvene the council, it resumed in 1559 under the direction of Pius IV (1559–1565). Its proceedings were dominated by the Jesuits. In these sessions several complaints raised by the Protestants—especially simony, nepotism, greed, and the violation of clerical celibacy—were addressed. A bishop was required to reside in his diocese. Other matters which drew Protestant ire, however, remained unchanged. Communion was to be given to the laity in only one kind (bread); the appointment of bishops had to be approved by the pope; prayer to saints was endorsed; purgatory was affirmed; and relics could be venerated. Even the indulgence system that first moved Luther to action was declared orthodox, though the council attempted to curb abuses. For example, it eliminated the office of indulgence seller. The council stated:

> Since the power of conferring indulgences has been granted to the Church by Christ, and since the Church has made use of this divinely given power even from the earliest

times, this holy Synod teaches and enjoins that the use of
indulgences, which is greatly salutary for Christian people
and has been approved by the authority of sacred Councils,
is to be retained in the Church.[9]

The Latin Vulgate, with the books of the Apocrypha, was
ruled to be the only true Scripture. Moreover, marriages between
Catholics and Protestants were forbidden. Heeding the concerns
of reforming humanists, the council decided that Catholic clerics
needed a better education so they could defend their beliefs against
the often better-trained Protestants. This decision led to the establishment of several Catholic universities and seminaries.

The council also reaffirmed the Index, a list of prohibited books
that included unauthorized versions of the Bible, the writings of
some humanists, the writings of specific Protestant Reformers, and
several scientific books:

> The books of those heresiarchs, who after the afore-
> said year [1515] originated or revived heresies, as well as
> those who are or have been the heads or leaders of her-
> etics, as Luther, Zwingli, Calvin, Balthasar Friedberg
> [Hubmaier], Schwenkfeld, and others like these, what-
> ever may be their name, title or nature of their heresy, are
> absolutely forbidden.[10]

Not only were these books not to be read, but in keeping with
church practice, they were to be destroyed. The Index was not
repealed until 1966. The council again went into recess and finally
closed in 1563.

The Council of Trent failed to bring the Protestants back into
the fold, but this was never really its purpose. Rather, it was meant
to define and strengthen Catholicism by countering Protestant
accusations. It signaled the Catholic Church's renewed emphasis on
piety and its pastoral role. In these regards, the Council of Trent
helped bring the church into the modern era.

The immediate post-Tridentine era was marked by new styles of music and architecture. The choirmaster of Saint Peter's in Rome, Giovanni da Palestrina (1524–1594), introduced polyphonic music to Catholic worship. Rather than the traditional one voice, this musical style consisted of two or more melodic voices. His masses and motets[11] provided musical dialogue characteristic of the revitalized spirituality that marked Tridentine Catholicism.

Giovanni Bernini (1598–1680) introduced Baroque architecture to Catholicism. This style's grandeur attempted to depict the triumph of the Catholic Church. Realistic statues and paintings made icons appear more lifelike. Bernini's most famous work was the altar of Saint Peter's Basilica.

REMAINING PROBLEMS

Prior to the Reformation, the Catholic Church was weakened by strong European monarchs who desired more control over ecclesiastical affairs. After Trent, even the church's strongest allies sought to take advantage of its weakened condition. In order to keep its allies, the Catholic Church made concessions that were inconceivable previously.

France had long been staunchly Catholic. But from the fourteenth century forward, it sought increased independence from the papacy without leaving Catholicism, a sentiment known as Gallicanism. The Gallicans triumphed at the Concordat of Bologna in 1516, when the papacy surrendered the right to nominate bishops and other high-ranking church officials to the French king. With the papacy trying to maintain its alliance in 1682, the Assembly of French Bishops adopted the *Gallican Declaration*, which stated that the pope had authority over spiritual matters but not temporal and civil ones.

The Gallican position grew in popularity and was codified at the Synod of Pistoria in 1786. Ultramontanists (meaning "beyond the mountains," a reference to Italy on the other side of the Alps) rejected Gallicanism and affirmed the authority of the pope over all temporal rulers. Often Jesuits, ultramontanists preferred papal control of the church over national independence. They depicted the Gallicans as heretical and as a primary cause of the French Revolution (1789–1799), which debilitated the Catholic Church in France. The Gallican Articles, however, held firm until the First Vatican Council in 1870. When the council ratified the doctrine of papal infallibility, it became impossible for France to uphold Gallicanism and remain in harmony with the Catholic Church.

The Thirty Years' War

Initially the Peace of Augsburg (1555) stopped military clashes between the Lutheran Schmalkaldic League and Holy Roman Emperor Charles V. But it was an uneasy truce at best. Any religious or political dispute had the potential to plunge Europe into war.

The event that broke the peace occurred in Bohemia, where Protestantism and nationalism were often one and the same. The Holy Roman Emperor Matthias (1612–1619) appointed Ferdinand (1578–1637), his cousin and a Catholic, as the king of Bohemia. During a meeting between Ferdinand's envoys and Bohemian nobles in 1618, the nobles became enraged and threw the king's representatives out a window. This Defenestration of Prague began the Thirty Years' War (1618–1648).

Realizing that the assault of his envoys would prompt Ferdinand to military action, the Protestants selected Frederick (1596–1632), elector of the Palatinate region, as their king. Ferdinand's army easily defeated Frederick's, and the victor declared that all Protestants in Bohemia were to convert to Catholicism or leave. In response England, the Netherlands, and Denmark formed an alliance against the Catholic forces and reinstituted Protestantism in Germany.

Eventually they were defeated by Catholic general Albert of Wallenstein (1583–1634).

The king of Sweden, the Lutheran Gustavus Adolphus (1594–1632), then invaded Germany. Adolphus's desire was not only to defend the Protestants of Germany but also to ensure that the Holy Roman Empire did not encroach on Sweden or thwart its desire to control the Baltic Sea. He won a series of victories over the Catholic forces and Wallenstein but died in battle in 1632. Tiring of war and with little means to continue it, the belligerents signed the Peace of Westphalia in 1648. Each ruler was permitted to choose his country's religion, and all Christian faiths were to be tolerated. Sweden gained land along the Baltic Sea. France gained land in the Rhineland, and the German princes gained greater autonomy from the emperor.

ORTHODOXY

The Reformation had little effect on the Eastern Orthodox churches. Outside of Russia, they struggled to remain viable under the Ottoman Empire. The most pressing internal problem was a Russian monastic dispute between those who favored endowments to support orphanages, hospitals, and poverty relief and those who believed a vow of poverty for their communities had to be maintained. Those who stressed the need for endowments eventually won. The Russian Orthodox had good relations with the Lutherans (who courted them), but no official affiliation developed. Attempts between Catholics and the Orthodox to heal the breach of 1054 also failed. Ivan IV (1533–1584) of Russia took the title *tsar*, or emperor, claiming he was the successor of the emperors of Rome and Constantinople. At the end of the sixteenth century, the prelate of Moscow took the title of patriarch, bolstering Russia's status as the capital of Orthodoxy in the East. Interactions of the Russian Church with both Catholics and Lutherans increased under Tsar Peter the Great (1682–1725) and his successors as the Russian Empire expanded westward and became a major European power.

CHAPTER TWENTY-ONE

CHRISTIANIZING
THE
NEW WORLD

Exploration of the New World and the changing face of Christianity were intertwined. The fall of Constantinople in 1453 proved to be a watershed, causing that city to lose its position as the center of the Orthodox faith and affecting trade routes, since Constantinople was the key port for moving Eastern spices and silk to the West. Its fall to Islam made the traditional trade route to the East much more difficult. Spain and Portugal were forced to find a new port and a new route to India and China.

The voyages of Marco Polo (1254–1324) convinced many explorers that the great sea he described off the coast of China might be the same ocean that touched Spain. Reaching the East, therefore, might be possible by sailing west. In the fifteenth century, Prince Henry the Navigator (1394–1460) sailed 600 miles down the West African coast looking for a route to India and setting up trade ports. Following Henry, the Portuguese reached Sierra Leone in 1460. In 1488, Bartolomeu Dias (1451–1500) sailed around the Cape of Good Hope and entered the Indian Ocean. Using this route, Vasco da Gama (1460–1524) was the first person to sail from Portugal to India in 1498.

A devout Catholic, Christopher Columbus (1451–1506) was looking for the western route to Asia when he landed in the

Bahamas on August 3, 1492. Sailing for Ferdinand and Isabella of Spain, Columbus's task also had religious aspects. When he encountered the indigenous people of the New World, he attempted to convert them to the Catholic faith. On his second voyage, Columbus celebrated the first Mass in the New World on January 6, 1494, and the first baptism occurred on September 21, 1494, at Isabella (now Haiti).

The timing of his arrival in the New World was important. Not even a generation after Columbus's achievement, the Protestant Reformation began. Because of the Catholic Church's loss of lands and revenue in Europe, Catholic exploration and exploitation of the New World intensified.

Spain and Portugal led the exploration and colonization of South America, Central America, and what are now Florida and Mexico. They imprinted the Catholic faith on the natives to such a degree that these regions remain predominantly Catholic. In Canada, France provided a firm foundation for the Catholic Church.

Protestant countries also wanted a share of the New World. Many of the earliest Protestants came to the New World for religious liberty. With a few exceptions, the evangelization of Native Americans was not a primary concern for them.

The East Coast of the modern United States was settled by Great Britain and Holland. British Puritans who settled in New England had the greatest influence on that region. They shaped New England's religion, commerce, and education well into the nineteenth century. The Church of England held sway in Virginia and the Carolinas but not as strongly as the Puritans in New England.

Spanish Influence

As the first countries to conquer and colonize the New World, Spain and Portugal often went to war against each other in South and Central America. To keep the Catholic powers at peace, Pope

Alexander VI issued five papal bulls that divided up the known world. The most important was issued on June 7, 1494. Alexander determined that all the lands 100 leagues (about 320 miles) west of the Cape Verde Islands belonged to Spain; the rest belonged to Portugal. This bull made much of Central America, South America, and the Caribbean Spanish, and Brazil Portuguese. The languages of these countries still reflect Alexander's decision.

Under the system of royal patronage, the papacy ceded church matters in the New World to the Spanish and Portuguese kings. The kings were to appoint church leaders, create dioceses, and direct missionary endeavors. In essence the state was an arm of the church.

The most famous Spanish conquistadors were Hernando Cortés (1460–1521), Juan Ponce de León (1474–1521), Vasco Núñez de Balboa (1475–1519), Hernando De Soto (1497–1542), and Francisco Vásquez de Coronado (1510–1554). They laid claims for the Spanish in what became Florida, Mexico, the Southwestern United States, and Peru. These conquistadors were interested in gold and silver, but they were endorsed by the Spanish monarchs, for whom the propagation of the Catholic faith was a secondary concern. Upon their first contact with natives, the conquistadors were required to read the *Requerimiento* to them, a summary of Christian history and a command that they obey the Spaniards and the pope. Read in Spanish, most natives didn't understand its meaning, and many of those who refused acquiescence were forcibly "evangelized."

Describing the evangelization process, Cortés wrote:

> Since as Catholic and Christians our principal intention ought to be the honor and service of God, and since the motive of the Holy Father in giving to the emperor the rule of the lands and the profit from them was that the people be converted to our Holy Catholic faith, we, therefore, require that all persons who have *repartimientos* [forced labor] of Indians be obliged to take away all their idols and warn them against further idolatrous practice, and that

they refrain from all sacrifice of human life to their gods. Failure to comply with the order will on the first offense be punished with a fine, the second offense with a double fine, and the third offense with the loss of the Indians.[1]

Exploitation occurred quickly, and the natives were robbed of their gold and land. Many were enslaved. To justify their actions, Spanish merchants claimed the natives were not people and did not have souls. The exploitation of the native Brazilians by Portuguese merchants was also widespread. Many members of the clergy were disturbed by the merchants' mistreatment of the natives.

Bartolomé de las Casas (1474–1566) and Junípero Serra (1713–1784) were two of the most important Spanish missionaries and Native American advocates. After arriving in Hispaniola as a conquistador in 1502, Las Casas became the first friar to be ordained as a priest in the New World. He became a Dominican in 1522 and served as bishop of Chiapas from 1543 to 1547. Las Casas was deeply concerned with people who had been enslaved. He particularly despised the *encomienda* labor system. State-sanctioned in the colonization of the Americas and the Philippine Islands, the system provided Spaniards with large land grants. They were to protect the natives on their land, teach them Spanish, and bring them into the Catholic faith. In exchange, Spanish landholders could take gold and silver and force the natives to labor without compensation for several months each year. Las Casas dedicated much of his ministerial effort to ending the *encomienda* system. Supporters of the *encomienda* system countered that natives were subhuman. Owning a native was no different from owning cattle. Las Casas appealed to the papacy on behalf of the Indians. As a result, Pope Paul III (1534–1549) issued *Sublimis Deus* in 1537 to keep merchants from enslaving the natives:

> We . . . consider, however, that the Indians are truly men and that they are not only capable of understanding

the catholic faith but, according to our information, they desire exceedingly to receive it. Desiring to provide ample remedy for these evils, we define and declare in our letters ... the Indians and all other people who may later be discovered by Christians, are by no means to be deprived of their liberty or the possession of their property, even though they may be outside the faith of Jesus Christ; and that they may and should, freely and legitimately, enjoy their liberties and the possessions of their property; nor should they be in any way enslaved; should the contrary happen, it shall be null and of no effect.[2]

Sublimis Deus was followed by King Charles V of Spain's "New Laws" in 1542 that were meant to stop the exploitation of natives by the *Encomenderos*. As a result slaveholders began to threaten Las Casas, and he was forced to return to Spain in 1547. Las Casas took part in what became known as the Valladolid Debates with Juan Ginés de Sepúlveda (1489–1573) in 1550–1551. Sepúlveda argued that the natives were natural pagans, inferior, and had to be subjugated by the Spanish. Las Casas argued that the natives were not natural pagans and should be peacefully evangelized. In 1552, he published *A Short Account of the Destruction of the Indies*. This book brought to light the mistreatment of the natives by the Spanish and helped cement the conquistadors' reputation as cruel and morally bankrupt.

A dedicated Franciscan friar and former professor, Junípero Serra ministered in New Spain. He arrived in Mexico City in 1750. After seventeen years he relocated to California, where he set up several missions, many of which evolved into large cities like San Diego, San Francisco, and Santa Clara. Missions were military and religious outposts on the fringes of Spanish territory. They not only provided natives the rudiments of an education, the basic teachings of Catholicism, and European customs but also protected them from hostile neighbors. A major objective of the mission system was to make Spaniards of the natives.

Serra was reported to have baptized 6,000 Indians and confirmed 5,000. While opposed to the military's treatment of the natives, Serra still treated them in a paternalistic manner. Natives who fled the mission were forcibly brought back. The Franciscans established twenty-one missions in California from 1769 to 1845 and baptized as many as 100,000 natives.

Many scholars have suggested that the natives' embrace of Catholicism was superficial at best and was little more than a veneer for their native customs, which did not mesh well with Spanish culture. In many instances they "adopted" the culture of their conquerors to receive food and protection. Only rarely were natives given leadership positions within a mission. They were often abused by the soldiers. Missions also proved to be incubators for European diseases against which the natives had no immunity. More often than not the promise of a better life as a Christian was an empty one.

French Influence

Because of the explorations of René-Robert Cavelier, Sieur de La Salle (1643–1687), France claimed all the territory from the Great Lakes to the Gulf of Mexico and as far west as the Mississippi River. France's strongholds in the New World were in the Saint Lawrence Valley, Quebec, and Louisiana. Unlike the gold-seeking Spanish who forced the natives to work in the mines or fields, French merchants tended to be fur traders who did not need slaves for their economic success. Like the Spanish the French merchants and colonists were not kind to the natives, but their treatment of them was better.

The Catholic Church followed French explorers into the New World. Cardinal Richelieu (1585–1642) appointed a Capuchin named Joseph Tremblay (1577–1638) to organize missions in the

French holdings. Tremblay sent the first Capuchin friars to the New World, where they worked in the Antilles, Port Royal (what is now Maine), and Guadeloupe.

Quebec was founded in 1608 and soon became the home of many Jesuits. François de Laval (1623–1708) became the first bishop of Quebec in 1658. A Jesuit, Laval founded a seminary to train clergy who would serve in Quebec. He also attempted to protect the natives from colonial exploitation by restricting the liquor trade. As a Jesuit, Laval disdained Gallicanism. His efforts helped ensure that Canadian Catholics were loyal to the papacy.

In 1673, Jesuit Father Jacques Marquette (1637–1675) began his work with the Illinois Indians in the Upper Mississippi River Valley. He may have been one of the first Europeans to see and map the northern expanses of the Mississippi River. Marquette also founded Sault Sainte Marie, the first European settlement in Michigan, in 1668.

Jean de Brébeuf (1593–1649) worked with the Hurons around Quebec. He evangelized, learned their language, and lived with them. His writings state that he converted thousands of them to the Christian faith. The Hurons were at war with Iroquois, and after a battle Brébeuf was captured. He was tortured for hours and finally died. His body was recovered, the skin removed, and his bones became relics.[3] Brébeuf was named the patron saint of Canada in 1930.

Accompanying LaSalle as his chaplain, Louis Hennepin (1626–1704) was a Franciscan and the first missionary to work in Minnesota. He preached to Native Americans and Catholic trappers throughout the Saint Lawrence countryside. He was the first person to describe Niagara Falls. Hennepin's historical accounts, however, are dubious at best. He made several claims, such as finding the mouth of the Mississippi River and being in charge of the LaSalle expeditions, which were false. Hennepin's evangelistic work in Minnesota paled in comparison to that of the Jesuits.

Catholic influence in Louisiana was also strong. The French founded New Orleans in 1718. It immediately became a Catholic stronghold and soon housed a girl's school run by the Ursuline Sisters. The impact of Catholicism can still be felt in Louisiana, which is divided into parishes rather than counties. Following its defeat in the French and Indian War (1756–1763), France ceased being a major factor in North America. Its Canadian possessions went to England, and Spain was given New Orleans and the territory west of the Mississippi as compensation for siding with France in the war. In 1803, the United States acquired the Louisiana Territory.

THE BRITISH INFLUENCE

Rather than the patronage system employed by Catholic nations, Britain used joint stock companies in its colonization. This allowed money gathered from different sources to underwrite the endeavor. The most prominent companies were the Massachusetts Bay Company and the Virginia Company. The purpose of these companies was to colonize, establish trade, and make a profit for their investors.

The Massachusetts Bay Company carried thousands of religious dissenters to New England who were fleeing the persecution of Archbishop William Laud (1573–1645). The overwhelming majority of these dissenters were Puritans. Because the colonies were so far removed from England, the Puritans were able to escape much of Laud's persecution and could worship as they pleased. In the middle colonies, particularly Pennsylvania and East New Jersey, the Quakers were prominent. Rhode Island had no official denominational ties. In the Southern colonies, the Church of England was the established faith. Maryland was established as a refuge for Catholics by the Calvert family, but Protestants soon outnumbered Catholics. Even so, Maryland was the center for Catholics in early America.

Each of these denominations attempted to evangelize the Native Americans, but other than John Eliot (1604–1690) of Massachusetts, there were few success stories. He evangelized the Algonquian Indians and gathered many of them together in towns. By 1674 he organized fourteen towns and claimed 3,600 converts. He also translated much of the Bible into Algonquin and wrote an Algonquin catechism.

Missionary overtures to the native population failed for many reasons. Native Americans who became Christians did not want to conform to English cultural standards. Wars occurred regularly. But the most important reason for native resistance to Christianity was that the colonists often employed unchristian measures to gain natives' land. Most Native Americans saw no reason to adopt the religion of such people. Many of those who did had pragmatic motivations.

NEW ENGLAND

The two major branches of English colonists were the dominant Congregationalist Puritans and a large Separatist minority. Also Calvinistic in theology, Presbyterians were present in some degree as well, but the Congregationalists looked down on them because of their views on church polity. Even when dealing with their fellow Calvinists, the Congregationalists were rigid. The majority of the Presbyterians in Massachusetts and Connecticut joined Congregational churches. The largest number who remained Presbyterian lived in New Jersey and New York.

Originally American Congregationalists did not demand that a person recount his or her conversion in order to qualify for church membership. This changed quickly, but initially every person in a community was considered a church member. All citizens were expected to attend church and to live moral lives. When New England churches began admitting only professed believers, they became the first state churches in history to practice regenerate church membership. To be a member of a Separatist church, a person had to recount his conversion.

Whether Puritan or Separatist, Calvinism was the dominant New England religious system. Both groups fled English persecution and hoped to set up a new and better England in America.

The Pilgrim Fathers were the first dissenters to arrive in America. Pastored by John Robinson, they were staunch Separatists who believed the Church of England was beyond repair. To escape religious persecution, they fled England in 1607 and settled in Amsterdam. Fearing the influence of the city's large Anabaptist population, however, they relocated to Leyden in 1609. But they still felt threatened by other faiths, worrying that their children would be led astray and cease to be English. Another more radical and distant move was necessary.

Many members of this congregation decided to move to Virginia led by William Brewster. They agreed to work for the Virginia Company, which secured their passage. On September 6, 1620, 102 passengers set sail for Virginia aboard the *Mayflower*. Only thirty-five were members of the Robinson congregation though. Blown off course, the *Mayflower* landed at Cape Cod on November 11, 1620. The Pilgrims resolved to stay and founded Plymouth Colony. As most of the *Mayflower* passengers were not members of the congregation, Pilgrims feared the nonmembers would be uncooperative. So before they left the ship, all male passengers signed the Mayflower Compact on November 11. Authored by William Bradford, the compact became the basis of civil government for the settlers of Plymouth Plantation. Those who signed it vowed to

> covenant and combine ourselves together in a civil body politic, for our better ordering and preservation and furtherance of the ends aforesaid; and by virtue hereof to enact, constitute, and frame such just and equal laws, ordinances, acts, constitutions, and offices from time to time, as shall be thought most meet and convenient for the general

good of the Colony, unto which we promise all due submission and obedience.[4]

The signatories agreed to follow the laws enacted by the community and work together for the betterment of all. In actuality, the Mayflower Compact was a Separatist church covenant that was adapted for the new civil government. It remained the constitution of Plymouth Plantation until it joined the Massachusetts Bay Colony in 1691.

The largest number of Puritans settled at Salem and Boston in 1630. An early governor of Massachusetts Bay, John Endicott (1589–1665), was a devout Puritan who brought many settlers to Salem in 1630. He banished anyone who was not a Puritan, beheaded four Quakers, and began the Pequot War (1634–1638), which nearly destroyed the entire Pequot nation. He even removed the cross from the English insignia because he believed it had Catholic connotations. As a Puritan, Endicott did not have good rapport with the Separatists at Plymouth. This relationship was eventually improved by a Separatist doctor named Samuel Fuller (1580–1633), who saved many lives in Salem.

Massachusetts Bay Colony received a royal charter in 1629. It encompassed much of what is now Massachusetts, Maine, New Hampshire, Connecticut, and Rhode Island. Plymouth Plantation and Salem colonies were absorbed into Massachusetts Bay Colony in 1691.

To escape the persecution of Charles I in England, thousands of Puritans poured into Massachusetts Bay from 1630 to 1640, and Boston became the capital. One of the most influential early Puritans, John Winthrop (1587–1649), preached aboard ship on his journey to America. His most famous sermon became known as "City on a Hill." It presented his belief that Boston would become a Christian city watched and admired by England and the entire world. Winthrop was elected governor of Massachusetts Bay Colony on October 20, 1629, and served several terms in office.

A theocratic government was established in 1631. Only members of the Congregational churches could vote in the colony. Having left England for religious liberty, they were now the majority and imposed their religious beliefs on everyone in the colony.

Under the leadership of Reverend Thomas Hooker (1586–1647), a critic of the Massachusetts leadership, Puritanism arrived in Connecticut in 1636. Early Connecticut leaders included John Davenport (1597–1670) and Theophilus Eaton (1590–1658), who organized the New Haven colony in Southern Connecticut. These men instituted a strict form of Puritanism. The Congregational Church was the established church, fines were levied against those who did not attend Sunday services, and taxes were collected to pay ministers and maintain churches. New Haven Colony merged with Connecticut in 1664.

The Puritan colonies outside of Massachusetts Bay (Plymouth, Connecticut, New Haven, and New Hampshire) adopted a system that became known as the New England Way. The leading Puritan divine in Boston, John Cotton (1585–1652), began to press for its adoption in 1636, and it soon became the standard in Congregational polity. To be a member of the Congregational church and vote in civil elections, a person had to describe or at least give credible evidence of his conversion. Only church members could be elected to public office. The New England Way wove Puritan ideology into the political and social fabric of New England.

RHODE ISLAND

Rhode Island was the notable exception to Puritan domination of New England. Banished from Boston, Salem, and Plymouth to Rhode Island for his Separatist teachings and for his belief that the natives were the true owners of the land, Roger Williams (1603–1683) settled a town he named Providence in 1638. Williams's settlement believed religion was a matter of individual conscience, not state determination. The state and the church were separate entities.

Roger Williams, not Thomas Jefferson (1743–1826), coined the term "wall of separation between church and state."

In a notable war of books with John Cotton, who believed in state-controlled religion, Williams wrote *Bloudy Tenent of Persecution* (1644), contending that state enforcement of religion tainted religion:

> God does not require any uniformity of religion to be enacted and enforced in any civil state; which enforced uniformity, sooner or later, is the greatest occasion of civil war, ravishing of conscience, persecution of Christ Jesus in his servants, and of the hypocrisy and destruction of millions of souls.[5]

Williams was briefly a Baptist and helped to form the first Baptist church in America at Providence in 1638. His time as a Baptist, however, was fleeting. After only a few months, he became a Seeker and never again affiliated with a denomination. He was responsible for securing Rhode Island's charter in 1644. Williams is still remembered as one of America's greatest spokesmen for religious liberty.

A Particular Baptist, John Clarke (1609–1676), founded the second Baptist church in America at Newport, Rhode Island, in 1644. He authored *Ill Newes from New England* (1652), condemning the Massachusetts Bay Congregationalists for persecuting Baptists. In graphic detail he described the whipping of Baptist leader Obadiah Holmes (ca. 1606–1682). This text won much sympathy for Baptists and sparked conversation concerning religious liberty. Clarke was responsible for acquiring Rhode Island's second charter in 1663.

Anne Hutchinson (1591–1643) was also banished from Massachusetts Bay Colony and briefly found refuge in Rhode Island. While in Boston, Hutchinson met with other women to discuss the sermons of her pastor and friend John Cotton. She argued that good works were not evidence of a person's salvation and said only the inward "seal of the Spirit" could evidence justification. She claimed that God communicated with her privately and said the Congregational ministers, Cotton excepted, taught a works-based faith. The colony's leaders frowned on her gatherings, especially after they began to attract a few men. Hutchinson was put on trial by Governor John Winthrop, accused of antinomianism, and expelled. Relocating to Rhode Island, she and her husband founded Portsmouth. After her husband's death she moved to New York, where she and all but one of her fifteen children were murdered by the Siwanoy Indians. The Puritans viewed her death as God's judgment.

The Middle Colonies

The middle colonies consisted of New Amsterdam, West Jersey, East Jersey, Pennsylvania, Delaware River, and Maryland. These colonies were not dominated by any one branch of Christianity. New Amsterdam had a large number of Dutch immigrants affiliated with the Dutch Reformed Church, which was formed in New Amsterdam in 1628. Unlike their Reformed brethren in Massachusetts Bay, they were less restrictive about who could live in their colony. In 1654 the Dutch even allowed twenty-four Jewish immigrants to settle in New Amsterdam. The Dutch Reformed Church also found a home in East Jersey. After the Third Dutch-Anglo War (1672–1674), New Amsterdam was ceded to England and renamed New York. The Church of England became the established church in 1693.

George Fox (1624–1691) founded the Society of Friends, popularly known as the Quakers. His teachings emphasized an inner light that could supersede Scripture, pacifism, and a ban on swearing oaths. These tenets made the Quakers a despised group by both Catholics and Protestants of Europe. Heavily persecuted by the Stuart monarchy, they sought a home in the New World. Those who migrated to New England were persecuted by the Puritans.

The Quakers ended up in Pennsylvania when Charles II (1660–1685) provided Quaker William Penn (1644–1718) with a land charter in 1681 to pay off a debt. Pennsylvania (Penn's Woods) became a haven not only for Quakers but for people of all persecuted religions. A large number of German Mennonites settled Germantown near Philadelphia. Scotch-Irish Presbyterians and Lutherans established themselves in the colony's western expanses.

MARYLAND

Unlike the other colonies, where Protestantism held sway, Maryland had a large Catholic population. A former secretary of state to James I, George Calvert (1579–1632), the first Lord Baltimore, converted to Catholicism in 1624 and resigned his government positions. However, he remained a loyal Englishmen and a member the King's Privy Council. In spite of Calvert's conversion, Charles I was determined to repay him for service rendered to James. So Charles granted the Calverts a royal charter in 1632 for land north of the Potomac River on the Chesapeake Bay. George Calvert, however, died before he could see his colony. His son Cecil Calvert (1605–1675) became the second Lord Baltimore and took charge of the colonial endeavor. Cecil Calvert named the colony after Charles I's Catholic wife Henrietta Maria (1625–1666) and the capital after his family's title. Even though there was a strong Jesuit presence in Maryland, Calvert did not make Catholicism the state-sanctioned religion. Wanting to increase trade and his family's income, he welcomed all religions into his colony. The Calverts' original charter was revoked in 1691, and they ceased to be the proprietors of Maryland. The Church of England became the official church of Maryland in 1702. After converting to Anglicanism, the fourth Lord Baltimore, Benedict Calvert (1679–1715), regained Maryland as a proprietary possession in 1715. It remained a Calvert possession until after the American Revolution.

The Southern Colonies

Anglicanism was the official religion of what became Virginia, North Carolina, South Carolina, and Georgia. The Virginia Company of London organized Virginia's first permanent city at Jamestown in 1607. The company dissolved in 1624, and Virginia became a royal colony. By 1625, Virginia was the most important of the Southern colonies as its tobacco farms proved prosperous. The Church of England attempted to set up a parish system in Virginia similar to that in England, with a set territory and its occupants under the guidance of one priest. Laws mandated church attendance, required Sabbath observance, and forbade irreverent lifestyles.

But several problems hampered the parish system and the enforcement of these laws. First, the Church of England failed to provide America with a bishop. This debilitated the American church since only a bishop could confirm full membership and ordain new ministers. As Virginia was the largest colony controlled by the Church of England, the ramifications of this failure were exacerbated. Second, the ministers that the Church of England supplied were often corrupt. Third, many of the colonists were more interested in turning a profit than religion. Fourth, with a lack of clergy and great distances between churches, parish churches were poorly attended. The Church of England, therefore, was not as strong a presence in Virginia as the Congregational Church was in New England.

An Anglican church was founded at Charleston in 1681, and in 1704 the Church of England became the established church in South Carolina. By 1725 it established thirteen parishes. Though the Church of England was the established church, South Carolina had a large number of Baptists and Huguenots. Prior to the Revolution, Charleston also had a Jewish community of approximately 500.

The Church of England had a much more difficult time establishing itself in North Carolina because the colony was inundated with Baptists, Quakers, and Presbyterians. The colonial assembly established the Church of England in 1701 and in 1705 passed a law that required citizens to pay taxes to support it. Dissenters often refused to pay those taxes and revolts were common. North Carolina became a royal colony in 1729, and the crown established the Church of England in 1741. Despite their illegal status, Shubal Stearns (1706–1771) organized a large group of Baptists at Sandy Creek by 1755. Destined to play a major role in American Baptist life, the Sandy Creek Association was formed in 1758.

Founded by James Oglethorpe (1696–1785) in 1733, Georgia was the last of the original thirteen colonies to be organized. Oglethorpe envisioned Georgia as a colony where debtors could work off their financial obligations without fear of arrest. The Church of England became the established church in 1758. In spite of the Anglican establishment, Georgia proved to be a safe haven for Baptists, Quakers, Lutherans, and other denominations. By 1733 a large number of Jews found sanctuary and freedom to worship in Savannah. Catholics were not permitted to worship in Georgia until 1777.

Despite the Church of England's difficulties in some Southern colonies, there were several Anglican success stories. Serving for fifty-four years, John Blair (1655–1743) was the commissary of the Church of England in Virginia. He founded William and Mary College in 1693 and relocated the capital to Williamsburg in 1698. One disappointment in Georgia proved to be a blessing. Anglican missionary John Wesley (1703–1791) came to Georgia in the mid-1730s and failed utterly in his evangelistic endeavors. He then returned to England and launched the Methodist movement.

Another notable heritage of the Southern colonies was slavery. Slaves were imported from Africa to work the tobacco farms, and without a strong religious presence to lobby for their better treatment, slavery in the Southern colonies was often brutal.

RELIGIOUS EDUCATION

Soon after settling in the New World, Protestant groups began to establish universities. Their purpose was to provide an education for Christian ministers. These universities have remained in continuous existence and are considered by many to be among the best in the United States. The oldest institution of higher learning in the United States, Harvard University, was founded by Congregationalists in Cambridge, Massachusetts, in 1636. Chartered in 1693 and located in Williamsburg, Virginia, William and Mary College is the second-oldest university in the United States. It was originally affiliated with the Church of England. Created to educate Congregational clergy, Yale University was founded in 1701 and located in New Haven, Connecticut. In 1746 Princeton University was established in Elizabeth, New Jersey, as the College of New Jersey. Though it had strong ties to the Presbyterian Church, it never had an official religious affiliation. Created in 1764 as Rhode Island College, Brown University was Baptist. These universities no longer have any affiliation with their founding denominations.

CHAPTER TWENTY-TWO

UNFORESEEN OPPOSITION

When Luther challenged the teachings of the Catholic Church, he opened the door for new assessments of age-old Christian beliefs. The Reformers, however, questioned the particulars of Catholic doctrine and tradition, not the validity of Christianity as a whole. By the end of the seventeenth century, carnage from the wars of religion and scientific breakthroughs prompted a more critical examination of Christianity.

The Age of Reason and the Enlightenment (1650–1800) produced a new type of philosopher. Largely from England, France, and Germany, Enlightenment thinkers believed science, mathematics, philosophy, observation, and reason were the basis of knowledge. Many Enlightenment thinkers concluded that the miracles of Christianity could either be explained by natural law or dismissed as mythical. Naturally, the conclusions of Enlightenment figures often clashed with the Bible.

THE DAWN OF THE AGE OF REASON

Catholics had long accepted the geocentric model of the universe, in which the sun revolved around a flat earth.[1] Psalm 93:1 was cited as proof that the earth was at the center of the universe: "The

LORD reigns! He is robed in majesty; the LORD is robed, enveloped in strength. The world is firmly established; it cannot be shaken." Joshua 10:12–13 was another text believed to suggest a flat earth:

> On the day the LORD gave the Amorites over to the Israelites, Joshua spoke to the LORD in the presence of Isra-. el: "Sun, stand still over Gibeon, and moon, over the Valley of Aijalon." And the sun stood still and the moon stopped until the nation took vengeance on its enemies. Isn't this written in the Book of Jashar? So the sun stopped in the middle of the sky and delayed its setting almost a full day.

A scholar of the late Renaissance, Nicholas Copernicus (1473–1543), was one of the first to challenge geocentrism. His 1543 book *De Revolutionibus Orbium Coelestium* argued that the movement of celestial objects demonstrated that the earth was not at the center of the universe. The earth revolved around the sun. The implications of this theory were enormous. If the earth was not the center of the solar system, then it seemed humanity was not at the center of creation. The Catholic Church placed the book on the Index in 1616. Copernicus's theories were also rejected by Protestants.

A professor of mathematics at Pisa and Padua, Galileo Galilei (1564–1642), took a keen interest in Copernicus's theories. Using a telescope, he observed celestial objects and proved that Copernicus's cosmology was correct. Galileo's assertion that the universe could be explained mathematically threatened to remove much of the mystery from the biblical story of creation. Moreover, this theory did not regard the Christian heaven as one of the many objects in the sky—a troubling notion for some. The papacy reacted by declaring that Galileo was in error and reaffirming the traditional geocentric cosmology. After he published a *Dialogue Concerning the Two Chief World Systems* in 1632, which asserted his heliocentric theories, Galileo was forced to recant and placed under house arrest for the remainder of his life. The Catholic Church's condemnation of Galileo damaged its reputation and typified its reaction to challenges. During the papacy of John Paul II (1978–2005) in 1992, the Catholic Church formally decreed that the authorities who condemned Galileo were in error.

Isaac Newton (1642–1727) confirmed the truth of Copernicus's and Galileo's theory. He maintained that the universe was governed by a set of immutable natural laws and compared its operation to the workings of a machine. In his 1687 book *Mathematical Principles of Natural Philosophy*, he presented the laws of motion and gravity, explaining why planets revolved around the sun. Newtonian principles were based on reason.

Following Newton's example, other European thinkers began to believe they could discover secrets of the universe by reason and observation. Some began to reject anything that could not be proved by the scientific method, including traditional Christian doctrines. Newton, for one, denied the divinity of Christ and the Trinity. He did, however, see God in the order of the universe. The transcendent God set natural laws in place and held complete authority over the universe, he said.

World exploration bolstered the idea that man could acquire transcendent truth merely by observing the universe. When explorers returned to Europe, they described Chinese and Native American religions that were similar in many ways to Christianity. Without the aid of churches or the Bible, these people often lived by the principles expressed in the Ten Commandments and believed in a great spirit that created the world. This led Enlightenment thinkers to conclude that a common ethic not dependent on Christianity was inherent in all humanity.

RATIONALISM AND EMPIRICISM

A politician and advisor to Queen Elizabeth I and King James I, Francis Bacon (1561–1626) was known as the Father of Empiricism.

(Empiricism is the belief that knowledge comes through sensory experience.) Bacon accepted no knowledge solely on the basis of authority. He demonstrated the validity of inductive reasoning in his *Novum Organum* (1620). According to Bacon, one first formed a hypothesis, then observed facts, checked them by experimentation, and developed a general law. Bacon's inductive method of reasoning challenged the older deductive method that dominated scholasticism. The deductive method taught that if the premises of a hypothesis were accepted, the hypothesis must be correct. Deductive reasoning was based on syllogisms and did not employ scientific experimentation. As the common philosophical example went, "Socrates is a man. All men are mortal. Therefore, Socrates is mortal." For Bacon, the problem was that often conclusions were based on false premises. Without experimentation, thinkers tended not to recognize their false premises.

In *Novum Organum* Bacon also outlined his theory of the four idols that hinder understanding. The "idols of the tribe" are the senses and human nature, which can be deceiving. The "idols of the cave" are presuppositions and prejudices that individuals develop based on their unique experiences. The "idols of the market" are a failure to understand the meaning of words. The "idols of the theater" are philosophical dogmas that people accept uncritically.

In religion, Bacon's inductive reasoning led him to conclude that God provided man with natural knowledge and a rational soul. Moreover, the universe was governed by natural laws that could be comprehended through reason. Man's rationality allowed him to understand something of God's purposes.

Trained as a Jesuit, René Descartes (1596–1650) was a French philosopher who believed human behavior was ruled by the mind and the body. The mind was spiritual. The body was composed of matter and functioned like a machine. When one physically sensed something, the mind discerned the proper reaction, Descartes said. Sometimes, however, passions caused humans to act without the guidance of the mind. The spiritual mind was always correct if the body did not lead it astray. The responsibility for one's actions rested with the individual alone. Descartes believed that if the passions of institutional religion were eliminated, minds could reason more effectively without undue interference.

As a rationalist (one who believed that reason, not sensory data, was the source of knowledge), Descartes believed knowledge had to be established through reason. He based his philosophy on the premise that everything except one's own consciousness should be doubted. The only foundational belief a person could reasonably hold was that he was thinking. As Descartes put it, *"Cogito ergo sum"* ("I think; therefore I am"). He wrote:

> I will now shut my eyes, stop my ears, and withdraw all my senses. I will eliminate from my thoughts all images of bodily things, or rather, since this is hardly possible, I will regard all such images as vacuous, false, and worthless. I will converse with myself and scrutinize myself more deeply; and in this way I will attempt to achieve, little by little, a more intimate knowledge of myself. I am a thing that thinks—that is, a thing that doubts, affirms, denies, understands a few things, is ignorant of many things, is willing, is unwilling, and also that imagines and has sensory perceptions. For, as I have noted before, even though the objects of my sensory experience and imagination may have no existence outside me, nonetheless the modes of thinking that I refer to as cases of sensory perception and imagination, insofar, as they are simply modes of thinking, do exist within me—of that I am certain.[2]

Descartes made several arguments for the existence of God. According to his ontological argument, man realized he was an imperfect being but still had the ability to entertain the idea of a perfect God. The idea had a greater cause than man. This greater cause was God. But Descartes's idea of God was mechanistic and based more on reason than biblical revelation.

Thomas Hobbes (1588–1679) argued that all matter remained in motion and all natural events were predetermined. As sensory beings, humans perceived the attributes of an object by its motions. A particular motion caused one's senses to determine, for example, that an odor was sour, a sound was loud, or the sun was bright. Innate knowledge did not exist; all knowledge came from one's senses.

Hobbes did not view humanity in terms of a body/mind dichotomy. The mind and the body were both composed of matter and worked together. There was no role for spirituality. The senses perceived something and sent the information to the mind, which produced physical perceptions of the object. Humans then perceived the object either in a positive way and desired it or in a negative way and were revolted by it.

Hobbes maintained that all people were egotists and acted in their personal interest at the expense of others. His belief in the egotistic nature of humanity became the basis of his political philosophy. In *Leviathan* (1651) he argued that people must obey their governments, even tyrannical governments, for without government the world would lapse into chaos. Man's ego would lead to murder, wars, theft, and other atrocities.

In Hobbes's native England, the acceptance of government was inseparable from obedience to the Church of England. He believed only troublemakers claimed the mind was spiritual. It was an excuse for them to say that God led them to act against the Church of England. According to Hobbes, reform advocates were "enthusiasts" acting on their physical desires.

John Locke (1632–1704) was perhaps the most influential empiricist. Published in 1690, his *An Essay Concerning Human Understanding* said that all human knowledge derived from sensation. There were no fixed or innate ideas such as time and space. A baby's mind, therefore, was a blank slate (*tabula rasa*). The baby's knowledge grew as it was enlightened by its senses and experience. The senses and the mind worked together and created understanding. This theory contradicted the belief that man had innate knowledge of God.

In his *Reasonableness of Christianity* (1695), Locke argued that the existence of God could be proved by cause and effect. Since nature was a system of causes, changes, and power, one could determine that a supreme being existed who caused the system. This idea was known as the cosmological argument. Locke also maintained that an idea of God could be developed by examining our own minds and their positive qualities, such as knowledge and wisdom. One could infinitely expand these qualities and arrive at an idea of God.

For Locke, the essence of Christianity included the acceptance of Christ as the Messiah. But he believed Christianity was merely a clear explanation of truths that everyone could discern with their natural faculties. Christ's role was to spread the knowledge of God and teach the moral duties that people owed to him. Man could prove Christ's identity as Messiah and his role as a moral guide. It was unreasonable to believe in Christ's divinity and miracles though.

Locke believed in religious toleration for everyone except Catholics and atheists. In *Letter Concerning Toleration* (1690) he asserted that it was impossible to evaluate the claims of competing religious viewpoints, that true belief could not be established by law, and that the coercion of religious uniformity would cause dissent. His *Two Treatises of Government* (1689) taught that humans had natural rights independent of government or society. People had the right to make choices concerning their lives, to be happy, and not to live in fear. People had the right to profit from the land they worked. The purpose of the government was to protect these rights. With these ideas Locke contributed to the rise of capitalism.

To protect inalienable rights, Locke developed his theory of the social contract. A government should arise from the consent of its people, he said. The task of a government was to protect the rights of its people. In turn, the people agreed to be governed. He saw no rational basis for the divine right of kings. Locke's concept of natural rights and social contract became cornerstones of the United States Constitution and Bill of Rights.

DEISM

Originating in sixteenth-century England, deism was the fruit of empiricism and the new sciences. It taught that God was transcendent and the first cause. He placed the world under natural laws and let it operate according to those laws, much as a child could pull the string on a top and watch it spin. The child was the first cause but did not interfere with the top's spinning. Humans were implanted with a moral compass and were to live by ethical laws discerned from the Bible. Christ was a moral teacher, not divine, and not a worker of miracles.

PROMINENT DEISTS

Many great thinkers of the sixteenth, seventeenth, and eighteenth centuries were deists. Among them were Edward Herbert (Lord Cherbury) (1583–1648), David Hume (1711–1776), François-Marie Arouet (1694–1778), Jean-Jacques Rousseau (1712–1778), and several of the Founding Fathers of the United States.

Advisor to Elizabeth I and James I, Edward Herbert was a soldier, an ambassador to France, and a deistic philosopher. His *On Truth* (1624) claimed that man was born with innate ideas that were the basis for all knowledge. He equated true religion with five tenets of deism in his 1663 book *Ancient Religion of the Gentiles*. First, there is a supreme being. Second, this supreme being must be worshipped. Third, virtue and piety must be a part of worshipping this supreme being. Fourth, humanity must repent. Fifth, the supreme being's justice will be applied in this world and the next.

David Hume disagreed with the rationalists. He did not believe in innate concepts. True knowledge came only through experience and observation, he said. Because men observed and experienced things through the lens of their own presuppositions, they never perceived the unadulterated truth. Absolute truth, therefore, could never be attained. Hume also held that personal sentiment, not abstract moral principles, was the basis for one's ethics.

In *Dialogues Concerning Natural Religion* (1779), Hume disagreed with the argument from design. Though it was possible to see that nature had an author, he believed this author also had an author. This led to infinite regression and made him question the existence of God. For Hume, it was "absurd to inquire for a general cause or first author."[3] He maintained that religion and miracles were nothing more than misunderstandings of human experience. Religion was perpetuated through fear and hope. Though he claimed to be a deist, Hume is more accurately described as an agnostic.

Better known by his pseudonym Voltaire, François-Marie Arouet's writings ridiculed traditional theology, the French government, and the Catholic Church. A deist, he believed in a supreme being that set the laws of nature but not the God of the Bible. Since man had no way of knowing God, he said, it was foolish to assume that one group had a better understanding of how to worship him than another. He concluded that all religions should be tolerated. For Voltaire, Christianity was nothing but superstition. God designed the world with natural laws and then let it run on its own.

Voltaire believed nations were of natural origin. Kings, therefore, were not appointed by God. The sovereign should be selected by the people. If the people believed the sovereign was corrupt or incompetent, he could and should be replaced. This belief, coupled with his railings against the Catholic Church, helped promote the French Revolution and an anticlericalism still evident in France.

A Genevan philosopher, Jean-Jacques Rousseau, believed that man was initially good, free, and happy. Society, however, corrupted humanity. In order to gain success, money, or position, a person had to appear to have the same desires as those in power. The result was a society built on hypocrisy.

Rousseau's *Social Contract* (1762) argued for government based on the general will. Although he believed Christians made inferior citizens, he was a strong advocate of religious toleration because religion was a means of enforcing social morality. As a deist, he saw God in creation. Creation was good because God was good. This goodness was marred by the influence of humans.

Freedom of religion in America owes much to deism. Influential American deists included Thomas Jefferson (1743–1826), Benjamin Franklin (1706–1790), and Thomas Paine (1737–1809). They maintained that man was naturally good and through reason could establish a better state. The Declaration of Independence reflects the influence of deism (though not all of the Founding Fathers were deists, and Christianity influenced them as well) in the lines: "We hold these truths to be self-evident, that all men are created equal, that they are endowed by their Creator with certain unalienable Rights, that among these are Life, Liberty, and the pursuit of Happiness." In *The Life and Morals of Jesus of Nazareth*, or as it became more popularly known, *The Jefferson Bible*, Jefferson removed the stories of the miracles and emphasized the ethical teachings of Christ. He did not believe Jesus was divine. Like Voltaire, these men maintained that nations established on the divine right of kings were based on unreasonable premises.

One of the most influential American books in support of deism was Thomas Paine's *Age of Reason: Being an Investigation of True and Fabulous Theology* (1794). Paine wrote:

> Deism, then, teaches us, without the possibility of being deceived all that is necessary or proper to be known. The creation is the Bible of the Deist. He there reads, in the handwriting of the Creator himself, the certainty of his existence and the immutability of his power, and all other

Bibles and Testaments are to him forgeries. The probability that we may be called to account hereafter will, to a reflecting mind, have the influence of belief; for it is not our belief or disbelief that can make or unmake the fact. As this is the state we are in, and which it is proper we should be in, as free agents, it is the fool only, and not the philosopher, or even the prudent man, that would live as if there were no God.[4]

Paine insisted that reason trumped revelation.

Of all the systems of religion that ever were invented, there is none more derogatory to the Almighty, more unedifying to man, more repugnant to reason, and more contradictory to itself than this thing called Christianity. Too absurd for belief, too impossible to convince, and too inconsistent for practice, it renders the heart torpid or produces only atheists or fanatics. As an engine of power, it serves the purpose of despotism, and as a means of wealth, the avarice of priests, but so far as respects the good of man in general it leads to nothing here or hereafter.[5]

Deism also had a strong influence on the French Revolution. After French leaders consulted with Thomas Jefferson, the *French Declaration of the Rights of Man and of Its Citizens* was published in 1789 and became the basis of the Revolution:

The Representatives of the French people, organized as a National Assembly, believing that the ignorance, neglect, or contempt of the rights of man are the sole cause of public calamities and of the corruption of governments, have determined to set forth in a solemn declaration the natural, unalienable, and sacred rights of man, in order that this declaration, being constantly before all members of the Social body, shall remind them continually of their rights and duties; in order that the acts of the legislative power, as well as those of the executive power, may be compared at any moment with the objects and purposes of all political institutions and may thus be more respected, and, lastly, in order that the grievances of the citizens, based hereafter upon simple and incontestable principles, shall tend to the maintenance of the constitution and redound to the happiness of all. Therefore the National Assembly recognizes and proclaims, in the presence and under the auspices of the Supreme Being, the following rights of man and of the citizen.[6]

OPPONENTS OF DEISM

In England, Joseph Butler (1692–1752) and William Paley (1743–1805) lost no time responding to the arguments of deists. The Anglican bishop of Durham, Butler believed the deist empirical method left too many questions unanswered. In *Analogy of Religion* (1736), he argued that natural religion and Christianity both advanced arguments based on probability. Natural religion was not superior but involved many of the same difficulties as revealed Christianity. This suggested that the same God was the author of both natural religion and Christianity. Wise people, therefore, should accept both, basing their theology on observation of the world and Scripture.

In addition to his arguments against deism, Paley offered an argument for God's existence that became famous. In *Natural Theology,* he wrote that if a man were walking on a beach and found a watch, he would realize that someone made it. In comparison, when a person examined the clocklike regularity of nature, he had to assume there was a designer:

> In crossing a heath, suppose I pitch my foot against a stone and were asked how the stone came to be there. I might possibly answer that, for anything I knew to the

contrary, it had lain there forever; nor would it perhaps
be very easy to show the absurdity of this answer. But suppose I had found a watch upon the ground and it should
be inquired how the watch happened to be in that place. I
should hardly think of the answer which I had given before,
that, for anything, I knew, the watch might have always
been there. Yet why should not this answer for the watch
as well as the stone? Why is it not admissible in the second
case, as in the first? For this reason, and for no other, namely, that when we come to inspect the watch, we perceive
(what we could not discover in the stone) that its several
parts are framed and put together for a purpose.[7]

The Enlightenment

The Enlightenment was an amalgamation of science, reason,
and deism. It emphasized humanity's goodness, progress, freedom, and innate rights. Some Enlightenment thinkers believed the
world's great questions were on the verge of being answered. They
distrusted tradition. Reason, observation, and experiment were
their authorities. The Bible was not exempt from critical examination. This manner of thinking led many to reject Christian concepts
such as the Trinity, revelation, miracles, and the incarnation.

A professor at the University of Königsberg, Prussia, Immanuel
Kant (1724–1804), held that human enlightenment had emerged,
replacing self-imposed immaturity that discouraged independent
thinking. He contended that religion was particularly guilty of lim-
iting thought and believed it had to be tested by experience.

Kant based his theories on the teachings of Locke and
Descartes. He asserted that sensory perception was the basis of
knowledge. Man had no *a priori* knowledge. Still, man's senses were
not totally accurate. They perceived the appearance of reality, not
reality itself. Kant called the sensory perception of an object the

phenomenon. An object's reality was the *noumenon. Noumena* could only be known indirectly, mediated by perception. To make sense of *noumena,* the mind shaped them into recognizable *phenomena* or categories of understanding.

In *Critique of Pure Reason* (1781) Kant argued that neither reason nor the senses allowed man to know the *noumenon* of God. Traditional Christian concepts like the deity of Christ and the truthfulness of the Bible were not the unmediated, absolute truth, according to Kant. He admitted that the existence of God could not be disproved. God, therefore, could not be dismissed. Still, if one chose to believe in God, he would have to admit that his belief was not based on reason or deduction. Kant wrote, "I have therefore found it necessary to deny knowledge, in order to make room for faith."[8]

For Kant the universal and unconditional Categorical Imperative, not religious dogma, was the basis of morality. According to the Categorical Imperative, humans should only act according to moral principles they willed to become universal laws. Put another way, the Categorical Imperative required people to treat others as ends, not as a means to reach personal and selfish goals.

The Positivity of the Christian Religion (1795), written by a philosopher in Berlin, Georg Hegel (1770–1831), maintained that Christianity had become legalistic and had forgotten Christ's moral teachings. True Christianity centered on God's love for man embodied in Christ. This love allowed humanity to be reconciled to God. According to Hegel, religious concepts were figurative representations depicted in rational terms. Hegel's influence was significant. He believed ideas were evolving continually. He called this process "dialectic." In Hegel's dialectic, one posed a "thesis," then questioned it with an "antithesis," and finally arrived at a third idea called a "synthesis" that combined whatever was of value in the first two. The entire process started over with the synthesis becoming a new thesis. At each dialectic level a deeper understanding evolved. Ideas that did not go through this process remained fragmented.

Hegel's most important application of dialectic was to religion. He believed Christianity was the "absolute religion," the culmination of religious development that summed up the most significant truths in other world religions. His book *Life of Jesus* presented Jesus as a rationalistic philosopher and his miracles as metaphors for doctrines.

CHAPTER TWENTY-THREE

EIGHTEENTH-CENTURY AMERICA

By the dawn of the eighteenth century, there was a notable decline in church attendance, spirituality, and morality throughout the colonies. There are many theories as to why this occurred. One is that the Enlightenment reached New England. This led to skepticism regarding supernatural events described in the Bible. Common sense and reason seemed more prudent than supernatural faith. In addition, the percentage of settlers who came to the New World in search of religious freedom dwindled. Seventeenth-century immigrants were among the first to seek the "American Dream": the idea that hard work would bring prosperity. Some immigrants were merchants seeking better business and commercial opportunities. Others were rugged adventurers who wanted to carve out a life in the American wilderness. These people had little interest in the Puritan ideas of election and moral rigidity. In the Southern colonies, the Church of England's parish system could do little for a population pushing westward. Other denominations such as the Baptists, however, began to make inroads in the Southern colonies.

After the initial surge of Puritan immigrants in the 1630s, the flow of Puritans from England slowed. Moreover, many of the children of the first Puritans did not exhibit the same religious zeal as their parents. They too were caught up in the American Dream. In

325

order to retain their control in both the civil and religious realms, the religious leaders of New England were forced to make several compromises. The Halfway Covenant was one such concession. Under the Halfway Covenant, second-generation Puritans who made no profession of conversion but still lived pious lives and remained committed to the church were considered halfway members. They were permitted to bring their children to be baptized and also become halfway members. Halfway members could not take the Lord's Supper and were not permitted to vote in the church. The Halfway Covenant weakened the commitment and spirituality of the Congregational churches somewhat but in doing so kept the church's power over society intact. The Halfway Covenant was ratified by a synod in 1662.

The brand of Puritanism that manifested itself in Salem, Massachusetts, in 1692 repelled many from the New England Way. Several girls in the town began behaving unusually, having fits and exhibiting strange contortions. When no medical causes for the behavior could be discovered, three local women were accused of bewitching the girls. This spawned a series of baseless accusations that various people in the community were involved in witchcraft. To make matters worse, the local pastor, Samuel Paris (1653–1720), invited ecclesiastical authorities from neighboring Puritan communities to Salem to investigate and help try accused witches. The leading Puritan divine of the day, Cotton Mather (1663–1728), approved several trials that were intended to uncover the identities of witches. The only way accused witches could avoid the gallows was to confess, repent, and then name other witches. Before order and reason returned to Salem, fourteen men and six women were hanged as witches. One man was pressed to death. The Salem witch trials became a hallmark of Puritan excess and a factor in the steady decline of the church in New England.

Several members of the clergy were dismayed by the religious lethargy that was becoming prevalent. Among them was

Solomon Stoddard (1643–1729), pastor of the Congregational church in Northampton, Massachusetts, and grandfather of Jonathan Edwards (1703–1758). In his sermon "Defects of Preachers Reproved," he accused the clergy of knowing Christianity but not practicing it, drawing a parallel between them and the biblical Pharisees. Ungodly preachers contributed to an ungodly laity, he said:

> There is great complaint in one country and in another, that there be but few converted; it is apparent by men's unsanctified lives and their unsavory discourses. This is one Reason, there is a great deal of preaching that does not promote it, but it is a hindrance to it. . . . In some towns there is no such thing to be observed for twenty years together. And men continue in a senseless condition, come to meeting and hear preaching, but are never the better for it.[1]

The Great Awakening

In the midst of this religious lethargy, one of the most unexpected transformations in American religious history occurred. A wave of awakenings swept the colonies in the mid-1720s, climaxed in the 1740s, and concluded prior to the American Revolution. This wave of religious fervor became known as the Great Awakening. It began with the Dutch Reformed and soon spread to the Congregationalists, Presbyterians, and other Protestant bodies. The flames were fanned by itinerant ministers who held revivals that denounced sin and called for a renewal of Christian devotion. Such revival meetings were often spontaneous and unorganized. Thousands of people attended Great Awakening revivals and displayed religious fervor that had never been seen in the colonies. The most influential Great Awakening leaders were Theodore Frelinghuysen (1691–1748), William Tennent (1673–1745), Gilbert Tennent (1712–1751), Jonathan Edwards, and George Whitefield (1714–1770).

Accounts of the Great Awakening first emerged in the Raritan Valley of New Jersey in 1726. They centered on the preaching of Dutch Reformed pastor Theodore Frelinghuysen. Influenced by Pietism, his sermons stressed that true Christians lived godly lives and could recount their conversion experiences. Anyone who could not recount his conversion or was living an immoral life was barred from the Lord's Supper. Frelinghuysen derided his fellow ministers for their vanity and lack of concern for the spiritual life of their congregations.

William Tennent and his son Gilbert were Presbyterian ministers in Pennsylvania and New Jersey. They emphasized grace, a true conversion experience, and assurance of one's salvation. They believed that unconverted clergy contributed to the spiritual lethargy in their region. This belief led to Gilbert's most famous sermon, "The Danger of an Unconverted Ministry," in which he attacked ministers who opposed the Great Awakening and accused them of not being true Christians:

> Sad experience verifies what has been now observed concerning the unprofitableness of the ministry of unconverted men. Look into the congregations of unconverted ministers, and see what a sad security reigns there; not a soul convinced that can be heard of, for many years together; and yet the ministers are easy; for they will say they do their duty![2]

To train ministers who were true Christians and open to the Great Awakening, William Tennent founded the Log College in 1726. The Log College became the foundation for Princeton University.

Known as the theologian of the Great Awakening, Jonathan Edwards was a graduate of Yale College, knowledgeable in the writings of the Enlightenment, an evangelical preacher, and a Calvinist. He was pastor of the Northampton Congregational Church in

Massachusetts. He was strict in his pastoral methods. An excellent but unemotional preacher, Edwards's sermons emphasized the need for a new spiritual birth. In 1734 his sermons were met with emotional outcries of repentance, and a revival began. The revival soon spread throughout the Connecticut River Valley. He published his *A Faithful Narrative of the Surprising Works of God* in 1737 describing his church's revivals. This book made Edwards known and admired throughout the colonies. Eventually he fell into disfavor with many of his parishioners and was dismissed from the Northampton Church in 1750. He then became a missionary to the Indians and served for less than a year as president of the College of New Jersey before his death in 1758.

In Edwards's 1746 *Treatise Concerning Religious Affections*, he argued that emotion and intellect both played a role in Christian conversion but said virtuous living, not emotional outbursts, were the evidence of true conversion. Edwards published *Freedom of the Will* in 1754. In it he argued that man possessed all the faculties necessary to turn to God but lacked the moral inclination to do so. When a person turned to God and was converted, it was because God provided him with supernatural grace that overcame his moral rebellion. Edwards's most famous sermon, and perhaps the most famous sermon in American history, was "Sinners in the Hands of an Angry God," which depicted man as a spider dangling by a thread over the flames of hell:

> O sinner! Consider the fearful danger you are in: it is a great furnace of wrath, a wide bottomless pit, full of the fire of wrath, that you are held over in the hand of God, whose wrath is provoked and incensed as much against you, as against many of the damned in hell. You hang by a slender thread, with the flames of divine wrath flashing about it, and ready every moment to singe it, and burn it asunder; and you have no interest in any Mediator, and nothing to lay hold of to save yourself, nothing to keep you

off the flames of wrath, nothing of your own, nothing that you can do, to induce God to spare you for one moment. ... Therefore let everyone that is out of Christ, now awaken and fly from the wrath to come. The wrath of Almighty God is now undoubtedly hanging over the great part of this congregation: Let everyone fly out of Sodom: "Haste and escape for your lives, look not behind you, escape to the mountain, lest you be consumed."[3]

"Sinners in the Hands of an Angry God" stressed that the only way to avoid the wrath of God was for the sinner to realize the enormity of his sins and turn to Christ for salvation. When Edwards delivered this sermon, people repented in droves.

George Whitefield was the greatest preacher of the Great Awakening. He came to Georgia in 1738. After a brief stay he returned to England to raise money for an orphanage and to be ordained by the Church of England. His return trip to Georgia was delayed so he preached throughout England in 1739. Because of his extemporaneous preaching, evangelistic fervor, and failure to claim that he was Anglican, many parish churches were closed to him. With traditional doors closed, he held open-air meetings where thousands came to hear him preach. His sermons stressed piety and the need for a spiritual rebirth.

Returning to America in 1740, he found that his reputation preceded him, and crowds clamored to hear his sermons. In his New England services of 1740, he preached 130 sermons, traveled more than 800 miles in seventy-three days, and saw thousands converted. After attending a service in Philadelphia with an estimated 30,000 attendees, the deist Benjamin Franklin complimented Whitefield's magnificent oratory and his ability to move crowds. A skeptical reporter for the *New England Weekly Journal* attended a Whitefield service in New York in 1739 and reported what he saw:

I went to hear him in the evening at the Presbyterian Church, where he expounded to about 2000 people within and without the doors. I never in my life saw so attentive an audience: Mr. Whitefield spoke as one having authority: All he said was Demonstration, Life, and Power! The people's eyes and ears hung on his lips. They greedily devoured every word. I came home astonished! Every scruple vanished. I never saw or heard the like, and I said within myself, surely God is with this man of Truth.[4]

Whitefield preached from New England to Georgia in front of crowds that numbered in the thousands. One experience many American colonists had in common was attending a Whitefield service. Because of his Calvinistic inclinations, Whitefield broke in 1741 from his former ministry partners, the Arminian Wesleys, though their relationship remained largely cordial.

RESULTS OF THE GREAT AWAKENING

The Great Awakening affected many aspects of American religion and life. The idea of individual transformation fit well with the developing concept of American individualism. Morality, public decency, and church attendance improved. Though reports vary, it has been estimated that between 30,000 and 40,000 people joined New England churches, and thousands more joined churches in the middle colonies.

The Great Awakening created a spiritual bond among the colonists, and many began to believe they did not need the oversight of British denominations. Many colonists also believed America was the new Promised Land. These beliefs contributed to the American Revolution.

The Great Awakening disrupted the traditional role of the minister in many communities. There had been revivals prior to the Great Awakening, but they were led almost exclusively by local pastors and confined to particular congregations. The success of the Great Awakening revivalists undercut the traditional role of the minister. To many it appeared that the local pastor could not attract crowds and usher in a powerful revival. Thousands of people left "cold" churches for those that appeared to be more spiritually vibrant. Baptist churches were among the primary beneficiaries of these defections.

The Great Awakening split Congregational churches between "old lights" and "new lights." Both claimed to be the theological descendants of New England Puritanism. Epitomized by Charles Chauncy (1705–1787), pastor of First Church Boston and a forerunner of Unitarianism, old lights did not like the emotional excesses that accompanied the Great Awakening. Chauncy believed many who claimed to have been converted merely had emotional experiences rather than authentic spiritual transformations. Members of the new lights saw in the Great Awakening a powerful work of God.

More than 100 congregations split over the Great Awakening. Eighty of these became Separate Baptist congregations. One of the most notable new light churches was that of Isaac Backus (1724–1806) in Middleborough, Massachusetts. Backus was also known for his indefatigable efforts to ensure religious liberty and the separation of church and state.

The American Revolution (1775–1783)

The Great Awakening may have created a common American spirituality, but American Puritanism provided a theological rationale for the American Revolution. Since the seventeenth century, Puritans had maintained that America possessed a special Christian destiny. Puritans and many other Christian Americans believed they had made a covenant with God. In exchange for the new home God granted them, they were to make America a shining city on a hill that would be an example to the world. Allowing England to dictate how Americans were to live would destroy this covenant. Many American Christians adopted this belief by 1776.

When the American Revolution began, Christian denominations chose sides. The majority of Baptists, Congregationalists, Presbyterians, and Catholics sided with the revolutionaries. The Church of England was split; the Anglicans in New England generally sided with the revolutionaries while those in the South supported the crown.

Following the American Revolution, most Anglicans realized that their denomination could not survive in America with the British monarch as its official head. Therefore, they created an American version. Organized by Samuel Seabury (1729–1796), the Protestant Episcopal Church was formed in 1789. Even so, it almost collapsed.

The Methodists faced similar problems. When the Revolution broke out, John Wesley, who was pro-British, ordered all his ministers to return to England. Most obeyed, but Francis Asbury (1745–1816) remained in America and became the father of American Methodism.

Though they were pacifists, the Mennonite, Amish, and Quaker denominations sympathized with the revolutionary cause.

THE CONSTITUTION AND DISESTABLISHMENT

When the American Revolution ended and the United States was born, the nonestablished denominations called for freedom of religion, including Methodists, Presbyterians, and Baptists. Pointing out a parallel between the Baptist plight and that of America before the Revolution, Baptist leader Isaac Backus argued that since Baptists did not attend the state churches, the tax dollars they were required to pay the establishment amounted to taxation without representation.

Many of the Founding Fathers supported religious liberty and disestablishment of religion. Among the strongest advocates for religious liberty were Thomas Jefferson, Benjamin Franklin, and James Madison (1751–1836). They wanted freedom of conscience for all citizens and realized that a national church would interfere with governance. The First Amendment, therefore, was meant in part to protect the government from the church.

The first act of disestablishment took place in Virginia. Advocated by Jefferson, the Virginia Statute for Religious Freedom was ratified in 1786. A forerunner of the First Amendment to the United States Constitution, the statute stipulated:

> We the General Assembly of Virginia do enact that no man shall be compelled to frequent or support any religious worship, place, or ministry whatsoever, nor shall be enforced, restrained, molested, or burthened in his body or goods, or shall otherwise suffer, on account of his religious opinions or belief; but that all men shall be free to profess, and by argument to maintain, their opinions in matters of religion, and that the same shall in no wise diminish, enlarge, or affect their civil capacities.
>
> And though we well know that this Assembly, elected by the people for their ordinary purposes of legislation only, have no power to restrain the acts of succeeding Assemblies, constituted with powers equal to our own, and that therefore to declare this act to be irrevocable would be of no effect in law; yet we are free to declare, and do declare, that the rights hereby asserted are of the natural rights of mankind, and that if any act shall be hereafter passed to repeal the present or to narrow its operation such act will be an infringement of natural right.[5]

The most important steps in securing freedom of religion on a national level were adopting Article Six of the U.S. Constitution and ratifying the First Amendment (1791). Article Six ensured that no denomination had a privileged position in America and that Protestantism would not be elevated over Catholicism or even atheism. It read, "No religious Test shall ever be required as a Qualification to any Office or public Trust under the United States."

The First Amendment took national religious liberty to its logical conclusion: "Congress shall make no law respecting an establishment of religion, or prohibiting the free exercise thereof." Unlike the Church of England, there would be no national church in the United States, and no citizen would be compelled to attend any church. Religion was voluntary. Each denomination stood on equal footing and would have to proselytize to survive and grow.

The religious provisions in the U.S. Constitution were unheard of in Europe. Though countries such as the Netherlands practiced religious toleration, no European country made religious freedom a national principle. All the European countries eagerly watched America's religious experiment.

While the U.S. Constitution guaranteed that there would be no national church, some of the states had established churches. In deference to states' rights, the disestablishment of these churches took place on a state level and was codified in state constitutions. Following the authors of the U.S. Constitution, many states disestablished quickly and without acrimony. Among them were Virginia, Maryland, New York, North Carolina, and South Carolina. Disestablishment took longer in other states, where the tradition of a government-sponsored church stretched back more than 200 years. The last states to give up their established churches were New Hampshire in 1817, Connecticut in 1818, and Massachusetts in 1833.

In spite of the First Amendment, some Christians still feared that America would establish a national church. In a letter to the

Baptists of Danbury, Connecticut, who feared that the government was merely tolerating them rather than granting them true religious liberty, President Thomas Jefferson said in 1802:

> Believing with you that religion is a matter which lies solely between Man and his God, that he owes account to none other for his faith or his worship, that the legitimate powers of government reach actions only, and not opinions, I contemplate with sovereign reverence that act of the whole American people which declared that their legislature should "make no law respecting an establishment of religion, or prohibiting the free exercise," thus building a wall of separation between Church and State. Adhering to this expression of the supreme will of the nation in behalf of the rights of conscience, I shall see with sincere satisfaction the progress of those sentiments which tend to restore to man all natural rights, convinced he had not natural right in opposition to his social duties.[6]

The Danbury Baptists were reassured by Jefferson's words. The United States was destined to be a country where all enjoyed freedom of religion. Conscience, not law, would reign supreme in matters of religion.

CHAPTER TWENTY-FOUR

NINETEENTH-CENTURY PROTESTANTISM IN ENGLAND

G reat Britain, ruler of the seas, was the world's most powerful state for 150 years. Though it lost its American colonies in the eighteenth century, the British Empire still held India, many Pacific Islands, Canada, Australia, and large areas in Asia and Africa. By 1920 one quarter of the world and between two-thirds and three-quarters of its population was under British rule. It was true that the "sun never set on the British Empire."

The attitude of British Christians toward the world was changing. Reports of explorations and colonization captivated them. Those reports alleged that many natives throughout Britain's holdings had never heard the name of Christ. In response, Christians felt a responsibility to evangelize them. The nineteenth century became known as the "Great Century" of Christian missions.[1]

England's government was also changing. The last vestiges of monarchial rule were disappearing, and democratization was on the rise. Parliament passed bills extending suffrage to more and more men. By the close of the century, the English monarch was merely a figurehead. True authority rested in the prime minister and Parliament's House of Commons.

England was changing its beliefs on human rights. Pressed by evangelical societies and far outpacing its former American colonies,

England outlawed the slave trade in 1807. Holding slaves anywhere in the British Empire was made illegal in 1833. Unlike the United States, where regional economies depended on slavery, Britain's territories were not reliant on slavery. For this reason, among others, manumission was accomplished throughout the British Empire without a civil war.

The Industrial Revolution was transforming England's lower- and middle-class work force. Prior to 1800 the overwhelming majority of the British populace lived in the countryside. With the Industrial Revolution rural workers migrated to cities to secure jobs in factories. By 1851 over half of the population lived in cities. Along with urban migration came slums, crowded living conditions, child labor, and dangerous working conditions, all of which spawned new Christian philanthropic organizations.

The Church of England underwent significant and surprising changes. It gained a new sense of spirituality through the ministry of John (1703–1791) and Charles Wesley (1707–1788). The Roman Catholic Relief Act of 1829 removed Catholicism as a barrier to high public office and emboldened Catholic-leaning Anglicans to call for more Catholic elements in the Anglican liturgy.[2] Other Anglicans wanted to make the Church of England open to all Protestant Christians. Though officially still the established church of Britain, the Church of England was losing influence and searching for its identity. As a result, many English Christians were attracted to Bible interpreters like John Nelson Darby (1800–1882) and great preachers like Charles Haddon Spurgeon (1834–1892).

METHODISM

The founder of the Methodist movement, John Wesley, attended the University of Oxford, where he, his brother Charles, George Whitefield, and several others established the Holy Club. They spent hours praying, taking Communion, reading devotional materials, closely examining their lives, and seeking signs that God was working in them. They were called "Methodists" because of the regimented manner or method in which they went about their spiritual exercises. John Wesley went to Georgia in 1735 but found his ministry unsuccessful and two years later returned to England.

John Wesley was influenced by the Moravian Brethren, a group founded by Count Nicholas von Zinzendorf (1700–1760) that emphasized piety, devotion to Christ, and missions. The Moravian influence and hearing Luther's Preface to Paul's Epistle to the Romans prompted Wesley's conversion experience on May 24, 1738, at Aldersgate Street, London, where he felt his "heart strangely warmed."[3]

Because many Anglican congregations closed their pulpits to him, Wesley followed Whitefield and began preaching in fields. His sermons found ready hearers and his popularity grew. Wesley and his lay ministers were always preaching and organizing, and by 1751 his movement was established throughout much of England. Wesley was an indefatigable minister. He traveled more than 200,000 miles on horseback, preached more than 40,000 sermons, and brought thousands of the urban middle class into the Methodist fold.

Wesley's concerns went beyond converting the lost to curing society's moral ills. He spoke out against liquor, gambling, slavery, and the appalling British penal system. In this regard he impacted John H. Howard (1726–1790), England's strongest advocate of prison reform. Howard's endeavors led to higher pay for prison guards so they would not resort to extorting prisoners to feed their families. Howard also sought to make prisons more rehabilitative.

Because of Wesley's passion for evangelism and social reform, Methodism flourished. The movement, however, encountered some resistance from Anglicans, prompting Wesley reluctantly to distance himself from the Church of England. He appointed Francis Asbury (1745–1816) and Thomas Coke (1747–1814) as cosuperintendents of the Methodist work in America. By the end of Wesley's life, Methodism was becoming a separate denomination from the Church of England. Wesley, however, insisted Methodists did not need to break with the established church. Following his death, Methodist churches formed were obviously independent of Anglicanism.

Doctrinally, Methodists held to justification by faith and Arminian soteriology.[4] Wesley taught that Christian perfection was attainable and man could be freed from willful sin. This concept became known as entire sanctification. Organizationally, Methodism was episcopalian, with ultimate authority residing in the conference. Among the hallmarks of Methodist worship services were intense preaching and hymn singing. Charles Wesley had a significant impact on Christian music. Of the more than 5,000 hymns he composed, "Jesus, Lover of My Soul" and "Hark! the Herald Angels Sing" are among the most famous.

THE CHURCH OF ENGLAND

Throughout much of the nineteenth century, the Church of England searched for an identity. The *via media* began to crumble with the formation of the Broad Church, Low Church, and High Church movements. The liberal wing of Anglicanism, the Broad Church movement or the "latitudinarians," allowed all professed Christians to enter or remain in the Church of England. Latitudinarians compared the church to Noah's ark, where all were welcome. Though the *Book of Common Prayer* and the Thirty-Nine Articles were retained as the church's worship and doctrinal standards, each person had freedom to interpret them, according to latitudinarians. The Low Church was the evangelical wing of Anglicanism, and its members put little stress on the sacraments, hierarchy, or clerical vestments. Instead, they emphasized evangelism, preaching, and ministering to the urban and rural working classes.

Many Low Church advocates left the Church of England, but many others remained Anglican.

The Clapham Sect was a prominent group within the Low Church. Named after the district of London in which most of its members resided, the Clapham Sect included wealthy and influential members of the local parish church. The members dedicated themselves to evangelism, living out the truths of the Bible, and alleviating social problems. The Clapham Sect created the private colony of Sierra Leone as a haven for freed slaves in 1787. William Wilberforce (1759–1833) was the most famous member of this group. Working through Parliament, he dedicated his life to the abolition of slavery. He was also prominent in the birth of British Bible societies and the promotion of missions in India.

To many Anglicans the combination of Enlightenment ideas, rationalism, and the effects of industrialism had stultified the Church of England. Longing to return to a mysterious, medieval manner of worship, the High Church movement sought to restore a more Catholic liturgy. These Anglo-Catholics emphasized the teachings of the church fathers, baptismal regeneration, the mystery of the sacraments, apostolic succession, the veneration of Mary, and clerical celibacy. They wanted the ruling monarch to remain the head of the Church of England.

Based at the University of Oxford, proponents of the Oxford Movement (1833–1845) were champions of high churchmanship. The movement's leaders were John Keble (1792–1866), Edward Bouverie Pusey (1800–1882), and John Henry Newman (1801–1890).

Among the movement's primary concerns was passing the Roman Catholic Relief Act of 1829, which abolished the requirement that government officials be Anglican. The Relief Act led many to fear that the Church of England, though still the established church, would lose its influence. This fear increased in 1833 when Parliament attempted to reduce the number of bishoprics in

Ireland by ten. In protest Keble delivered a sermon at Saint Mary's Church, Oxford, which asserted the church's divine origin and the validity of apostolic succession.

In their *Tracts for the Times* (1833), Oxford Movement authors stressed the Church of England's traditional ties to Rome, the *Book of Common Prayer* as a rule of faith, the authority of the early church fathers, and transubstantiation. For these men there was no *via media*. While retaining the Church of England's independence from Rome, a move back to the Catholic teachings was necessary, they said. Theologians and politicians ridiculed the Oxford Movement, but it caused many people to leave the Church of England for the Catholic Church.

John Henry Newman was the most influential member of the Oxford Movement. He became a fellow at Oriel College, Oxford, and vicar of Saint Mary's in 1829. The author of twenty *Tracts for the Times*, he argued that the Thirty-Nine Articles, the most Protestant aspect of Anglicanism, were not critical of Catholicism itself but only of its abuses. In Article 90 Newman wrote:

> The framers constructed them [the Thirty-Nine Articles] in such a way as best to comprehend those who did not go so far in Protestantism as themselves. Anglo-Catholics then are but the successors and representatives of those moderate reformers; and their case has been directly anticipated in the wording of the Articles. It follows that they are not perverting, they are using them, for an express purpose for which among others their authors framed them.[5]

Because of Article 90, Newman was silenced and condemned by the bishop of Oxford. He became a Catholic in 1845. In 1864, he defended his actions in *Apologia pro Vita Sua*. In essence, Newman saw the Roman Catholic Church as the culmination of Christianity. Newman was made a cardinal in 1879 and declared venerable in 1991.

THE SALVATION ARMY

While serving as a Methodist minister, Salvation Army founder William Booth (1829–1912) dedicated himself to meeting the spiritual and physical needs of the poor and destitute of London. He left the Methodists in 1861 because they disapproved of the forcefulness of his evangelistic techniques. Cut off from Methodist pulpits, Booth became a street preacher. In 1865 he began holding well-attended evangelistic meetings in London's East End. He then started his own revivalist movement, the Christian Mission, in the Whitechapel district. The Mission emphasized evangelism, social ministries, and benevolence. Booth set forth a holistic view of ministry:

> If we help the man it is in order that we may change him. The builder who should elaborate his design and erect his house and risk his reputation without burning his bricks would be pronounced a failure and a fool. Perfection of architectural beauty, unlimited expenditure of capital, unfailing watchfulness of his labourers, would avail him nothing if the bricks were merely unkilned clay. Let him kindle a fire. And so here I see the folly of hoping to accomplish anything abiding, either in the circumstances or the morals of these hopeless classes, except there be a change effected in the whole man as well as in his surroundings. To this everything I hope to attempt will tend. In many cases I shall succeed, in some I shall fail; but even in failing of this my ultimate design, I shall at least benefit the bodies, if not the souls, of men; and if I do not save the fathers, I shall make a better chance for the children.[6]

Booth became the general superintendent of his movement, but his followers called him the "General," and converts became known as "soldiers of Christ"—leading to the name Salvation Army. The group quickly established a strong presence in England and claimed the conversion of more than a quarter million people from 1881 to 1885. From its beginning the Salvation Army was involved in philanthropy and social work. It has provided food and clothing to the poor, established programs to help alcoholics, and performed disaster relief around the world.

MISSIONS

A desire to evangelize the natives of Britain's far-flung colonies was the impetus for the British mission movement. Almost overnight Congregationalists, Baptists, and other Protestant denominations created missionary societies. Two of the more influential were the Baptist Missionary Society and the London Missionary Society.

Known as the Father of Modern Missions, William Carey (1761–1834) grew up in the Church of England. In his early twenties, Carey met several influential Baptists, including Andrew Fuller (1754–1815), who persuaded him to become a Baptist in 1783. At this time many Particular Baptists fell into the error of hyper-Calvinism, stressing predestination and election so strongly that they denied the universal command to repent and believe in Christ, and said Christians should not call people to salvation until they gave evidence of being elect. Hyper-Calvinists viewed evangelism and missions as challenges to God's sovereignty in election. Many hyper-Calvinists became antinomians, maintaining they were not liable for sinful actions because all actions were foreordained by God. Fuller was one of the first Particular Baptists to question this view. In his *Gospel Worthy of All Acceptation* (1785), he declared that the gospel was meant for all and that every Christian had the responsibility to proclaim it.

After reading Fuller's book, the *Voyages of Captain Cook*,[7] and the *Account of the Life of David Brainerd*,[8] Carey concluded that he had a responsibility to spread the gospel throughout the world.

At a meeting of Baptist ministers in 1786, Carey asked if it was the responsibility of Christians to evangelize all over the world. A minister is reported to have replied: "Sit down young man. You are an enthusiast! When God pleases to convert the heathen, He will do it without consulting you or me."[9] Carey was undeterred. In 1792 he published his groundbreaking missionary manifesto, *An Enquiry into the Obligations of Christians to Use Means for the Conversion of the Heathens.* This work called for Christians to realize that the Great Commission was not merely given to the apostles, as proposed by many Particular Baptists, but to all Christians. Carey wrote:

> If the command of Christ to teach all nations extend only to the apostles, then, doubtless, the promise of divine preference in this work must be so limited; but this is worded in such a manner as expressly precludes such an idea. Lo, I am with you always, to the end of the world.[10]

Carey delivered the "Deathless Sermon" to the meeting of the Nottingham Baptist Association on May 31, 1792. His text was Isaiah 54:2–3, and the theme was "Expect Great Things from God; Attempt Great Things for God." This sermon led to the birth of the Particular Baptist Society for Propagating the Gospel Among the Heathen later that same year. Soon afterward it was more concisely renamed the Baptist Missionary Society.

With his wife Dorothy (1752–1807) and son Felix (1786–1822), Carey arrived in India in 1793. He spent the remaining forty-one years of his life ministering there. At first he managed an indigo plant. Because of his linguistic skills, he was appointed professor of Bengali and Sanskrit at Fort Williams College in Calcutta in 1801, a position he held for thirty-one years. These jobs gave him the means to fund his missionary endeavors. Seven years passed though before the first Indian was converted.

Carey was an indefatigable worker. He translated the Bible into Bengali and more than twenty other Asian languages. These languages were spoken by approximately one-third of the world's population. By 1814 he established twenty churches and mission stations in India. With the aid of William Ward (1769–1823) and Joshua Marshman (1768–1837), Carey founded Serampore College in 1818.[11] The work of these men led to the conversion of more than 700 Indians. During his time in India, Carey preached thousands of sermons in the vernacular, mastered several Indian dialects, and inspired others to dedicate their lives to foreign missions.

Inspired by Carey, the London Missionary Society was founded in 1795. Its members were Anglicans, Presbyterians, Methodists, and Congregationalists. The differing forms of church government practiced by member denominations were to be set aside so as not to interfere with evangelism. The society's work centered on several Pacific Islands, China, and Africa. The society's first twenty-nine missionaries were stationed in Tahiti.

Assigned by the London Missionary Society, Robert Morrison (1782–1834) was the first Protestant missionary to China. He arrived in 1807 and remained there for twenty-seven years. Based in Canton, Singapore, and Penang, he learned Chinese, wrote a Chinese grammar and dictionary, and translated the Bible into Chinese. His main contributions to missions in China were his many printing endeavors.

Congregational pastor and explorer David Livingstone (1813–1873) was the London Missionary Society's most famous missionary. Barred from China because of the Opium War, he accepted an appointment to South Africa. He moved away from the coast and pushed deep into the central African interior because he wanted to evangelize where no other Europeans had gone. Livingstone was one of the first white people to explore the Zambia River, was believed to be the first white person to see Victoria Falls (which he named after his queen), and outlined the geographical features of

Lake Ngami, Lake Malawi, and Lake Bangweulu. His exploits were recorded in British and American newspapers, and he developed a large following on both sides of the Atlantic. Upon returning to Britain, where he was greeted as a hero, he resigned his missionary position and accepted a position with the Royal Geographic Society.

When he was fifteen years old, James Hudson Taylor (1832–1905) decided to be a missionary to China. He prepared himself for the hardships by sleeping on the floor, constantly exercising, and eating as little as possible. While studying to become a physician and medical missionary, Taylor taught himself several Chinese dialects. After being appointed to China, he founded the nondenominational China Inland Mission in 1865. In the hope of being accepted by the Chinese, Taylor adopted Chinese culture and preached in Chinese. This did not sit well with Taylor's fellow missionaries, who refused to assimilate. One can easily see why Taylor's ministry was more successful than theirs.

The Great Century of Christian missions culminated in 1910, when 1,200 representatives of foreign missionary societies met in Edinburgh, Scotland. In a spirit of ecumenism, the delegates determined to spread the gospel by working together. They vowed not to interfere with one another's work or to convert the natives from one Protestant denomination to another. Unity was to be the theme of the twentieth century.

THE LEGACY OF NINETEENTH-CENTURY CHRISTIAN MISSIONS

For some Christian missionaries, evangelism was only one reason for their presence. They also sought to introduce Western culture and values, believing Christianity and European ways went hand in hand. This belief did much to undermine missionary endeavors.

Many natives were willing to accept or at least feign the acceptance of Christianity in exchange for learning about European agricultural and industrial methods. This led many natives to perceive Christianity as just another aspect of European culture rather than a spiritual relationship with Christ. Known as imperialistic Christianity, this meshing of spiritual transformation and Western culture often cast the missionary, consciously or not, as merely a tool of the British government.

Though contemporary Christians are averse to imperialistic Christianity, it was not without strengths. The presence of the British government and the European worldview allowed missionaries to press for women's rights, help stop indigenous tribal warfare, and end the African slave trade. Often supplied by the government, missionaries were able to introduce modern medicine into Africa and curtail the spread of malaria and cholera. In India, missionaries were able to press for women's rights and abolish ritual suicide (*sati*) by widows.

JOHN NELSON DARBY (1800–1882)

One of the founders of the Plymouth Brethren, John Nelson Darby taught that world history was divided into seven ages or dispensations. The final and imminent dispensation was to be the restoration of the nation of Israel. The Christian church and Israel, however, were distinct entities. He also taught that there would be a period of tribulation prior to Christ's return and a pretribulational rapture. In a time when scientific discoveries were challenging traditional Christian beliefs, Darby's dispensationalism was meant to demonstrate that God was still in control of history. In the United States his system was popularized and expanded by the Scofield Reference Bible, which described the dispensations in its study notes. Dispensationalism found a home among many twentieth-century fundamentalists and evangelicals in America.

CHARLES HADDON SPURGEON (1834–1892)

The most influential evangelical in England in the nineteenth century, Charles Haddon Spurgeon, pastored the New Park Street Baptist Church, London, from 1854 until his death in 1892. Spurgeon was renowned for his sermons, which were often transcribed and published in newspapers throughout England and the United States. Thousands were converted under his preaching. He delivered sermons in everyday English and stressed the teachings of Christ. Spurgeon's sermons often stressed the sinfulness of man and the necessity of Christ. Because of the popularity of his sermons, the New Park Street Church outgrew its facilities. The members constructed a new building in 1861, the Metropolitan Tabernacle, which seated 5,000 and was frequently filled to capacity.

Spurgeon was also known for his antipathy toward liberalism. In 1887 he became involved in the prolonged and divisive Downgrade Controversy with moderate and liberal British Baptists that continued until his death. Spurgeon believed English Baptists had "downgraded" their beliefs concerning the Bible and holy living. His primary opponent, John Clifford (1836–1923), was Arminian in soteriology, concerned for social problems, and a liberal politician. He was also pastor of the Westbourne Baptist Chapel in London, president of the London Baptist Association in 1879, of the Baptist Union in 1888 and 1889, and of the National Council of Evangelical Churches in 1898.

Spurgeon also founded the Stockwell Orphanage, the Pastor's College (renamed Spurgeon's College), and published dozens of books, including his forty-nine-volume *Sermons on the Bible*.

THE FIRST DECADES OF THE TWENTIETH CENTURY

The optimism of the Edinburgh Conference came to an abrupt halt in 1914 with the beginning of World War I. The passion for

Christian missions and philanthropy so prevalent in nineteenth-century England was replaced by war mobilization. Immanuel Kant was wrong: humanity was not advancing. Following World War I, Christianity in England never recovered its missionary zeal.

CHAPTER TWENTY-FIVE

THE SECOND GREAT AWAKENING AND ITS AFTER-EFFECTS

The Second Great Awakening (1790–1830) had three distinct but interrelated phases. The first occurred at Yale College and affected New England Congregationalism. The second, on the western frontier of Kentucky, Missouri, and Tennessee, was noted for its intense revivals. The third was dominated by Charles Finney's ministry and revivals.

YALE AND THE NEW ENGLAND PHASE

President Timothy Dwight of Yale College (1752–1817), the grandson of Jonathan Edwards, is credited with starting the Congregational phase of the Second Great Awakening. Dwight feared that Yale students were more interested in Deism than Christianity. So along with other professors, he began lecturing and preaching on the truths of Christianity. A revival began in 1802. When it ended, more than seventy of the 225 students at Yale had been converted. The Yale revival then spread to other colleges throughout the United States.[1] As Dwight hoped, the revival helped stop the spread of Deism at Yale and in the United States.

Nathaniel Taylor (1786–1858), a student at Yale during the revivals, set forth what came to be known as "Taylorism" or "New

Haven Theology." He spoke against the rigid predestination of old-school Calvinism, believing the revivals demonstrated that human freedom played a role in conversion. Everyone was a sinner, but Adam's sin was not imputed to others, he said. Each human was responsible only for his own sin, and man had the ability to choose whether or not to sin. In 1822 Taylor was named professor of didactic theology at the newly established Yale Divinity School. The father of author Harriet Beecher Stowe (1811–1896), Lyman Beecher (1775–1863) was the most influential proponent for of New Haven theology.

While still Calvinistic, New Haven theology represented a step toward Arminianism and continued America's drift from the theology of its first Puritan settlers. By amending the traditional Calvinist doctrines of original sin and imputation,[2] New Haven theology bolstered a developing movement of dissenters from Calvinist orthodoxy. Among the dissenters were Unitarians, who rejected traditional orthodoxy in favor of rationalism and an emphasis on human freedom.

Unitarianism advanced in notable ways during the nineteenth century. In 1805 the Hollis Professor of Divinity chair at Harvard College was filled by Henry Ware (1764–1845), an avowed Unitarian. The American Unitarian Association was formed in 1825. Horace Bushnell (1802–1876), pastor of the North Congregational Church in Hartford, Connecticut, did much to complement Unitarianism, though he was not a Unitarian himself. He continued to liberalize Congregationalism by arguing that man had the ability to cure the sins of society and that all theological language was merely a metaphor for religious experience, not a statement of propositional truth. Bushnell's teachings informed Washington Gladden's (1836–1918) social gospel.

To combat Unitarianism, Reformed denominations attempted to produce more trained ministers. This led to the birth of

Princeton Seminary in 1812. By then, however, Unitarianism had a strong foothold in the Northeastern United States.

New Haven theology also promoted social reform. Its adherents were known for their support of abolitionism and Christian philanthropic societies.

THE WESTERN PHASE

The First Great Awakening was orderly, based mainly in larger towns or cities, undertaken by educated ministers, and Calvinistic in theology. The western phase of the Second Great Awakening was its polar opposite. It took place in the rural West; the ministers were generally uneducated; the services were rambunctious; and the soteriology was Arminian, consistent with the emerging American belief that individuals could forge their own destiny.

Under the leadership of Presbyterian minister James McGready (1763–1817), the awakening began at a Communion service in Logan County, Kentucky, in 1800. McGready announced the service in advance, and people came as far as 100 miles to attend. Prior to serving Communion, McGready questioned each candidate to ensure his worthiness to participate. People who were denied Communion began to beg God for salvation and forgiveness. Others were moved by the passionate preaching and claimed to have been forgiven and saved by Christ. The great revival movement in Kentucky had begun.

Pastor of a small Presbyterian church in Cane Ridge, Bourbon County, Kentucky, Barton W. Stone (1772–1844) witnessed the events in Logan County and hoped to emulate them. He scheduled a Communion service for August 1801. Presbyterian, Baptist, and Methodist ministers all publicized and participated in it.

Though accounts vary, this six-day revival may have attracted as many as 25,000 attendees. People who came from other regions camped in the field where the revival was held. Stone and his fellow

ministers examined candidates for the Lord's Supper. Those found
unworthy were distraught and began to weep over their condition
and cry out for salvation. Preachers delivered highly emotional sermons throughout the large field that were meant to lead individuals
to repentance. While listening to these sermons, people began to
bark like dogs, roll on the ground, run aimlessly, fall down, swoon,
and have convulsions. These "physical exercises" became the hallmark of the Cane Ridge revival. Thousands claimed to be instanta-
neously converted. James Campbell, who participated in the Cane
Ridge revival, described what he saw:

> Sinners dropping down on every hand, shrieking,
> groaning, crying for mercy, convoluted; professors [of
> religion] praying, agonizing, fainting, falling down in dis-
> tress, for sinners, or in raptures of joy! Some singing, some
> shouting, clapping their hands, hugging, and even kissing,
> laughing; others talking to the distressed, to one another,
> or to opposers of the work, and all this at once—no specta-
> cle can excite a stronger sensation. And with what is doing,
> the darkness of the night, the solemnity of the place, and of
> the occasion, and the conscious guilt, all conspire to make
> terror thrill through every power of the soul, and rouse it
> to awful attention.[3]

Following the example of Cane Ridge, other ministers began
to hold "camp meetings" throughout the West. Itinerant Methodist minister Peter Cartwright (1785–1872) was a prominent camp
meeting evangelist in Kentucky and Tennessee. His hatred of slavery caused him to relocate to Illinois, where he continued his ministry. Cartwright's charisma and energetic sermons were reported to
have brought thousands to Christianity.

Not all religious leaders believed these revivals were an act of
God. It seemed to many Presbyterian ministers that these gatherings
were chaotic and excessively emotional. They were also troubled by

revivalists' lack of theological training. Pro-revival Presbyterians broke away from their denomination and formed the Cumberland Presbyterian denomination in 1810.

Denominations with a more populist mentality, such as Baptists and Methodists, were comfortable with the new revivalism, and they grew. Methodists were the greatest numerical beneficiaries and employed camp meetings across the western frontier. Denominations that resisted the new revivals saw their numbers dwindle. The awakening's resonance with populist-minded denominations was due, at least in part, to the theology that underlay it. Indeed, the Second Great Awakening shifted American soteriology. The free will of Arminianism replaced Calvinistic predestination, a shift that seemed consistent with the American Dream. People were not predestined to a situation or status, but with the aid of God could shape their own destiny.

Though many leaders of the Second Great Awakening were Presbyterians, this shift in soteriology was unacceptable to Old School Presbyterians. As a result Presbyterians in America split between the New School, which supported the awakening and adopted a modified form of Calvinism, and the Old School, which opposed revivalism and held a more traditional form of Calvinism. Old School Presbyterians lost many members to pro-revival denominations. They survived the Second Great Awakening but could not keep pace with the ever-growing number of Methodists and Baptists. In the twentieth century the Presbyterian Church suffered several modernist-fundamentalist schisms. The largest Presbyterian denomination in America is the Presbyterian Church, USA, which is noted for being theologically progressive.

CHARLES GRANDISON FINNEY (1792–1875)

An ordained Presbyterian minister, Charles Grandison Finney was the greatest revivalist in the first half of the nineteenth century and the father of modern revivalism. Finney's own conversion laid the foundation for his beliefs. One day in 1821 he decided to become a Christian, so he went to the woods and prayed for salvation. He allegedly had a vision of Jesus and received a baptism of the Spirit. This experience taught him that anyone who desired could come to Christ.

Finney began to hold revivals in Oneida County, part of the "Burned-Over District" in Western New York. This area became the site of many intense revivals, the birthplace of several denominations and sects,[4] and was characterized by an unusual degree of religiosity. Building on the success of his revivals there, Finney held other large revivals in New York, Philadelphia, Rochester, and Boston from 1827 to 1832.

During his revivals Finney used what he called "New Measures." To attract large crowds, he announced his meetings well in advance. The services lasted for several days to build momentum. Finney's sermons were dramatic. He called out known sinners by name and prayed for them from the pulpit. But his most lasting new measure was the "anxious bench." He reserved the front bench for those who were "anxious" over their spiritual condition. While Finney preached, those who felt compelled to ask for prayer came forward to the anxious bench, where members of the congregation prayed for them. The anxious bench was the clear precursor of "coming forward" in the modern altar call system. Finney's New Measures demonstrated his belief that people could be induced to accept Christ. For Finney a revival was the proper use of human means to draw people to Christ.

Finney was also a social activist. Rather than becoming involved in politics though, he believed social problems could be eradicated by Christians' faithfully applying the gospel to their lives. A postmillennialist, he maintained that a true Christian would care for his fellowman and help usher in the kingdom of God. He denounced slavery and believed drinking to be a sin of the soul that could be cured through conversion. Because of his popularity, Finney helped galvanize development of abolitionist and temperance societies.

Finney served as a model for future evangelists. His successors adopted and elaborated on his techniques. The revivalist tradition was continued by Dwight Lyman Moody (1837–1899), Billy Sunday (1862–1935), and William (Billy) Graham (b. 1918).

REFORM MOVEMENT

The teachings of Timothy Dwight and Charles Finney promoted reform movements. For these men, conversion was just the first step in a Christian's life. The new Christian must dedicate himself to correcting the ills of society, they believed. This took many forms.

BIBLE AND TRACT SOCIETIES

Inspired by the Second Great Awakening, the New York Bible Society, later renamed the American Bible Society (ABS), was created in 1809. ABS was governed by Protestant laymen with the explicit purpose of evangelism. It was popular from the outset, and within a year forty-one organizations were affiliated with it. Between 1829 and 1831, ABS published and distributed more than a million Bibles and, by 1986, 290 million.

Founded in 1899, the Christian Commercial Travelers' Association, better known as the Gideons, is the world's best-known Bible distribution organization, consisting primarily of lay professionals with a strong belief in evangelism. They began placing Bibles in hotel rooms, prisons, hospitals, and trains in 1908. The Gideons have placed or distributed more than 1.8 billion complete Bibles and New Testaments in more than 190 countries around the world.

Tracts were an innovative and inexpensive way to evangelize, often costing less than a penny each. They usually presented in a brief, pointed, and simple manner the gospel of Christ, along with the address of a church where the reader could go for spiritual help.

Tracts were effective because they could be left anywhere, distributed by hand, and passed along to multiple readers. Baptists created a General Tract Society in 1824, and the ecumenical American Tract Society was formed in 1825.

ABOLITIONISM

Finney's sermons against slavery did much to promote abolitionist societies. Owning human beings was incompatible with Christian perfectionism, natural rights, reform, and the desire for a postmillennial return of Christ, he said. Many abolitionist societies were dominated by Christians who adopted these beliefs. Some Baptist and Methodist associations would not allow slave owners to become members. Few denominations went as far as the Quakers, however, who explicitly condemned slavery and forbade anyone who owned slaves from joining the Society of Friends.

Other Christians, particularly those in the South, rejected abolitionists' reasoning. They maintained that the Bible supported slavery. Some of their favorite proof texts were the letter to Philemon and Colossians 4:1, "Masters, supply your slaves with what is right and fair, since you know that you too have a Master in heaven." Another justification for slavery was that if left in Africa, slaves would never have had opportunity to hear the gospel. Christian proponents of slavery emphasized that slaves had to be treated fairly. A Baptist minister from Charleston, South Carolina, for whom Furman University was later named, Richard Furman (1755–1825) wrote: "For though they are slaves, they are also men; and are with ourselves accountable creatures; having immortal souls, and are being destined to future eternal reward. Their religious interests claim a regard from their masters of the most serious nature; and it is indispensable."[5]

Furman also noted that "slavery, when tempered with humanity and justice, is a state of tolerable happiness; equal, if not superior, to that which many poor enjoy in countries reputed free."[6] Though the slave trade ended in 1808, that did nothing for those who were already enslaved.

A convert of Charles Finney, Theodore D. Weld (1803–1895), held abolitionist meetings and applied the evangelistic "New Measures" to convert his hearers to abolitionism. He implored Americans to repent of slavery and immediately free all slaves. Influenced by a Quaker friend, William Lloyd Garrison (1805–1879) was another prominent abolitionist. In 1831 he founded *The Liberator*, which soon became the voice of radical abolitionism. Under Garrison, the militant American Anti-Slavery Society was formed in 1832. In its constitution the Society made its rationale for abolition clear:

> Those for whose emancipation we are striving—constituting at the present time at least one-sixth part of our countrymen—are recognized by the law, and treated by their fellow beings, as marketable commodities, as goods and chattels, as brute beasts; are plundering daily of the fruits of the toil without redress; really enjoying no constitutional nor legal protection from licentious and murderous outrages upon their persons; are ruthlessly torn asunder— the tender babe from the arms of its frantic mother—the heart-broken wife from her weeping husband—at the caprice or pleasure of irresponsible tyrants. For the crime of having a dark complexion, they suffer the pangs of hunger, the infliction of stripes, and the ignominy of brutal servitude. They are kept in heathenish darkness by laws expressly enacted to make their instruction a criminal offense.[7]

Ministers such as William Ellery Channing (1780–1842) and Elijah P. Lovejoy (1802–1837) called from their pulpits for manumission. Channing's *Slavery* (1835) and *Address at Lennox* (1842) were eloquent pleas for freeing the slaves. Lovejoy published an abolitionist paper in St. Louis but was met with such harassment that he moved to Alton, Illinois, in 1836, where he published the *Alton Observer*. His press in Alton was destroyed three times, and he was threatened for defending a black man who had been condemned by a judge for inciting slaves to riot. He also did not endear himself to the community when he condemned slave owners for raping female slaves. Lovejoy was killed by a mob in 1837.

Harriet Beecher Stowe's *Uncle Tom's Cabin* (1852) was one of the more poignant and important abolitionist statements. Empathy for the main characters, who were slaves, prompted many Americans to support abolition.

SOCIAL GOSPEL

The Industrial Revolution created an increasingly materialistic society. With the aid of machines, production of goods increased exponentially. Private economic ventures seemed to spring up everywhere. Perhaps more than ever, people embraced capitalism and pursued the American dream of prosperity and success.

For those in the emerging middle and upper classes, the Industrial Revolution brought a higher standard of living than at any point in recorded history. A person of low station by birth could ascend to the middle or even upper class through economic success. For those who climbed the economic ladder, income was no longer solely dedicated to necessities. They could afford luxury items. But not everyone benefitted from the boom in production. To increase their profits, factory owners often paid their employees the lowest possible wages, resulting in poverty for those at the bottom of the social heap. Though different from the medieval class system, the Industrial Revolution led to new levels of economic disparity between the upper and lower classes.

In response labor unions, antimonopoly laws, and higher taxes on the rich emerged in an attempt to create a more equitable American society. The social gospel was also born out of the inequalities created by industrialization. Prominent in the late nineteenth and early twentieth centuries, proponents of the social gospel such as Washington Gladden and Walter Rauschenbusch (1861–1918) were liberal theologians who believed the gospel needed to be recast as an antidote to social ills rather than merely a message of individual salvation. The immanence of God, Christ as the measure of ethics, the unity of society, a progressive view of man's ability, and the postmillennial return of Christ were key beliefs of social gospelers. The Lord would not return, they thought, until humanity rid itself of social evils. Yet salvation was not the primary goal of the social gospel. The movement hoped to improve the lives of America's urban poor. Social-gospel advocates helped organize unions, pass restrictions on child labor, and lobby for better living conditions in urban apartment complexes. The social gospel aimed for a Christian society based on compassion rather than greed and class conflict.

Rauschenbusch described this Christian society as the kingdom of God. In *A Theology of the Social Gospel* (1917), he wrote:

> The Kingdom of God is humanity organized according to the will of God. Interpreting it through the consciousness of Jesus we may affirm these convictions about the ethical relations within the Kingdom: (a) Since Christ revealed the divine worth of life and personality, and since his salvation seeks the restoration and fulfillment of even the least, it follows that the Kingdom of God, at every stage of human development, tends toward a social order which will best guarantee to all personalities their freest and highest development. This involves the redemption of social life from the cramping influence of religious bigotry, from the repression of self-assertion in the relation of upper and lower classes, and from all forms of slavery in which human beings are treated as mere means to serve the ends of others.[8]

According to its critics, the social gospel stressed social activism at the expense of spiritual change. Indeed, social gospelers like Rauschenbusch believed traditional Christian orthodoxy was inadequate and advocated adjusting it to fit the needs of the day. Because they spoke out against the worst aspects of capitalism, social-gospel advocates often were accused of being socialist or communist. The most active social-gospel proponents were Baptists, Methodists, and Congregationalists.

The Oneida Community

Born in Brattleboro, Vermont, John Humphrey Noyes (1811–1886) was a preacher and social activist. While studying law at Dartmouth College, he was converted at a revival in the Burned-Over District and resolved to become a minister. He studied at Andover Theological Seminary and Yale Divinity School. After studying the Bible, he concluded that Christ returned to earth in AD 70 and enabled humans to attain spiritual perfection.

These beliefs cost him his ministerial license in 1834. But he gathered some thirty followers at Putney, Vermont. In order to achieve perfection, Noyes taught that all property should be held in common. In 1846 he announced his theory of "complex marriage," which promoted cohabitation and denounced monogamy. Noyes frequently matched partners together to produce the best offspring. Complex marriage incensed many people, and his socialistic community relocated to Oneida, New York, in 1848. The Oneida Community thrived for thirty years, had more than 200 members, and generated a sizable income from manufacturing silver place settings and its joint stock company. Outsiders in Oneida did not care for the complex marriage practiced in the community. To lessen the burden on his community or to escape arrest, Noyes relocated to Canada in 1876. The Oneida Community began to lose its vision and ceased to exist in 1881. Its joint stock company Oneida, however, continues to produce silverware.

SECOND GREAT AWAKENING
DENOMINATIONS—AMERICAN ORIGINALS

Revivals in the first half of the nineteenth century led to growing expectation of Christ's return. Basing their position on a postmillennial interpretation of Revelation 20:1–10, many Christians began to believe Christ's second coming would occur after the gospel had been preached to the whole world. Christians who witnessed the Second Great Awakening believed that if they worked hard enough, the whole world would soon hear of Christ. One result was the birth of several millennial denominations.

DISCIPLES OF CHRIST

A Scotch-Irish Presbyterian who emigrated from Northern Ireland, Alexander Campbell (1788–1866) and his father, Thomas Campbell (1763–1854), started the Christian Association of Washington in Washington County, Pennsylvania, in 1809. The association adopted no formal creed or confession but rather accepted the single statement, "Where the Scriptures speak we speak; where the Scriptures are silent we are silent." In 1811, Alexander and Thomas left the Presbyterian Church after Alexander would not allow his infant son to be baptized and formed the Brush Run Church in Brush Run, Pennsylvania. Accepting immersion in 1813, Campbell and his church joined the Redstone Baptist Association. Campbell's church broke away from the Baptists in 1827 and formed groups of "Disciples." With Campbell as their leader, the Disciples promoted a church based on the book of Acts, rejection of confessions other than the Bible, the inferiority of the Old Testament, and rigid primitivism.

Barton W. Stone soon discovered that the Presbyterian Church did not welcome the belief in free will and emotionalism displayed at Cane Ridge and elsewhere. For this reason, he led a group of Presbyterians out of the Synod of Kentucky. Rejecting all contrived names, they were simply known as "Christians." Stone's "Christians" joined Campbell's "Disciples" in 1832 to create the Disciples of Christ.

The Disciples of Christ were "Restorationists" who hoped to return to the earliest form of Christian worship and church polity. They believed that by returning to the model provided in the book of Acts, they would usher in the millennium.

Disciples of Christ maintained that the Lord's Supper should be held each week, that baptism of believers by immersion was necessary for salvation, and that there was no creed but the Bible. In its formative stages the movement's ministers lived off the benevolences offered by their congregations. Other than the Church of Jesus Christ of Latter Day Saints, no American religious group grew faster than the Disciples of Christ in the nineteenth century. Theological schisms over modernism and the use of musical instruments in worship led to creation of three branches: the Christian Church (Disciples of Christ), Christian Church/Churches of Christ, and the noninstrumental Churches of Christ.

SEVENTH-DAY ADVENTISTS

The millennial teachings of William Miller (1782–1849) gave rise to Adventism. By using a mathematical formula that he applied to the symbolic numbers in the book of Daniel, Miller determined that Jesus would return on March 21, 1843. Christ would then bring about the final judgment, destroy the world, and usher in a new heaven and earth. Miller's formula fit well into the antebellum worldview. Many believed that since man was progressing, he should be able to discern even the most hidden truths of the Bible. Thousands of people believed Miller and awaited the arrival of

Christ. When Christ did not return in 1843, Miller corrected his calculations and announced the date as October 22, 1844. When Christ still did not return, his prediction became known as the "Great Disappointment." But Miller's failure did not squelch the notion that others might be able to predict Christ return, and so millennialism remained strong.

A self-proclaimed prophet, Ellen White (1827–1915) took up Miller's mantle. After the Great Disappointment, she supposedly began to have visions about the millennium. Millerites accepted her visions as authentic, and she gained many followers. Under her leadership some Millerites formed the Seventh-day Adventist Church in 1863. The name of the denomination refers to their worship on the Jewish Sabbath (Saturday) rather than Sunday. White said an angel informed her that failure to observe the Sabbath had delayed the return of Christ. Seventh-day Adventists believed in an imminent return of Christ, that they were the righteous remnant mentioned in Revelation 12:17, and that White's prophecies were valid.

Because of White's poor health, Seventh-day Adventists advocated eating only grains and vegetables. A disciple of White, John Harvey Kellogg (1852–1943) developed cereals that were suited to the Seventh-day Adventist diet. Though prominent in the United States, most of the growth of Seventh-day Adventists was in Europe.

AMERICAN SECTS

SHAKERS

Jane and James Wardley (fl. 1747) of England were the first Shakers. The origin of Shakers in America, however, is tied to Ann Lee (1736–1784), who led a small group of Shakers or "Dancing Quakers" to Manchester, New York, in 1774.

Beginning in 1770, Mother Ann, as she was called, supposedly received a series of revelations that all human sin was rooted in sexual intercourse. She said the millennium had begun and that God required celibacy of all. The Shakers lived in communities in which all things were shared and men and women lived separately, though they were regarded as equal. Shakers maintained that Christ had already returned and that Lee was his female counterpart.

They also believed God was both Father and Mother, maintained a strong spirituality, composed original hymns, and performed energetic dances. They believed Christian truths were being revealed through their leaders and through their worship. Few people converted to the Shaker belief system, and because of their celibacy, a second generation of Shakers never emerged. At the movement's pinnacle there were no more than 5,000 Shakers in the United States. Of the nineteen Shaker communities, the most prominent were in New York and Kentucky. Only one Shaker community, in Sabbathday Lake, Maine, existed as of 2012. Many know the Shakers for their skill in making furniture.

JEHOVAH'S WITNESSES

A former Adventist, Charles Taze Russell (1852–1916) formed several Bible study groups in Pittsburgh, Pennsylvania, in the 1870s. While teaching these Bible studies, he questioned the doctrine of the Trinity, the validity of confessions and church tradition, and the existence of hell. By 1880, Russell formed thirty Bible study classes. These classes came together in 1884 to form the Zion's Watch Tower and Tract Society. Russell headquartered the group in New York in 1909 and was elected pastor of approximately 500 congregations.

In 1876 Russell, along with Nelson H. Barbour (1824–1905), published *Three Worlds*. In 1879 Russell began publishing *Zion's Watch Tower and Herald of Christ's Presence* to announce the return of Christ. In this publication he stated that Christ returned to Earth as an invisible spirit in 1874 and inaugurated the "Millennial Dawn." Russell also taught that a 2,520-year period called "the Gentile Times" would end in 1914. The world would then end and God's kingdom would be inaugurated. Russell died in 1916, unable to amend the errors in his calculations. Citing Isaiah 43:10–12,[9] the group changed its name to Jehovah's Witnesses in 1931.

Jehovah's Witnesses believed in the imminent return of Christ, progressive revelations from their leader, and that they were the 144,000 of Revelation 14 who would be in heaven. Jehovah's Witnesses not numbered among the 144,000 would live in a paradise on earth, they said. Other Jehovah's Witness teachings included the exclusive use of the word *Jehovah* for God, the necessity of refusing blood transfusions,[10] pacifism, and the illegitimacy of any state or church. They were also well known for door-to-door evangelism and distribution of the *Watch Tower*. Jehovah's Witnesses have their own version of the Bible, the New World Translation, with "Jehovah" replacing "Lord" in the New Testament. The reported membership[11] of the Jehovah's Witnesses was 7.2 million in 2010.

CHURCH OF JESUS CHRIST OF LATTER-DAY SAINTS

The Church of Jesus Christ of Latter-day Saints arose from the Second Great Awakening, millennial expectations, and the creativity of Joseph Smith (1805–1844). Born to a land speculator and a doting mother, Smith grew up in Palmyra, New York, in the Burned-Over District. Not only was it home to revivalists, reform groups, millennial sects, and utopian societies, the region was also known for a strong belief in magic, the occult, and buried treasure. Tapping into the religious and mystical hysteria, Smith formed a uniquely American religion.

In 1820, when he was fourteen years old, Smith claimed he received a vision of a "Father" and "Son" informing him that all religious denominations were wrong. Moreover, he was to restore the primitive church and the Old Testament priesthood. In 1823, Smith claimed to have been told by the angel Moroni that golden tablets were buried in Manchester, New York, on Hill Cumorah. He reported that the tablets were written in hieroglyphics but two seer stones (*Urim* and *Thummim*) allowed him to interpret them.

Smith said he began to translate the tablets in 1827 and had his findings published in 1830. Allegedly viewed only by Smith and eleven of his followers, these tablets contained the *Book of Mormon*, which described the American Indians as the lost tribes of Israel and chronicled their history from 600 BC to AD 421. After his resurrection Christ appeared to these tribes and formed a church among them, Smith said. This culture ended at the close of the fifth century, but its history was recorded by the Prophet Mormon—hence the title *Book of Mormon* and the group being labeled Mormons. Smith's claims were met with derision, but he still managed to gather a large group of followers. He told them they were reviving the faith created by Christ in America and were the true saints who would enter heaven.

On April 6, 1830, Smith and his followers founded the Church of Jesus Christ of Latter-day Saints in Fayette, New York. Naturally, Smith was named the church's leader and prophet. He claimed to have further revelations that were recorded in *The Book of Commandments* (1833), the *Doctrines and Covenants* (1835), and *The Pearl of Great Price* (1842). In these texts he taught human progression to divine status, elaborate temple ceremonies, baptism of the dead by proxy, eternal marriage, and polygamy.

Many citizens of Palmyra believed Smith to be a charlatan and castigated his new movement. He then said God had revealed to him that Kirtland, Ohio, was to be the Mormon holy city. Upon their arrival in 1831, Smith's followers began work on their first temple, which was dedicated in 1836. Soon their numbers swelled, and Smith controlled the town. They built an outpost in Independence, Missouri, which they named Zion.

While in Kirtland, Smith established a city government, a militia, a bank, and began to dominate regional politics by having his followers vote as a bloc. But his bank collapsed, and some of his most trusted members left the church. Smith and his followers left Kirtland for Independence, Missouri, in 1837. The Missouri years were bloody, with Mormons suffering defeat to locals in the "Mormon War." Smith then prophesied that his group should relocate to Nauvoo, Illinois. After arriving in Nauvoo in 1839, Smith took precautions to protect his church. He established a private militia, again dominated local politics, and announced that he was going to run for president of the United States. While in Nauvoo, Smith claimed a revelation that became section 132 of *Doctrines and Covenants*. In verses 61–62 Smith brought into Mormon law the principle of polygamy:

> And again, as pertaining to the law of the priesthood—
> if any man espouse a virgin, and desire to espouse another,
> and the first give her consent, and if he espouse the second,
> and they are virgins, and have vowed to no other man, then
> is he justified; he cannot commit adultery for they are given
> unto him; for he cannot commit adultery with that that
> belongeth unto him and to no one else. And if he have ten
> virgins given unto him by this law, he cannot commit adul-
> tery, for they belong to him, and they are given unto him;
> therefore is he justified.

Though only practiced by the leadership and kept secret, polygamy was exposed by former members in local newspapers. Smith became incensed that the innermost secrets of Mormonism were being printed in the Nauvoo newspaper and ordered it destroyed. Soon Smith was arrested and placed in the Carthage, Illinois, jail. A mob broke into the jail on June 27, 1844, and murdered Smith and his brother Hyrum (1800–1844).

After an internal dispute, Brigham Young (1801–1877) was selected as the new prophet and leader of Latter-day Saints. Young realized that as long as Mormons lived in territories that were already settled, they would face persecution. Starting in 1846, Young led a large group across the United States to the Great Salt Basin in the Utah Territory.[12] Far removed from other settlers, they built Salt

Lake City and established the church's headquarters. Young led the
Mormon Church until his death in 1877.

Latter-day Saints believed that the *Book of Mormon* and Joseph
Smith's prophecies were equal in authority to the Bible. Smith was
reported to have had forty-nine wives and Young fifty-five. But a
new prophecy in 1890 suspended polygamy. The prophecy coincid-
ed with Utah's attempt to gain statehood, which could not happen
if polygamy was legal. Mormons displayed strong patriotism, evangelistic impulse, and concern for family values. They also consumed
no caffeine and placed a high value on material property. Each
young man was encouraged to participate in a two-year mission
involving personal evangelism. As of 2010 the worldwide Mormon
population exceeded fourteen million, with approximately eight
million in the United States. In Utah, the LDS Church numbered
one and one-half million, 60 percent of the state's population. A
smaller group that claims Smith never taught polygamy, the Reorganized Church of Jesus Christ of Latter-day Saints, is headquartered
in Independence, Missouri. In addition, there are fundamentalist
Mormons who still practice polygamy. Because polygamy is illegal,
these groups attempt to stay out of the mainstream. The president
of the Fundamentalist Church of Jesus Christ of Latter-day Saints,
Warren Jeffs (b. 1955), is the most prominent polygamist leader in
the United States and is currently in prison for sexual assault and
aggravated sexual assault of children.

CHAPTER TWENTY-SIX

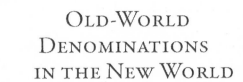

OLD-WORLD DENOMINATIONS IN THE NEW WORLD

Joining the American originals in the religious fabric of the New World were the older, established Protestant denominations of Europe. While many of them found state sanction and support in Europe, they had to make their way in America without government aid. The most prominent Old World denominations in America were the Presbyterians, Lutherans, and Methodists. Methodists gave birth to the Holiness and Pentecostal churches. Though there were Baptists in Europe, the first American Baptists tended to be converts from other groups. But since Baptists had much in common with Old World denominations, they are covered in this chapter.

PRESBYTERIANS

In 1706, the first American presbytery was formed in Philadelphia. Over the next fourteen years two presbyteries were added in the Philadelphia area. These three presbyteries formed the Synod of Philadelphia in 1717—comprised of forty churches and 3,000 members. The Synod of Philadelphia adopted the Westminster Confession as its rule of faith in 1729. The first General Assembly of the Presbyterian Church in the United States of America was held in Philadelphia in 1789. Other areas of Presbyterian influence

371

were in the South. Scotch-Irish Presbyterians came to America in large numbers beginning in the early 1720s and settled in the southern Piedmont region (an area encompassing parts of Virginia, the Carolinas, Georgia, and Alabama). They were strongest where there was little Church of England influence. Southern Presbyterians were more enthusiastic in their worship services than their northern brethren. Most were also staunch supporters of slavery.

After the Great Awakening, a schism developed within the Presbyterian Synod. Those who embraced the revivals constituted the New Side, and those who rejected them were called the Old Side. The Gilbert Tennent-led New Side was removed from the Philadelphia Synod in 1741. The two factions reunited in 1758 and formed a General Assembly. In 1801, Presbyterians came together with Congregationalists and created the Plan of Union, which called for joint evangelization of the West.

The Second Great Awakening splintered Presbyterians again. Old School Presbyterians objected to the intense emotionalism, supposedly instantaneous conversions, and physical manifestations that occurred along the western frontier. They also objected to uneducated clergymen-leading the revivals. Presbyterians who favored the revivals and did not believe that clergy needed a formal education formed the Cumberland Presbyterian branch in 1810. Cumberland Presbyterians were located largely in the frontier regions of Tennessee and Kentucky. In the North, the Old and New School Presbyterians split into several denominations.

As in many antebellum denominations, the issue of slavery led to a schism among Presbyterians. In the South, Old School Presbyterians formed the Presbyterian Church in the Confederate States of America. After the Civil War, they took the name Presbyterian Church in the United States. In the North, the Old and New School Presbyterians reunited in 1870 and became the Presbyterian Church in the United States of America.

In the late nineteenth century, Presbyterians became embroiled in controversy over the advance of liberal theology, referred to as modernism at the time. Charles Augustus Briggs (1841–1913), a professor of Hebrew and biblical theology at the Presbyterian Union Seminary in New York, denied the historical accuracy of several biblical passages. He also denied Mosaic authorship of the Pentateuch and argued that Isaiah had more than one author. After a three-year trial he was expelled from the Presbyterian ministry and became an Episcopalian. However, he remained at Union Seminary, which broke its ties with the Presbyterian Church.

Princeton Seminary was the stronghold of conservative theology. Led by Charles Hodge (1797–1878), his son Archibald Hodge (1823–1886), and Benjamin B. Warfield (1851–1921), Princeton theologians held that the Bible was inerrant, divinely inspired, and completely trustworthy. Professor of New Testament John Gresham Machen (1881–1937) was adamant in objecting to liberal theology. Because he believed liberal doctrine was finding its way into Princeton, he founded Westminster Seminary in Philadelphia in 1929. Machen attracted many followers and they founded the Presbyterian Church of America in 1936, which later became the Orthodox Presbyterian Church.

Despite these controversies, many Presbyterian bodies reunited in the twentieth century. In 1910, a majority of the Cumberland Presbyterian Church joined with the northern United Presbyterian Church in the United States of America (UPCUSA). In turn the Presbyterian Church in the United States of America merged with the United Presbyterian Church of North America in 1958 to form the United Presbyterian Church in the United States of America. In 1983 the southern Presbyterian Church in the United States (PCUS) and the northern UPCUSA merged to create the Presbyterian Church, USA (PCUSA). A minority of the PCUS, however, viewed their northern brethren as too doctrinally and socially liberal and formed the Presbyterian Church in America.

The PCUSA is now the largest Presbyterian denomination, with a membership of 2.3 million and churches in each state. Since the 1983 unification, the PCUSA has had several theological debates. The most divisive of these concerned the ordination of homosexuals and whether Presbyterian ministers could perform homosexual marriages.

LUTHERANS

Lutherans in America tend to be ethnically diverse due to immigration and adhere to traditional Lutheran creeds. The largest Lutheran groups are the Evangelical Lutheran Church in America (ELCA) with 4.5 million members and the Lutheran Church Missouri Synod with 2.4 million members.

The ELCA was formed on January 1, 1988, with the merger of the American Lutheran Church (ALC), the Lutheran Church in America (LCA), and the Association of Evangelical Lutheran Churches (AELC). It affirmed the Augsburg Confession and the *Book of Concord* as its doctrinal standards. The ELCA is perhaps the least conservative Lutheran group in America. It allows the ordination of female and homosexual pastors.

The Lutheran Church Missouri Synod (LCMS) was founded in Chicago in 1847. Composed of German immigrants in the upper Midwest, German was the dominant language in LCMS worship services. For this reason it originally took the name German Evangelical Lutheran Synod of Missouri, Ohio, and Other States. Because of anti-German backlash during World War I, "German" was dropped from the name in 1917, and English became more prominent in worship services. The LCMS affirms all the sixteenth-century Lutheran creeds, the infallibility of the Bible, and a male-only clergy.

BAPTIST, METHODIST, HOLINESS, AND PENTECOSTAL DENOMINATIONS

BAPTISTS

Baptists have been in New England since the mid-seventeenth century, with the Great Awakening prompting their growth. Riding this momentum and pushing westward, they were in most areas east of the Mississippi River by the beginning of the nineteenth century. The strongest centers of Baptist activity from 1780 to 1820 were Philadelphia, Charleston, and Sandy Creek, North Carolina. Established in 1764 in Providence, Rhode Island, Brown University became the first Baptist institution of higher education.

Created in 1814, the General Missionary Convention, later renamed the Triennial Convention, was the first national organization of Baptists in the United States. Its purpose was to support the missionary work of Adoniram Judson (1788–1850) and Luther Rice (1783–1836) in India. Loosely associated with the Triennial Convention, the Baptist General Tract Society was formed in 1824 followed by the American Baptist Home Mission Society in 1832. These societies were based in northern cities and placed under the supervision of northern Baptists.

As with Presbyterians, slavery divided the Triennial Convention. Baptists in the South supported it while those in the North pressed for manumission. Southerners left the Triennial Convention and formed the Southern Baptist Convention in 1845.

The SBC is currently composed of more than 45,000 churches and sixteen million members who jointly support missions, theological education, and cultural engagement. Each church is autonomous and voluntarily associates on a local, state, and national level. The SBC operates several entities and committees that operate year-round even though the convention is in session just two days per year. To fund Southern Baptist ministries on the state and national levels, the Cooperative Program was developed in 1925. Under this program local churches forward a percentage of their undesignated receipts to their state conventions, which in turn forward a percentage to the Southern Baptist Convention. Local churches and state conventions are autonomous from the SBC and determine on their own the percentage they forward to denominational causes.

Though the name suggests an emphasis on the American South, the SBC includes churches in all fifty states. One hallmark of Southern Baptists has been their emphasis on both home and foreign missions. Almost immediately after organizing in 1845, the SBC began mission work in China and Africa. Following World War II, Southern Baptists expanded their mission work across the world and have been particularly active in the Third World. As of 2014, the SBC had more than 5,000 international missionaries. It supports six seminaries, and its state convention partners are affiliated with more than fifty colleges and universities. In the last two decades of the twentieth century, the SBC became known for its conservative theology and inerrantist view of the Scriptures. A moderate group of Southern Baptists left the SBC in 1991 and formed the Cooperative Baptist Fellowship (CBF). The CBF has 1,800 affiliated churches and fifteen theological schools.

Baptists in the North came together in 1907 to form the Northern Baptist Convention. They took the name American Baptist Convention (ABC) in 1950. These Baptists suffered several schisms over modernism and fundamentalism. They never truly recovered from the breakup of the Triennial Convention and the modernist-fundamentalist controversy. Their membership steadily declined in the twentieth century. In 2008 what is now called the American Baptist Churches USA reported a membership of 1.3 million. It is affiliated with six theological schools and fifteen colleges.

The first black Baptist church was founded in Augusta, Georgia, in 1773. Following the Civil War, most black Baptists chose to organize their own churches rather than join the SBC or a northern society. Formed in 1895, the National Baptist Convention (National

Baptist Convention, USA, Inc.) was the first black Baptist convention. A group left the NBC in 1915 over a dispute concerning the ownership of a publishing house and named itself National Baptist Convention of America.[1] The National Baptist Convention USA split again in 1961 when two factions disagreed on whether to support Martin Luther King Jr. (1929–1968) and the Civil Rights Movement. The group that supported King formed the Progressive National Baptist Convention. A fourth convention, the National Missionary Baptist Convention of America, was created in 1988. The NBC USA remains the largest of the black Baptist conventions and reported an approximate membership of 5 million in 2011.

Martin Luther King Jr. is the most influential black Baptist to date. Born in Atlanta, Georgia, King received his education at Morehouse College (BA, 1948), Crozer Theological Seminary (BD, 1951), and Boston University (PhD, 1955). During his studies he was drawn to Mahatma Gandhi's (1869–1948) teachings on nonviolent resistance to social and political oppression. King was called as pastor of the Dexter Avenue Baptist Church in Montgomery, Alabama, in May 1954. Because of his speaking ability and earned doctorate, King immediately became a respected member of the city's black community. The following year, Rosa Parks (1913–2005) sparked the modern civil rights movement when she refused to move to the segregated section of a Montgomery bus. A meeting of ministers chose King to lead the movement to boycott the city's buses. The boycott began on December 5, 1955, and ended on November 13, 1956, after the United States Supreme Court declared Alabama's segregation laws to be unconstitutional.

The following year King was named head of the Southern Christian Leadership Conference. Because of the bus boycott victory, King became the recognized leader of the civil rights movement. His *Letter from a Birmingham Jail*, written in 1963, is one of the most eloquent descriptions of the plight of blacks in America:

We have waited for more than 340 years for our constitutional and God given rights. The nations of Asia and Africa are moving with jetlike speed toward gaining political independence, but we still creep at horse and buggy pace toward gaining a cup of coffee at a lunch counter. Perhaps it is easy for those who have never felt the stinging darts of segregation to say, "Wait." But when you have seen vicious mobs lynch your mothers and fathers at will and drown your sisters and brothers at whim; when you have seen hate filled policemen curse, kick and even kill your black brothers and sisters; when you see the vast majority of your twenty million Negro brothers smothering in an airtight cage of poverty in the midst of an affluent society; when you suddenly find your tongue twisted and your speech stammering as you seek to explain to your six year old daughter why she can't go to the public amusement park that has just been advertised on television, and see tears welling up in her eyes when she is told that Funtown is closed to colored children, and see ominous clouds of inferiority beginning to form in her little mental sky, and see her beginning to distort her personality by developing an unconscious bitterness toward white people; when you have to concoct an answer for a five year old son who is asking: "Daddy, why do white people treat colored people so mean?"; when you take a cross county drive and find it necessary to sleep night after night in the uncomfortable corners of your automobile because no motel will accept you; when you are humiliated day in and day out by nagging signs reading "white" and "colored"; when your first name becomes "nigger," your middle name becomes "boy" (however old you are) and your last name becomes "John," and your wife and mother are never given the respected title "Mrs."; when you are harried by day and haunted by night by the fact that you are a Negro, living constantly at tiptoe stance, never quite knowing what to expect next, and are plagued with inner fears and outer resentments; when you are forever fighting a degenerating sense of "nobodiness"— then you will understand why we find it difficult to wait. There comes a time when the cup of endurance runs over, and men are no longer willing to be plunged into the abyss of despair. I hope, sirs, you can understand our legitimate and unavoidable impatience. You express a great deal of anxiety over our willingness to break laws. This is certainly a legitimate concern. Since we so diligently urge people to obey the Supreme Court's decision of 1954 outlawing segregation in the public schools, at first glance it may seem rather paradoxical for us consciously to break laws. One may well ask: "How can you advocate breaking some laws and obeying others?" The answer lies in the fact that there are two types of laws: just and unjust. I would be the first to advocate obeying just laws. One has not only a legal but a moral responsibility to obey just laws. Conversely, one has a moral responsibility to disobey unjust laws. I would agree with St. Augustine that "an unjust law is no law at all."[2]

In August 1963 King led a march of 250,000 people on the Mall in Washington D.C., where he delivered his famous "I Have a Dream" speech:

> Let us not wallow in the valley of despair, I say to you today, my friends. And so even though we face the difficulties of today and tomorrow, I still have a dream. It is a dream deeply rooted in the American dream. I have a dream that one day this nation will rise up and live out the true meaning of its creed: "We hold these truths to be self-evident, that all men are created equal." I have a dream that one day on the red hills of Georgia, the sons of former slaves and

the sons of former slave owners will be able to sit down together at the table of brotherhood. I have a dream that one day even the state of Mississippi, a state sweltering with the heat of injustice, sweltering with the heat of oppression, will be transformed into an oasis of freedom and justice. I have a dream that my four little children will one day live in a nation where they will not be judged by the color of their skin but by the content of their character.[3]

Following the March on Washington, King received the Nobel Peace Prize in 1964.

In March 1965, King led a march from Selma, Alabama, to Montgomery, Alabama. Unprovoked, 600 peaceful and unarmed marchers were attacked by police officers with clubs and tear gas. Several marchers were hospitalized. Because much of the police brutality was televised, the civil rights movement gained nation-wide sympathy and adherents. Two days later King led a symbolic march to the bridge where the attacks took place. Two weeks later, 3,200 marchers left Selma. By the time they arrived in Montgomery, their number had risen to more than 25,000.

While supporting the unionization of black garbage collectors in Memphis, Tennessee, King was assassinated on April 4, 1968. His message of nonviolent protest, justice, equality, and love did much to break down legalized segregation in the United States.

Many of these Baptist groups are members of the worldwide Baptist World Alliance (BWA). Organized in 1905, the BWA pro-motes unity among Baptist denominations, religious liberty, evan-gelism, separation of church and state, and disaster relief. The SBC withdrew from the BWA in 2004 over concerns that the BWA tol-erated liberal theology.

The SBC, ABC, CBF, NBC, and NBCA are the largest Baptist bodies in the United States, but there are many other smaller groups. Among these are the General, Regular, Duck River, Hardshell, Seventh-day, and Separate Baptists. Though there are exceptions, most Baptists believe in the Bible as the sole authority for doctrine and practice, separation of church and state, the offices of pastor and deacon in the local church, the autonomy of the local church, congregational polity, the priesthood of all believers, the ordinances of baptism and the Lord's Supper, and soul competency. In matters of soteriology, Baptists can be found in all theological camps—Calvinist, Arminian, and others.

METHODISTS

The Methodist movement in America began with Wesley's sending of Francis Asbury to work in the colonies in 1771. Upon his arrival, Asbury found that there were not enough ministers to assign one to each preaching point. So he sent itinerant ministers into the countryside to serve at multiple preaching points on a rotating basis and to set in motion the Methodist pattern of "circuit riding." When the American Revolution began, Wesley sided with the British and summoned his ministers to do the same. Other than Asbury, almost all Methodist ministers returned to England. Because he remained, the Methodist Church avoided being labeled as Tory, which could have been its death knell in America.

The Methodist Episcopal Church began to take shape in 1784 when Wesley appointed Thomas Coke as the first superintendent of the Methodist movement in America. Wesley instructed Coke that upon his arrival in America he was to ordain Asbury. Knowing the anti-American implications of appointing an Englishman, Asbury called a conference in Baltimore, Maryland, on December 24, 1784. At this "Christmas Conference," the representatives elected Asbury and Coke as cosuperintendents. Much to Wesley's chagrin, Asbury changed their titles from superintendent to bishop. Wesley resisted an official break from the Anglican Church, but by the end of his life, Methodism was obviously a separate denomination.

Under Asbury's leadership Methodists developed preaching circuits in the western expanses of America. Whenever frontiersmen created a new settlement, a Methodist minister was not far behind. Asbury himself was an itinerant preacher for forty-five years. He reportedly traveled more than 300,000 miles, delivered more than 16,500 sermons, and ordained 4,000 ministers. By 1844, the Methodist Episcopal Church reported 4,400 circuit riders.

Like Presbyterians and Baptists, the Methodist Church split over slavery. The Methodist Episcopal Church of the North opposed it, and the Methodist Episcopal Church of the South supported it. Unlike the Baptists, these factions reunited in 1939 and created the Methodist Church.

There were also black Methodist denominations. The African Methodist Episcopal (AME) Church was started by Richard Allen (1760–1831) in Philadelphia in 1816. A slave who had purchased his freedom, Allen began his own church because he believed he was not being treated as a full member of the St. George's Methodist Episcopal Church in Philadelphia. He purchased a black-smith shop and founded the Bethel Church in 1793. Saint George's Church attempted to assert its authority over Bethel Church, but Allen was able to retain its independence. Asbury ordained Allen as the church's deacon in 1799. In 1816, representatives of black Methodist churches met at Bethel and formed the AME Church. Asbury then ordained Allen as its first bishop. The AME Church now supports seven colleges, three seminaries, and a university in Liberia. It is also active in foreign missions, with a strong missionary presence in Africa, South America, and the Caribbean. As of 2010, AME membership was approximately 2.5 million.

The African Methodist Episcopal Zion (AMEZ) Church formed in New York City in 1821. Its founders were several black members of the John's Street Methodist Episcopal Zion Church who did not like their secondary status in the congregation. Asbury approved their separation, and with six other black Methodist churches they formed the AMEZ Church. It supports one college and one seminary. In 2010, it reported a membership of 1.5 million.

The Evangelical United Brethren Church joined with the Methodist Church and became the United Methodist Church in 1968. In 2007, the United Methodist Church estimated its membership in America at eight million. The Methodist Church is associated with one hundred colleges and universities.

HOLINESS CHURCHES

Holiness churches have their roots in Methodism. After the Civil War, many Methodists began to abandon Wesley's idea of Christian perfection. Other Methodists, who gave rise to the Holiness churches, emphasized perfection and taught a "second blessing" of the Holy Spirit following salvation that brought believers to a higher level of spirituality.

One of the most important early Holiness leaders, Phoebe Palmer (1807–1874), taught that in the second blessing the Holy Spirit perfected the will of a believer and enabled him or her to achieve "entire sanctification."

In 1894 the Methodist Episcopal Church denied entire sanctification, and many churches left it to form Holiness denominations. The largest Holiness churches are the Free Methodist Church, the Church of God (Anderson, Indiana), and the Church of the Nazarene.

PENTECOSTAL CHURCHES

Most Pentecostal churches stemmed from the Holiness churches. The Pentecostal movement began on New Year's Day in 1901 when Charles Parham's (1873–1929) students at Bethel Bible College in Topeka, Kansas, supposedly received the spiritual gift of tongues (*glossolalia*). Citing Acts 2, Parham taught that receiving the Holy Spirit had to be evidenced by speaking in tongues. Soon others experienced *glossolalia*, and Parham organized the Apostolic Faith Mission, which quickly grew to 25,000 members. Parham later opened a Bible Institute in Houston, Texas.

For a short time in 1905, William Seymour (1870–1922) was one of Parham's students at the Houston Bible Institute. He brought Pentecostalism to Los Angeles, California, leading what became known as the Azusa Street Revival in Los Angeles in 1906. The revival lasted for three years and was marked by speaking in tongues and miraculous healings. From Azusa Street, the Pentecostal movement spread across the United States.

There are now more than 300 Pentecostal denominations in the United States. The largest are the Assemblies of God, Church of God (Cleveland, Tennessee), and Church of God in Christ. Most Pentecostal churches believe in a spiritual baptism that is evidenced by speaking in tongues. They also believe in the truth of the Bible, practice evangelism, believe in faith healing, and expect an imminent millennium. The members of Pentecostal churches are racially diverse, and women frequently assume leadership roles.

CHAPTER TWENTY-SEVEN

CATHOLICISM AND ORTHODOXY IN THE MODERN ERA

C atholicism faced many unforeseen problems in the modern world. It had to cope with the end of absolute monarchies that depended on the church for their legitimacy. It had to contend with revolutions, the loss of the Papal States, two world wars, and rising anti-Catholic prejudice. Economic systems such as Marxism, communism, socialism, and in some instances capitalism displaced the church as the center of life. Liberation theology and feminism challenged traditional Catholic positions. In response to these changes, the Catholic Church held major councils in both the nineteenth and twentieth centuries.

The Orthodox churches also had their share of problems. During the communist era, the Russian Orthodox Church suffered from the Soviet Union's determination to create an atheistic society. Other Orthodox churches remained small; many struggled to maintain their influence in Islamic nations; and the majority had little influence outside their nation's borders.

CATHOLICISM IN FRANCE

The French Revolution (1789–1799) permanently changed Catholicism in France. Though French monarchs were largely

responsible for their nation's abject poverty in the late eighteenth
century, the Catholic Church bore a share of responsibility. Philosophers such as Voltaire and Rousseau rarely missed an opportunity to point out the church's culpability. Since Catholicism was
the national church, many French citizens viewed it as part of the
government and resented paying forced tithes to it. They despised
monks who did little for the church or society yet continued to live
off their state-provided income. Opulence in the church and among
monarchs put France on the verge of bankruptcy.

     When the monarchy weakened in 1789, so did the Catholic
Church, as the National Assembly confiscated church property in
the name of the state. In 1790 the monasteries were dissolved. The
National Assembly limited the number of bishops to eighty-three,
one for each province, and bishops were selected by civil officials. To
the pope's chagrin, the church was forced to vow loyalty to the revolutionary government. Protesting this assault of papal authority,
thousands of clergy left France.

     When the First Republic was declared on September 21, 1792,
many citizens wanted to punish the church for its ties to the dis-
credited monarchy. Following Louis XVI's (1774–1792) execution on January 21, 1793, French priests faced the Reign of Terror
(1793–1794). Hundreds if not thousands of them were killed by
the Republic and vengeful mobs. Under Maximilien de Robespierre's
(1758–1794) Committee for Public Safety, a "cult of reason" developed that emphasized worship of the Supreme Being. Notre Dame
Cathedral and other churches were used for ceremonies dedicated
to the cult of reason.

     Hoping to gain the Catholic population's support, Napoleon
Bonaparte (1769–1821) signed the Concordat of 1801 with Pope
Pius VII (1800–1823). The Concordat reinstated Catholicism as
the state church and provided it with financial support. The Catholic Church, however, remained under the direction of the state,
and its property was not returned. Education was also taken out of

its hands and placed under state control. According to the Organic Articles of 1802, the Catholic Church could not call a synod or publish papal bulls concerning France without permission from the government.

Napoleon's coronation by Pius VII as emperor on December 2, 1804, reinforced the government's authority over the church. Hoping to emulate the coronation of Charlemagne, but only to an extent, Napoleon unexpectedly took the crown from Pius's hand and crowned himself and then his wife. Napoleon did not want to give the impression that he was answerable to the church.

Pius VII suffered the wrath of Napoleon for refusing to endorse his war with England. Napoleon retaliated by annexing the Papal States. When he was defeated at Waterloo in 1815 and sent into exile, the Papal States were returned.

Fortunately for Catholics, the French Revolution did not affect the church as much as radicals desired. Though clearly weakened, it remained a bulwark of steadiness and assurance in uncertain times.

Relations with Protestantism

The Catholic Church did not forget about the descendants of Martin Luther. Pius VII condemned Protestant Bible societies in 1816. Leo XII (1823–1829) likewise denounced Bible societies and referred to their translations as the "devil's gospel." He also clarified the Catholic Church's position concerning Protestantism, maintaining that anyone not a part of the Catholic Church was not a Christian and under God's wrath. Pius VIII (1829–1830) denounced liberty of conscience, and his successor Gregory XVI (1831–1846) announced that freedom of religion was nothing short of insanity.

Pius IX (1846–1878)

The reign of Pius IX was the longest in papal history. It was also one of the most important. Pius was concerned about changes happening in the world and wanted to retain traditional Catholicism against these pressures. As a result, much of his reign was reactionary. Against the Protestant advance, he reasserted in 1854 that there was no salvation outside the Catholic Church. In his encyclical *Quanto conficiamur moerore* (1863), Pius condemned Protestantism as heresy along with every other teaching that conflicted with Catholic doctrine.

In addition, he decreed *Ineffabilis Deus* (Latin for "Ineffable God"), which officially defined the doctrine of the Immaculate Conception of Mary. This doctrine developed over centuries and declared that Mary was born free of original sin. *Ineffabilis Deus* stated:

> We declare, pronounce and define that the doctrine which holds that the Most Blessed Virgin Mary, in the first instant of Her conception, by a singular grace and privilege granted by Almighty God, in view of the merits of Christ Jesus the Savior of the human race, was preserved free from all stain of original sin, is a doctrine revealed by God and therefore to be firmly and constantly believed by all the faithful.[1]

Pius published the *Syllabus of Errors* in 1864. It condemned eighty political and social ideas pertaining to marriage, Bible societies, public schools, freedom of conscience, capitalism, separation of church and state, and other modern phenomena. The *Syllabus* made clear that the Roman pontiff would not reconcile himself to "progress, liberalism, and civilization as lately introduced."[2]

The most significant event in Pius's reign was Vatican Council I. Pius convened the council on December 8, 1869, and adjourned it on October 20, 1870. The cardinals who attended, like the pope, were concerned with liberal trends in society and the church's declining authority. They sought to retain traditional Catholicism.

Vatican I's "Dogmatic Constitution" listed doctrines that had to be accepted and condemned philosophies at odds with Catholic dogma. The Bible's divine inspiration, the seven sacraments' power to impart grace, and the primacy of the pope had to be accepted. Rationalism, naturalism, pantheism, atheism, materialism, and rejection of creation *ex nihilo* were in opposition to the Catholic Church.

The most famous pronouncement of Vatican I was the doctrine of papal infallibility. It stated that the pope was the successor of Peter and could make unchallengeable pronouncements when speaking *ex cathedra* on matters of faith and morals. Such statements had to be accepted as true. The doctrine stated:

> We, adhering faithfully to the tradition received from the beginning of the Christian faith—with a view to the glory of our Divine Saviour, the exaltation of the Catholic religion, and the salvation of Christian peoples (the sacred Council approving), teach and define as dogma divinely revealed: That the Roman Pontiff, when he speaks *ex cathedra* (that is, when—fulfilling the office of Pastor and Teacher of all Christians—on his supreme Apostolic authority, he defines a doctrine concerning faith or morals to be held by the Universal Church), through the divine assistance promised him in blessed Peter, is endowed with that infallibility, with which the Divine Redeemer has willed that His Church—in defining doctrines concerning faith and morals—should be equipped: And therefore, that such definitions of the Roman Pontiff of themselves—and not by virtue of the consent of the Church—are irreformable. If any one shall presume (which God forbid!) to contradict this our definition; let him be anathema.[3]

Though not defined officially until 1870, papal infallibility was a majority opinion among Catholics long before that. Pius applied it when he asserted the Immaculate Conception of Mary without approval of a council in 1850.

By codifying papal infallibility, the council intended to lift the prestige of the papacy and contain dissent within the church. After much discussion papal infallibility was approved with only two votes of opposition, including one by a bishop from Arkansas. A small group known as the "Old Catholics" broke away from Rome over papal infallibility. They were strongest in Switzerland and Austria but never became a viable alternative to Rome.

Pius XII (1939–1958) spoke *ex cathedra* in 1950 when he decreed the doctrine of the Assumption of Mary. This doctrine stated that the virgin Mary was taken to heaven in body and soul at the end of her earthly life. Pius's wording was ambiguous regarding whether she died before her assumption or was assumed without having to experience death. The church allowed Catholics to hold either position. According to Pius:

> Therefore, the majestic Mother of God, from all eternity united in a mysterious way with Jesus Christ by "one and the same decree" of predestination, immaculate in her conception, in her divine motherhood a most unspotted virgin, the noble ally of the Divine Redeemer who bore off the triumph over sin and its supporters, finally achieved, as the supreme crown of her privileges, that she should be preserved immune from the corruption of the tomb, and, like her Son before her, having conquered death, should be carried up, in body and soul, to the celestial glory of Heaven, to reign there as Queen at the right hand of her Son, the immortal King of the ages. . . . Therefore we . . . declare and define, as a dogma revealed by God, that the Immaculate Mother of God, ever-Virgin Mary, on the completion

of her course of her earthly life, has been taken up, in body and soul, to the glory of heaven.[4]

While Vatican I was in session, the Franco-Prussian War began. To defend itself, France recalled its soldiers who were protecting the Papal States. The Italian king, Victor Emmanuel (1861–1878), then annexed the Papal States. The papacy was left with only the Lateran Palace, Vatican City, and Castel Gandolfo. Pius lived in the Vatican for the final eight years of his reign, where he plotted to regain the lost territories. His successor, Leo XIII (1878–1903), was also incensed over the loss of the Papal States. He refused to recognize Italy as a nation and forbade Catholics from voting in national elections.

REACTION TO VATICAN I AND OTHER PAPAL PRONOUNCEMENTS

Many European nations responded harshly to Pius's dictums. The German chancellor and a devout Protestant, Otto von Bismarck (1815–1898) began to view the Catholic Church as a rival for the loyalty of the German people. He believed the church was interfering with German unification, which had been achieved at the close of the Franco-Prussian War. Bismarck launched the *Kulturkampf*, or "struggle for civilization," to enforce German nationalism and weaken the Catholic Church. He expelled the Jesuits in 1872 and instituted the Falk Laws in 1873. Enforced only in Prussia, these laws required the government rather than the church to perform all marriages, forced clerical education to take place in state universities, and placed all education in the hands of the government. But, aware that he needed the full support of Catholics against socialism, Bismarck rescinded most of the laws by 1880.

While Pius X (1903–1914) was pope, France passed laws that limited the clergy's role in public education, placed convents and monasteries under government control, and made civil rather than ecclesiastical marriage mandatory. France and the Vatican ended official relations in 1904, and the following year France passed legislation separating church and state. All church property became state property, and the Catholic Church no longer received a governmental stipend.

MARXISM

Marxism was a major threat not just to Catholicism or to Christianity in general, but to all religions. Developed by Karl Marx (1818–1883), what came to be known as Marxism was an extreme reaction to capitalism. Marx believed that religious, social, and political institutions were products of a society's economic organization. As technology improved a society's means of production, he said, existing forms of social organization became inefficient and led to class conflict. Ultimately, class conflict led to social revolution, according to Marx. As examples, he cited the transition from feudalism to capitalism and the revolutions in England and France. Because profits were taken from the laborers who created it, Marx maintained that capitalism was an unfair system. Capitalism also led to the concentration of private property, which further alienated the wealthy from the poor, according to Marx. As an alternative he advocated socialism, a system based on cooperative ownership of the means of production and distribution of wealth based on each worker's contribution to the system.

Marx claimed that religion was merely a tool to provide hope for the powerless and the poor:

> Man makes religion, religion does not make man. In other words, religion is the self-consciousness and self-feeling of man who has either not yet found himself or has already lost himself again. But man is no abstract being squatting outside the world. Man is the world of man, the state, the society. This state, this society, produces

religion, a reversed world-consciousness, because they are in a reversed world.[5]

Man created God. According to Marx, "Religion is the opiate of the people." In a more egalitarian world, free of the powerless and the poor, religion would no longer be necessary.

To create economic balance, Marx advocated a society where no one owned private property. His system became known as communism. It would eliminate greed and selfishness, he said. To make this new society work, people had to eliminate their personal beliefs and ambitions and replace them with a desire to advance the system as a whole.

For most of the twentieth century, Marxist regimes ruled the Soviet Union, China, Cuba, and several Eastern European countries. Though all the popes from Pius XI (1922–1939) onward condemned communism, none was more vehement against it than John Paul II (1978–2005).

Pius XI (1922–1939)

During the reign of Pius XI there was a dramatic rise of fascism, national socialism, and communism. In Italy, Benito Mussolini (1883–1945) and Pius appeared to have a cordial relationship. In return for the pope's not condemning fascism, remaining out of Italian politics, and not insisting on the return of the Papal States, Mussolini approved the Lateran Concordat and Treaty of 1929 that recognized the Vatican as a sovereign state.

Pius XII (1939–1958)

Elected six months prior to the outbreak of World War II, Pius XII could not have become pope at a worse time. He had been papal nuncio to Bavaria and had drawn up concordats with Bavaria,

Prussia, and Nazi Germany. His close ties to Germany did not help his cause or legacy.

Pius never denounced Germany's anti-Semitic laws and never made public statements supporting the Jews, but he did condemn the extermination of a race. In 1943 he did little to stop the Nazis from sending the Jews of Rome to concentration camps. Following the war, Pius claimed that denouncing Nazis' treatment of Jews would have made their plight worse. Though it is hard to imagine that the Jewish plight could have been any worse, perhaps Pius was thinking of his predecessor's condemnation of Hitler's policies. When the Nazis pressured Catholic clerics to accept their beliefs, Pius XI penned an encyclical entitled "With Burning Anxiety" that condemned Nazi beliefs and called Hitler mad. He had the encyclical smuggled into Germany and read on Palm Sunday of 1937. Hitler responded with a crackdown on Catholic clerics.

Some historians have reevaluated the reign of Pius XII, claiming that he may have saved thousands of Jews by hiding them in Vatican City and in churches throughout Europe. While most historians believe he was at least neglectful of his obligations, defenders claim that his inaction saved the church from possible extermination in Nazi-controlled territories. This theory, however, appears flawed. There is more evidence of high-ranking Catholic officials helping to secure passports for Nazi leaders and aiding their relocation to safe countries after World War II.

INFLUENTIAL THEOLOGIANS

Yves Congar (1904–1995) and Karl Rahner (1904–1984) were among the most influential Catholic theologians of the twentieth century. Their thought had a strong influence on Vatican II (1962–1965). In many ways these theologians began the process of bringing the Catholic Church into the modern era.

A Dominican theologian, Congar understood that much of the Catholic Church's tradition and dogma came about in response to political and cultural circumstances. He maintained that Catholic tradition needed to be understood in its historical context. For Congar, the ever-changing state of the world made it difficult for theologians of previous eras to speak adequately regarding the future. He suggested in *True and False Reform in the Church* (1950) that the church place more emphasis on Scripture than on tradition, an idea that promoted reconciliation with Protestants. Many of his writings were suppressed by the Congregation of the Doctrine of the Faith. Under the pontificate of John XXIII (1958–1963), however, Congar found favor and served as a theological consultant and influential participant in Vatican II.

A prolific author, Rahner was one of the best-known Catholic scholars around the time of Vatican II (1962–1965). His most influential works were the twenty-three-volume *Theological Investigations* (1961–1992) and *Foundations of the Christian Faith* (1978).

Rahner argued that all great world religions taught dependence on a divine creator who offered the hope of freedom through a divine redeemer. Though followers of these religions all believed in deliverance through a redeemer, many did not know his name, Rahner said. He called them "anonymous Christians" and said they may receive God's saving grace. Rahner maintained, however, that Christianity was the clearest and fullest expression of God's grace.

Rahner held that Christians of each age had to interpret Scripture and tradition in relation to their world. He argued that the mystery of God, which permeated all things, including Scripture and tradition, spoke to all people in all ages and was not static. While recognizing the primacy of the pope, Rahner asserted that ministers throughout the world must be able to speak to the cultures in which they ministered.

Vatican II (1962–1965)

Held in Rome over four sessions, Vatican II was the only ecumenical council in the twentieth century. It was called by John XXIII, who ministered in Bulgaria, Turkey, Germany, and France and saw firsthand the atrocities of war and the impact of Islam on Christianity. When John died during the proceedings, Pope Paul VI (1963–1978) continued the council. In a Catholic sense, Vatican II was truly ecumenical. European bishops were joined by bishops from Latin America, Africa, and Asia. Representatives from the world's major Protestant denominations also attended, but had no voting rights.

The pronouncements of Vatican II touched virtually every aspect of Catholicism. The virgin Mary was declared to be the mother of the church, vernacular languages replaced Latin in the liturgy, hymn singing was introduced, and Communion in both kinds was mandated for the laity. The Index of forbidden books was eliminated. Several modern translations of the Bible were approved, and the laity was encouraged to read them. In a dramatic turnabout, Vatican II supported religious liberty:

> The Vatican council declares that the human person has a right to religious freedom. Freedom of this kind means that everyone should be immune from coercion by individuals, social groups and every human power so that, within due limits, no men or women are forced to act against their convictions nor are any persons to be restrained from acting in accordance with their convictions in religious matters in private or public, alone or in association with others. The council further declares that the right to religious freedom is based on the very dignity of the human person as known through the revealed word of God and by reason itself.[6]

The council resolved to open avenues of dialogue with some of the Protestant denominations, referred to as "separated brethren." Moreover, Jews did not inherit the guilt of Christ's death, according to Vatican II. The council said, "Even though the Jewish authorities and those who followed their lead pressed for the death of Christ (see John 19:6), neither all Jews indiscriminately at that time, nor Jews today, can be charged with the crimes committed during his passion."[7]

The Catholic Church said it respected that which was true in all religions. Jesus, however, was the clearest manifestation of God, and the other religions manifested merely a "ray" of truth. Such teachings helped bring the Catholic Church into the modern world.

Swiss theologian Hans Küng (b. 1928), however, believed Vatican II did not go far enough and challenged papal infallibility in his *Infallible? An Inquiry* (1971). He also taught that non-Christian religions might provide a path to God and thus a manner of salvation. The Sacred Congregation for the Doctrine of the Faith censured Küng in 1979 and rescinded his license to teach as a Catholic theologian.

Other Catholics believed Vatican II went too far. More conservative Catholics believed the church had capitulated too much to modernism and culture. Many such priests and bishops defied the council and continued to perform the Latin Mass. On the opposite end of the spectrum, some American Catholics began to speak in favor of birth control and against clerical celibacy. In Latin America, the council's empathy for the poor and oppressed gave rise to liberation theology. Deeply committed to Catholic tradition, Pope John Paul II modified some of Vatican II's dictums.

LIBERATION THEOLOGY

Since the sixteenth century, the Catholic Church has been active in South America and has long been the largest Christian denomination on the continent. However, Catholicism often was tied to oppressive and authoritarian regimes that kept citizens in poverty. Church leaders told people they should count it a privilege to suffer as Christ had suffered and they should obey their masters. Their reward for obedience and suffering would be in heaven.

But in the late 1960s, the Catholic Church changed its posture toward oppressive regimes. In his *Populorum Progressio* of 1967, Pope Paul VI blamed the crushing poverty in South America on economic injustice and said it had to be abolished. He wrote:

> The same duty of solidarity that rests on individuals exists also for nations: "It is the very serious duty of the developed nations to help the under-developed." It is necessary to put this teaching of the Council into effect. Although it is normal that a nation should be the first to benefit from the gifts that Providence has bestowed on it as the fruit of the labour of its people, still no country can claim on that account to keep its wealth for itself alone. Every nation must produce more and better quality goods to give to all its inhabitants a truly human standard of living, and also to contribute to the common development of the human race. Given the increasing needs of the under-developed countries, it should be considered quite normal for an advanced country to devote a part of its production to meet their needs, and to train teachers, engineers, technicians and scholars prepared to put their knowledge and their skill at the disposal of less fortunate peoples.[8]

Such pronouncements helped give rise to liberation theology, an ideology that depicted the gospel primarily as a means to free people from unjust political, economic, and social conditions. At the Second Latin American Bishops' Conference at Medellín, Columbia, in 1968, Gustavo Gutiérrez (b. 1928), the most significant liberation theologian, rose to prominence. In his *A Theology of Liberation* (1971), Gutiérrez argued that Christians must alleviate oppression throughout the world. For Gutiérrez, liberation required eliminating the political and social causes of poverty and denouncing selfishness. Gutiérrez concluded that if one knew God (orthodoxy), one had to practice justice (orthopraxis).

Other liberation theologians expanded on the work of Gutiérrez. Leonardo Boff (b. 1938) said the church must be concerned with the physical welfare of man, not just his spiritual needs. The kingdom of Jesus meant not only a future hope but a present deliverance from oppression, he said. The church, therefore, must support the poor whenever possible. According to liberation theology, God's posture toward people is determined largely by their economic condition.

Liberation theologians often cited the biblical story of the exodus. Since God led his people out of slavery and Pharaoh's oppression, he obviously does not want his people to live in spiritual or physical oppression, they said. In this regard many South American governments were perceived as no less tyrannical than Pharaoh.

From the New Testament, liberation theology emphasized Jesus' opposition to social and religious structures that burdened people and kept them in a state of need. In the Beatitudes, liberation theologians said, Jesus blessed those who were poor. Because Christ was oppressed and died at the hands of a cruel government, the crucifixion was a sign to many liberation theologians that Jesus identified with the victims of repressive governments.

Oscar Romero (1917–1980) was a martyr of the liberation movement in Latin America. Initially suspicious of liberation theology, he sympathized with the poor after becoming bishop of the rural diocese of Santiago de María in El Salvador in 1975. He became archbishop of San Salvador in 1977 and began to preach against the government's neglect of the poor. In 1980 he was murdered by government assassins while saying Mass.

The results of liberation theology were varied. John Paul II condemned various aspects of it. Headed by Cardinal Joseph Ratzinger (b. 1927), who became Pope Benedict XVI (2005–2013), the Sacred Congregation of the Doctrine of the Faith criticized liberation theology. The Sacred Congregation noted that ultimate liberation is liberation from sin, not from social constructs. It also noted that liberation theology has a tendency to become more concerned with activism than with spirituality and condemned Gutiérrez for emphasizing orthopraxis at the expense of orthodoxy. Catholics have also expressed concern that liberation theology relies on Marxist principles, identifies the church with the privileged, and advocates "structured violence" at times.[9]

Liberation theology has spread beyond South America and the Catholic Church. Its ideas gave rise to black and feminist theologies that can be found in both Catholic and Protestant denominations. Black theology developed in the racially charged 1960s as some black Christians rejected Martin Luther King's philosophy of nonviolent resistance for a more aggressive approach.

James Cone (b. 1938) has become black theology's most influential scholar. Heavily influenced by Malcolm X (1925–1965) and an advocate of black power, Cone took King to task for accommodation and placing too much emphasis on heavenly rewards at the expense of black people's dignity in this world. In 1970 Cone wrote *A Black Theology of Liberation*. He maintained that racism was a sin. Just as humans had a propensity to sin because of the fall, society had a propensity toward prejudice, he said. Just as Jesus redeemed sinners, he could also free humanity from its racist inclinations. Cone also believed Christ should be viewed as black:

> To suggest that Christ has taken on a black skin is not theological emotionalism. If the Church is a continuation of the Incarnation, and if the Church and Christ are where the oppressed are, then Christ and his Church must totally identify with the oppressed to the extent that they too

suffer for the same reasons persons are enslaved. In America, blacks are oppressed because of their blackness. It would seem, then, that emancipation could only be realized by Christ and his Church becoming black. Thinking of Christ as nonblack in the twentieth century is as theologically impossible as thinking of him as non-Jewish in the first century. God's Word in Christ not only fulfills his purposes for man through his elected people, but also inaugurates a new age in which all oppressed people become his people. In America, that people is a black people. In order to remain faithful to his Word in Christ, his personal manifestation must be the very essence of blackness.[10]

There are at least two schools of Catholic feminist theology. One wants to bring women into church leadership roles; the other thinks the church is too patriarchal to change. Each group critiques theological language that depicts God exclusively in masculine terms. Since God transcends gender, one should be able to envisage him in masculine or feminine terms, feminists argue. The church should employ feminine depictions of God and realize that the differences between men and women are purely biological, not based on any aspect of God. According to feminist theologians, depicting God as feminine would help Catholics address issues of concern to women.

Two prominent feminist theologians are Mary Daly (1928–2010) and Rosemary Radford Ruether (b. 1936). In *The Church and the Second Sex* (1968), Daly argued that traditional Christian theology wrongly suggested that women were inferior to men. She cited as examples the singular use of male symbols for God and male church leaders. Her feminist theology moved her away from the Catholic Church. In *Sexism and God Talk* (1983), Ruether contended that the church used masculine language to keep women from rising to prominent positions. She helped begin the "Women-Church" movement.

Slavery also plays a role in feminist arguments. Just as slavery was permitted in the biblical era but abandoned in the modern era, feminists say, patriarchal religion was the norm in the Bible but should be abandoned in the modern era.

POPE JOHN PAUL II

John Paul II was the first non-Italian to be elected pope since the Reformation. Beloved around the world, he visited more countries and traveled more miles than any previous pope.[11] He appointed 231 cardinals, entertained heads of state on more than 700 occasions, and addressed millions at his Wednesday public audiences at the Vatican.

John Paul was a participant and advisor at Vatican II, but he was more conservative than many participants and partially backtracked Vatican II's tenuous steps into the modern world. Even though he appointed more cardinals than any previous pope, he was the final authority on all matters. Some of his decisions were controversial. Despite the AIDS crisis, John Paul remained adamant against the use of condoms. He was largely silent regarding clergy convicted of sexual abuse.

John Paul's greatest legacy was his concern for the poor and his role in the fall of communism in Eastern Europe. His dedication to the virgin Mary was well documented. When he was shot and seriously wounded on May 13, 1981, he credited the virgin Mary of Fatima with diverting the bullet from his vital organs.

After suffering from Parkinson's disease for more than a decade, John Paul II died on April 2, 2005. His successor, Benedict XVI, was also conservative and dedicated to defending traditional Catholic dogma. When Benedict resigned in 2013, Francis, formerly Jorge Mario Bergoglio of Argentina, succeeded him. Francis was the first Latin American pope.

CATHOLICISM IN AMERICA

During the mid-nineteenth century, immigration from Eastern European countries made the Catholic Church the largest denomination in the United States. Between 1820 and 1860, 2 million Catholic immigrants arrived. In the 1840s, 800,000 came from Ireland alone where the potato famine destroyed their primary source of income and subsistence. By 1860, more than 3 million Catholics lived in the US. After the Civil War, Catholic immigration continued, and by 1910 the Catholic population in America exceeded 15 million.

Following the American Revolution, the Vatican allowed the American clergy to nominate their first bishop. They selected John Carroll (1735–1815), a Jesuit from Maryland. He was approved by Pius VI (1775–1799)in 1789 and named bishop of the see of Baltimore. Carroll was a strong bishop who had to cope with uniquely American difficulties. Because of a lack of clergy, many Catholics built their own churches and were led by laity. When clergy arrived, church ownership and governance became points of contention, a problem known as trusteeism. In addition, many American Catholics wanted to choose their own priests, preferably ones who spoke the same language as their congregations. These issues were not completely resolved until the early twentieth century.

Carroll had to appease many different immigrant groups with different patron saints, feast days, and customs. This often led to different nationalities living and worshipping in different parishes. A Catholic national identity was difficult to develop. Despite these difficulties, Carroll placed Catholicism in America on a firm foundation.

Still, Catholics often were treated with hostility by their Protestant neighbors. With the notable exception of Maryland, America was dominated by Protestantism. Because many early colonists came from England where the Reformation had only recently ended, they had no love for Catholicism. Many Puritans considered the

Catholic Church a tool of the Antichrist. In fact, Catholic immigration to Massachusetts Bay Colony was forbidden by law in 1647.

One of the primary allegations against Catholics was that they could not be good Americans because their first loyalty was to the papacy, which was against separation of church and state. Newspapers, cartoons, and books warned Protestant Americans about the dangers of the papal minions. In *A Plea for the West* (1835), the great revivalist Lyman Beecher (1775–1863) argued that freedom would be threatened if Catholic immigration were not checked in the western territories.

Stories of sexually depraved monks, priests, and nuns contributed to misconceptions. Written by a former nun, *The Awful Disclosures of the Hotel Dieu Nunnery* (1836) was one of the most popular books in America. It described how nuns were forced to have sex with priests who portrayed it as almost a sacramental act, had abortions, and suffered terrible corporal punishment. Though the book proved to be untrue, by the outbreak of the Civil War, it had sold more than 600,000 copies.

An anti-Catholic political organization formed in 1849, the Order of the Star-Spangled Banner, made halting Catholic immigration a cornerstone of its platform. When asked about their principles, members of the order often said they "did not know." For this reason they were known as the Know Nothings. They changed their name to the American Party in 1852 and managed to elect seventy-five congressmen to the House of Representatives in 1854. After their initial success, the Know Nothings lost much of their following as the issue of slavery took precedence over Catholic immigration.

At the turn of the twentieth century, the Catholic population in America exceeded 12 million. Immigration was the major factor in Catholicism's continued growth, with the majority of Catholic immigrants arriving from Eastern and Southern Europe. During World War I, Catholics worked with other denominations, provided chaplains, recruited soldiers, raised funds, and worked in a myriad of war-associated benevolent societies.

This era of relative peace for Catholics came to an end with passage of the National Origins Act in 1924, stopping immigration from Eastern and Southern Europe. Since the majority of potential immigrants were Catholic, the act had anti-Catholic overtones. But if weakening Catholicism was the goal, it failed. With the tide of diverse immigrants stemmed, the Catholic Church was better able to organize those already in America.

Anti-Catholicism surfaced in 1928 when the Democratic Party nominated the Catholic governor of New York, Alfred E. Smith (1873–1944), as its candidate for president. Protestants brought back their old arguments, accusing Smith of being the pope's puppet, wanting to make Catholicism the national religion, and hoping to repeal Prohibition. Opponents aired these accusations in sermons, posters, on the radio, and in newspapers. Smith was resoundingly defeated, even in his home state, by Herbert Hoover (1874–1964), a Quaker.

Once again Catholicism found itself under attack in the 1960 presidential election when the Democratic Party nominated John F. Kennedy (1917–1963). Though Americans were more pluralistic than they had been in 1928, many Protestants wondered if the Catholic Kennedy would be more loyal to the pope than to America. After Kennedy affirmed his dedication to separation of church and state, he defeated Richard Nixon (1931–1994) in a close election. Kennedy's election did not end anti-Catholicism in America, but it certainly helped.

Following Vatican II's pronouncements approving separation of church and state and religious freedom, Catholics finally were able to reconcile their faith with their identity as Americans. Vatican II also reinvigorated many lay American Catholics, increasing the popularity of organizations like Opus Dei and the Knights of

Columbus. Many Catholic high schools, colleges, and universities became nationally renowned for their academic excellence.

In recent decades many Catholics sought federal aid for their private schools, but some Americans viewed this as a violation of the First Amendment. The Catholic Church was also forced to acknowledge several scandals involving sexual abuse of children. In spite of these setbacks, the Catholic Church remains the largest Christian denomination in the United States. Catholic presence is particularly strong in New England industrial cities and southwestern states. In 2011, the Catholic population of the United States exceeded 77 million. As of 2012, six of the nine Supreme Court justices were Catholic.

ORTHODOXY

In the twenty-first century the Orthodox Church is a communion of autocephalous[12] churches, defined by region and ruled by a council of bishops. The patriarch of Constantinople only holds authority over the Orthodox in Turkey, Crete, and a few other locations. In the United States the Greek Orthodox Church had more than 2 million members in the 1980s.

Beginning in 1721 with the reign of Peter the Great (1682–1725) and closing with the Revolution of 1817, the Russian Orthodox Church was a department of the state. It was governed by bishops appointed by the czar. Orthodoxy in Russia, therefore, developed with little input from Rome. In fact, when Catholicism appeared in Russia, it met with resistance. For example, in 1819 to keep Catholic influence from spreading, Russia expelled the Jesuits. In Russia, belief in the tradition handed down from Constantinople and pride in the Orthodox Church led to the belief that it was the only true church. Thousands of young men became monks, and the number of monasteries in Russia grew from 452 in 1810 to more than a thousand in 1914.

Wars in the Balkans and the rise of communism posed threats to Orthodoxy in the twentieth century. In the Soviet Union the state revoked the church's right to own property in 1918 and confiscated many priceless icons and treasures in 1921. By 1929 atheistic state rallies replaced the church services, and the distribution of Bibles was forbidden. Thousands of Russian clergy were martyred.

In an attempt to rally Russian nationalism during World War II, Joseph Stalin (1928–1953) resurrected the Russian Orthodox Church. During the next fifteen years more than 22,000 Russian Orthodox churches opened their doors. Nikita Khrushchev (1958–1964) disestablished the Russian Orthodox Church in 1957 and persecution resumed. Many of the Orthodox immigrated to America. In 1970, descendants of the Russian Orthodox Church formed the Orthodox Church in America (OCA) and claimed more than a million members in 2010.

After the fall of communism in 1989, millions of Christians came out of hiding and reestablished the Russian Orthodox Church. The modern Russian Orthodox Church is ecumenical and carries on interfaith dialogues with the Lutheran Church. Its tradition and liturgy, however, remain uniquely Russian.

CHAPTER TWENTY-EIGHT

MODERN PROTESTANTISM

I n the modern era Protestants refined their theological focus in response to Enlightenment teachings, critical examinations of the Bible, new scientific theories, and two world wars. While some Protestants attempted to reconcile Christianity with culture, science, and reason, others tried to maintain the doctrines of the Reformation in spite of cultural pressures. They emphasized the fundamentals of the faith above science, biblical criticism, and modernism. Others hoped to create a worldwide Protestant organization. As a result, modern Protestantism has taken many forms.

NINETEENTH-CENTURY LIBERAL THEOLOGIANS

Nineteenth-century liberal theology attempted to adapt the Christian faith in order to reclaim those who had been drawn away from it by Enlightenment thinking. Popular in Germany and grounded in the teachings of Immanuel Kant, liberal Protestantism emphasized reason or experience over revelation. It reflected the optimism of the times as democracies replaced monarchies and science appeared to explain the world in a more definitive way than the Bible. For liberals, the Bible was just another book that should be studied critically. Reason or experience could judge revelation.

In the nineteenth century human efforts seemed to make the world more ethical, and liberal thinkers adjusted their theology to reflect the progress of culture. The doctrine of original sin seemed obsolete, so many cast it aside. Liberals began to teach that God could be found through introspection. Man was inherently good but had been led astray by society. Among the most influential liberal theologians were Friedrich Schleiermacher (1768–1834) and Albrecht Ritschl (1822–1899).

Considered the father of Protestant liberalism, Schleiermacher was a German Reformed pastor who believed feeling was the basis for religion. In 1799 he published *On Religion: Speeches to Its Cultured Despisers*. The purpose of this book was to draw educated skeptics back to Christianity. Schleiermacher maintained: "Religion's essence is neither thinking nor acting, but intuition and feeling. It wishes to intuit the universe, wishes devoutly to overhear the universe's own manifestations and actions, longs to be grasped and filled by the universe's immediate influences in childlike passivity."[1] He argued that all people felt the presence of the Infinite of the universe and that the greatest religious experience one could have was to be in harmony with the Infinite.

In *The Christian Faith* (1821–1822, 2nd ed. 1830–1831), Schleiermacher contended that religion was not based on church authority but rather on man's understanding that he was only a small part of the universe. Christianity pointed man to the reality that he was utterly dependent on God. To have a religious experience, man needed only to depend on God. Christ served as the mediator of this dependence. The church and tradition were unnecessary. Schleiermacher held that all monotheistic religions were valid, but Christianity was the highest.

Another German theologian, Albrecht Ritschl, asserted that religion was the social consciousness of dependence. Religion was not based on reason but on value judgments. Acceptance of all the biblical accounts was a value judgment. The Bible was a record of human consciousness, not God's objective word.

Ritschl advocated the "kingdom of God," a society built on morals and ethics. He believed God guided history toward perfection through an evolutionary process. Certain historical figures, such as Christ, were deliverers of God's plan. Christ's life was meant to serve as a moral example to humanity. Humans had the ability and the responsibility to create the kingdom of God.

BIBLICAL CRITICISM

Biblical criticism refers to the scholarly study of the Bible using historical-critical methods that arose from seventeenth- and eighteenth-century Enlightenment thought. It has often been divided into the subcategories of "higher" and "lower" criticism. Higher criticism examines such matters as the authorship, historical background, and literary sources of each biblical book. Lower criticism attempts to determine whether the current texts of the biblical books represent their original texts. Many Bible scholars have embraced some of these historical-critical methods. However, conservative scholars largely reject forms of biblical criticism and its conclusions when its practitioners operate from rationalistic presuppositions, deny the possibility of the supernatural, and, thus, undermine the Bible's authority and reliability.

Some of the first scholars who used biblical criticism to question traditional views of the Old Testament were Jean Astruc (1684–1766), Johann G. Eichhorn (1752–1827), Karl H. Graf (1815–1869), and Julius Wellhausen (1844–1918). Among the first to question traditional views of the New Testament using biblical criticism were Hermann Samuel Reimarus (1694–1768), Ferdinand Christian Baur (1792–1860), and David Strauss (1808–1874).

A French theologian, Jean Astruc was one of the first scholars to question the Mosaic authorship of Genesis. Because it used both

Jehovah and Elohim as names for God, he concluded that the book was a compilation of two different documents from two different traditions with at least two different authors. Moses, therefore, was not the only author of Genesis.

Johann Eichhorn applied Astruc's theories to other books in the Hexateuch (Genesis through Joshua). He believed the miracles of the Old Testament could be explained as natural events. Because of the superstitious mind-set of the ancient world, he maintained that unusual events were accepted as miracles.

Karl Graf and Julius Wellhausen developed the "documentary hypothesis." They held that sections of the Pentateuch which used Jehovah as the name of God were the earliest documents (J). Sections that employed Elohim (E) as the name of God originated later. Sections that consisted of laws were known as D for Deuteronomy, and sections concerning sacrifices and the temple were dubbed P for their priestly origins. These texts were compiled by different authors with different purposes. The documentary hypothesis not only challenged traditional biblical authorship, but it also depicted the Bible as nothing more than a great work of literature.

A professor of Oriental languages at Hamburg, Hermann Samuel Reimarus applied biblical criticism to the New Testament. He rejected the possibility of miracles in his *Fragments* (1778), maintaining that biblical writers had the best intentions when depicting miracles but propagated fiction.

The founder of the Tübingen School in Germany, F. C. Baur, also applied biblical criticism to the New Testament, which he said depicted competing Jewish and Pauline versions of Christianity. Taught by Jesus and his twelve disciples, Jewish Christianity emphasized keeping the law, the high value of women, and a reorientation of rather than a break from Judaism. Pauline Christianity denied the value of the law, had misogynistic overtones, and pushed for a complete break from Judaism. Baur claimed that Matthew was written by Judaizers and that John was an overreaction to Gnosticism.

He insisted the Pastoral Epistles (1 and 2 Timothy and Titus) could not have been written by Paul in the first century. Instead, he dated them to the second century. According to Baur, Paul wrote only Galatians, 1 and 2 Corinthians, and Romans.

In his *Life of Jesus* (1835), David Strauss concluded that Paul distorted the meaning of Jesus and his teachings. Strauss depicted Jesus as an ethical teacher who believed he was the Messiah. Jesus was not divine and did not perform miracles. All the miracles attributed to him were invented by his followers to prove his divinity. Strauss believed Paul was mainly responsible for the myth of Jesus' divinity and his role in redemption.

After Strauss, several additional works explored the life of Jesus. The most influential was Albert Schweitzer's (1875–1965) *The Quest of the Historical Jesus* (1906). A theologian, physician, and organist from Germany, Schweitzer found all the previous work on the life of Christ to be inadequate. He argued that Jesus was a Jewish apocalyptic prophet who believed God was on the verge of establishing his kingdom on earth. Jesus believed the "Son of Man" would inaugurate this kingdom. When the Son of Man did not appear, Jesus took this role upon himself. Schweitzer maintained that when Jesus was about to die, he realized he had been mistaken. Schweitzer believed Christianity's creeds were written to prove the divinity of Christ in the absence of scriptural proof. For Schweitzer, Jesus was either a failed apocalyptic prophet or a completely unknowable person.

EVOLUTION

Charles Darwin (1809–1882) was the driving force behind the theory of evolution. A student of medicine and theology, Darwin traveled around the world from 1831 to 1836 aboard the *Beagle*. Published in 1859, *Origin of Species by Means of Natural Selection* detailed his observations and corresponding hypotheses. He concluded that all species descended from common ancestry. Darwin determined that some animals developed characteristics that were favorable to survival. Through natural selection these animals passed on these traits to their offspring, who evolved to survive in their environment. Species that did not evolve eventually died out.

In *Descent of Man* (1871), Darwin applied this theory to man, asserting that man evolved from the common ancestry of all species. This theory contravened the idea of man's being made in the image of God as described in Genesis 1–2. Moreover, the new science of geology seemed to demonstrate that natural features like mountains formed by gradual processes, not by catastrophic events like a divine flood. Evolution and geology argued that the earth was much older than Archbishop James Ussher's (1581–1656) date of Sunday, October 23, 4004 BC. Darwin's theory implied that God and the Bible were nothing more than evolutionary products of man's consciousness. It appeared that Darwin had declared war on God and the Bible. Reaction to *Descent of Man* was intense. Christian denominations denounced Darwin and his work. His advocates defended him and several conflicts ensued.

Perhaps the most famous clash over Darwin's theories occurred in Dayton, Tennessee, in 1925. The "Scopes Monkey Trial" involved a teacher named John Scopes (1900–1970), who, against Tennessee state law, taught evolution in his class and was fired. The American Civil Liberties Union (ACLU) had promised to defend anyone fired for teaching evolution, and city boosters who wanted to attract attention to Dayton encouraged Scopes to teach evolution. With the aid of the ACLU, he then sued the State of Tennessee for wrongful termination.

An advocate of evolution, an agnostic, and one of the most brilliant lawyers of the early twentieth century, Clarence Darrow (1857–1938) defended Scopes. A former candidate for president and advocate of biblical creationism, William Jennings Bryan (1860–1925) represented the state. As the trial unfolded, it became apparent that Scopes was irrelevant. He was merely the means used by the evolutionists to argue against the Tennessee law. In actuality the Bible was placed on trial, and Bryan allowed himself to be cross-examined. Though the court found against Scopes and imposed a minor fine, Darrow made Bryan and his beliefs seem foolish. Bryan was broken by the trial and died soon afterward. To many it appeared that biblical creationism died with its champion, but this proved to be untrue.

Neoorthodoxy

Prominent from the 1920s through the early 1960s, neoorthodoxy was a reaction to liberal Protestantism. Neoorthodox theologians did not hold as optimistic a view of man and his progress as did liberals. They sought to overturn liberal relativism and return to Reformation doctrine based on historical revelation. Sin, biblical revelation, and God's omnipotence and omniscience were strong neoorthodox themes. Because neoorthodoxy affirmed critical approaches to biblical scholarship, many conservative Christians opposed it. The best-known neoorthodox theologians were Karl Barth (1886–1968), Emil Brunner (1889–1966), Reinhold Niebuhr (1892–1971), H. Richard Niebuhr (1894–1962), and Dietrich Bonhoeffer (1906–1945).

A Swiss theologian, Karl Barth is regarded as the father of neoorthodoxy. He was a pastor and then a professor at the German universities of Göttingen, Münster, and Bonn. While teaching at these universities, Barth observed the rise of the Third Reich. Originally, he considered Nazi ideology irrelevant to Christianity. As long as the gospel could be preached, Barth paid the Nazis little mind. While he was at Bonn, however, the Nazis took control of German churches. Pastors were required to place Hitler's name in liturgies and, in many cases, even to replace the cross with the swastika. Many German pastors acquiesced.

Barth was alarmed by their willingness to allow culture to shape Christianity. He joined the Confessing Church, which formed in opposition to the denominations that cooperated with Hitler. He also helped write the Barmen Declaration (1934), which stated that the church would not allow any government, political group, or ideology to distort the gospel. When the Nazis tried to force Barth to swear an oath of allegiance to Hitler, he refused and moved to Basel, Switzerland, in 1935.

Originally a proponent of liberal theology, Barth lost confidence in it because of World War I and the rise of totalitarianism throughout Europe. The use of modern technology to cause so much death made clear that man was not advancing the kingdom of God. Barth believed liberalism was too concerned about human experience and amalgamating theology and culture. It improperly downplayed the relationship between God and man, he thought. Barth, therefore, determined to break the liberal hold on Christianity.

A staunch Calvinist and proponent of Reformation thought, Barth was dedicated to Paul's teachings. He maintained that all human knowledge was revealed to man through Christ. Natural revelation could not lead a person to Christ. All theology, therefore, must be based solely on the Bible, which was a witness to God's revelation. The Bible could be examined critically.

In his commentary on Romans, Barth argued that liberalism led man away from Reformation themes and into a culture-based faith. To remedy liberalism, he emphasized the sovereignty of God, sin, and the judgment of God:

> It then becomes clear that God is the God of all men, the God of the Gentiles and of the Jews; He is not an element in spiritual experience or in the course of history; He is, rather, the ground of all elements, by whom they are measured and in whom they are contained. He differs absolutely from all light and properties and abilities. This being so, the everlasting power and divinity ([Rom] 1:20) of God

shines forth ever more clearly. When therefore we use the word "God," we do not say something but everything, not the last truth but one, but the last truth of all. It is the word of judgment, of the challenge of hope; it is directed, to all, and is significant—of supreme significance for all.[2]

In *The Word of God and the Word of Man* (1928), Barth noted that the Word of God frequently did not support man's reason. In fact, it often conflicted with worldly thinking. Man was faced with a choice. Did he live according to the Word of God, which was demanding, or the word of man, which was more accommodating to culture? For Barth the answer was obvious. Man had to follow the Word of God.

Barth's most influential work was his multivolume *Church Dogmatics* (1932–1967). The most prominent Protestant systematic theology since the Reformation, *Church Dogmatics* argued that theology had nothing to do with culture and could never be comprised. The God of the Bible was "wholly other," and man could never find God by examining himself or the natural world. For Barth, God was transcendent. There was nothing man could do to bring about God's kingdom. The Bible became especially relevant when the Holy Spirit inspired the reader during "moments of crisis," Barth said. At such moments of crisis, man truly encountered God.

Because religion was a creation of man, Barth condemned it as idolatrous and arrogant. God's truth was manifested in Jesus, his crucifixion, and his resurrection. Only through Christ's grace did Christianity provide salvation. Barth believed living the gospel was far more important than organized religion.

A Swiss theologian, Emil Brunner briefly served as a pastor before being named chairman of systematic theology at the University of Zurich (1924–1955). A prolific author, Brunner's most influential works included *The Mediator* (1934), *Man in Revolt: A Christian Anthropology* (1937), and his three-volume *Dogmatics* (1946–1960). Differing with Barth, Brunner held that there was a natural knowledge of God in all mankind and that humans could know God through his creation. If Genesis 1:27[3] is correct, there must be a place where revelation and reason intersect, he said.

Brunner emphasized revelation of truth through a personal encounter with the divine that inwardly transformed the individual. The individual became aware of the inward change when he placed his faith in Christ, according to Brunner. He taught that God demanded commitment to Christ that ruled one's life.

Neoorthodoxy was also prominent in the United States. Reinhold Niebuhr was a pastor in Detroit and then professor of applied Christianity at Union Theological Seminary in New York (1928–1960). Like Barth, he sought to turn Christian theology away from liberalism and back to biblical revelation. In *Does Civilization Need Religion?* (1927), Niebuhr attacked the liberal view that the modern world was in tune with God's will. In his *Moral Man and Immoral Society* (1932), he noted the reality of original sin and the tendency of societies to perpetuate injustice. For Niebuhr, the Christian's role was to serve as a prophet confronting modern culture. Based on his 1939 Gifford Lectures at the University of Edinburgh, Niebuhr's, seminal work was *The Nature and Destiny of Man* (1941–1943), in which he delineated the consequences of sin, the importance of the Bible for Western civilization, and the danger of uncontrolled capitalism. Niebuhr's theories concerning "just war" and his belief that foreign affairs should be based on realism rather than idealism affected many American politicians such as Jimmy Carter (b. 1924), Barack Obama (b. 1961), and John McCain (b. 1936).

Reinhold's brother H. Richard Niebuhr was a professor at Yale Divinity School. He held that religion was not based on experience. Man could not comprehend all the truths of God, Richard Niebuhr said. God's claims did not change, but the claims of religion were always changing.

Richard Niebuhr argued that American Protestant denominations did not reflect the gospel but rather ethnic, social, and economic divisions. The church was being shaped for the comfort of the middle class rather than for the needs of the poor. American Christianity had become a capitalistic and national religion. In his 1937 book *The Kingdom of God in America*, Niebuhr made his most damning attack on Protestant liberalism. He charged liberalism with teaching that "a God without wrath brought men without sin into a kingdom without judgment through the ministrations of Christ without a cross."[4]

Dietrich Bonhoeffer was a Lutheran pastor in Germany and a signer of the Barmen Declaration. When the Nazis began their rise to power, Bonhoeffer relocated to London, where he served as a pastor. Regretting having left Germany in a time of crisis, he returned and led a Confessing Church Seminary in Finkenwalde, Pomerania. Eventually he was forbidden to preach and banished from Berlin.

Bonhoeffer wrote *The Cost of Discipleship*, his most influential book, in 1937. Arguing against "cheap grace" that is given and received with no consequence, he believed grace often came at the expense of suffering for one's Christianity.

Bonhoeffer joined the German resistance to Hitler in 1942. He then attempted to form ties with the British government. His activities were discovered, and he was arrested and imprisoned in 1943. Bonhoeffer was hanged as a traitor in February 1945.

In his posthumously published *Letters and Papers from Prison* (1951), Bonhoeffer discussed the possibility of a "religionless" Christianity, drawing a distinction between faith and religion. He saw the decline of religion as an opportunity for the renewal of true Christianity. In describing Christianity's responsibility to impact the world, Bonhoeffer wrote:

> During the last year or so I've come to know and understand more and more the profound this-worldliness of Christianity. The Christian is not a *homo religiosus*, but

simply a man, as Jesus was a man—in contrast, shall we say, to John the Baptist. I don't mean the shallow and banal this-worldliness of the enlightened, the busy, the comfortable, or the lascivious, but the profound this-worldliness, characterized by discipline and the constant knowledge of death and resurrection. I think Luther lived a this-worldly life in this sense.[5]

Because of his writings concerning religionless Christianity, Bonhoeffer has unfairly been called the father of the "Death of God" theology.[6] More than likely, this is a distortion of what Bonhoeffer meant. In discussing "religionless Christianity," he did not intend to suggest that belief in God had become unnecessary.

PAUL TILLICH (1886–1965)

A Lutheran pastor and German chaplain in World War I, Paul Tillich taught at several German universities. After the Nazis gained power, he came to Union Theological Seminary in New York and later taught at Harvard University and the University of Chicago. His greatest work is the three-volume *Systematic Theology* (1951, 1957, 1963), though some call it a "systematic philosophy."

Tillich held to what he called the "method of correlation." He maintained that the purpose of theology was to correlate the ultimate questions humans asked about life with the answers revealed by God. Philosophy identified questions that were important to contemporary culture, he said. Theology then attempted to answer them. In order for Christianity to be relevant, according to Tillich, theology had to listen to and answer the questions being asked by modern culture.

Tillich held that God was the nontheistic "ground of being" in which all life had its foundation. God was not a being, as Christian theology traditionally maintained, Tillich said. God was simply the source of all being. He superseded all concepts and could not be described as having the traditional divine attributes. Tillich argued that his conception of God helped men and women who considered the traditional doctrine of God, found it wanting, and rebelled against it. Man encountered the ground of being in an existential manner, according to Tillich. Traditional Christian doctrines were symbols that pointed to God, not literal statements about him. All literal statements about God involved setting limits to the transcendent. God was not personal, Tillich said.

Tillich employed many traditional Christian terms but redefined them in nontraditional ways. He used some of the same concepts and phrases as the contemporary new age movement, and many evangelicals regard him as a pantheist or even an atheist.

EVANGELICALISM

Evangelicalism originated in Great Britain in the 1730s. A Protestant theological system but not a denomination, evangelicalism stresses the importance of being born again, biblical inerrancy, and conservative theology. Since evangelicalism crosses denominational lines, evangelicals are not committed to any particular ecclesiology.

Emphasizing individual repentance and conversion, William (Billy) Graham (b. 1918) was the most influential evangelical of the twentieth century. His career launched in 1949 at a tent-revival meeting in Los Angeles that was given great attention by the Hearst newspapers. In 1957 Graham preached to more than 2 million people at a crusade in New York that lasted twelve weeks and witnessed more than 60,000 decisions for Christ. He held a five-day crusade in Seoul, South Korea, in 1973, with more than 3 million people attending. He preached regularly to millions across the world live and on television. His most famous television event was a five-night crusade in 1995 from San Juan, Puerto Rico. It was broadcast live to 185 countries and to more than 10 million people. More than

1 million decisions were reported. Located in Charlotte, North Carolina, and founded in 1950, the Billy Graham Evangelistic Association produced a radio program known as *The Hour of Decision*, television specials, and Christian movies. Graham also had close ties with many United States presidents, and many Protestant Americans saw him as the nation's spiritual leader. According to the Graham organization, more than 2 million people have accepted Christ at Graham revivals.

Other leading evangelicals included Carl F. H. Henry (1913–2003), Bernard Ramm (1916–1992), John Stott (1921–2011), Donald Bloesch (1928–2010), and Millard Erickson (b. 1932). Two of the most influential evangelical organizations are the National Association of Evangelicals (1942) and *Christianity Today*, a magazine Graham helped establish with Henry as the first editor.

At the request of Graham and others, the International Congress on World Evangelization was held at Lausanne, Switzerland, in 1974, attended by more than 2,300 evangelicals from 150 countries. Attendees signed the Lausanne Covenant, which affirmed that they would work together to spread the message of Christ throughout the world. Evangelicalism encompasses many Protestant denominations and is particularly prevalent among Baptists, Presbyterians, and Methodists.

FUNDAMENTALISM

Fundamentalism was conservative Christianity's reaction to biblical criticism, evolution, and theological liberalism. In most cases it was countercultural. It began in Bible conferences throughout the United States, the most important of which was the 1895 Niagara Bible Conference in southern Ontario, Canada, where conservative Christians adopted fourteen principles. Five of these, the so-called five principles of fundamentalism, are the truthfulness of the Bible, Jesus' deity, the virgin birth, the substitutionary theory of the atonement, and the bodily return of Christ.

A series of ninety essays in twelve volumes entitled *The Fundamentals* did much to advance fundamentalism. The essays were published between 1910 and 1915 by A. C. Dixon (1854–1925) and Reuben A. Torrey (1856–1928). They promoted Protestantism and the five tenets of fundamentalism. They attacked modernism, socialism, evolution, Catholicism, biblical criticism, and other systems that were antithetical to the fundamentals. The essays were financed by Lyman Stewart (1840–1923), who had free copies mailed to Protestant ministers and missionaries. The World Christian Fundamentals Association was formed in 1919 and held rallies throughout the United States. In 1920 a Baptist minister, Curtis Lee Laws (1868–1946), editor of *The Watchman-Examiner*, coined the term *fundamentalist*. He said a fundamentalist was a person who was ready "to do battle royal for the fundamentals of the faith."[7] Other early influential fundamentalists included William Bell Riley (1861–1947) and John Franklyn Norris (1877–1952).

In the twentieth and twenty-first centuries, fundamentalists have been among the most visible ministers in the United States. They are active not only in their own congregations but also in the realms of education, mass media, and politics. Fundamentalist schools include Bryan College in Dayton, Tennessee, Patrick Henry College in Purcellville, Virginia, and Bob Jones University in Greenville, South Carolina.

The son of a United States senator, Pat Robertson (b. 1930) has become one of the most famous fundamentalists in America. He is the founder of the Christian Broadcasting Network, the widely viewed *700 Club*, the American Center for Law and Justice, and Regent University. Robertson has constantly spoken out against homosexuality, the ACLU, and abortion. He has also been one of the most politically active fundamentalists. After being defeated in a bid for the Republican nomination for the United States presidency in 1988, Robertson founded the Christian Coalition to support conservative candidates for public office. With more than 2 million members, the Christian Coalition's backing is important for conservative candidates. Because of IRS investigations into his holdings and controversial statements in which he blamed the terrorist attack of September 11, 2001, and the 2005 devastation of Hurricane Katrina on liberal aspects of American society, Robertson lost much of his influence.

Pastor of the Thomas Road Baptist Church in Lynchburg, Virginia, and founder of Liberty University, Jerry Falwell (1933–2007) gained fame through his television program the *Old-Time Gospel Hour*. Falwell founded the Moral Majority in 1979, a political organization of conservative Christians with diverse theological beliefs that endorsed conservative candidates. Some analysts maintained that the Moral Majority was influential in electing Ronald Reagan (1911–2004) and George H. W. Bush (b. 1924) to the presidency. The Moral Majority dissolved in 1989.

ECUMENISM

Since the beginning of the mission movement in the early nineteenth century, Protestants have attempted to work together to advance Christianity. Many of the first such efforts failed because of denominational rivalries and doctrinal differences. Following World War II, the ecumenical movement once again developed a strong following, with many hoping the cooperative efforts of Christians could prevent future wars. Delegates at a conference in the Netherlands in 1938 drafted a constitution for the World Council of Churches in Process of Organization (WCC). After World War II delayed the effort, the WCC was officially established in Amsterdam in 1948. Representatives of 147 churches from forty-four countries attended the initial meeting. Members of a general assembly to oversee the organization were elected, and delegates decided that the organization would convene every six to eight years.

In many ways the WCC is a Christian version of the United Nations. No single ecclesiology was adopted. Its first projects were evangelism and aiding postwar European reconstruction. The WCC's headquarters is in Geneva, Switzerland. In 1961, many of the Orthodox churches joined the WCC. In 1968 the WCC became more involved in social, economic, and political issues and less involved in missions and evangelism.

Though the WCC's numbers began to decline in the 1970s, its denominational membership represents more than 590 million people in more than 120 countries. Most of its members are liberal Protestants. More conservative denominations, such as the Roman Catholic Church, the Southern Baptist Convention, and the Lutheran Church Missouri Synod, have never been members.

New Trends in Protestantism

Megachurches

Before 1990 there were only fifty megachurches—congregations with more than 2,000 members—in the world, but in 2011 there were more than 1,300 in the United States alone. The world's largest church, the Yoido Full Gospel Church in Seoul, and several others in South Korea have memberships of more than 1 million. Among the largest megachurches in the United States are Lakewood Church in Houston, Texas, pastored by Joel Osteen (b. 1963), with an average of 43,000 attending weekly services; Life Church in Edmond, Oklahoma, pastored by Craig Groeschel (b. 1967), with an average weekly attendance of more than 27,000; Willow Creek Community Church in South Barrington, Illinois, pastored by Bill Hybels (b. 1951), with an attendance of 24,000; and Saddleback Church in Lake Forest, California, pastored by Rick Warren (b. 1954), with an attendance of 20,000. Most megachurches are charismatic in worship style, have a compelling pastor, and have upbeat, unconventional worship services. Megachurches are also technologically driven and broadcast worldwide.

THE PROSPERITY GOSPEL

Also known as the "Word of Faith," the prosperity gospel teaches that worldly wealth and physical health are promised to all believers who have faith. It teaches that poverty and illness are not caused by humans but rather by the devil. Advocates base these beliefs primarily on their interpretations of Bible passages such as 3 John 2: "Dear friend, I pray that you may prosper in every way and be in good health physically just as you are spiritually." Another often-cited passage is John 14:13–14: "Whatever you ask in My name, I will do it so that the Father may be glorified in the Son. If you ask Me anything in My name, I will do it." Prosperity theology has grown in popularity because of charismatic ministers such as Kenneth E. Hagin (1917–2003), Kenneth Copeland (b. 1936), Joyce Meyer (b. 1943), T. D. Jakes (b. 1957), Creflo Dollar (b. 1962), and Joel Osteen.

MODERN EVANGELICALS

Evangelicalism has taken on new dimensions in this new century. At least three evangelical streams can be identified, two of which are new. First, there are traditional evangelicals who emphasize the Bible, being born again, and biblical truths. Second, many middle-aged evangelicals are adopting a "seeker-sensitive" approach to church. Their worship services are casual and informal, secular music has been adapted for church use, and doctrine, especially concerning sin and hell, is often softened so people feel more comfortable. The third evangelical stream is the "missional" church. Beginning in the late twentieth century and now popular among young Christians, missional evangelicals stress the importance of becoming a missionary in one's own culture or neighborhood. Rather than attempt to attract people to a church through programs, they reach out to their community through clubs, food drives, neighborhood cleanups, community block parties, and child-friendly park events.

CHAPTER TWENTY-NINE

THE NEW CHRISTIAN WORLD— GLOBALIZATION IN THE TWENTIETH AND TWENTY-FIRST CENTURIES

The "Great Century" of Protestant missions began in 1792 with William Carey's *An Enquiry into the Obligations of Christians to Use Means for the Conversion of the Heathen* and ended with the Edinburgh Missions Conference of 1910. In those years, much of the previously unevangelized world was introduced to the gospel. As detailed in previous chapters, missionary societies sent their representatives around the globe. Not only did they bring the gospel but also medicine, new agricultural techniques, and education. Particularly in the Global South and much of what was once considered the Third World, these missionaries laid the foundation for Christianity's astonishing growth in the twentieth and twenty-first centuries.

According to the Operation World Database (OWD),[1] there were 2.2 billion Christians in the world in 2011, more than twice the number in 1900. Though the world population has grown sevenfold since 1900, Christianity's growth is still amazing. Before 1900 most Christians lived in Europe and North America. This proportion, however, was soon to change.

In 2011, 522 million Christians lived in Europe and 271 million in North America. With European church attendance estimated below 10 percent, most of these nominal Christians do not attend services. Much of Europe is post-Christian and secular. Church attendance is higher in North America, but secularism has made strong inroads, and many denominations are weak.

The opposite is occurring in the Global South. There are now 503 million Christians in Latin America, 503 million in Africa, and 368 million in Asia. In the last quarter of the twentieth century, these numbers grew by more than a quarter of a billion. By 2011, Christians comprised 24 percent of the population of these continents (1.3 billion people). The majority of the world's Christians, therefore, now live in the Global South. Australia is the exception to Christianity's vibrancy in the Southern Hemisphere. Similar to the situation in Europe, nearly 70 percent of Australians openly identify with Christianity, but only 10 percent attend worship services.

Whether Catholic, evangelical, or Pentecostal, the overwhelming majority of Christians in the Global South are conservative in theology, believe in supernatural manifestations such as divine healing, and regard the Bible as true in all that it says.

SOUTH AND LATIN AMERICA

Since the arrival of the explorers and conquistadors, Catholicism has been the largest Christian denomination in Latin America. Nearly half of all baptized Catholics live in Latin America, and Brazil, in South America, is the largest Catholic country in the world. The majority of South American and Brazilian Catholics, however, rarely attend mass or practice their faith. After Brazil won its independence from Portugal in 1822, it severed formal ties with the Catholic Church, and Protestants won religious freedom. Protestant missionaries, such as Southern Baptists, arrived en masse at the close of the nineteenth century and have made significant inroads. They have also found success in Mexico, El Salvador, Puerto Rico,

Guatemala, Argentina, and Chile. Pentecostal churches and Pentecostal expressions of worship are growing faster in Latin America than any other form of Christianity. In fact, many Roman Catholic churches have incorporated Pentecostal practices into their worship services.

The reason for this growth has much to do with Catholicism. For more than 400 years, Latin Americans were forced to live under governments that had little regard for their needs. Many critics accused the Catholic Church of siding with oppressive regimes. Liberation theologians sought to correct this situation, but since the Vatican viewed the movement with suspicion, it had little effect on most oppressed Christians. Whereas liberation theology sought social and economic equality, Pentecostalism appealed directly to the spiritual needs of the poor. In other words, Pentecostalism promised what liberation theology could not: spiritual liberation for oppressed people.

The first signs of a Latin American Pentecostal movement appeared in 1909 at the Methodist Episcopal Church in Valparaiso, Chile, and quickly spread to Brazil the following year. Like North American Pentecostalism, the Latin American version was marked by *glossolalia*, exorcism, spiritual healings, prophecy, and the prosperity gospel. Today, the largest churches in Latin America are Pentecostal. The Jotaceche Pentecostal Church in Santiago, Chile, has more than 150,000 members, and the Congregação Cristã in São Paolo, Brazil, numbers more than 60,000. The desire for a fresh encounter with the Holy Spirit while maintaining an attachment to their traditional faith has driven many Latin American Catholics to accept aspects of the Pentecostal and charismatic movements. Undergirded by a vibrant Pentecostalism, the growing Christian populations of other Latin American countries resemble that of Brazil. Not all of Latin America, however, has accepted Pentecostalism to the same extent as Brazil. It is not as prevalent in Mexico,

Venezuela, Colombia, and Peru, where traditional Catholicism remains dominant.

AFRICA

In Africa there were forty times more Christians in 2000 than there were in 1900. In 2000 an average of 2,300 people a day converted to Christianity. Because of Islam's dominance in North Africa since the seventh century, Christianity's growth has been almost exclusively relegated to the sub-Saharan region. A significant Christian minority, however, survives in North Africa in the Coptic Church of Egypt. Sub-Saharan Christianity has not totally escaped the effects of militant Islam. In Nigeria, the sizable Christian population faces intense and increasingly frequent violence from the Islamic majority.

Though the coastal nations of Mozambique and Angola were colonized by Catholic countries in the 1400s, it was not until the late eighteenth century that serious attempts were made to evangelize the African interior. One of the first places Christianity gained a foothold was Sierra Leone, where the Anglican Church established a colony in 1792. The first mission stations were organized by missionaries from Sierra Leone in the early 1800s. Evangelistic efforts in sub-Saharan Africa were fueled at least in part by the influence of missionary David Livingstone. Thanks to his writings, newspaper coverage, and encounter with Henry Morton Stanley (1841–1904), the idea of being a missionary in Africa was romanticized, and the number of volunteers swelled.

Since its arrival in 1652, the Dutch Reformed Church has been influential in South Africa. In the nineteenth and twentieth centuries, it was associated with apartheid, with many pro-apartheid government officials holding church membership. For this reason the World Alliance of Reformed Churches expelled the Dutch Reformed Church in the early 1980s. The Anglican archbishop of

Cape Town, Desmond Tutu (b. 1931), was a leading spokesman against apartheid in the 1980s. The Church reversed its pro-apartheid position in 1986 and desegregated. Since then several branches of the Dutch Reformed Church have apologized for their racism. As of 2011, nearly 75 percent of the South African population self-identified as Christian. South Africa has thousands of independent churches, most of which are associated with Pentecostalism.

The Berlin Conference of 1884 that apportioned Africa among the European powers had an enormous effect on Christianity on the continent. Colonization provided Christian missionaries an entrance to and some manner of protection in previously unevangelized areas. In many locations missionaries planted Christianity with some level of success. But because of their ties to occupying powers, many Africans viewed Christian missionaries with suspicion and perceived them as arrogant. Some Africans felt compelled to tolerate Christianity in order to get along with colonial authorities. This often led to paternalism and false professions of conversion. When discussing missionaries and colonialism, the first prime minister of Kenya, Jomo Kenyatta (1894–1978), said, "When the missionaries came to Africa they had the Bible and we had the land. They said, 'Let us pray.' We closed our eyes. When we opened them we had the Bible and they had the land."[2]

Still, missionaries made many positive contributions to Africa. They not only brought the gospel but also medicine, modern agricultural techniques, and education. In addition, missionaries helped mediate tribal wars and disputes with Europeans. Missionaries like Livingstone highlighted the horrors of the slave trade and helped bring it to an end. By 1900, most of the sub-Saharan African interior had been introduced to Christianity.

The situation in sub-Saharan Africa began to change in the mid-twentieth century with the end of colonial empires. This led to the birth of many new African nations, forty-two of which joined the United Nations by 1975. Within many of these new countries, such as the Republic of the Congo, Uganda, Kenya, and Swaziland, Christianity put down deep roots, and it is now the dominant religion. Independence spawned new, indigenous churches that have grown exponentially. Denominations tied to the colonial powers remain relevant in Africa but have been outpaced by indigenous movements.

Pentecostalism is the largest Christian movement in Africa. Because of similarities to tribal religions, the Pentecostal concepts of spiritual healing, prophecy, and other supernatural manifestations are attractive. Instead of being officially bound to Western Pentecostal denominations, African Pentecostals prefer to form their own denominations. Zimbabwe is dominated by the Assemblies of God, for instance, but the Zimbabwean denomination is independent from the American one.

Though predominantly independent, African Pentecostal churches often have strong relationships with the American Assemblies of God and Church of God (Cleveland, Tennessee) denominations. American Pentecostal televangelists such as Gordon Lindsay (1906–1973), Kenneth Hagin (1917–2003), T. L. Osborne (b. 1923), and James Bakker (b. 1940) made frequent trips to and are popular in Africa. Their popularity is attributable in part to their emphasis on prophecy, spiritual healing, and economic prosperity. One of the largest churches in Africa, the Church of God Mission International of Benson Idahosa in Benin City, Nigeria, has more than 300,000 members, a large Miracle Center for divine healings, and stresses the prosperity gospel. Its founder, Benson Idahosa (1938–1988) claimed to have raised twenty-eight people from the dead; and when preaching about economic prosperity, he frequently stated that his "God is not poor."

Another reason for the popularity of independent Pentecostal churches is that they can shape their own theological systems without approval from a denomination. Some African Pentecostals, for example, participate in ancestor worship and maintain other aspects of traditional African religions, practices that would never be acceptable in American Pentecostalism. Not all African Pentecostal churches mix Christian spirituality with pagan religious traditions though. Many indigenous Pentecostal churches are thoroughly orthodox.

William Wade Harris (1860–1929) and Samuel Kimbangu (1887–1951) were two notable Pentecostal leaders who opposed traditional African religions practices. Harris dressed in white, abstained from alcohol, carried a bamboo cross, and identified with the prophet Elijah. He spoke out against tribal practices and often burned objects believed to have magical powers. According to some reports, when he touched pagan shrines or amulets, they burst into flames. He did, however, practice polygamy. He led a major revival along the Ivory Coast in 1913 and 1914 that resulted in more than 100,000 converts. After his death in 1929, the majority of his followers gravitated to more established churches.

A former Baptist, Simon Kimbangu started a mass movement in the Congo in 1921. His followers claimed he performed miracles such as healing the sick and raising the dead. Suspected of leading an insurrection against Belgian colonial authorities, he was arrested shortly after launching his movement and spent the rest of his life in prison. His followers were persecuted and fled to safe havens throughout central Africa, taking the miraculous stories of Kimbangu with them. The government permitted his followers to hold services in 1959, and their numbers soared. By 2011 they became known as the Church of Jesus Christ on Earth, with an estimated 5.5 million members in Africa, Europe, and North America. Those who claim Kimbangu as their spiritual forefather continue to proclaim his miracles and hail him as a prophet. The Church of Jesus Christ on Earth forbids tribal syncretism, tribal dances, polygamy, ancestor worship, witchcraft, and violence.

Perhaps more than in any other place in the world, indigenous African churches are having great success and bearing much fruit. If the increase in African Christians continues at its current rate, Africa will be home to the world's largest Christian population by 2025. The majority of these Christians will be affiliated with a uniquely indigenous and independent version of Pentecostalism.

ASIA

Christianity was born in Palestine in the Middle East region of Asia and, despite seasons of intense persecution, still exists there. Several traditions claim Christianity spread early to central and far east Asia. One claims the apostle Thomas brought Christianity to India. Another claims Jesus himself brought his teachings to India. There is strong archeological evidence that Nestorian Christianity arrived in China by 635. Catholic missionaries began their work in Asia in the thirteenth century and in many locations still have a small presence. Arriving with the Dutch navy, Protestant missionaries began to work in Asia in the early seventeenth century, with their strongest endeavors in the late nineteenth century. Christianity, however, is weaker in Asia than in any other continent. With a population of 4.1 billion, Asia is by far the most populous continent in the world, but only 368 million, about 9 percent of the population, are Christians. There are several reasons for these sparse numbers.

First, Asia had fully developed religions such as Buddhism and Hinduism that were engrained into its culture well before the great Protestant mission emphasis of the late nineteenth century. In India, the low percentage of Christians (just 6 percent of the population) has much to do with the Hindu caste system. As Christianity speaks to the poor and oppressed, the majority of Indian Christians have been from the lower castes. Among these lower castes Mother Teresa (1910–1997) performed her ministry in Calcutta. This has made Christianity unappealing to many Indians, especially those in higher castes. The Lord's Supper is a prime example of an unappealing Christian practice since higher-caste Indians are reticent to share a table with those from the lower castes. Many Indians perceive missionaries as foreign agitators seeking to build an egalitarian society. Those in higher castes find this counter to their personal interests. As a result, missionaries still find it difficult to be issued a visa in India.

Several countries in Asia have large Muslim populations that became more militant when the colonial powers began to leave in the 1950s. In countries such as Iran, Pakistan, and Bangladesh, the small Christian population lives under constant threat of persecution. A once thriving community, Christians in Lebanon face the threat of being killed for their faith. Although the population of Turkey is overwhelmingly Muslim, the government grants freedom of religion. Anglicanism and Eastern Orthodoxy are the country's strongest Christian denominations, but Christians comprise less than 1 percent of the population.

With the largest Muslim population in the world (187 million), Indonesia also grants freedom of religion—though Christians experience some persecution. After gaining its independence from the Dutch in 1949, Indonesia enacted a policy of equality among its five major religions: Islam, Buddhism, Hinduism, Catholicism, and Protestantism. Confucianism also has some standing. With the rise of Islamic sentiment in the 1960s, the government attempted to promote Islam by forcing all its citizens to declare one of the five religions. The plan failed, and the result was more than two million Muslims converting to Christianity. In 2011, Indonesian Christians numbered nearly 50 million but faced persecution in the areas of Maluku and central Sulawesi.

Another reason for the sparse presence of Christianity in Asia is that it has several authoritarian regimes that persecute Christians. China and North Korea are two prime examples. Though more than 105 million Christians live in China, they account for only 6 percent of the population. To receive government sanction, Chinese Christians must register with one of the authorized Chinese

Christian organizations: the Three-Self Patriotic Movement (Protestant), the China Christian Council (Protestant),[3] the Chinese Patriotic Catholic Association, and the Chinese Catholic Bishops Council. The Chinese government interferes with the affairs of these organizations. During the Cultural Revolution (1966–1976), when communism was being pressed, the government closed churches affiliated with these organizations. This led millions of Christians to worship secretly in house churches or, as they are more widely known, "underground churches." When the Cultural Revolution ended and state-sanctioned Christian organizations became legal again, many Christians remained loyal to their underground churches. Since these churches are illegal, when their members are discovered, they face loss of property, imprisonment, and other forms of persecution. As the numbers in these churches are unreported, it is impossible to determine how many Christians are truly in China. The number would be several million more than those who self-reported to the government. During the 1980s and 1990s, China introduced economic reforms and became a major player in the world's economy. A somewhat less repressive attitude toward Christianity was a necessary concession for economic development.

North Korea remains strictly communist, is ruled by dictators, and forbids Christianity. The small Christian population of North Korea is forced to worship in secret.

As mentioned in previous chapters, Francis Xavier brought Christianity to Japan in 1549. Dominicans and Franciscans arrived at the end of the sixteenth century. In spite of internecine fighting among the orders, they were nominally successful in their evangelistic efforts. Christianity was outlawed in 1587 and persecution followed. Twenty-six Christians were crucified in 1597, and Catholicism was outlawed until 1873. Protestants began to work in Japan in the late nineteenth century but with meager results. In modern Japan there is little interest in Christianity; the work of Francis Xavier and his successors is a distant memory. Though

Shinto has seen a revival of sorts, the Japanese people could be considered nonreligious.

Overall, the number of Christians in Asia has increased more than tenfold since 1900. The main reason for this growth is the overwhelming success of Christianity in South Korea and the Philippines.

The first known Christian mission work in Korea was performed by the Jesuits in the eighteenth century. They converted thousands to Christianity. Throughout much of the nineteenth century, however, Korea moved toward isolationism, earning the nickname "the Hermit Kingdom." Wanting to remove vestiges of the West, brutal persecutions of Christians occurred (1839–1846; 1866–1867) that led to thousands of people being martyred. A year after Korea ended its isolation in 1883, Presbyterian missionaries arrived. Their work ended in 1910, when Japan colonized Korea and imposed Shintoism. Christianity began to grow in Korea after World War II. During the Korean War, Christians moved from North to South Korea to escape communism.

In South Korea, Christianity has flourished and claims some 30 percent of the population as adherents. Korean Christians are known for their evangelistic zeal. With more than 12,000 foreign missionaries, South Korea is second only to the United States in foreign missionaries sent. Active in more than 160 countries, Korean missionaries serve throughout the Middle East, Africa, central and east Asia, and the United States.

Most Korean Christians are Protestants and associate with some manner of Pentecostalism. Korean Pentecostalism emphasizes faith healing and is marked by a strong belief in the prosperity gospel.[4] The largest church in the world, with more than one million members, is the Central Full Gospel Church in Seoul. The church's pastor, David Yonggi Cho (b. 1936), emphasizes the importance of faith healing, evangelism, and asking God for material blessings.

Spain introduced Christianity to the Philippines in 1542 when it seized the islands and forcibly attempted to Christianize the natives. The overwhelming majority of Filipino Christians in the twenty-first century are Catholic. Their great hero is Jaime Cardinal Sin (1928–2005), who was the county's spiritual leader and helped depose President Ferdinand Marcos (1917–1989). With 92 percent of the population professing Christianity, the Republic of the Philippines has the highest percentage of Christians in the world.

The Unreached

Despite the growth of Christianity in Asia and Africa, most unreached people groups still live in the "10/40 Window," the region between ten and forty degrees of longitude. It consists of sixty-two countries in Africa, Asia, and parts of southern Europe. Approximately half of the world's population, 3.1 billion, lives in the window, including 82 percent of the world's poorest people. Along with being largely deprived of the gospel, they are often illiterate, malnourished, and susceptible to disease. Because the window encompasses strongholds of militant Islam, Buddhism, and Hinduism, Christians who live there often face persecution. They are also stymied by laws that forbid evangelism. In spite of harsh conditions, missionaries and indigenous Christians have found ways to evangelize in some regions within the window.

The New Face of Christianity

In the nineteenth century, the stereotype of a Christian was a Caucasian male from the Global North. In the twenty-first century, the average Christian is a darker-skinned female from the Global South. For more than a thousand years Christianity has been a largely Western religion, but this is no longer true. Missionaries are being sent from countries such as Brazil and South Korea to traditional Christian countries like the United States. In a little more than one hundred years, the locus of Christianity has shifted. The words of John Mbiti (b. 1931), a Christian philosopher in Uganda, are proving to have merit: "The centers of the church's universality are no longer in Geneva, Rome, Athens, Paris, London, New York, but Kinshasa, Buenos Aires, Addis Ababa and Manila."[5] Perhaps the reason for this global shift is that God goes where he is most wanted.

Endnotes

Chapter 2

1. Tertullian, *Apology* 50, in *The Faith of the Early Fathers*, ed. William A. Jurgens (Collegeville, MN: Liturgical Press, 1970), 1:282.
2. *1 Clement* 21:3–6, in *The Apostolic Fathers: Greek Texts and English Translations*, 3rd ed., ed. Michael Holmes (Grand Rapids: Baker Academic, 2007), 75.
3. The *Muratorian Canon* (ca. 170), however, identified him as the brother of Pius, the bishop of Rome (ca. 142–146 or ca. 157–161).
4. *The Letter of Ignatius to the Magnesians* 6:1 in *The Apostolic Fathers*, 207.
5. *The Epistle of Ignatius to the Romans* 4:1 in *The Apostolic Fathers*, 229.
6. *The Martyrdom of Polycarp* 9:3 in *The Apostolic Fathers*, 317.
7. Tacitus, *Annals* 15.44.
8. Pliny, *Epistles* 10.96–97. Cited in *Documents of the Christian Church*, 3rd ed., ed. Henry Bettenson and Chris Maunder (New York: Oxford University Press, 1999), 4.

CHAPTER 3

1. *Gospel of Thomas,* in *Readings in the History of Christian Theology,* ed. William C. Placher (Philadelphia: Westminster, 1988), 1:12.
2. *Gospel of Truth,* in *The Gnostic Bible: Gnostic Texts of Mystical Wisdom from the Ancient and Medieval Worlds—Pagan, Jewish, Christian, Mandaean, Manichaean, Islamic, and Cathar,* ed. Willis Barnstone and Marvin Meyer (Boston: Shambhala Publications, 2003), 243.
3. *Gospel of Thomas* 1 in *Readings in the History of Christian Theology,* 1:12.
4. *Gospel of Truth,* in *The Gnostic Bible,* 245.

CHAPTER 4

1. Irenaeus, *Against Heresies* 1.10.1, in *The Ante-Nicene Fathers: The Writings of the Fathers Down to A.D. 325,* ed. Alexander Roberts and James Donaldson (Grand Rapids: Eerdmans, 1873), 1:330.
2. Hippolytus, *Apostolic Tradition* 21, in *The Faith of the Early Fathers,* ed. William A. Jurgens (Collegeville, MN: Liturgical Press, 1970), 1:169–70. The passage was written in a question-and-answer format between a presbyter and a candidate for baptism. For purpose of content and information, I have paraphrased the passage to make it more easily understood.
3. Eusebius, *Expositions of the Oracles of the Lord,* in *Documents of the Christian Church,* 3rd ed., ed. Henry Bettenson and Chris Maunder (New York: Oxford University Press, 1999), 30.
4. Irenaeus, *Against Heresies* 1.2.2, in *Ante-Nicene Fathers,* 1:331.
5. Irenaeus, *Against Heresies* 3.3.2, in *Ante-Nicene Fathers,* 1:415–16.
6. Irenaeus, *Demonstration of the Apostolic Preaching* 33, in *A New Eusebius: Documents Illustrating the History of the Church*

to AD 337, 5th ed., ed. J. Stevenson (Cambridge: Cambridge University Press, 1993), 120.

7. Tertullian, *On the Flesh* 5, in *Ante-Nicene Fathers*, 3:525.

8. Cyprian, *On the Unity of the Church* 6, in *The Faith of the Early Fathers*, 1:221.

9. Clement of Alexandria, *Stromata* 1.5, in *Ante-Nicene Fathers*, 2:305.

10. Origen, *On First Principles* 1:6, in *Ante-Nicene Fathers*, 4:260.

CHAPTER 5

1. Justin Martyr, *First Apology*, 67, in *The Faith of the Early Fathers*, ed. William A. Jurgens (Collegeville, MN: Liturgical Press, 1970), 1:55–56.

2. *Shepherd of Hermas, Similitude* 9.16, in *The Faith of the Early Fathers*, 1:88.

3. *Didache*, 7.1, cited in *The Faith of the Early Fathers*, 1:2.

4. Justin Martyr, *First Apology* 66, in *The Ante-Nicene Fathers: The Writings of the Fathers Down to A.D. 325*, ed. Alexander Roberts and James Donaldson (Grand Rapids: Eerdmans, 1873), 1:185.

5. Tertullian, *Apology* 39, in *Ante-Nicene Fathers*, 3:47.

6. Eusebius of Caesarea, *Commentary on Psalm 64,* in S. J. Robert Taft, *The Liturgy of the Hours in East and West: The Origins of the Divine Office and Its Meaning for Today,* 2nd ed. (Collegeville, MN: Liturgical Press, 1993), 33.

7. *Didache* 8.1.

CHAPTER 6

1. Eusebius, *Life of Constantine* 1.28, in *Nicene and Post-Nicene Fathers*, First Series, ed. Philip Schaff and Henry Wace (Grand Rapids: Eerdmans, 1900), 1:490.

2. Ibid.

3. Eusebius, *Life of Constantine* 2.24, in ibid., 1:546.

4. Arius to Eusebius of Nicodemia, in *Readings in the History of Christian Theology*, ed. William C. Placher (Philadelphia: Westminster, 1988), 1:52.

5. Nicene Creed, in *Readings in the History of Christian Theology*, 1:53.

6. "'If you want to be perfect,' Jesus said to him, 'Go, sell your belongings and give to the poor, and you will have treasure in heaven. Then come, follow Me.'"

7. Athanasius, *Life of Antony* 5, in *Nicene and Post-Nicene Fathers*, 4:197.

Chapter 7

1. Athanasius, *On the Incarnation,* in *Documents of the Christian Church*, 3rd ed., ed. Henry Bettenson and Chris Maunder (New York: Oxford University Press, 1999), 37.

2. Athanasius, *On the Incarnation,* in *Nicene and Post-Nicene Fathers*, First Series, ed. Philip Schaff and Henry Wace (Grand Rapids: Eerdmans, 1900), 4:65.

3. Basil the Great, *On the Holy Spirit,* in *The Faith of the Early Fathers*, ed. William A. Jurgens (Collegeville, MN: Liturgical Press, 1970), 2:16.

4. Apollinaris, *Fragment 45*, in *Readings in the History of Christian Theology*, ed. William C. Placher (Philadelphia: Westminster Press, 1988), 1:64.

5. Gregory of Nazianzus, *Letter 101,* in *Nicene and Post-Nicene Fathers*, 7:440.

6. Nestorius, *First Sermon Against the Theotokos,* in *Readings in the History of Christian Theology*, 1:69.

7. Ibid.

8. *The Definition of Chalcedon,* in *Readings in the History of Christian Theology*, 1:75.

CHAPTER 8

1. John Chrysostom, *Against the Judaizers,* in *Christianity in Late Antiquity, 300–450 CE: A Reader*, ed. Bart Ehrman and Andrew S. Jacobs (New York: Oxford University Press, 2004), 230.

2. Ambrose, *Sermon Against Auxentius,* in *The Faith of the Early Fathers*, ed. William A. Jurgens (Collegeville, MN: Liturgical Press, 1970), 2:165.

3. Ibid.

4. Jerome, *The Life of Malchus, the Captive Monk,* in *Nicene and Post-Nicene Fathers*, First Series, ed. Philip Schaff and Henry Wace (Grand Rapids: Eerdmans, 1900), 6:315.

5. Jerome, *The Perpetual Virginity of Mary,* in *Readings in the History of Christian Theology*, ed. William C. Placher (Philadelphia: Westminster, 1988), 1:127.

6. Jerome, *Against Jovian,* in *Readings in the History of Christian Theology*, 1:128.

7. Jerome, *Against Vigilantius*, in *Readings in the History of Christian Theology*, 1:125–26.

8. Augustine, *On the Grace of Christ* in *Readings in the History of Christian Theology*, 1:114.

9. Pelagius, *De peccato originali* 1, in *Documents of the Christian Church*, 3rd ed., ed. Henry Bettenson and Chris Maunder (New York: Oxford University Press, 1999), 58.

10. Augustine, *On Grace,* in ibid., 59–60.

11. Augustine, *City of God,* in *Readings in the History of Christian Theology*, 1:120–21.

CHAPTER 9

1. *Codex Theodosius* XVI.10.16, in *Creeds, Councils, and Controversies: Documents Illustrating the History of the Church AD 337–461*, ed. J. Stevenson, rev. W. H. C. Frend (London: SPCK, 1980), 153.

2. *Leo to the Bishops of the Province of Vienne*, in *The Faith of the Early Fathers*, ed. William A. Jurgens (Collegeville, MN: Liturgical Press, 1970), 3:269.

3. Valentinian III, *Edict*, in *Documents of the Christian Church*, 3rd ed., ed. Henry Bettenson and Chris Maunder (New York: Oxford University Press, 1999), 25.

4. Gelasius I, *Letter to Emperor Anastasius*, in *Readings in the History of Christian Theology*, ed. William C. Placher (Philadelphia: Westminster, 1988), 2:123.

5. Ambrose, *On the Mysteries of the Sacraments*, in *The Faith of the Early Fathers*, 2:176.

6. *The Martyrdom of Polycarp*, in *The Faith of the Early Fathers*, 3:31.

7. Cyprian, *Epistles*, in *The Ante-Nicene Fathers: The Writings of the Fathers Down to A.D. 325*, ed. Alexander Roberts and James Donaldson (Grand Rapids: Eerdmans, 1873), 5:315.

8. Augustine, *City of God*, in *The Faith of the Early Fathers*, 3:97.

9. Jerome, *Letter to Riparius*, in *Nicene and Post-Nicene Fathers*, First Series, ed. Philip Schaff and Henry Wace (Grand Rapids: Eerdmans, 1900), 6:212.

CHAPTER 10

1. Bede, *A History of the English Church and People*, trans. Leo Sherley-Price (New York: Penguin, 1986), 69.

2. Gregory the Great, *Dialogues*, in *The Faith of the Early Fathers*, ed. William A. Jurgens (Collegeville, MN: Liturgical Press, 1970), 3:320.

3. With the introduction of the stirrup from the East in the eighth and ninth centuries, the mounted knight replaced the foot soldier as the most important element in battle.

CHAPTER 11

1. *Codex Junis Civilis*, cited in Nicolas Zernov, *Eastern Christendom* (London: Weidenfeld & Nicolson, 1961), 66.

2. *Nov. 146, Justinian to Arebindas*, cited in J. Parkes, *The Conflict of Church and Synagogue: A Study in the Origins of Anti-Semitism* (1934; repr., New York: Meridian, 1961), 392–93.

3. *Procopius Describes the Hagia Sophia* (dedicated by Justinian in 537), cited in *The Church of the St. Sophia Constantinople*, trans. W. Lethaby and H. Swainson (New York: Macmillan, 1984), 24.

4. *The Third Council of Constantinople, 681*, in *Documents of the Christian Church*, 3rd ed., ed. Henry Bettenson and Chris Maunder (New York: Oxford University Press, 1999), 101.

5. John of Damascus, *On the Worship of Images*, in *Readings in Church History,* vol. 1: *From Pentecost to the Protestant Revolt*, ed. Colman J. Barry (New York: Newman, 1960), 312.

6. John of Damascus, *On the Worship of Images* IV, in Hugh T. Kerr, ed., *Readings in Christian Thought* (Nashville: Abingdon, 1990), 73.

7. Athanasius, *On the Incarnation,* in *The Faith of the Early Fathers,* ed. William A. Jurgens (Collegeville, MN: Liturgical Press, 1970), 1:322.

8. John of Damascus, *On the Dormition of Mary*, Sermon 2, cited in *On Holy Images, Followed by Three Sermons on the Assumption,* trans. Mary H. Allies (London: Thomas Baker, 1898).

9. Ibid.

10. *Patriarch Photius of Constantinople: Encyclical Letter to the Archiepiscopal Sees of the East, 866,* in *Readings in Church History* (New York: Newman Press, 1959), 317.

CHAPTER 12

1. In 962, the Kingdom of Germany became a part of the Holy Roman Empire until 1806.
2. A deacon was assigned the task of speaking for the deceased Formosus.
3. This act closed all churches, disallowed the celebration of Mass, and banned burial in consecrated ground. Baptism of infants was still permitted, and extreme unction could be given to the dying.
4. Innocent III, "The Sun and the Moon," in *Documents of the Christian Church*, 3rd ed., ed. Henry Bettenson and Chris Maunder (New York: Oxford University Press, 1999), 123.
5. Fourth Lateran Council (1215), in *Enchiridion Symbolorum Definitionum et Declarationum*, 33rd ed., ed. Henry Denzinger and Adolph Schönmetzer (Freiburg: Herder, 1965), 260.
6. Decrees of the Fourth Lateran Council (1215), in *Medieval Religion: A Sourcebook*, ed. Roberta Anderson and Dominic Aidan Bellenger (New York: Routledge, 2007), 82.
7. Scholars differ on the number of Crusades. What some scholars separate into two campaigns, others consider two aspects of the same campaign.
8. Pope Urban II: The Call to the First Crusade, November 26, 1095, in *Readings in Church History*, vol 1: *From Pentecost to the Protestant Revolt*, ed. Colman J. Barry (New York: Newman Press, 1960), 1:328.
9. Ibid.
10. The number of children on the Children's Crusade varies. Some sources have the number of children as high as 50,000.

CHAPTER 13

1. Anselm, *Proslogion*, in *Documents of the Christian Church*, 3rd ed., ed. Henry Bettenson and Chris Maunder (New York: Oxford University Press, 1999), 151.
2. Quoted in Ray C. Petry, *A History of Christianity: Readings in the History of the Church* (Grand Rapids: Baker, 1962), 1:396.
3. The Pseudo-Dionysius was once believed to be Dionysius the Areopagite mentioned by Paul in Acts 17:34. In reality he was a Neoplatonist who lived in the late fifth century.
4. Thomas à Kempis, *The Imitation of Christ*, quoted in Robert A. Baker and John M. Landers, *A Summary of Christian History*, rev. ed. (Nashville: B&H, 1994), 170.
5. This text was believed to be the first English language work written by a woman.
6. Julian of Norwich, *God Our Mother*, in *Medieval Religion: A Sourcebook*, ed. Roberta Anderson and Dominic Aidan Bellenger (New York: Routledge, 2007), 233.

CHAPTER 14

1. Boniface VIII, Unam Sanctum, in *Documents of the Christian Church*, 3rd ed., ed. Henry Bettenson and Chris Maunder (New York: Oxford University Press, 1999), 127.
2. Francesco Petrarch, *The Papal Court at Avignon*, quoted in Robert A. Baker and John M. Landers, *A Summary of Christian History*, rev. ed. (Nashville: B&H, 1994), 157.
3. The Decree of the Council of Constance, *Sacrosancta*, April 1415, in *Documents of the Christian Church*, 149.
4. John Wycliffe, *On Indulgences*, in *Great Voices of the Reformation: An Anthology*, ed. Harry Emerson Fosdick (New York: Modern Library, 1952), 23–24.

5. Jean le Bel, *True Chronicles*, for 1347–1348, in Jean Comby, *How to Read Church History*, trans. J. Bowden and M. Lydamore (New York: Crossroad, 1985), 1:182.
6. Dante Alighieri, *The Divine Comedy: Paradiso,* Canto V (London: Penguin, 2007), 41.
7. Desiderius Erasmus, *In Praise of Folly*, trans. Betty Radice (Harmondsworth, UK: Penguin, 1509), 164–65.
8. Savonarola was so popular that he convinced many Florentines to toss their worldly possessions into a bonfire. This became known as the "Bonfire of the Vanities."

Chapter 15

1. From Peter Lombard, *The Four Books of Sentences*, quoted in Alister McGrath, *Christian Theology: An Introduction*, 5th ed. (West Sussex, UK: Wiley-Blackwell, 2011), 404.
2. Thomas Aquinas, *Summa Theologica*, in David Ayerst and A. S. T. Fisher, *Records of Christianity*, vol. II: *Christendom* (New York: Oxford University Press, 1977), 217.
3. Quoted in R. W. Southern, *Western Society and the Church in the Middle Ages* (London: Penguin, 1990), 226.
4. Suger of Saint Denis, *Sumptuous Receptacles for the Sacred Bodies of Patron Saints*, in *Abbot Suger on the Abbey Church of St. Denis and Its Art Treasures*, ed. and trans. E. Panofsky (Princeton: Princeton University Press, 1946), 57.
5. Thomas Aquinas, *The Three Greatest Prayers: Commentaries on the Our Father, the Hail Mary and the Apostles' Creed*, trans. Laurence Shapcote (Westminster, MD: Newman, 1956), 32–33.

CHAPTER 16

1. Capitalism is an economic system based on private ownership of the means of production and the creation of goods or services for profit.

2. Quoted in James Kittelson, *Luther the Reformer* (Minneapolis: Augsburg Fortress, 1986), 53.

3. According to tradition, the Holy Stairs (*Scala Santa*) were the steps that led to the *praetorium* of Pontius Pilate in Jerusalem. They were believed to be the stairs Jesus climbed during his passion. They were brought to Rome by Helena, the mother of Constantine, in the fourth century. To emulate the passion of Jesus, pilgrims climbed the stairs on their knees praying on each step. The stairs were located in the Old Lateran Palace.

4 Romans 1:17 references Habakkuk 2:4: "Look, his ego is inflated; he is without integrity. But the righteous one will live by his faith."

5. Martin Luther, "Luther's Conversion," from *Luther's Works*, ed. Jaroslav Pelikan and Helmut T. Lehmann (Minneapolis: Augsburg Fortress, 1955–1986), 34:336–37.

6. It was against church law to hold more than one archbishopric. Albert, therefore, was forced to pay Leo X for a dispensation that allowed him to gain the archbishopric of Mainz.

7. Martin Luther, "The 95 Theses," in *The European Reformation Sourcebook*, ed. Carter Lindberg (Malden, MA: Blackwell, 2000), 33.

8. Luther, *An Open Letter to the Christian Nobility in Three Treatises*, trans. Charles M. Jacobs (Philadelphia: Muhlenberg, 1960), 13–14.

9. Martin Brecht, "Luther, Martin" in *Oxford Encyclopedia of the Reformation*, ed. Hans J. Hillerbrand (New York: Oxford University Press, 1996), 1:460.

10. He began to work on the Old Testament when he returned to Wittenberg. His translation of the entire Bible did not appear until 1534.

11. The Zwickau Prophets were Nicholas Stork, Thomas Dreschel, and Markus Stübner.

12. Martin Luther, *Against the Robbing and Murdering Hoards of Peasants*, quoted in Roland H. Bainton, *Here I Stand: A Life of Martin Luther* (New York: Meridian Printing, 1995 ed.), 217.

13. Martin Luther, "A Might Fortress Is Our God" (1529).

CHAPTER 17

1. "He [Peter] became hungry and wanted to eat, but while they were preparing something, he went into a visionary state. He saw heaven opened and an object that resembled a large sheet coming down, being lowered by its four corners to the earth. In it were all the four-footed animals and reptiles of the earth, and the birds of the sky. Then a voice said to him, 'Get up, Peter; kill and eat!' 'No, Lord!' Peter said. 'For I have never eaten anything common and ritually unclean!' Again, a second time, a voice said to him, 'What God has made clean, you must not call common.' This happened three times, and then the object was taken up into heaven" (Acts 10:10–16).

2. Ulrich Zwingli, *Of Freedom of Choice in the Selection of Food,* in *A Reformation Reader: Primary Texts with Introductions,* 2nd ed., ed. Denis R. Janz (Minneapolis: Fortress, 2008), 187.

3. William L. Lumpkin, *Baptist Confessions of Faith,* rev. ed. (Philadelphia: Judson, 1969), 25.

4. Ibid., 28.

5. Henry C. Vedder, *Balthasar Hubmaier: The Leader of the Anabaptists* (New York: Putnam, 1905), 108.

6. *The Complete Writings of Menno Simons,* ed. John Wenger, trans. Leonard Verduin (Scottsdale, PA: Mennonite Publishing House, 1956), 671.

CHAPTER 18

1. Gerard may have been excommunicated.
2. John Calvin, *Commentary on Psalms,* cited in T. H. L. Parker, *John Calvin: A Biography* (Philadelphia: Westminster, 1975), 163.
3. Olivétan was the first person to translate the Bible into French from the Hebrew and Greek texts. It was published in 1535 as *La Bible Qui Est Toute la Saincte Scripture.*
4. Protestants placed placards throughout Paris and other cities condemning the Catholic mass. The Catholic reaction was violent and resulted in a mass exodus of Protestants from France.
5. Calvin and Farel wanted the Lord's Supper to be celebrated each week but were forced to compromise with a monthly, mandatory observance.
6. J. K. S. Reid, trans., *John Calvin: Theological Treatises* (Philadelphia: Westminster, 1954), 231.
7. John Calvin, *The Ecclesiastical Ordinances,* cited in *The European Reformation Sourcebook,* ed. Carter Lindberg (Malden, MA: Blackwell, 2000), 171.
8. Calvin completed commentaries on all the books of the New Testament except 2 John, 3 John, and Revelation.
9. John Calvin, *Institutes of Christian Religion,* trans. Henry Beveridge (Grand Rapids: Eerdmans, 1933), 3.21.5.
10. John Calvin, *Institutes of Christian Religion,* 4.7, in *Documents of the Christian Church,* 3rd ed., ed. Henry Bettenson and Chris Maunder (New York: Oxford University Press, 1999), 238.

11. J. H. S. Burleigh, *A Church History of Scotland* (New York: Oxford University Press, 1960), 154.

12. The origin of the term *Huguenot* is unknown.

CHAPTER 19

1. Tyndale was the first person to translate the Bible into English from Greek and Hebrew. Under pressure from the papacy and the English monarchy, he was strangled to death, and then his body was burned by church authorities in Brussels, Belgium.

2. At this time Britain was composed of two countries. England was ruled by the Tudors, and Scotland was ruled by the Stuarts.

3. "If a man marries his brother's wife, it is impurity. He has shamed his brother; they will be childless."

4. *The Act of Supremacy*, 1534, in *Documents of the Christian Church*, 3rd ed., ed. Henry Bettenson and Chris Maunder (New York: Oxford University Press, 1999), 252.

5. Reports of the number of participants vary from 8,000 to 30,000 participants.

6. *Marian Injunctions*, March 4, 1554, in *Documents of the English Reformation*, ed. Gerald Bray (Minneapolis: Fortress, 1994), 317.

7. *The Thirty-Nine Articles*, 1563, in *A Reformation Reader: Primary Texts with Introductions*, ed. Denis R. Janz (Minneapolis: Fortress, 2008), 374.

8. J. R. Tanner, ed., *Constitutional Documents of the Reign of James I, A.D. 1603–1625, with an Historical Commentary* (Cambridge: Cambridge University Press, 1930), 67.

9. Thomas Helwys, *A Short Declaration of the Mystery of Iniquity*, in Joe Early Jr., *The Life and Writings of Thomas Helwys* (Macon, GA: Mercer University Press, 2009), 209.

CHAPTER 20

1. His Targum translation covered only the first five books of the Old Testament.

2. Ximénez's New Testament was completed in 1515 and thus preceded Erasmus's edition by one year. Ximenez's edition, however, was not published until papal permission was received in 1520.

3. Girolamo Savonarola, *On the Renovation of the Church*, 1495, in *The European Reformation Sourcebook*, ed. Carter Lindberg (Malden, MA: Blackwell, 2000), 241–42.

4. *Constitution of the Jesuit Order,* in *Documents of the Christian Church*, 3rd ed., ed. Henry Bettenson and Chris Maunden (New York: Oxford University Press, 1999), 275.

5. Ignatius of Loyola, *Spiritual Exercises,* in *Documents of the Christian Church*, 272.

6. *Proposal of a Select Committee of Cardinals and Other Prelates Concerning the Reform of the Church, Written and Presented by Order of His Holiness Pope Paul III*, 1537, in *The European Reformation Sourcebook*, 247–48.

7. Attendance: 187 Italians, 31 Spaniards, 26 French, 2 Germans.

8. Decree and Canons Concerning Justification, January 13, 1547, cited in *The European Reformation Sourcebook*, 254.

9. *The Council of Trent*, session XXV, in *Documents of the Christian Church*, 281.

10. "Ten Rules Concerning Prohibited Books Drawn up by the Fathers Chosen by the Council of Trent and Approved by Pope Pius IV," in *The European Reformation Sourcebook*, 258.

11. A motet is a song with parts for different voices.

Chapter 21

1. *Colección de Documentos Ineditos Relativos al Descumbrimiento Conquista y Colonización on de las Posesiones Españolas* (Madrid: 1885), 26:141–42.
2. *Sublimis Deus*, cited in *A Documentary History of Religion in America to the Civil War*, ed. Edward S. Gaustad (Grand Rapids: Eerdmans, 1993), 64.
3. Brébeuf's bones can still be viewed at the Church of Saint Joseph near Midland, Ontario.
4. *The Mayflower Compact*, 1620, in *The Great Documents of Western Civilization*, ed. Milton Viorst (New York: Barnes & Noble, 1994), 165.
5. Roger Williams, *The Bloudy Tenent of Persecution*, 1644, in *Readings in Baptist History: Four Centuries of Selected Documents*, ed. Joseph Early Jr. (Nashville: B&H Academic, 2008), 21.

Chapter 22

1. Isaiah 11:12 says, "He will lift up a banner for the nations and gather the dispersed of Israel; He will collect the scattered of Judah from the four corners of the earth." Revelation 7:1 says, "After this I saw four angels standing at the four corners of the earth, restraining the four winds of the earth so that no wind could blow on the earth or on the sea or on any tree."
2. René Descartes, *Meditations on First Philosophy*, in *Fifty Readings in Philosophy*, 4th ed., ed. Donald C. Abel (New York: McGraw-Hill, 2012), 152.
3. David Hume, *Dialogues Concerning Natural Religion*, in *Fifty Readings in Philosophy*, 53.
4. Thomas Paine, *Age of Reason: Being an Investigation of True and Fabulous Theology* (1794; repr., New York: Books, Inc., n.d.), 231.

5. Ibid., 233.
6. *Declaration of the Rights of Man and of the Citizen*, 1789, in *The Great Documents of Western Civilization*, ed. Milton Viorst (New York: Barnes & Noble Books, 1994), 190.
7. William Paley, *Natural Theology*, in *Fifty Readings in Philosophy*, 55–56.
8. Immanuel Kant, *Critique of Pure Reason*, 2nd ed., trans. N. K. Smith (London: Macmillan, 1933), 29.

CHAPTER 23

1. Solomon Stoddard, *The Defect of Preachers Reproved in a Sermon Preached at Northampton, May 19, 1723*, in *The Great Awakening: Documents of the Revival of Religion, 1740–1745*, ed. Richard L. Bushman (New York: Atheneum, 1970), 15.
2. Gilbert Tennent, "The Danger of an Unconverted Ministry, 1740", in *The Great Awakening: Documents of the Revival of Religion*, 91.
3. Jonathan Edwards, "Sinners in the Hands of an Angry God," in *Jonathan Edwards: Representative Selections*, ed. Clarence H. Faust and Thomas H. Johnson (New York: Hill & Wang, 1962), 161, 172.
4. "A Report on Whitefield in New York," *The New England Weekly Journal*, 1739, in *The Great Awakening: Documents of the Revival of Religion*, 23.
5. Quoted in *No Establishment of Religion: America's Original Contribution to Religious Liberty*, ed. T. Jeremy Gunn and John Witte Jr. (New York: Oxford University Press, 2012), 166.
6. Thomas Jefferson, *Letter to Danbury Baptist Association, 1 January 1802*, in *Readings in Baptist History: Four Centuries of Selected Documents*, ed. Joseph Early Jr. (Nashville: B&H Academic, 2008), 75.

Chapter 24

1. The Great Century began when William Carey was commissioned as a missionary to India in 1793 and concluded with the World Missionary Conference held in Edinburgh, Scotland, in 1910. Kenneth Scott Latourette coined the phrase "Great Century" in his seven-volume *History of the Expansion of Christianity* (New York: Harper, 1937–1945).

2. Dissenting religious denominations, such as Baptists, were legalized in 1828.

3. John Wesley, *The Works of John Wesley*, 3rd ed. (Grand Rapids: Baker Books, 1999), 1:103. Some argue that Wesley's conversion occurred before this experience.

4. Influenced by Whitefield, some Welsh Methodists, however, were Calvinistic.

5. John Henry Newman, *Tract 90*, cited in *Documents of the Christian Church*, 3rd ed., ed. Henry Bettenson and Chris Maunder (New York: Oxford University Press, 1999), 358.

6. William Booth, *In Darkest England, and the Way Out* (1890; repr., Champaign, IL: Project Gutenberg, [1996]), Preface, accessed December 18, 2013, http://www.gutenberg.org/cache/epub/475/pg475.html.

7. Carey was particularly concerned with the natives Cook encountered that had no knowledge of Christ.

8. David Brainerd (1718–1747) was an American missionary to the Delaware Indians in New Jersey.

9. Quoted in H. Leon McBeth, *The Baptist Heritage: Four Centuries of Baptist Witness* (Nashville: Broadman, 1987), 185.

10. William Carey, *An Enquiry into the Obligations of Christians to Use Means for the Conversion of the Heathens* (Leicester, 1792), cited in H. Leon McBeth, *A Sourcebook for Baptist Heritage* (Nashville: Broadman, 1990), 136.

11. Carey, Ward, and Marshman were known as the Serampore Trio.

CHAPTER 25

1. Prior to the Yale revivals, Hampden-Sidney College in Virginia had a similar revival in 1787.

2. Imputation is the idea that Adam's sin and Christ's righteousness could be credited to others.

3. Paul K. Conkin, *Cane Ridge: America's Pentecost* (Madison: University of Wisconsin Press, 1989), 93–94.

4. Loosely, the Burned-Over District covers the westernmost region of New York between the Finger Lakes and Lake Erie. Groups originating in the Burned-Over District include the Shakers, Mormons, Adventists, and the utopian Oneida Community.

5. Richard Furman, *Exposition of the Views of the Baptists Relative to the Coloured Population of the United States in a Communication to the Governor of South Carolina*, Charleston, South Carolina, 24 December 1822, in James A. Rogers, *Richard Furman: Life and Legacy* (Macon, GA: Mercer University Press, 2001), 283–84.

6. Ibid., 285.

7. *The Declaration of Sentiments and Constitution of the American Anti-Slavery Society*, New York, 1837, in *American Christianity: Interpretation and Documents, 1820–1960*, ed. H. Shelton Smith, Robert T. Handy, and Lefferts A. Loetscher (New York: Charles Scribner's Sons, 1963), 2.

8. Walter Rauschenbusch, *A Theology for the Social Gospel* (New York: Macmillan, 1917), 131–45.

9. "'You are My witnesses'—this is the Lord's declaration—'and My servant whom I have chosen, so that you may know and believe Me and understand that I am He. No god was formed before Me, and there will be none after Me. I, I am Yahweh, and there is no other Savior but Me. I alone declared, saved, and proclaimed—and not some foreign god among you. So

you are My witnesses'—this is the LORD's declaration—'and I am God.'"

10. This belief was based on Acts 15:28–29: "For it was the Holy Spirit's decision—and ours—to put no greater burden on you than these necessary things: that you abstain from food offered to idols, from blood, from eating anything that has been strangled, and from sexual immorality. You will do well if you keep yourselves from these things."

11. The members of the Jehovah's Witnesses who are involved in evangelism are known as publishers.

12. At this time the Utah Territory was a part of Mexico.

CHAPTER 26

1. Now the National Baptist Convention of America, Inc.
2. Martin Luther King Jr., "Letter from a Birmingham Jail," April 16, 1963, in *A Documentary History of Religion in America Since 1865*, ed. Edwin S. Gaustad (Grand Rapids: Eerdmans, 1993), 495–96.
3. King, "I Have a Dream," August 28, 1963, in *A Documentary History of Religion in America Since 1865*, 496–97.

CHAPTER 27

1. *The Doctrine of the Immaculate Conception*, 1854, in *Documents of the Christian Church*, 3rd ed., ed. Henry Bettenson and Chris Maunder (New York: Oxford University Press, 1999), 286.
2. *The Papal Syllabus of Errors, 1864*, in *The Creeds of Christendom*, ed. Philip Schaff (New York: Harper, 1919), 2:233.
3. *The Doctrine of Papal Infallibility*, 870 in *Documents of the Christian Church*, 288–89.

4. *The Doctrine of the Assumption of the Blessed Virgin Mary*, 1950, in *Documents of the Christian Church*, 297–98.
5. Karl Marx and Friedrich Engels, "Contributions to the Critique of Hegel's Philosophy of Right," in *On Religion* (Moscow: Foreign Languages Publishing House, 1955), 41.
6. *Declaration of Religious Liberty, December 1965*, in *Documents of the Christian Church*, 366.
7. *Declaration on the Relation of the Church to Non-Christian Religions, 28 October 1965*, in *Documents of the Christian Church*, 365.
8. *Populorum Progressio, 1967*, in *Documents of the Christian Church*, 397–98.
9. The doctrine of structured violence teaches that a person who does not take action against oppression is just as guilty as the oppressor.
10. James Cone, *Black Theology and Black Power* (Maryknoll, NY: Orbis, 1997), 69.
11. It is estimated that John Paul II traveled in excess of 750,000 miles.
12. Independent and autonomous.

CHAPTER 28

1. Friedrich Schleiermacher, *On Religion: Speeches to Its Cultured Despisers* [1799], trans. Richard Crouter (Cambridge: Cambridge University Press, 1988), 101–2.
2. Karl Barth, *The Epistle to the Romans*, 6th ed., trans. Edwyn C. Hoskyns (Oxford: Oxford University Press, 1968), 113.
3. "So God created man in His own image; He created him in the image of God; He created them male and female."
4. H. Richard Niebuhr, *The Kingdom of God in America* (1937; repr., Middletown, CT: Wesleyan University Press, 1988), 193.

5. Dietrich Bonhoeffer, *Letters and Papers from Prison* (New York: Macmillan, 1971), 369.

6. In the nineteenth century, German philosopher Friedrich Nietzsche was the first to use the phrase "death of God."

7. Curtis Lee Laws, "Convention Side Lights," *Watchman-Examiner* 8, July 1, 1920, 834.

CHAPTER 29

1. Research entities that supply information concerning Christian populations in the world, continents, and countries often vary in their calculations. To be consistent, I have chosen to use the Operation World Database for all of my population numbers (www.operationworld.org).

2. Philip Jenkins, *The Next Christendom: The Coming of Global Christianity*, 3rd ed. (New York: Oxford University Press, 2011), 52.

3. The Three-Self Patriotic Movement is associated with the China Christian Council and is commonly known as *lianghui* or "two organizations."

4. The prosperity gospel stresses that financial blessings are the will of God for Christians.

5. John Mbiti as quoted in Kwame Bediako, *Christianity in Africa* (Edinburgh: Edinburgh University Press, 1995), 154.

BIBLIOGRAPHY

WORKS CITED AND CONSULTED

PRIMARY SOURCE DOCUMENTS AND BOOKS WHERE PRIMARY SOURCE DOCUMENTS ARE QUOTED

Abel, Donald C., ed. *Fifty Readings in Philosophy.* 4th ed. New York: McGraw-Hill, 2012.

Allies, Mary H., trans. *On Holy Images, Followed by Three Sermons on the Assumption.* London: Thomas Baker, 1898.

Anderson, Roberta, and Dominic Aidan Bellenger, eds. *Medieval Religion: A Sourcebook.* New York: Routledge, 2007.

Aquinas, Thomas. *The Three Great Prayers: Commentaries on the Our Father, the Hail Mary and the Apostles' Creed.* Translated by Laurence Shapcote. Westminster, MD: Newman Press, 1956.

Ayerst, David, and A. S. T. Fisher, eds. *Records of Christianity, Vol. II: Christendom.* New York: Oxford University Press, 1977.

Bainton, Roland H. *Here I Stand: A Life of Martin Luther.* 1950. Reprint, New York: Meridian Printing, 1995.

Barnstone, Willis, and Marvin Meyer, eds. *The Gnostic Bible: Gnostic Texts of Mystical Wisdom from the Ancient and Medieval Worlds—Pagan, Jewish, Christian, Mandaean, Manichaean, Islamic, and Cathar.* Boston: Shambhala Publications, 2003.

Barry, Colman J., ed. *Readings in Church History: From Pentecost to the Protestant Revolt.* New York: Newman Press, 1960.

Barth, Karl. *The Epistle to the Romans.* 6th ed. Translated by Edwyn C. Hoskyns. Oxford: Oxford University Press, 1968.

Bede. *A History of the English Church and People.* Translated by Leo Sherley-Price. New York: Penguin Books, 1986.

Bediako, Kwame. *Christianity in Africa.* Edinburgh: Edinburgh University Press, 1995.

Bettenson, Henry, and Chris Maunder, eds. *Documents of the Christian Church,* 3rd ed. New York: Oxford University Press, 1999.

Bonhoeffer, Dietrich. *Letters and Papers from Prison.* New York: Macmillan, 1971.

Booth, William. *In Darkest England, and the Way Out.* Champaign, IL.: Project Gutenberg, [1996?]. http://www.gutenberg.org/cache/epub/475/pg475.html (accessed December 18, 2013).

Bray, Gerald, ed. *Documents of the English Reformation* Minneapolis: Fortress, 1994.

Brecht, Martin. "Luther, Martin." In *Oxford Encyclopedia of the Reformation,* ed. Hans J. Hillerbrand. New York: Oxford University Press, 1996.

Burleigh, J. H. S. *A Church History of Scotland.* Oxford: Oxford University Press, 1960.

Bushman, Richard L., ed. *The Great Awakening: Documents of the Revival of Religion, 1740–1745.* New York: Atheneum, 1970.

Calvin, John. *Institutes of Christian Religion.* Translated by Henry Beveridge. Grand Rapids: Eerdmans, 1933.

Coakley, John W., and Andrea Sterk, eds. *Readings in World Christian History, Volume 1: Earliest Christianity to 1453.* Maryknoll, NY: Orbis, 2004.

Colección de Documentos Ineditos Relatrivos al Descumbrimiento Conquista y Colonizacion on de las Posesions Españolas. Madrid, 1885.

Cone, James. *Black Theology and Black Power.* Maryknoll, NY: Orbis Books, 1997.

Conkin, Paul K. *Cane Ridge: America's Pentecost.* Madison: University of Wisconsin Press, 1989.

Dante. *The Divine Comedy: Paradiso.* London: Penguin, 2007.

Denzinger, Henry, and Adolph Schönmetzer, eds. *Enchiridion Symbolorum Definitionum et Declarationum,* 33rd ed. Frieburg: Herder, 1965.

Didache 8.1

Dupré, Louis, and James A. Wiseman, ed. *Light from Light: An Anthology of Christian Mysticism.* 2nd ed. New York: Paulist, 2001.

Early, Joseph, Jr., ed. *Readings in Baptist History: Four Centuries of Selected Documents.* Nashville: B&H Academic, 2008.

———. *The Life and Writings of Thomas Helwys.* Macon, GA: Mercer University, 2009.

Ehrman, Bart D., ed. *After the New Testament: A Reader in Early Christianity.* New York: Oxford University Press, 1998.

———, and Andrew S. Jacobs, eds. *Christianity in Late Antiquity, 300–450 CE: A Reader.* New York: Oxford University Press, 2004.

Erasmus, Desiderius. *In Praise of Folly.* Translated by Betty Radice. Harmondsworth, UK: Penguin, 1509.

Faust, Clarence H., and Thomas H. Johnson, eds. *Jonathan Edwards: Representative Selections.* New York: Hill&Wang, 1962.

Fosdick, Harry Emerson, ed. *Great Voices of the Reformation: An Anthology.* New York: Modern Library, 1952.

Gaustad, Edwin S., ed. *A Documentary History of Religion in America to the Civil War.* Grand Rapids: Eerdmans, 1993.

———, ed. *A Documentary History of Religion in America Since 1865.* Grand Rapids: Eerdmans, 1993.

Gunn, T. Jeremy, and John Witte Jr., eds. *No Establishment of Religion: America's Original Contribution to Religious Liberty.* New York: Oxford University Press, 2012.

Holmes, Michael, ed. *The Apostolic Fathers: Greek Texts and English Translations,* 3rd ed. Grand Rapids: Baker Academic, 2007.

Janz, Denis R., ed. *A Reformation Reader: Primary Texts with Introductions.* Minneapolis: Fortress, 2008.

Jenkins, Philip. *The Next Christendom: The Coming of Global Christianity.* 3rd ed. New York: Oxford University Press, 2011.

Jurgens, William A., ed. *The Faith of the Early Fathers.* 3 vols. Collegeville, MN: The Liturgical Press, 1970.

Kant, Immanuel. *Critique of Pure Reason.* 2nd ed. Translated by N. K. Smith. London: Macmillan, 1933.

Kerr, Hugh T., ed. *Readings in Christian Thought.* Nashville: Abingdon, 1990.

Kittelson, James. *Luther the Reformer.* Minneapolis: Augsburg Fortress, 1986.

Lethaby, W., and H. Swainson, trans. *The Church of St. Sophia Constantinople.* New York: n.p., 1894.

Lindberg, Carter, ed. *The European Reformation Sourcebook.* Malden, MA: Blackwell, 2000.

Lumpkin, William L. *Baptist Confessions of Faith.* Revised ed. Philadelphia: Judson, 1969.

Luther, Martin. *An Open Letter to the Christian Nobility in Three Treatises.* Translated by Charles M. Jacobs. Philadelphia: Muhlenberg, 1960.

———. "A Mighty Fortress Is Our God." 1529.

Maffly-Kipp, Laurie F. *American Scriptures: An Anthology of Sacred Writings.* New York: Penguin, 2010.

Marx, Karl, and Friedrich Engels. *On Religion.* Moscow: Foreign Languages Publishing House, 1955.

McBeth, H. Leon. *The Baptist Heritage: Four Centuries of Baptist Witness.* Nashville: Broadman, 1987.

———. *A Sourcebook for Baptist Heritage.* Nashville: Broadman, 1990.

McGinn, Bernard, ed. *The Essential Writings of Christian Mysticism.* New York: Modern Library, 2007.

McGrath, Alister. *Christian Theology: An Introduction.* 5th ed. West Sussex, UK: Wiley-Blackwell, 2011.

Munron, D. C. *Translations and Reprints from the Original Sources of European History.* Series 1. Vol. 3, no. 1, rev. ed. Philadelphia: University of Pennsylvania Press, 1912.

Neibuhr, H. Richard. *The Kingdom of God in America.* 1937. Reprint, Middleton, CT: Wesleyan University Press, 1988.

Paine, Thomas. *Age of Reason: Being an Investigation of True and Fabulous Theology.* New York: Books, Inc., 1794.

Panofsky, E., ed. and trans. *Abbot Suger on the Abbey Church of St. Denis and Its Art Treasures.* Princeton: Princeton University Press, 1946.

Parker, T. H. L. *John Calvin: A Biography.* Philadelphia: Westminster, 1975.

Parkes, James. *The Conflict of Church and Synagogue: A Study in the Origins of Anti-Semitism.* New York: Jewish Publication Society, 1934.

Pelikan, Jaroslav, and Helmut T. Lehmann, eds. *Luther's Works.* Minneapolis: Augsburg Fortress, 1955–1986.

Petry, Ray C. *A History of Christianity: Readings in the History of the Church.* Vol. 1. 1962. Reprint, Grand Rapids: Baker Book House, 1981.

Placher, William C., ed. *Readings in the History of Christian Theology.* 2 vols. Philadelphia: Westminister, 1988.

Queen, Edward L., II, Stephen R. Prothero, and Gardiner H. Shattuck Jr., eds. 2 vols. *The Encyclopedia of American Religious History.* New York: Proseworks, 1996.

Rauschenbusch, Walter. *A Theology for the Social Gospel.* New York: Macmillan, 1917.

Reid, J. K. S., trans. *John Calvin: Theological Treatises.* Philadelphia: Westminster, 1954.

Roberts, Alexander, and James Donaldson, eds. *The Ante-Nicene Fathers: The Writings of the Fathers Down to A.D. 325.* Grand Rapids: Eerdmans, 1873.

Rogers, James A. *Richard Furman: Life and Legacy.* Macon, GA: Mercer University Press, 2001.

Schaff, Philip. *The Creeds of Christendom.* 3 vols. New York: Harper, 1919.

———, and Henry Wace, eds. *Nicene and Post-Nicene Fathers,* 14 vols. First Series. Grand Rapids: Eerdmans, 1900.

Schleiermacher, Friedrich. *On Religion: Speeches to Its Cultured Despisers* [1799]. Translated by Richard Crouter. Cambridge: Cambridge University Press, 1988.

Smith, H. Shelton, Robert T. Handy, and Lefferts A. Loetscher, eds. *American Christianity: Interpretation and Documents, 1820–1960.* 2 vols. New York: Charles Scribner's Sons, 1963.

Southern, R. W. *Western Society and the Church in the Middle Ages.* London: Penguin Books, 1990.

Stevenson, J., ed. *Creeds, Councils, and Controversies: Documents Illustrating the History of the Church AD 337–461.* Revised by W. H. C. Frend. London: SPCK, 1980.

———, ed. *A New Eusebius: Documents Illustrating the History of the Church to AD 337.* 5th ed. Cambridge: Cambridge University Press, 1993.

Tacitus, *Annals* 15.44.

Taft, S. J. Robert. *The Liturgy of the Hours in East and West: The Origins of the Divine Office and Its Meaning for Today.* 2nd ed. Collegeville, MN: Liturgical Press, 1993.

Tanner, J. R., ed. *Constitutional Documents of the Reign of James I, A.D. 1603–1625, with an Historical Commentary.* Cambridge: Cambridge University Press, 1930.

Tierney, Brian, ed. *The Middle Ages: Sources of Medieval History.* 5th ed. New York: McGraw Hill, 1992.

Toulouse, Mark G., and James O. Duke. *Makers of Christian Theology in America.* Nashville: Abingdon, 1997.

———. *Sources of Theology in America.* Nashville: Abingdon, 1999.

Vedder, Henry C. *Balthasar Hubmaier: The Leader of the Anabaptists.* New York: Putnam, 1905.

Viorst, Milton, ed. *The Great Documents of Western Civilization.* New York: Barnes & Noble, 1994.

Wenger, John, ed. *The Complete Writings of Menno Simons.* Translated by Leonard Verduin. Scotsdale, PA: Mennonite Publishing House, 1956.

Wesley, John. *The Works of John Wesley*. 3rd ed. Grand Rapids: Baker Books, 1999.

Zernov, Nicolas. *Eastern Christendom*. London: Weidenfeld&Nicolson, 1961.

Encyclopedias, Dictionaries, and Reference Works

Ashbrook, Susan Harvey, and David Hunter, eds. *The Oxford Handbook of Early Christian Studies*. New York: Oxford University Press, 2008.

Chadwick, Henry, and Gillian R. Evans, eds. *Atlas of the Christian Church*. New York: Facts on File, 1987.

Farmer, David H., ed. *The Oxford Dictionary of the Saints*. 4th ed. New York: Oxford University Press, 2003.

Ferguson, Everett, ed. *Encyclopedia of Early Christianity*. 2nd ed. New York: Garland, 1999.

Hillerbrand, Hans J., ed. *The Oxford Encyclopedia of the Reformation*. 4 vols. New York: Oxford University Press, 1996.

Johnston, William W., ed. *Encyclopedia of Monasticism*. 2 vols. Chicago: Fitzroy Dearborn, 2000.

Kelly, J. N. D. *Oxford Dictionary of Popes*. New York: Oxford University Press, 1986.

Livingstone, Elizabeth A., ed. *The Oxford Dictionary of the Christian Church*. 3rd ed. New York: Oxford University Press, 1997.

McBrien, Richard, and Harold Attridge, eds. *The HarperCollins Encyclopedia of Catholicism*. San Francisco: Harper San Francisco, 1995.

McFarland, Ian A., David A. S. Fergusson, Karen Kilby, and Iain R. Torrance, eds. *Cambridge Dictionary of Christian Theology*. Cambridge: Cambridge University Press, 2011.

Murray, Peter, and Linda Murray, eds. *The Oxford Companion to Christian Art and Architecture*. New York: Oxford University Press, 1996.

Parry, Ken, David Melling, Sidney Griffith, and Dimitri Brady, eds. *A Dictionary of Eastern Christianity*. Oxford: Blackwell, 1999.

Patte, Daniel, ed. *Cambridge Dictionary of Christianity*. Cambridge: Cambridge University Press, 2010.

Pelikan, Jaroslav. *The Christian Tradition: A History of the Development of Doctrine*. 5 vols. Chicago: University of Chicago Press, 1974, 1978, 1984.

Journals and Newspapers

Laws, Curtis Lee. "Convention Side Lights." *Watchman-Examiner,*
    July 1, 1920.
The New England Weekly Journal, 1739
Sword and Trowel, August 1887

General Surveys of Church History

Baker, Robert A., and John M. Landers. *A Summary of Christian History.*
    Revised. ed. Nashville: B&H, 1994.
Bokenkotter, Thomas. *A Concise History of the Catholic Church.* New York:
    Doubleday, 2004.
Comby, Jean. *How to Read Church History.* Vol. 1. Translated by John
    Bowden and Maragret Lydamore. New York: Crossroad, 1985.
Gonzalez, Justo. *A History of Christian Thought: From the Beginnings to the
    Council of Chalcedon.* Revised ed. Nashville: Abingdon, 1988.
———. *A History of Christian Thought: From Augustine to the Eve of the
    Reformation.* Revised ed. Nashville: Abingdon, 1988.
———. *A History of Christian Thought: From the Protestant Reformation to
    the Twentieth Century.* Revised ed. Nashville: Abingdon, 1988.
Green, Vivian. *A New History of Christianity.* New York: Continuum, 2000.
Hinson, Glenn E. *The Early Church: Origins to the Dawn of the Reformation.*
    Nashville: Abingdon, 1996.
MacCulloch, Diarmaid. *Christianity: The First Three Thousand Years.* New
    York: Penguin, 2009.
Payne, Robert. *The Making of the Christian World: From the Birth of Christ
    to the Renaissance.* New York: Dorset, 1990.
Schaff, Philip. *History of the Christian Church.* 8 vols. Grand Rapids: Eerd-
    mans, 1979.
Shelley, Bruce L. *Church History in Plain Language.* Updated 2nd ed. Dallas:
    Word Publishing, 1995.
Spickard, Paul R., and Kevin M. Cragg. *God's Peoples: A Social History of
    Christians.* Grand Rapids: Baker, 1994.
Walker, Williston, Richard A. Norris, David W. Lotz, and Robert T. Handy.
    A History of the Christian Church. 4th ed. New York: Charles Scribner's
    Sons, 1985.

NAME INDEX

SUBJECT INDEX

Matthew 45
Matthias (emperor of the Holy Roman Empire) 288
Matthys, Jan 240–41
Maxentius (emperor of Rome) 69
Maximian (emperor of Rome) 68–69
Maximilla 37
Maximinus Daia (emperor of Rome) 69
Maximus the Confessor 141
Mayflower 272, 300
"Mayflower Compact" 300–1
Mbiti, John 441–42
McCain, John 418
Mecca 132
Medici family 275
Medicis 194, 198
megachurches 425–26
Melchiorite Christology 240
Melitian Schism 85
Melitius of Antioch 97
Memphis, Tennessee 380
Mendicant Orders 171–74
Mennonites 239–40, 272, 305, 333
Merici, Angela 277
Merovingians 128
Mesopotamia 102
Messiah 2–4, 7, 9, 28, 34, 315, 413
Methodism 338–40, 343, 362
Methodist Episcopal Church 381–82
Methodists 307, 333, 346, 353–55, 358, 371, 375, 381–83, 422
Methodius 143
Mexico 292, 296, 430–31
Mexico City 295
Meyer, Joyce 426
Michael III (emperor of Byzantine) 146
Michael III (king of Byzantium) 143
Michelangelo, Nicolo 195, 198–99
Michigan 297
Middle Colonies 304–5
Mieczyslaw I (prince of Poland) 184
mikvah 60

Milan 86, 101, 103, 107–8, 155
Millenarian Revolutionary Radical Reformers 235, 240–42
Millenary Petition 268
Miller, William 364–65
Minnesota 297
minor offices 66
Miracles of the Virgin 208
missions 295–97, 344–47, 376, 433, 436–37, 439–40
Missouri 351, 368
Mithras 8, 13, 70
modalism 50, 74, 243
Modalistic Monarchianism (Patripassianism) 36
Monarchianism 31, 35–36
monasticism 72, 76–82, 79, 98, 102–3, 108, 114, 119, 124–26, 153, 158, 169–74, 182–83, 212–15, 218, 229, 262–63, 274–77, 279, 281, 289
monastic schools 174
Mongols 165
Monica 106, 108
Monophysitism 93, 95, 135–36, 137, 145
Monothelites 137
Montanism 31, 37, 47, 49, 135
Montanus 36
Montgomery, Alabama 377, 380
Moody, Dwight Lyman 357
Moors 129, 150
Moral Majority 424
Moravia 143, 236, 238–39
Moravian Brethren 339
More, Thomas 262, 280
    Utopia 280
Morrison, Robert 346
Moscow 289
Moses 1–2, 21, 29, 51, 132, 412
Mother Teresa 436
Mozambique 432
Muhammad 131–32, 138
Münster, Germany 241–42, 415
Münster Rebellion 241–42
Müntzer, Thomas 222, 235
Muratorian Canon 46
music 287

Puritanism   *257–59, 266, 268–69, 271, 292, 298–304, 325–27, 332, 352, 403–4*
Pusey, Edward Bouverie   *341*

Q

quadrivium   *130, 174*
Quakers   *301, 304–08, 333, 358–59, 405*
Quartodeciman controversy   *21*
Quebec   *296–97*
quietism   *281–83*
Qumran   *4*
Qur'an   *132*

R

Radical Reformation   *234–43*
Radical Reformers   *227, 230, 233, 233–43*
Rahner, Karl   *394–95*
  Foundations of the Christian Faith   *395*
  Theological Investigations   *395*
Ramm, Bernard   *422*
Raphael   *198–99*
rationalism   *311, 313*
Ratislav   *143*
Rauschenbusch, Walter   *361*
  A Theology of the Social Gospel   *361*
reader   *66*
Reagan, Ronald   *424*
realism   *175–80*
Reformation   *289*
refrigariums   *57*
Regent University   *423*
Regular Baptists   *380*
reichskirche   *131*
Reimarus, Hermann Samuel   *411–12*
  Fragments   *412*
Reinhart, Anna   *230*
relics   *72, 103, 105–6, 119–21, 138, 164, 166–67, 190, 201, 206–7*
religious humanism   *194, 196–97*
Remonstrants   *256*

Renaissance   *130, 147, 166, 180, 185, 193–99, 212*
Republic of Congo   *434*
Republic of the Philippines   *440–41*
Requerimiento   *293–94*
Restraint of Annates (England)   *262*
Reublin, William   *236*
Reuchlin, Johannes   *196*
  Rudiments of Hebrew   *196*
Reynolds, John   *268*
Rhineland   *181*
Rhode Island   *298, 301–4*
Ricci, Matteo   *279*
Rice, Luther   *375*
Richard I (king of England)   *164, 166*
Richard II (king of England)   *191*
Richelieu, Cardinal Armand Jean de Plessis   *296*
Riley, William Bell   *423*
Ritschl, Albrecht   *410–11*
Robber's Synod   *93*
Robert of Molesme   *170*
Robert of Normandy   *163*
Robertson, Pat   *423–24*
Robinson, John   *270–71, 300*
Rochester, New York   *356*
Roman Empire   *8, 15–16, 27, 29*
Roman Inquisition   *284*
Romanus of Subiaco   *81*
Rome (city)   *16, 18–20, 32–33, 36, 38–40, 42, 47–51, 53, 57, 65, 69, 71, 76, 81, 86, 91, 93, 95, 103, 107, 110, 113, 115–17, 120–21, 123–27, 126, 129, 133–34, 151–54, 156–58, 160, 173, 186–88, 190, 197–98, 206, 211, 213–14, 217, 228–29, 261–63, 267, 276–77, 280, 282, 284, 289, 394, 406*
Romero, Oscar   *399*
Rothmann, Bernhard   *241*
Rousseau   *386*
Rousseau, Jean-Jacques   *316–17*
  Social Contract   *318*
Royal Injunctions (England)   *265*
royal patronage   *293*
Ruether, Rosemary Radford   *401*

Scripture Index